Legal Rights of Teachers and Students

Martha M. McCarthy
Indiana University

Nelda H. Cambron-McCabe
Miami University of Ohio

Stephen B. Thomas
Kent State University

PEARSON

Boston • New York • San Francisco
Mexico City • Montreal • Toronto • London • Madrid • Munich • Paris
Hong Kong • Singapore • Tokyo • Cape Town • Sydney

Senior Editor: *Arnis E. Burvikovs*
Editorial Assistant: *Christine Lyons*
Marketing Manager: *Tara Whorf*
Production Editor: *Michelle Limoges*
Compositor: *TKM Productions*
Composition and Prepress Buyer: *Linda Cox*
Manufacturing Buyer: *Andrew Turso*
Cover Designer: *Kristina Mose-Libon*

For related titles and support materials, visit our online catalog at www.ablongman.com.

Library of Congress Cataloging-in-Publication Data

McCarthy, Martha M.
Legal rights of teachers and students / Martha M. McCarthy, Nelda H. Cambron-McCabe, Stephen B. Thomas.
p. cm.
Rev. and condensed ed. of: Public school law / Nelda H. Cambron-McCabe, Martha M. McCarthy, Stephen B. Thomas. 5th ed. c2004.
Includes bibliographical references and index.
ISBN 0-205-35449-1
1. Teachers—Legal status, laws, etc.—United States. 2. Students—Legal status, laws, etc.—United States. I. Cambron-McCabe, Nelda H. II. Thomas, Stephen B. III. Cambron-McCabe, Nelda H. Public school law. IV. Title.

KF4119.M388 2004
344.73'078—dc21 2003051824

Printed in the United States of America

10 9 8 7 6 5 4 3 2 08 07 06 05 04

Contents

Preface

It has never been more imperative for teachers to understand the law. Since World War II, lawmakers have significantly reshaped educational policy. Most school personnel are aware of the escalating litigation and legislation, and some are familiar with the names of a few landmark Supreme Court decisions. But many educators do not understand basic legal principles that are being applied to educational questions. As a result, they are uncertain about the legality of daily decisions they must make in schools. Information provided in this book should help alleviate concerns voiced by educators who feel that the scales of justice have been tipped against them.

Material in *Legal Rights of Teachers and Students* is drawn from the fifth edition of *Public School Law: Teachers' and Students' Rights* (2004) that the three of us also authored. For this condensed book, we have selected topics particularly pertinent to classroom teachers. In analyzing specific school situations, we have explored the tension between government controls and individual freedoms in the school context. Implications of legal mandates are discussed, and guidelines are provided for educators. Throughout the chapters, we have highlighted in bold type or boxes some of the most important legal concepts. Also, we have included a number of tables, figures, and scenarios to make the information more meaningful.

We have attempted to cover the topics thoroughly but in a nontechnical manner, avoiding the extensive use of legal terms. However, the topics are documented in footnotes that appear at the bottom of pages if the reader wants to explore specific cases or points of law in greater detail. These notes provide additional information on selected cases and should assist the reader in understanding specific concepts. Also, a glossary of basic legal terms and a table of selected Supreme Court cases are provided at the end of the book.

A few comments about the nature of the law might assist the reader in using this book. Laws are not created in a vacuum; they reflect the social and philosophical attitudes of society. Moreover, individuals who have personal opinions and biases make laws. Although one may prefer to think that the law is always objective, personal considerations and national political trends do have an impact on the development and interpretation of legal principles.

Also, the law is not static, but rather is continually evolving as courts reinterpret constitutional and statutory provisions and as legislatures enact new laws. In the 1960s and early 1970s, courts and legislative bodies tended to focus on the expansion of personal rights through civil rights laws and constitutional interpretations favoring the individual's right to be free from unwarranted government intrusions. However, since 1975, judicial rulings have supported government authority to impose restraints on individual freedoms in the school context in the interest of the collective welfare. Although the themes of educational equity and individual rights, which dominated litigation earlier, remain important, efforts to attain educational excellence have generated a new genre of legal activity pertaining to teachers' qualifications and performance standards for students.

In this book, much of the discussion of the law focuses on court cases because the judiciary plays a vital role in interpreting constitutional and legislative provisions. Decisions are highlighted that illustrate points of law or legal trends, with particular emphasis on recent litigation. A few cases are pursued in depth to provide the reader with an understanding of the rationale behind the decisions. Reviewing the factual situations that have generated these controversies should make it easier for educators to identify potential legal problems in their own school situations.

As we complete this book, judicial decisions are being rendered and statutes are being proposed that may alter the status of the law vis-à-vis teachers and students. Additionally, some questions confronting school personnel have not yet been addressed by the Supreme Court and have generated conflicting decisions among lower courts. It may be frustrating to a reader searching for concrete answers to learn that in some areas the law is far from clear.

In spite of unresolved issues, certain legal principles have been established and can provide direction in many school situations. It is important for educators to become familiar with these principles and to use them to guide their decisions. Although the issues generating legal concern will change over time, knowledge of the logic underlying the law can make teachers more confident in dealing with questions that have not been clarified by courts or legislatures.

We have attempted to arrange the chapters in logical sequence for those reading the book in its entirety or using it as a text for school law courses. An introductory chapter establishes the legal context for the subsequent examination of students' and teachers' rights, and a concluding chapter provides a summary of the major legal principles. Subheadings appear within chapters to facilitate using this book for reference if a specific issue is of immediate interest. The reader is encouraged, however, to read the entire text because some topics are addressed in several chapters from different perspectives, and many of the principles of law transcend chapter divisions. Taken together, the chapters provide an overall picture of the relationship among issues and the applicable legal principles.

The material will assist school personnel in understanding the current application of the law, but it is not intended to serve as a substitute for legal counsel. Educators confronting legal problems should always seek the advice of an attorney. Also, there is no attempt here to predict the future course of courts and legislatures. Given the dynamic nature of the law, no single text can serve to keep teachers abreast of current legal developments. If we can provide an awareness of rights and responsibilities, motivate educators to translate the basic concepts into actual practice, and generate an interest in further study of the law, our purposes in writing this book will have been achieved.

Acknowledgments

A number of individuals contributed to the completion of this book. We are extremely grateful to our students who reacted to various drafts of the chapters and assisted in checking citations. Our sincere thanks go to several education graduate students and law students who provided valuable assistance in reviewing drafts of chapters, locating legal materials, and verifying citations: Rozlind Gallaspie, Tonya Gendin, Lisa Lee, Jennifer Nobles, and Ran Zhang. In addition, we appreciate the cheerful and conscientious assistance provided by staff members Peggy Bower, Jan Clegg, Susan Hanns, and Stephanie Maynard.

This book would not have been completed without the support of our families. Our parents offered constant encouragement, as they do in all our professional endeavors. The contributions of our spouses, George Kuh, Harry McCabe, and Yvonne Thomas, simply cannot be measured. They assumed far more than their share of family responsibilities during the writing of this book. Also, throughout this project, our children, Kari and Kristian Kuh, Patrick McCabe, and Kyle Thomas, provided support as well as much needed diversions from long hours of legal research.

1

Legal Framework of Public Education

The authority for the establishment and control of American public education, which serves about 46,900,000 students, is grounded in law. State and federal constitutional and statutory provisions provide the framework within which school operational decisions are made. Policies and practices at any level of the educational enterprise must be consistent with legal mandates from higher authorities. The overlapping jurisdictions of federal and state constitutions, Congress and state legislatures, federal and state courts, and various government agencies (including local school boards and school-based councils) present a complex environment for educators attempting to comply with legal requirements. In an effort to untangle the various legal relationships, this chapter describes the major sources of law and how they interact to form the legal basis for public education. This overview establishes a context for subsequent chapters in which legal principles are discussed more fully as they apply to specific school situations.

State Control of Education

> Since the United States Constitution does not authorize Congress to provide for education, the legal control of public education resides with the state as one of its sovereign powers.

The Tenth Amendment to the United States Constitution stipulates that "the powers not delegated to the United States by the Constitution, nor prohibited by it to the states, are reserved to the states respectively, or to the people." The Supreme Court repeatedly has affirmed the comprehensive authority of the states and school officials to control public schools as long as actions are consistent with fundamental federal constitutional safeguards. The state's authority over education is considered comparable to its powers to tax and to provide for the general welfare of its citizens. Although each state's educational system has unique features, many similarities are found across states.

Legislative Power

All state constitutions specifically address the legislative responsibility for establishing public schools. Usually the legislature is charged with providing for a uniform, thorough and efficient, or adequate system of public education. In contrast to the federal government, which has only those powers specified in the United States Constitution, state legislatures retain all powers not expressly forbidden by state or federal constitutional provisions. Thus, **the state legislature has plenary, or absolute, power to make laws governing education.**

Presently, all 50 states require that students between specified ages (usually 6 to 16) attend a public or private school or receive equivalent instruction to ensure an educated citizenry. States can authorize exemptions to compulsory attendance (e.g., married students) and can attach conditions to school enrollment (e.g., vaccination against communicable diseases). In addition, legislatures are empowered to create, consolidate, and abolish school districts; raise revenue and distribute educational funds; control teacher certification; prescribe curricular offerings; impose fees for textbooks; establish pupil performance standards; and regulate specific aspects of public school operations.

Legislatures also can authorize other school governance arrangements, such as state-funded charter schools that operate outside many regulations on the basis of a charter granted by the state or local board of education or other entities. The charter school movement has been characterized as one of the fastest growing education reform efforts nationally. **Since 1991, 39 states and the District of Columbia have enacted laws authorizing charter schools, usually specifying a cap on the number of charters granted to existing public or private schools or groups starting new schools.**[1] The number of charter schools range from one in a few states to more than 200 in Arizona and California. Charter schools account for less than 1 percent of all students, but their enrollment continues to increase as states approve new legislation and expand existing laws.

In some instances, when state laws are subject to several interpretations, courts are called on to clarify legislative intent or to assess the constitutionality of provisions. A state's attorney general also may be asked to interpret a law or to advise school boards on the legality of their actions, and such opinions are binding unless overruled by the judiciary.

Although the state legislature cannot relinquish its law-making powers, it can delegate to subordinate agencies the authority to make rules and regulations necessary to implement laws. These administrative functions must be carried out within the guidelines established by the legislature. Some states are quite liberal in delegating administrative authority, whereas other states prescribe detailed standards that must be followed by subordinate agencies. **It is a widely held perception that local school boards control public education, but local boards have only those powers conferred by the state.** Courts consistently have reiterated that the authority for public education is not a local one, but rather is a central

1. Center for Education Reform, *Charter School Highlights and Statistics,* 2002 (http://edreform.com/pubs/chglance.htm).

power residing in the state legislature. School buildings are considered state property, local school board members are state officials, and teachers are state employees. Public school funds, regardless of where collected, are state funds.

State Agencies

Since it has been neither feasible nor desirable to include in statutes every minor detail governing public schools, all states except Wisconsin have established a state board of education that typically supplies the structural details to implement broad legislative mandates. In most states, members of the state board of education are elected by the citizenry or appointed by the governor, and the board usually functions immediately below the legislature in the hierarchy of educational governance.

Accreditation is an important tool used by state boards to compel local school districts to abide by their directives. School districts often must satisfy state accreditation requirements as a condition of receiving state funds. Although models vary among states, the most common approach involves the establishment of minimum standards in areas such as curriculum, teacher qualifications, instructional materials, and facilities. In some states, different grades of school accreditation exist, with financial incentives to encourage local schools to attain the highest level. **Since the mid-1980s, there has been a movement toward performance-based accreditation under which a school's performance is assessed against predicted outcomes calculated for the school in areas such as pupil achievement, absenteeism, and retention.**

Within legislative parameters, the state board of education can issue directives governing school operations. In some states, rules pertaining to such matters as proficiency testing for students and programs for children with disabilities are embodied in state board rules rather than state law. The judiciary generally has upheld decisions made by state boards of education, unless they have violated legislative or constitutional mandates.

State boards of education, however, cannot abrogate powers delegated by law to other agencies. In 1991, the North Carolina Supreme Court held that the state board's prohibition on local board contracts with Whittle Communications interfered with school districts' statutory authority to enter into contracts for supplementary materials.[2] The school board's contract to air daily classroom broadcasts of Channel One (a news program including advertisements) in return for television equipment was within the local board's delegated authority.

In addition to the state board, generally considered a policymaking body, all states have designated a chief state school officer (CSSO), who often is known as the superintendent of public instruction or commissioner of education and functions in an executive capacity. The duties of the CSSO include engaging in research and long-range planning, monitoring reform initiatives, and adjudicating educational controversies. When considering an appeal of a CSSO's decision, courts will not judge the wisdom of the decision or overrule such a decision unless it is clearly arbitrary or against the preponderance of evidence. Each state also has established a state department of education, consisting of educa-

2. State v. Whittle Communications & Thomasville City Bd. of Educ., 402 S.E.2d 556 (N.C. 1991), *reh'g denied,* 404 S.E.2d 878 (N.C. 1991).

tional specialists who provide consultation to the state board, CSSO, and local school boards.

Local School Boards

Although public education in the United States is state controlled, it is for the most part locally administered. All states except Hawaii have created local school boards in addition to state education agencies and have delegated certain administrative authority over schools to these local boards. **Nationwide, there are approximately 14,900 local districts, ranging from a few students to several hundred thousand.** Some states, particularly those with a large number of small school districts, have established intermediate or regional administrative units that perform regulatory or service functions for several local districts.

As with the delegation of authority to state agencies, delegation of powers to local school boards is handled very differently across states. Some states with a deeply rooted tradition of local control over education (e.g., Colorado) give local boards a great deal of latitude in making operational decisions about schools. In states that tend toward centralized control of education (e.g., Florida), local boards must function within the framework of detailed legislative directives. **State legislatures retain the legal responsibility for education and can restrict the discretion of local boards by enacting legislation to that effect.**

The citizenry within the school district usually elects local school board members. The United States Supreme Court has recognized that the Equal Protection Clause requires each qualified voter to be given an opportunity to participate in the election of board members, with each vote given the same weight as far as practicable. When board members are elected from geographical districts, such districts must be established to protect voting rights under the "one person, one vote" principle. If "at-large" elections result in a dilution of the minority vote, an abridgment of the federal Voting Rights Act may be found.[3] However, the Supreme Court in 1996 struck down congressional redistricting plans drawn on the basis of race,[4] so the creation of race-based voting districts to ensure that a majority of the voters for designated school board seats are people of color would likely abridge the Fourteenth Amendment.[5]

The state legislature can specify the qualifications, method of selection, terms and conditions, and procedures for removal of local school board members. A local board must act as a body; individual board members are not empowered to make policies or perform official acts on behalf of the board. School boards have some discretion in adopting operational procedures, but they are legally bound to adhere to such procedures once established. **Although courts are reluctant to interfere with decisions made by boards of education and will not rule on the wisdom of such decisions, they will invalidate any board action**

3. 42 U.S.C. § 1971, *et seq.* (2003). Section 1973 states that "no practice or procedure shall be imposed or applied . . . in a manner which results in a denial or abridgment of the right . . . to vote on account of race."
4. Bush v. Vera, 517 U.S. 952 (1996); Shaw v. Hunt, 517 U.S. 899 (1996).
5. *See, e.g.,* Cannon v. N.C. State Bd. of Educ., 917 F. Supp. 387 (E.D.N.C. 1996) (holding that creation of race-based single board member voting districts threatened equal protection rights).

that is arbitrary, capricious, or outside the board's legal authority (i.e., an *ultra vires* act).

School board meetings and records must be open to the public. Most states have enacted "sunshine" or "open meeting" laws that specify exceptions, such as allowing school boards to meet in executive session to discuss matters that threaten public safety or pertain to pending or current litigation, personnel matters, collective bargaining, or the disposition of real property. Discussion of these matters may take place in closed meetings, but statutes usually stipulate that formal action must occur in open meetings.

Local school boards hold powers specified or implied in state law and other powers considered necessary to achieve the purposes of the express powers. These delegated powers generally encompass the authority to determine the details of the curriculum offered within the school district, raise revenue to build and maintain schools, select personnel, and enact other policies necessary to implement the educational program pursuant to law. Courts have recognized that even without specific enabling legislation, local boards have discretionary authority to enter into contracts and make decisions necessary to operate the schools.[6] However, local school boards cannot delegate their decision-making authority to other agencies or associations.

School-Based Councils

Since the mid-1980s, the notion of decentralizing many operational decisions to the school level (site-based management) has received considerable attention. Several legal controversies have focused on the composition and authority of these councils. In 1995, the Seventh Circuit upheld an Illinois law creating elected school councils, empowered to hire personnel and approve budgets and programs, in the Chicago public schools.[7]

The 1990 Kentucky Education Reform Act entailed major changes in school funding, curriculum, and governance, including the creation of school-based councils with authority for policy decisions affecting school sites. Whereas local school boards retain many of their traditional powers—such as establishing schools, setting tax rates and budgets, and maintaining facilities—the school-based councils are authorized to hire the building principal, select textbooks, and make policy decisions in other areas such as curricular offerings, staff assignments, and student discipline. In 1994, teachers challenged a local board's decision to require school-based councils to obtain board approval before implementing school improvement plans. Noting some overlap in duties between local boards and school councils, the Kentucky Supreme Court reasoned that the state did not delegate to local boards approval authority over council decisions pertaining to school improvement plans.[8] The court reasoned that the state law granting school-based councils independent policymaking

6. In recent years, corporations such as Education Alternatives, Inc. and the Edison Project have attracted substantial attention because of their contracts to manage public schools and school districts. Also, a number of companies, such as Sylvan Learning Systems, Britannica Learning Centers, and Berlitz Language Schools, have more limited contracts with public school districts to provide intensive tutoring or specialized instruction.

7. Pittman v. Chi. Bd. of Educ., 64 F.3d 1098 (7th Cir. 1995).

8. Bd. of Educ. v. Bushee, 889 S.W.2d 809 (Ky. 1994).

powers constituted a clear delegation of legislative authority to the school level. Decisions of school-based councils have the force of law and will not be invalidated by the judiciary unless the councils act beyond their scope of delegated authority or impair protected rights.

Local boards of education and, in some jurisdictions, school-based councils are authorized to perform discretionary duties (i.e., those involving judgment), whereas school employees (e.g., superintendents, principals, teachers) can perform only ministerial duties necessary to carry out policies. Hence, a superintendent can recommend personnel to be hired and propose a budget, but the school board, or in some instances the school council, must make the actual decisions. Although it might appear that educators at the building level retain little decision-making authority, administrators as well as classroom teachers can enact rules and regulations, consistent with policies and laws from higher authorities, to ensure the efficient operation of the school or class under their supervision.

Federal Role in Education

> The federal government influences public education through its funding powers and the enforcement of constitutional rights.

Unlike state constitutions, the Federal Constitution is silent regarding education; hence, individuals do not have an inherent federally protected right to an education.[9] The United States Constitution, however, does confer basic rights on individuals, and these rights must be respected by school personnel. Furthermore, Congress exerts control over the use of federal education aid and regulates other aspects of schools through legislation enacted pursuant to its constitutionally granted powers.

United States Constitution

A *constitution* is a body of precepts providing the system of fundamental laws of a nation, state, or society. The U.S. Constitution establishes a separation of powers among the executive, judicial, and legislative branches of government. These three branches form a system of checks and balances to ensure that the intent of the Constitution is respected. The Constitution also provides a systematic process for altering the document, if deemed necessary. Article V stipulates that amendments may be proposed by a two-thirds vote of each house of Congress or by a special convention called by Congress on the request of two-thirds of the state legislatures. Proposed amendments then must be ratified by three-fourths of the states to become part of the Constitution.

9. San Antonio Indep. Sch. Dist. v. Rodriguez, 411 U.S. 1 (1973) (holding that there is no explicit or implied fundamental right to an education under the Federal Constitution).

The U.S. Constitution is the supreme law in this nation, and state authority over education must be exercised in a manner consistent with its provisions. All federal constitutional mandates affect public education to some degree, but the following provisions have had the greatest impact on public school policies and practices.

General Welfare Clause. Under Article I, Section 8, of the Constitution, Congress has the power "to lay and collect taxes, duties, imposts and excises, to pay the debts and provide for the common defense and general welfare of the United States." In 1937, the Supreme Court declared that it will not interfere with the discretion of Congress in its domain, unless Congress exhibits a clear display of arbitrary power.[10]

Using the general welfare rationale, Congress has enacted legislation providing substantial federal support for research and instructional programs in areas such as science, mathematics, reading, special education, vocational education, career education, and bilingual education. Congress also has provided financial assistance for the school lunch program and for services to meet the special needs of various groups of students, such as the educationally and culturally disadvantaged. In addition, Congress has responded to national health and safety concerns with legislation such as the 1980 Asbestos School Hazard Detection and Control Act and the 1988 Indoor Radon Abatement Act, which require the inspection of school buildings and, if necessary, remedial action to assure the safety of students and employees. As addressed in Chapter 4, given the increasing use of the Internet, the federal government has attempted to protect the welfare of minors by policing the suitability of materials made available to them electronically.

Obligation of Contracts Clause. Article I, Section 10, of the Constitution stipulates that states cannot enact any law impairing the obligation of contracts. Administrators, teachers, and noncertified personnel are protected from arbitrary dismissals by contractual agreements. School boards also enter into numerous contracts with individuals and companies in conducting school business. The judiciary often is called on to evaluate the validity of a given contract or to assess whether a party has breached its contractual obligations.

First Amendment. **The Bill of Rights, comprising the first 10 amendments to the United States Constitution, safeguards individual liberties against government encroachment.** The most preciously guarded of these liberties are contained in the First Amendment's protection of speech, press, assembly, and religious liberties. The religion clauses have evoked a number of lawsuits challenging government aid to and regulation of nonpublic schools and contesting public school policies and practices as advancing religion or impairing free exercise rights. Cases involving students' rights to express themselves and to distribute literature have been initiated under First Amendment guarantees of freedom of speech and press. Moreover, teachers' rights to academic freedom and to speak out on matters of public concern have precipitated numerous lawsuits. The right of assembly has been the focus of litigation involving student clubs and employees' rights to organize and engage in collective bargaining.

10. Helvering v. Dains, 301 U.S. 619, 644–645 (1937).

Fourth Amendment. This amendment guarantees the right of citizens "to be secure in their persons, houses, papers, and effects against unreasonable searches and seizures." It safeguards individuals against arbitrary government intrusions and has frequently appeared in educational cases involving drug-testing programs and searches of students' lockers, cars, and persons. A few cases also have involved alleged violations of school employees' Fourth Amendment rights by school officials.

Fourteenth Amendment. **The Fourteenth Amendment, adopted in 1868, is the most widely invoked constitutional provision in school litigation because it specifically addresses state action.** In part, the Fourteenth Amendment provides that no state shall "deny to any person within its jurisdiction, the equal protection of the laws." This clause has been significant in school cases involving alleged discrimination based on race, gender, ethnic background, and disabilities. In addition, some school finance litigation often has been based on the Equal Protection Clause.

The Due Process Clause of the Fourteenth Amendment, which prohibits states from depriving citizens of life, liberty, or property without due process of law, also has played an important role in school litigation. Property rights are legitimate expectations of entitlement created through state laws, regulations, or contracts. Compulsory school attendance laws confer on students a legitimate property right to attend school, and the granting of tenure gives teachers a property entitlement to continued employment. Liberty rights include interests in one's reputation and fundamental rights related to marriage, family matters, and personal privacy. In addition, the Supreme Court has interpreted Fourteenth Amendment liberties as incorporating the personal freedoms contained in the Bill of Rights.[11] Thus, the first 10 amendments, originally directed toward the federal government, have been applied to state action as well. Although the concept of "incorporation" has been criticized, Supreme Court precedent supports the notion that the Fourteenth Amendment restricts state interference with fundamental constitutional liberties. **This incorporation principle is particularly important in school litigation since education is a state function; claims that public school policies or practices impair personal freedoms (e.g., First Amendment free speech guarantees) often are initiated through the Fourteenth Amendment.**

The federal judiciary has identified both procedural and substantive components of due process guarantees. Procedural due process ensures fundamental fairness if the government threatens an individual's life, liberty, or property interests; minimum procedures required by the Constitution are notice of the charges, an opportunity to refute the charges, and a hearing that is conducted fairly. Substantive due process requires that state action be based on a valid objective with means reasonably related to attaining the objective. In essence, substantive due process shields the individual against arbitrary government action that impairs life, liberty, or property interests.

Since the Fourteenth Amendment protects personal liberties against unwarranted state interference, private institutions, including private schools, usually are not subject to these restrictions. For practices of private schools and other private entities to be challenged successfully under the Fourteenth Amendment, there must be sufficient government

11. *See* Cantwell v. Connecticut, 310 U.S. 296, 303 (1940); Gitlow v. New York, 268 U.S. 652, 666 (1925).

involvement in the private school to constitute "state action." This is difficult to establish unless a private entity performs state functions. For example, in 2001, the Supreme Court ruled that private organizations regulating interscholastic sports and other activities among private and public schools are considered state actors if sufficiently involved with state school officials.[12] Thus, private high school athletic associations can be liable for constitutional violations. It is unlikely, however, that a private school would meet the criteria to be considered a state actor.

Federal Legislation

Congress is empowered to enact laws to translate the intent of the United States Constitution into actual practices. **Laws reflect the will of the legislative branch of government, which, theoretically, in a democracy represents the citizenry.** Because the states have sovereign power regarding education, the federal government's involvement in public schools has been one of indirect support, not direct control.

Funding Laws. Federal legislation affecting public education was enacted prior to ratification of the Constitution. The Ordinances of 1785 and 1787, providing land grants to states for the maintenance of public schools, encouraged the establishment of public education in many states. However, it was not until the mid-twentieth century that Congress began to play a significant role in stimulating targeted educational reform through its spending powers under the General Welfare Clause.

The most comprehensive law offering financial assistance to schools, the Elementary and Secondary Education Act of 1965 (ESEA), in part supplied funds for compensatory education programs for economically disadvantaged students. With passage of the ESEA, federal aid to education doubled, and the federal government's contribution increased steadily until reaching its high point of over 9 percent of total public education revenue in 1981. In 2000, the federal share was 7.3 percent.[13]

Congress and federal administrative agencies have exerted considerable influence in shaping public school policies and practices through categorical funding laws and their accompanying administrative regulations. Individual states or school districts have the option of accepting or rejecting such federal assistance, but if categorical aid is accepted, the federal government has the authority to prescribe guidelines for its use and to monitor state and local education agencies to ensure fiscal accountability.

Much of the federal categorical legislation enacted during the 1960s and 1970s provided funds to assist school districts in attaining equity goals and addressing other national priorities. For example, the Bilingual Education Act of 1968 and the Education for All Handicapped Children Act of 1975 (which became the Individuals with Disabilities Education Act of 1990) have provided federal funds to assist education agencies in offering services for students with special needs. Although in the 1980s Congress shifted away from its

12. Brentwood Acad. v. Tenn. Secondary Sch. Athletic Ass'n, 531 U.S. 288 (2001).
13. National Center for Education Statistics, Revenues and Expenditures for Public Elementary and Secondary Education (Washington, DC: U.S. Department of Education, 2002) (http://nces.ed.gov/pubs2002/20002367).

heavy reliance on categorical federal aid by consolidating some categorical programs into block grants with reduced funding and regulations, aid for economically disadvantaged and English-deficient students and children with disabilities has remained categorical in nature.

In 2002, President Bush signed into law the No Child Left Behind Act, the most comprehensive reform of the ESEA since it was enacted in 1965.[14] This law, directed at improving the performance of public schools, pledges that no child will be left in a failing school. Specifically, the law requires states to implement accountability systems with higher performance standards in reading and mathematics along with annual testing of all students in grades 3 through 8. Furthermore, assessment data must be categorized by poverty, ethnicity, race, disability, and limited English proficiency to ensure that no group of children is left behind. The law greatly expands choices for parents of children attending Title I schools that do not meet state standards. If students are in a school that has been identified as low performing, they must be given the option of attending a better school within the district, including charter schools. For students attending persistently failing schools (failure to make adequate yearly progress in three of the four preceding years), the school district must permit the students to use Title I funds to obtain supplemental educational services (e.g., tutoring, after-school or summer programs) from either public or private providers. Persistently failing schools face mandated reconstitution if they do not make adequate yearly progress.

Civil Rights Laws. In addition to laws providing financial assistance to public schools, Congress has enacted legislation designed to clarify the scope of individuals' civil rights. **Unlike the discretion enjoyed by state and local education agencies in deciding whether to participate in federal funding programs, educational institutions must comply with these civil rights laws.** Some federal antidiscrimination laws are enacted to enforce constitutional rights and have general application. Others apply only to recipients of federal financial assistance. Various federal agencies are charged with monitoring compliance with these laws and can bring suit against noncomplying institutions. Under some civil rights laws, individuals also can initiate private suits to compel compliance and, in some instances, to obtain personal remedies.

Several laws enacted in the latter part of the nineteenth century to protect the rights of African American citizens were seldom the focus of litigation until the mid-twentieth century. Since the 1960s, these laws, particularly 42 U.S.C. Section 1983, have been used by students and teachers to gain relief in instances where their federal rights have been violated by school policies and practices. **Section 1983 provides a private right to bring suit for damages against any person who, acting under color of state law, impairs rights secured by the United States Constitution and certain federal laws.**[15] Although Section 1983 does not confer specific substantive rights, it has been significant in school cases because it allows individuals to obtain damages from school officials and school districts for

14. 20 U.S.C. § 6301 *et seq.* (2003).

15. School boards as well as school officials are considered "persons" under 42 U.S.C. § 1983 (2003). *See* text accompanying note 88, Chapter 12.

abridgments of federally protected rights. However, Section 1983 cannot be used to enforce federal laws where congressional intent to create private rights is not explicit.[16]

Subsequent civil rights laws enacted since the 1960s do confer substantive rights to protect citizens from discrimination. The vindication of employees' rights in school settings has generated substantial litigation under Title VII of the Civil Rights Act of 1964, which prohibits employment discrimination on the basis of race, color, sex, religion, or national origin. Modeled in part after Title VII, the Americans with Disabilities Act of 1990 provides specific protections in employment and public accommodations for individuals with disabilities. Also, the Age Discrimination in Employment Act of 1967 protects employees over age 40 against age-based employment discrimination. Other civil rights laws pertain only to institutions housing programs that receive federal funds, such as Title VI of the Civil Rights Act of 1964 (prohibiting discrimination on the basis of race, color, or national origin), Title IX of the Education Amendments of 1972 (barring gender discrimination against participants in education programs), the Rehabilitation Act of 1973 (prohibiting discrimination against otherwise qualified persons with disabilities), and the Age Discrimination Act of 1975 (barring age discrimination in federally assisted programs or activities). Courts often have been called on to interpret these acts and their regulations as they apply to educational practices.

Still other federal laws offer protections to individuals in educational settings and place responsibilities on school officials. For example, the Family Educational Rights and Privacy Act guarantees parents access to their children's school records and safeguards the confidentiality of such records. Federal laws also protect human subjects in research projects and require parental consent before students participate in federally supported psychiatric or psychological examination, testing, or treatment designed to reveal information in specified sensitive areas. Courts have played an important role in interpreting the protections included in these laws and ensuring compliance with the federal mandates.

Federal Administrative Agencies

Similar to state governments, much of the regulatory activity at the federal level is conducted by administrative agencies. In 1980, the Department of Education was created; its secretary, who serves as a member of the president's cabinet, is appointed by the president with the advice and approval of the Senate. Regulations promulgated by the Department of Education to implement funding laws have had a significant impact on many schools. The department administers regulations for over 100 different programs ranging from services for Native American students to projects for school dropouts.

Through their regulatory activities, numerous federal agencies influence state and local education policies. For example, the Office for Civil Rights and the Equal Employment Opportunity Commission have reviewed claims of discrimination in public schools and have initiated suits against school districts that are not in compliance with civil rights

16. *See* Gonzaga Univ. v. Doe, 536 U. S. 273 (2002) (finding that Congress did not intend to create privately enforceable rights under the Family Education Rights and Privacy Act); text accompanying note 92 , Chapter 4.

laws. The Environmental Protection Agency also has placed obligations on schools in connection with asbestos removal and maintenance of safe school environments. School districts can face the termination of federal assistance if they do not comply with such federal regulations.

Function and Structure of the Judicial System

> Courts do not initiate laws, but they influence the law by interpreting the meaning of constitutional and statutory provisions.

Judicial decisions are usually cited in conjunction with statutory and constitutional provisions as a major source of educational law. As early as 1835, Alexis de Tocqueville noted that "scarcely any political question arises in the United States that is not resolved, sooner or later, into a judicial question."[17] Courts play an important role in applying principles of law to settle disputes. The terms *common law* and *case law* refer to judicially created legal principles that are relied on as precedent when similar factual situations arise.

Although most constitutional provisions and statutory enactments never become the subject of litigation, some provisions require judicial clarification. Since federal and state constitutions set forth broad policy statements rather than specific guides to action, courts serve an important function in interpreting such mandates and in determining the legality of various school policies and practices.

The Supreme Court has articulated specific guidelines for exercising the power of judicial review. The Court will not decide hypothetical cases and will not render an opinion on issues in nonadversarial proceedings. A genuine controversy must be initiated by a party with standing to sue. To achieve such standing, the party must have a "real interest" in the outcome of the case, such as having been adversely affected by the challenged practice. The Court also will not anticipate a constitutional question or decide a case on constitutional grounds if there is some other basis for resolving the dispute. **In applying appropriate principles of law to specific cases, the Court generally follows the doctrine of *stare decisis* (abide by decided cases), and thus relies on precedents established in previous decisions.** On occasion, however, the Court does overrule a prior opinion.

Procedures vary somewhat by type of suit and jurisdiction, but a plaintiff typically initiates a suit by filing a complaint with the appropriate court clerk. After a period of *discovery* when evidence is gathered, the defendant may submit a *motion to dismiss,* arguing that the plaintiff failed to state a legal claim or that the claim was barred by the applicable statute of limitations (i.e., the plaintiff failed to file within time restrictions). Furthermore, either party may request *summary judgment,* noting that facts of the case are not in dispute

17. Alexis de Tocqueville, *Democracy in America,* rev. ed. (New York: Alfred A. Knopf, 1960), vol. 1, p. 280.

and that the party is entitled to judgment based on applicable law. If summary judgment is not granted, the plaintiff's case then is presented. At that point, a *directed verdict* (state trials) or *judgment as a matter of law* (federal trials) may be awarded if either the plaintiff fails to establish a legal violation or the defendant is unsuccessful in identifying a proper defense. When a directed verdict is not granted, the defendant's case is then presented.

In cases argued before a judge, the trial judge holds a hearing to make findings of fact based on the evidence presented and then applies legal principles to those facts in rendering a judgment. If the case involves a jury trial, the jury renders a verdict, identifying the prevailing party and appropriate awards. Either party may file a motion for a *judgment notwithstanding the verdict* if believed that the jury made an error as a matter of law. Also, either party may file a motion for a new trial, alleging that proper procedures were not followed, or appeal the decision to a higher court. Figure 1.1 displays the steps (civil procedure) that typically are followed at the trial court level.

If the ruling is appealed, the appellate court must accept the trial court's findings of fact unless they are clearly erroneous. The appeals court reviews the written record of the evidence but does not hold a hearing for witnesses to be questioned. The appellate court may accept the trial court's findings of fact but disagree with the conclusions of law.

In addition to individual suits,[18] education cases often involve class-action suits brought on behalf of all similarly situated individuals. To be certified as a class action, the suit must satisfy rules of civil procedure that specify prerequisites to establish class members' commonality of injury and circumstances.

Various remedies are available through court action. In some suits, a court-ordered injunction is sought to compel school officials to cease a particular action or to remove restraints they have imposed on protected freedoms. For a court to issue an injunction, evidence must indicate that the complainant would likely prevail in a trial on the merits of the case. Judicial relief also can take the form of a declaration that specific rights must be respected. In addition, courts can order personal remedies, such as reinstatement and removal of material from school records. Moreover, courts can award damages to compensate individuals for the deprivation of their rights, and punitive damages at times can be assessed against state officials if such deprivations constitute a willful or reckless disregard of protected rights. Under certain circumstances, attorneys' fees can be awarded.

In interpreting constitutional and statutory provisions, courts have developed various criteria to evaluate whether the law has been violated. These judicially created standards or "tests" are extremely important and in some instances appear to go beyond the original intent of the constitutional or statutory provision in question. Judicial standards for assessing claims under various constitutional and statutory provisions are continually evolving and being refined by courts. The judiciary thus occupies a powerful position in shaping the law through its interpretive powers.

18. Most educational litigation involves civil suits, initiated by individuals alleging injury by another private party. Civil suits often involve claims for damages or requests for specific conduct to cease because it impairs the individual's protected rights. In contrast, criminal suits are brought on behalf of society to punish an individual for committing a crime, such as parents who violate compulsory school attendance laws.

FIGURE 1.1 *Civil Procedure*

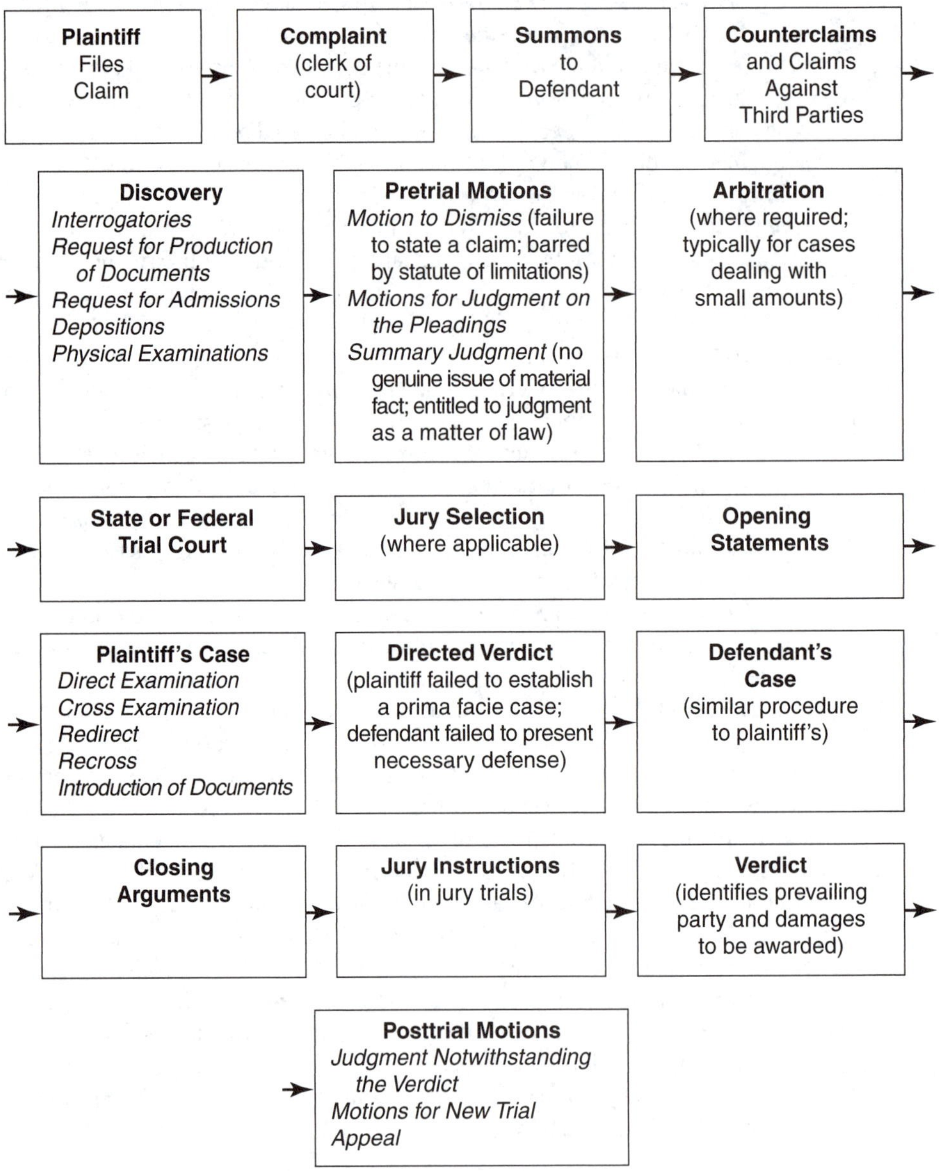

Courts, however, will not intervene in a school-related controversy if the dispute can be settled in a legislative or administrative forum. All state educational systems provide some type of administrative appeals procedure for aggrieved individuals to use in disputes involving internal school operations. Many school controversies never reach the courts because they are settled in these administrative forums. Under most circumstances, courts require such administrative appeals to be exhausted before court action is brought. Also, some courts will direct parties to participate in arbitration in an effort to resolve the dispute and avoid a trial.

In evaluating the impact of case law, it is important to keep in mind that a judicial ruling applies as precedent within the geographical jurisdiction of the court delivering the opinion. It is possible for two state supreme courts or two federal courts to render conflicting decisions on an issue, and such decisions are binding in their respective jurisdictions. Only decisions of the United States Supreme Court have national application.

State Courts

State courts are established pursuant to state constitutional provisions, and the structure of judicial systems varies among states. In contrast to federal courts, which have only those powers granted by the United States Constitution, state courts can review most types of controversies unless restricted by state law. State judicial systems usually include trial courts of general jurisdiction, courts of special jurisdiction, and appellate courts. All states have a court of last resort, and decisions rendered by state high courts can be appealed to the United States Supreme Court.

In most states, the court of last resort is called the supreme court or supreme judicial court. However, in New York and Maryland, the highest court is the Court of Appeals, and in West Virginia, it is the Supreme Court of Appeals. Courts occupying the next level in the state judicial system usually are referred to as appeals courts or superior courts. State trial courts of general jurisdiction often are called district or circuit courts, but in New York, trial courts are referred to as supreme courts of their respective counties. The most common special jurisdiction courts are juvenile, probate, domestic relations, and small claims courts. State judges are either elected or appointed by the governor.

Federal Courts

Article III, Section I, of the United States Constitution establishes the Supreme Court and authorizes Congress to create other federal courts as necessary. The federal court system contains courts of special jurisdiction such as the Claims Court, Tax Court, and Court of International Trade. There are three levels of federal courts of general jurisdiction: district courts, circuit courts of appeal, and the Supreme Court. The number of federal district courts in a state is based on population. Each state has at least one federal district court; many states have two or three; and California, New York, and Texas have four each. Judgments at the district court level are usually presided over by one judge.

On the federal appeals level, the nation is divided into 12 geographic circuits, each with its own federal circuit court of appeals.[19] A thirteenth federal circuit court has national jurisdiction to hear appeals regarding specific claims (e.g., customs; copyrights, patents, and trademarks; international trade). Most federal circuit courts have from 15 to 20 judges, but the largest (Ninth Circuit) has more than 40 judges. Circuit decisions usually are rendered by a panel of the court, but in some instances the entire court *(en banc)* will rehear a case. Although a federal circuit court decision is binding only in the states within that circuit, such decisions often influence other appellate courts when dealing with similar questions. The jurisdiction of the federal circuits is as follows:

- *First Circuit:* Maine, Massachusetts, New Hampshire, Rhode Island, and Puerto Rico;
- *Second Circuit:* Connecticut, New York, and Vermont;
- *Third Circuit:* Delaware, New Jersey, Pennsylvania, and the Virgin Islands;
- *Fourth Circuit:* Maryland, North Carolina, South Carolina, Virginia, and West Virginia;
- *Fifth Circuit:* Louisiana, Mississippi, Texas, and the Canal Zone;
- *Sixth Circuit:* Kentucky, Michigan, Ohio, and Tennessee;
- *Seventh Circuit:* Illinois, Indiana, and Wisconsin;
- *Eighth Circuit:* Arkansas, Iowa, Minnesota, Missouri, Nebraska, North Dakota, and South Dakota;
- *Ninth Circuit:* Alaska, Arizona, California, Idaho, Hawaii, Montana, Nevada, Oregon, Washington, and Guam;
- *Tenth Circuit:* Colorado, Kansas, New Mexico, Oklahoma, Utah, and Wyoming;
- *Eleventh Circuit:* Alabama, Florida, and Georgia;
- *DC Circuit:* Washington, DC;[20] and
- *Federal Circuit:* National jurisdiction on specific claims.

The United States Supreme Court is, of course, the highest court in the nation, beyond which there is no appeal. **It has been firmly established that the Supreme Court has the ultimate authority in interpreting federal constitutional guarantees.**[21] If the Supreme Court finds a specific practice unconstitutional (e.g., intentional school segregation), this judicial mandate applies nationwide. If the Court, however, concludes that a given activity does not impair federal constitutional guarantees (e.g., corporal punishment in public schools), states and local school boards retain discretion in placing restrictions on the activity. In the latter instances, legal requirements will vary across jurisdictions.

When the judiciary interprets a statutory enactment contrary to legislative intent, the law can be amended to clarify its purpose. Congress has done so with a number of civil rights laws in response to Supreme Court rulings. However, the legislative branch does not have this discretion in connection with constitutional interpretations. If the Supreme Court rules that a federal law conflicts with a provision of the United States Constitution, the only

19. In 1981, the Fifth Circuit was divided into the Fifth and Eleventh Circuits.
20. Washington, DC, has its own federal district court and circuit court of appeals; only federal laws apply in this jurisdiction.
21. *See* Marbury v. Madison, 5 U.S. (1 Cranch) 137 (1803).

recourse to keep the law is to amend the Constitution. Given the significance of Supreme Court decisions and the nine justices' lifetime appointments, the composition of the Court is critically important.

The Supreme Court has original jurisdiction in cases in which a state is a party or cases that involve federal ambassadors and other public ministers. The Court has appellate jurisdiction in other cases arising under the Constitution or federal laws or entailing disputes between states or parties residing in different states.[22] The Supreme Court disposes of approximately 5,000 cases a year, but renders a written opinion on the merits in less than 5 percent of these cases. The Court often concludes that the topic of a case is not appropriate or of sufficient significance to warrant Supreme Court review. It requires concurrence of at least four justices for a case to be accepted, and denial of review *(certiorari)* does not infer agreement with the lower court's decision even though that decision stands. Since the Supreme Court has authority to determine which cases it will hear, many issues are left for resolution by lower courts. Accordingly, precedents regarding some school controversies must be gleaned from federal circuit courts or state supreme courts and may differ from one jurisdiction to another.

An individual need not exhaust state administrative appeals before initiating a federal suit if the abridgment of a federally protected right is involved, but some federal laws specify administrative procedures that must be pursued before commencing court action. Suits involving federal issues also may be heard by state courts, and the United States Supreme Court may review the interpretation of federal rights by the state judiciary. Individuals have a choice whether to initiate a federal or state suit in these circumstances, but they cannot relitigate an issue in federal court if they have been denied relief by the state judiciary. In essence, a federal suit cannot be initiated if the state judiciary has already adjudicated the issue or it could have been raised in the prior state litigation.

Judicial Trends

Traditionally, the federal judiciary did not address educational concerns; fewer than 300 cases involving education had been initiated in federal courts prior to 1954.[23] However, starting with the landmark desegregation decision, *Brown v. Board of Education of Topeka* (1954),[24] federal courts assumed a significant role in resolving educational controversies. By 1970, litigation was clearly viewed as an important tool to influence social policies, and more legal challenges to school practices were initiated in the 1970s than in the preceding seven decades combined.[25] Since the 1960s, courts have addressed nearly every facet of the educational enterprise. Much of this judicial intervention has involved the protection of individual rights and the attainment of equity for minority groups.

The volume of federal cases pertaining to school issues reached its zenith in the 1970s. Since then, it has stabilized or declined slightly in most areas (e.g., employment concerns,

22. *See* text accompanying note 94, Chapter 12, for a discussion of Eleventh Amendment restrictions on federal lawsuits brought by citizens against the state.

23. John Hogan, *The Schools, the Courts, and the Public Interest* (Lexington, MA: D. C. Heath, 1985), p. 11.

24. 347 U.S. 483 (1954).

25. William Bennett, "Excessive Legalization in Education," *Chicago Daily Law Bulletin* (February 22, 1988), p. 2.

student discipline), except for litigation dealing with church/state issues and the rights of children with disabilities. Indeed, cases involving children with disabilities have increased at a phenomenal rate since 1980.

There has been a notable shift in the posture of the federal judiciary during the past two decades. In the 1960s and early 1970s, federal courts expanded constitutional protections afforded to individuals in school settings, but since the 1980s, the federal judiciary has exhibited more deference to the decisions of the legislative and executive branches and greater reluctance to extend the scope of civil rights. **When the Supreme Court strikes down a practice under the Constitution, standards become more uniform nationally, but when the Court defers to local boards, standards vary, reflecting local perspectives.** If the federal judiciary continues to exhibit restraint, volatile political controversies will be assured, because policymakers will have to grapple with issues that formerly were settled through judicial pronouncements.

The Rehnquist Court's strong federalism stance is redefining the balance of power between the federal government and states. In sharply divided decisions, the Supreme Court has strengthened states' sovereign immunity by precluding federal lawsuits against states unless Congress has abrogated state immunity through legislation enacted to enforce the Fourteenth Amendment. Such congressional intent, however, must be explicit in the federal legislation. For example, in recent cases, the Court held that Congress exceeded its authority in imposing liability on states under the Age Discrimination in Employment Act[26] and the American with Disabilities Act.[27] Although the new federalism limits suits against states, school districts will not benefit from the immunity unless they are considered an arm of the state for Eleventh Amendment purposes.[28]

The debate will likely continue over whether courts have the competence to play a key role in shaping educational policies and whether it is legitimate for courts to play such a role, but it cannot be questioned that courts influence school policies. Despite some deceleration in federal litigation, the volume of school cases is still substantial, far outstripping school litigation in any other nation.

Conclusion

Public schools in the United States are governed by a complex body of regulations that are grounded in constitutional provisions, statutory enactments, agency regulations, and court decisions. Since the mid-twentieth century, legislation relating to schools has increased significantly in both volume and complexity, and courts have played an important role in interpreting statutory and constitutional provisions. Although rules made at any level must be consistent with higher authority, administrators and teachers retain considerable latitude in establishing rules and procedures within their specific jurisdictions. As long as educators act reasonably and do not impair the protected rights of others, their actions will be upheld if challenged in court.

26. Kimel v. Fla. Bd. of Regents, 528 U.S. 62 (2000).
27. Bd. of Trs. v. Garrett, 531 U.S. 356 (2001).
28. See text accompanying note 95, Chapter 12.

2

Tort Liability

Tort law offers civil rather than criminal remedies to individuals for harm caused by the unreasonable conduct of others. **Generally, a *tort* is described as a civil wrong, independent of breach of contract, for which a court will provide relief in the form of damages.** Tort cases primarily involve state law and are grounded in the fundamental premise that individuals are liable for the consequences of their conduct that result in injury to others. Most school tort actions can be grouped into three categories: negligence, intentional torts, and defamation.[1]

Negligence

> The propriety of an educator's conduct in a given situation is gauged by whether a reasonably prudent teacher (with the special skills and training associated with that role) would have acted in a similar fashion under like conditions.

Negligence is a breach of one's legal duty to protect others from unreasonable risks of harm. The failure to act, or the commission of an improper act, that results in injury or loss to another person, can constitute negligence. To establish negligence, an injury must be avoidable by the exercise of reasonable care. Additionally, each of the following four elements must be present to support a successful claim (see Figure 2.1):

- The defendant has a *duty* to protect the plaintiff,
- The *duty is breached* by the failure to exercise an appropriate *standard of care,*

1. A fourth category of tort cases is termed *strict liability.* This type of tort occurs when an injury results from the creation of an unusual or extreme hazard. Because such torts are uncommon in educational settings, they are not discussed in this chapter.

FIGURE 2.1 *Negligence: Elements and Defenses*

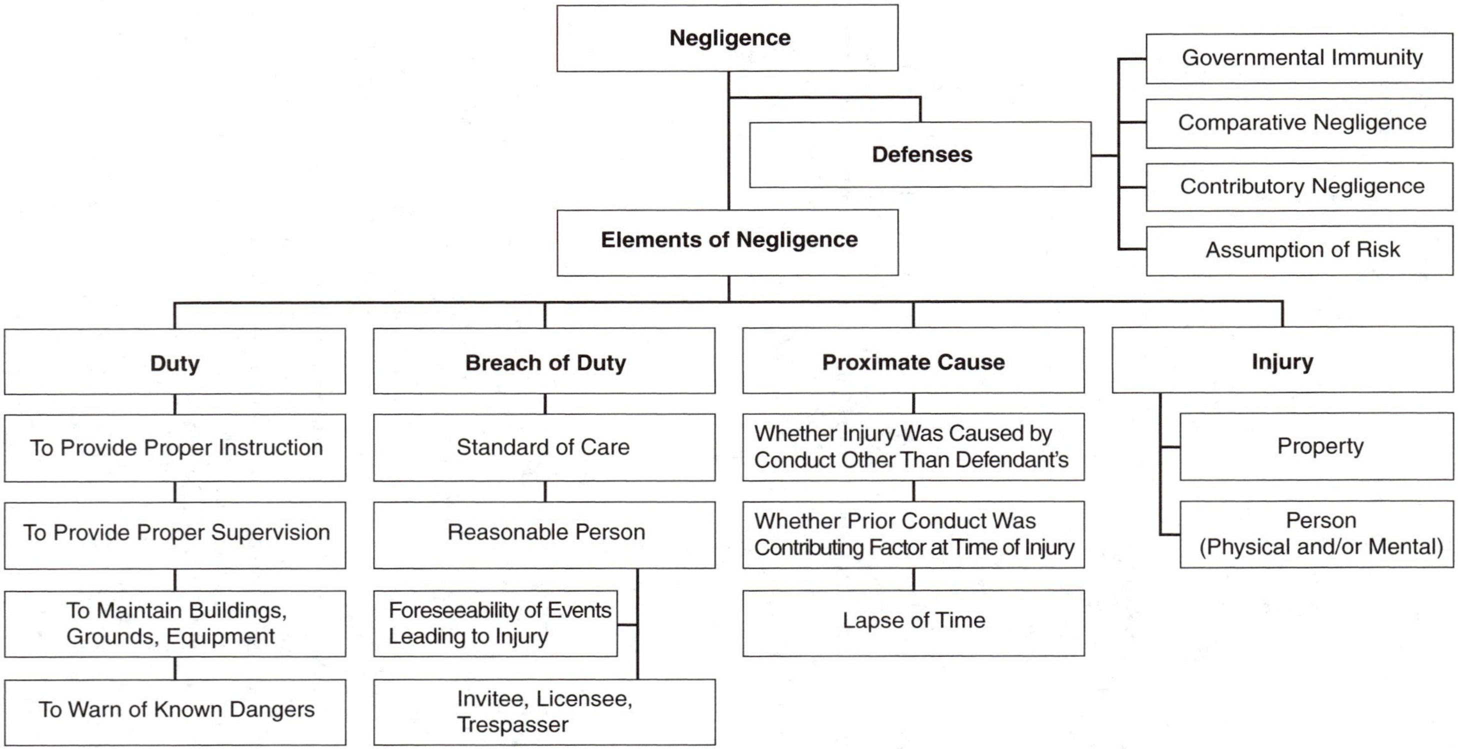

- The negligent conduct is the *proximate or legal cause* of the injury, and
- An actual *injury* occurs.

Duty

School officials have a common law duty to anticipate foreseeable dangers and to take necessary precautions to protect students entrusted in their care. **The specific duties that school personnel owe students are to give proper instruction; provide adequate supervision; maintain equipment, facilities, and grounds; and warn students of known dangers**.

Instruction. Teachers have a duty to provide students with adequate and appropriate instruction prior to commencing an activity that may pose a risk of harm—the greater the risk, the greater the need for thorough instruction. Following such instruction, an effort should be made to determine whether the material was heard and understood. This can be accomplished through assessments appropriate for the activity, such as paper and pencil tests, oral tests, and observations. A Nebraska case focused on inadequate instructions and failure to make protective aprons available to the students, as was recommended for welding class activities. The instructor had informed the students simply to wear old shirts and stated on four separate occasions that it was not his responsibility to ensure that students wore protective clothing. "Safety garments" as a topic was briefly mentioned in one of many handouts distributed in class, but the instructor made no effort to determine whether students read or understood the material and never prevented a student from participating based on the type of clothing worn.[2]

Supervision. Although state statutes require educators to provide proper supervision, school personnel are not expected to have every child under surveillance at all times during the school day or to anticipate every possible accident or incident that might occur. Moreover, there is no set level of supervision (i.e., there is no predetermined student-teacher ratio mandated by courts) required under common law for each activity or population.

In assessing if adequate supervision has been provided, courts will determine whether the events leading up to the injury foreseeably placed the student at risk and whether the injury could have been prevented by proper supervision. Two student injury cases involving rock-throwing incidents illustrate this point. In one instance where student rock throwing had continued for almost 10 minutes before the injury occurred, the court found the supervising teacher liable for negligence.[3] But, when a teacher aide had walked past a group of students moments before one child threw a rock that was deflected and hit another child, no liability was assessed.[4] The court concluded that the teacher aide had provided adequate supervision and had no reason to anticipate the event that caused the injury.

2. Norman v. Ogallala Pub. Sch. Dist., 609 N.W.2d 338 (Neb. 2000).
3. Sheehan v. Saint Peter's Catholic Sch., 188 N.W.2d 868 (Minn. 1971).
4. Fagan v. Summers, 498 P.2d 1227 (Wyo. 1972). *See also* Janukajtis v. Fallon, 726 N.Y.S.2d 451 (App. Div. 2001) (finding that even with intense supervision, officials could not have prevented a child from being injured when struck in the eye with a stick thrown by a fellow student).

The school district's duty to supervise also includes the duty to protect pupils and employees from foreseeable risks posed by other students or school personnel, as well as persons not associated with the district. Depending on the circumstances of a particular case, districts can meet this duty by warning potential victims, increasing the number of supervisory personnel, and/or providing increased security where assaults, batteries, or other violent acts are reasonably foreseeable. Courts do not expect schools to ensure the safety of students, but do require that officials respond promptly and professionally when confronted with potentially dangerous circumstances.[5]

If conduct of an individual violator, and not the negligent supervision of the district, is the proximate cause of the injury, most courts have rejected school district tort liability. Even if the alleged violator is a school employee, conduct such as battery and sexual assault represent independent acts outside an individual's scope of employment. Nonetheless, districts may be found liable for negligence in hiring or in retaining employees where school officials had knowledge of prior or continuing misconduct.[6]

It is important to note that there may be times when students pass out of the "orbit of school authority" even though they are physically present on campus. This often occurs today, given the wide range of uses of school buildings (e.g., meetings for nonschool groups such as Scouts). In such a case, an Indiana appeals court found that a district had no duty to supervise male students who secretly videotaped female lifeguards in their locker room in various stages of undress. The tape later was circulated at the school, and the victims claimed that the school district's negligence caused their emotional distress. The lifeguard class, although held in school facilities, was not part of the public school curriculum (i.e., it was sponsored by the Red Cross), and school employees neither taught nor supervised the course. Once school officials learned what had transpired, they investigated, identified, and suspended those responsible and confiscated the one remaining tape. The incident was found to be unforeseeable, and no special duty was established for the district either to provide security or to supervise the class.[7]

Supervision of students en route to and from school also has generated considerable litigation. Over the years, parents have argued that school officials are responsible for their children from the time they leave home until the time they return. Although such a bright-line test would assist courts in rendering uniform decisions, in this instance it clearly would result in the placement of an unrealistic demand on school resources and an unfair burden

5. *See, e.g.,* David XX v. Saint Catherine's Ctr. for Children, 699 N.Y.S.2d 827 (App. Div. 1999) (denying summary judgment where a 6-year-old was sexually abused by a 13-year-old during transport to school; the parents had informed officials on numerous occasions that an aide had not accompanied the driver, as was required, and that the older child had a history of aggressive sexual dysfunction).

6. *See, e.g.,* Doe v. Cedar Rapids Cmty. Sch. Dist., 652 N.W.2d 439 (Iowa 2002) (holding that under state law the hiring, retention, and supervision of a middle school teacher was not a discretionary function entitled to immunity). But, failure to conduct a background check before hiring a staff member will result in liability only if such failure is shown to be the proximate cause of the injury. *See* Kendrick v. E. Delavan Baptist Church, 886 F. Supp. 1465 (E.D. Wis. 1995).

7. Roe v. N. Adams Cmty. Sch. Corp., 647 N.E.2d 655 (Ind. Ct. App. 1995).

on personnel. Unless specifically required under state statute, courts instead focus on whether:

- The events that caused the injury were foreseeable,
- The district had an express or implied duty to provide supervision on and off school grounds before and after school hours, and
- The child was injured due to a breach of that duty.

If school districts are not responsible for transporting a child, proper supervision still should be provided at pick-up and drop-off areas. Moreover, crossing guards should be stationed at nearby intersections for walkers, and assistance should be provided to parents and children to help identify safe routes to and from school. If any known dangers exist that cannot be removed (e.g., criminal elements within the neighborhood, busy roads, an attractive nuisance maintained at a construction site), parents should be notified and students should be given safety instructions. Moreover, parents need to be informed as to the earliest time supervision will be provided before school (e.g., 20 minutes prior to the beginning of the school day), so that students will not arrive earlier than school personnel.[8]

In cases where the district is responsible for providing transportation (e.g., school bus, disability van), officials should ensure that staff are properly trained and that district procedures are communicated and practiced. Such procedures should include license requirements, background checks, maintenance schedules, driving practices (e.g., stopping at railroad crossings), loading and unloading procedures, student conduct during transport, and criteria for assigning aides. Designated procedures were not followed in a Washington case where a bus driver was found negligent in the death of a 13-year-old who was killed by a car after she had exited the bus.[9] The driver failed to use either the stop sign or flashing lights as the student left the bus and then permitted the student to cross behind the bus instead of in front, as required by state law.

In addition, school officials also have a duty to provide supervision during field trips and school sponsored off-campus activities. As with other supervisory roles, school officials accompanying the students need to assess foreseeable risks associated with each activity (both planned and spontaneous) and be aware of the abilities of their students.

However, when the activity is neither curricular nor school sponsored, liability is less likely, given the difficulty of identifying a continuing duty on the part of school officials to provide supervision. No continuing duty was identified in a Washington case where school officials failed to supervise students participating in a party during "senior release day."[10] A student left the party intoxicated and was killed in a car accident on her way home. School personnel were not involved in planning or financing the party nor did they attend. Furthermore, knowledge that there would be a party did not create a duty to supervise.

As a general rule, school districts are not expected to protect truant and nonattending students. This is true for those who never arrive at school as well as for those who exit school grounds during the school day without permission, notwithstanding an appropri-

8. *See, e.g.,* Glaser v. Emporia Unified Sch. Dist. No. 253, 21 P.3d 573 (Kan. 2001).

9. Yurkovich v. Rose, 847 P.2d 925 (Wash. Ct. App. 1993).

10. Rhea v. Grandview Sch. Dist., 694 P.2d 666 (Wash. Ct. App. 1985).

ate level of surveillance of the school building and grounds as determined by the age and ability of the students. In a New York case, the court declared that "nothing short of a prison-like atmosphere with monitors at every exit could have prevented [a student] from leaving the school grounds."[11] The court declined to require such security measures and further concluded that once a truant student is beyond the legal control of the school district there was no duty to supervise. In fact, extreme measures to keep students at school may themselves result in liability. In Kentucky, a teacher chained a student by the ankle and later, when he "escaped," chained him by the neck to a tree to prevent him from leaving school grounds. The student had come late or skipped class on numerous occasions. The appeals court determined that the lower court erred in granting a directed verdict to the teacher and that proof of emotional damages should be submitted to the jury on remand.[12]

Maintenance of Buildings, Grounds, and Equipment. By law, some states protect frequenters of public buildings from danger to life, health, safety, or welfare. These *safe place statutes* may be used successfully by individuals to obtain damages from school districts for injuries resulting from defective conditions of school buildings and grounds. Moreover, school officials have a common law duty to maintain facilities and equipment in a reasonably safe condition. Districts can be held liable where they are aware of, or should be aware of, hazardous conditions and do not take the necessary steps to repair or correct the conditions. For example, school districts are responsible for the removal or encasement of asbestos materials;[13] failure to do so can result in injury and tort suits. Because state and federal support for asbestos removal has been limited, numerous districts have sued asbestos manufacturers and suppliers to recover extraction costs.[14] Such providers typically failed either to test the materials to determine whether they were hazardous or to warn consumers of potential dangers.

The duty to provide reasonable maintenance of facilities does not place an obligation on school personnel to anticipate every possible danger or to be aware of and correct every minor defect as soon as the condition occurs. If dangers are known, however, damages may be awarded where injuries result from unsafe building or playground conditions. But, if the conduct of the injured party, rather than the unsafe condition of the grounds, is found to be the primary cause of the injury, the school district may not be liable for negligence. To illustrate, a California appeals court concluded that a district was not liable for the death of a student on school grounds after regular school hours.[15] Although the playground was accessible to the public, unsupervised, and in disrepair, the court concluded that the student's death resulted from his own conduct in attempting to perform a hazardous skateboard activity, not from defective playground conditions.

11. Palella v. Ulmer, 518 N.Y.S.2d 91, 93 (Sup. Ct. 1987).
12. Banks v. Fritsch, 39 S.W.3d 474 (Ky. Ct. App. 2001).
13. Asbestos School Hazard Detection and Control Act, 20 U.S.C. § 3601 *et seq.* (2003); Asbestos Hazard Emergency Response Act (AHERA) of 1986, 15 U.S.C. § 2641 *et seq.* (2003).
14. *See, e.g., In re* Asbestos Sch. Litigation, Pfizer, 46 F.3d 1284 (3d Cir. 1994).
15. Bartell v. Palos Verdes Peninsula Sch. Dist., 147 Cal. Rptr. 898 (Ct. App. 1978).

In addition to maintaining buildings and grounds, school personnel also are required to maintain equipment and to use it safely, whether in woodshop, science labs, or athletics.[16] In a Kentucky case, a coach was found liable for the electrocution death of a student who had been using a whirlpool. The coach had "modified" the equipment but had failed to install a ground fault interrupter, although one was required by the national electric code. His negligence was found to be the substantial factor causing the student's death.[17]

Duty to Warn. In nearly all states, courts have recognized either a statutory or common law duty to warn students and/or parents of known risks they may encounter. This duty has been identified in areas such as physical education and interscholastic sports, vocational education, laboratory science, and other occasions when a student uses potentially dangerous machinery or equipment.[18] Informing, if not warning, students and parents of known dangers is necessary so that the participants then may "assume" the usual risks associated with the activity. (See discussion later in this chapter under "Assumption of Risk.")

In addition to the somewhat traditional warnings connected with sports or the use of equipment, school psychologists and counselors have a duty to warn parents, potential victims, and others as appropriate when they learn through counseling or therapy that clients intend to harm themselves or others. Those in receipt of such information are required to inform potential victims or to notify parents if students threaten to injure themselves. This requirement supersedes claims of professional ethics or discretion, therapist-client privilege, or confidentiality. But, school officials will not typically be found liable when acts of violence are unforeseeable (i.e., the threat of suicide was neither explicitly stated nor apparent), even if they knew that a particular student was under stress or seemed depressed or preoccupied.[19]

Breach of Duty/Standard of Care

Once a duty has been established, the injured individual must show that the duty was breached by the failure of another to exercise an appropriate standard of care.[20] **The degree of care teachers owe students is determined by the age, experience, and maturity level**

16. *See, e.g.,* Arteman v. Clinton Cmty. Unit Sch. Dist. No. 15, 740 N.E.2d 47 (Ill. App. Ct. 2000) (identifying the independent duty of the district to provide appropriate safety equipment to students; the injured student had been assigned "experimental" roller blades with the brake on the toe).
17. Massie v. Persson, 729 S.W.2d 448 (Ky. Ct. App. 1987).
18. *See, e.g.,* Mangold v. Ind. Dep't of Natural Res., 720 N.E.2d 424 (Ind. Ct. App. 1999) (finding no negligence where a student was injured when he tried to take a shotgun shell apart using a hammer; his hunting course instructor had directed him not to handle guns or shells without parental or instructor supervision).
19. *See, e.g.,* McMahon v. St. Croix Falls Sch., 596 N.W.2d 875 (Wis. Ct. App. 1999) (finding that although school officials had failed to inform the parents that their son had been crying at school, had received low grades and been removed from the basketball team, and failed to come to school the day of his death, the purported negligence of school personnel was found too remote to render the district liable).

of the students; the environment within which the incident occurs; the type of instructional or recreational activity; and the presence of external threats. For example, primary-grade students will generally require closer supervision and more detailed and repetitive instructions than high school students, and a class in woodwork will require closer supervision than a class in English literature.

Reasonable Person. In assessing whether appropriate care has been taken, courts consider whether the defendant acted as a "reasonable person" would have acted under the circumstances. The reasonable person is a hypothetical individual who has:

- The physical attributes of the defendant;
- Normal intelligence, problem-solving ability, and temperament;
- Normal perception and memory with a minimum level of information and experience common to the community; and
- Such superior skill and knowledge (e.g., first aid training) as the defendant has or purports to possess.

Courts will not assume that a defendant possesses any predetermined physical attributes (e.g., size, strength, agility), but rather will consider each defendant's actual physical abilities and disabilities in determining whether the defendant was responsible for a plaintiff's injury. Accordingly, if a child is attacked by another student, a different expectation to intervene will exist for a large, physically fit teacher as compared to a small, frail teacher.

Even though defendants' actual physical characteristics and capabilities are used in determining whether their conduct was reasonable, that is not the case when considering mental capacity. Courts will assume that all adult individuals have normal intelligence, problem-solving ability, and temperament, even when the evidence indicates that they do not possess such attributes.[21] Although this may initially appear unfair, it would be judicially unmanageable for courts to attempt to determine each person's mental abilities and capabilities. The current approach (i.e., the assumption of normal intelligence) provides a more objective procedure and requires defendants to be responsible for injuries they cause others. Moreover, courts will expect the defendant to have a normal perception of the environment (e.g., be aware that the rear of the school yard is bordered by a small river) and an accurate memory of what has occurred within that environment (e.g., recalling that the playground floods following a heavy rain).

Courts also will consider whether the defendant had or purported to have any superior knowledge or skill in its effort to determine whether the defendant acted as a reasonable person. Teachers, being college graduates and state licensed, are expected to act like reasonable persons with similar education. In addition, any special training an indi-

20. *See, e.g.,* Weber v. William Floyd Sch. Dist., 707 N.Y.S.2d 231 (App. Div. 2000) (affirming decision in favor of school district where a cheerleader was injured in an attempt to perform a straddle jump; she failed to show that school personnel did not exercise ordinary reasonable care).

21. W. Page Keeton, Dan B. Dobbs, Robert E. Keeton, and David G. Owen, *Prosser and Keeton on Torts,* 5th ed. (St. Paul, MN: West, 1988), p. 177.

vidual has received also may affect whether a given act is found reasonable. Accordingly, a teacher with an advanced degree in chemistry may be held to a higher standard of care than others with lesser skills and training where chemicals in a school laboratory are mixed improperly and ignite.

Invitee, Licensee, Trespasser. In determining whether an appropriate standard of care has been provided, courts consider whether an injured individual was an invitee, licensee, or trespasser, with invitees receiving the greatest level of care and trespassers receiving the least. In a school setting, an *invitee* is one who enters the school premises on the expressed or implied invitation of the school district or one of its agents. The district then has an affirmative duty to exercise reasonable care for the safety of invitees commensurate with the risks and circumstances involved. Furthermore, invitees must be protected against known dangers as well as those that might be discovered with reasonable care. Under most circumstances, students, teachers, and administrators are invitees of the district. Students who break into a school after hours, however, have exceeded the "period of invitation" and become trespassers.[22]

When permission to be on school premises is requested and permitted, the person becomes a *licensee* (e.g., requests by salespersons, parents, newspersons). Even school children may qualify as licensees under certain circumstances (e.g., while engaged in activities of a local nonschool organization that has been permitted evening or weekend use of a school classroom). Such persons enter the building or grounds facing the same conditions and threats as the occupier. Nevertheless, districts still need to warn licensees of known dangers and not injure intentionally or by willful, wanton, or reckless conduct.

If the individual has been neither invited nor received consent, the person is guilty of *trespass* upon accessing school property. Although state laws often blur the distinction between licensee and trespasser, less care has to be provided for the safety of trespassers. Adult trespassers in particular have no right to a safe place and must assume the risk of what they may encounter. Generally, the owner owes no duty to trespassers other than to refrain from willfully or wantonly injuring them (e.g., by setting traps). In selected jurisdictions, however, if the owner knows that trespassers are on the premises (e.g., vagrants living in an abandoned school building), the owner must use reasonable care not to expose the trespasser to an environment that is known to be dangerous. When the trespasser is a child, as often is the case on school property, it is prudent to take additional steps to restrict access or to remove known dangers. This is particularly true where an attractive nuisance may exist on school property (e.g., swimming pool, easily climbed architectural structure) that will foreseeably attract children. In such narrow instances, there is little legal distinction between a trespasser and a licensee in regard to the standard of care required.

22. *See, e.g.,* Howard County Bd. of Educ. v. Cheyne, 636 A.2d 22 (Md. Ct. App. 1994) (holding that a 4-year-old was an invitee when she initially entered a gym to attend a sports function, but that a question remained for the jury to determine whether she had exceeded the scope of her invitation at the time of injury).

Proximate Cause

For liability to be assessed against a school district, the negligent conduct of school personnel must be the proximate or legal cause of injury. ***Proximate cause*** **has been defined as "that which in a natural and continuous sequence, unbroken by any efficient intervening cause, produces the injury, and without which the result would not have occurred."**[23] In determining proximate cause, courts will:

- Consider factors other than the defendant's conduct that contributed to producing the injury,
- Ascertain whether the challenged conduct created a force that was in operation up to the time of the injury, and
- Assess the lapse of time between the conduct and the occurrence of the injury.

Accordingly, not every seemingly negligent act results in liability, even when an injury results, unless the act was, in fact, the cause of the injury.

Injury

Legal negligence does not exist unless actual injury is incurred either directly by the individual (e.g., broken arm) or by the individual's property (e.g., broken window). Most often, an individual will know of the injury as soon as it occurs; in some instances, however, the individual may not be aware of the injury for many months or even years (e.g., development of asbestosis due to exposure to asbestos 20 years earlier). In most states, there is a statute of limitations (i.e., a period of time within which suit must be filed) of one to three years on tort claims, although the actual time can be greater *if* the limitations period does not begin until the plaintiff reaches the age of majority or becomes aware of the injury.

When students are injured in the school setting, school personnel have a duty to provide reasonable assistance commensurate with their training and experience. When reasonable treatment is provided, no liability will generally be assessed even if the treatment later is found to be inappropriate. State *Good Samaritan laws* often shield individuals from liability when they provide care in emergency situations. Acts that a reasonable person would not have taken, however, are not protected. In a Pennsylvania case, two teachers were held personally liable for administering medical treatment to a student by holding his infected finger under boiling water. The superior court concluded that the action was unreasonable and noted that the situation did not necessitate emergency first aid.[24]

Defenses against Negligence

Several defenses are available to school districts when employees have been charged with negligence. At times, districts have identified procedural defects (e.g., the failure to adhere to statutory requirements regarding notice of claim), or have proposed that plaintiff's injury

23. Anselmo v. Tuck, 924 S.W.2d 798, 802 (Ark. 1996).
24. Guerrieri v. Tyson, 24 A.2d 468 (Pa. Super. Ct. 1942).

was caused by uncontrollable events of nature in an effort to thwart liability claims. More commonly, however, defenses such as governmental immunity, contributory negligence, comparative negligence, or assumption of risk have been asserted.

Governmental Immunity. In the rare cases where this defense is comprehensively applied, governmental entities (including school districts) cannot be sued for any reason. Governmental immunity is available to employees only when specifically conferred by state law for acts within the scope of employment, or courts interpret the law as doing so. However, immunity is seldom comprehensively applied today, as nearly all states either have limited its use or have qualified its application based on various factors. For example, districts in some states are immune if:

- Claims are related to the maintenance of the school building or property,
- Contested acts are governmental rather than proprietary,[25]
- Decisions qualify as discretionary rather than ministerial,[26]
- School property is being used for recreational instead of educational purposes,[27] or
- The injury is compensable under the state's workers' compensation laws (employees only).[28]

Contributory Negligence. In states that recognize contributory negligence as a defense, plaintiffs are denied recovery if their actions are shown by the defendant to have been substantially responsible for the injury; it makes no difference that the defendant was negligent

25. *Governmental functions* are those that are performed in discharging the agency's official duties (e.g., hiring faculty, maintaining a building), which are generally considered immune from liability. On the other hand, *proprietary functions* are those that are only tangentially related to the curriculum, can as easily be performed by the private sector, and often require the payment of a fee (e.g., community use of school pool, catering services, plant sales); these activities have been permissible targets for tort actions.
26. *Discretionary functions* are those that require consideration of alternatives, deliberation, judgment, and the making of a decision (e.g., the discretion used in the selection of a new teacher); in contrast, *ministerial functions* are those performed in a prescribed manner, in obedience to legal authority, and without discretion (e.g., procedures used for stopping a school bus at a railroad crossing). As a rule, districts will be liable for negligence involving ministerial duties but be immune from liability for negligence associated with actions that are discretionary. *See, e.g.,* Pauley v. Anchorage Sch. Dist., 31 P.3d 1284 (Alaska 2001) (granting qualified immunity to a principal who had released a student to his noncustodial mother; the good faith, discretionary decision was neither malicious nor corrupt); Trotter v. Sch. Dist. 218, 733 N.E.2d 363 (Ill. App. Ct. 2000) (concluding that the persons who were responsible for supervising a freshman swim class were entitled to discretionary function immunity in the drowning death of a student).
27. *See, e.g.,* Auman v. Sch. Dist., 635 N.W.2d 762 (Wis. 2001) (concluding that the recreational immunity statute did not shield the district from liability for injuries to a student during mandatory recess). Also, in some states, school districts still may be liable when a recreational injury is the result of a ministerial function.
28. Under workers' compensation, liability exists regardless of negligence or fault on the part of the employer or employee, provided that the injury was accidental *and* arose out of and in the course of employment.

and also partially at fault. In most jurisdictions today, a slight degree of fault will not prevent a plaintiff from prevailing; typically, the contributory negligence must be significant, although it need not be dominant.

In assessing whether contributory negligence exists, children are not necessarily held to the same standard of care as adults. Rather, their actions must be reasonable for persons of similar age, maturity, intelligence, and experience. Many courts then make individualized determinations as to whether a minor plaintiff appreciated the risks involved and acted as a reasonable person of like characteristics and abilities. Other courts have established age ranges in an effort to more objectively and uniformly determine whether children have the capacity to contribute to or cause their own injuries. Although courts vary greatly and designated ages may seem arbitrary, the most commonly used ranges are:

- Children from birth to age 7 are considered incapable of negligence (although this limit sometimes is as low as age 4);
- Youth between ages 7 and 14 are considered incapable of negligence, but this presumption can be rebutted; and
- Students age 14 and over are generally presumed capable of negligence, although this presumption, too, can be rebutted.

In a school setting, educational personnel have been successful in claiming contributory negligence only when they have been able to show that the injured student was sufficiently mature, intelligent, and experienced to understand the consequences of specific actions and nonetheless engaged in dangerous conduct.[29]

Comparative Negligence. Under the contributory model just discussed, only the injured party bears financial responsibility if found ultimately responsible for the act leading to an injury. **Under the comparative model, the plaintiff and/or one or more defendants bear responsibility in proportion to fault**. For example, in Louisiana, a school bus driver permitted two girls to exit his bus even though he knew one had threatened to injure the other. He initially exited with them, held them apart, and told a teacher to summon the principal. Instead of waiting for the principal or a teacher to arrive, however, he reentered the bus to move it since he was blocking traffic. When he pulled away, one student proceeded to stomp the other student's ankle; the injury was so severe that three screws were required to align the broken bones. The court reasoned that the driver should not have left the students unsupervised under the circumstances and assessed 15 percent liability against him (85 percent against the attacking student).[30]

Assumption of Risk. This defense can be either express or implied. ***Express assumption*** **occurs when the plaintiff consents in advance to take his or her chances of injury given a known danger** (e.g., signing an agreement to assume the risks associated with participa-

29. *See, e.g.,* Aronson v. Horace Mann-Barnard Sch., 637 N.Y.S.2d 410 (App. Div. 1996) (holding that a senior who was an experienced diver and swimmer was contributorily negligent as she alone was responsible for her injuries when she executed a shallow dive).

30. Bell v. Ayio, 731 So. 2d 893 (La. Ct. App. 1999).

tion in high school football). This assumes, of course, that the risks have been disclosed or are apparent and understood. ***Implied assumption*** **occurs without an express written or oral agreement, yet is logically assumed given the plaintiff's conduct** (e.g., when spectators at a baseball game elect to sit in unscreened seats, they assume the risk of possible injury even if they failed to sign an agreement).

Although inherent risks are associated with athletics or recreation, all participants will not necessarily understand those risks. Understanding risks often is associated with age, maturity, and experience. As a result, school personnel must exercise reasonable care to protect students from unassumed, concealed, or unreasonably high risks. This duty can be met when participation is voluntary (i.e., there is no evidence of compulsion to participate) and the student is knowledgeable of and assumes the risks associated with the activity.[31]

Note, however, that student athletes are assuming only those risks that occur during normal participation in the sport; they are not assuming unknown risks associated with a coach's negligence. Moreover, they are not assuming that they will be exposed to intentional torts (e.g., battery) or conduct that represents a reckless disregard for the safety of others. But, penalties and poor judgment by other participants generally will not qualify as intentional torts and most often will be viewed as occurring commonly, if not routinely, in the sport (e.g., being clipped in football, being hit by a pitched ball in baseball).[32]

Some educators are under the mistaken impression that parents may waive their child's right to sue for negligence by signing forms granting permission for their children to participate in particular activities. Such permission slips indicate that the student assumes normal risks associated with the activity, but parents cannot waive their child's entitlement to appropriate supervision and instruction. Accordingly, students may assume some risk of potential injury by engaging in a dangerous sport (e.g., hockey) or by participating in a field trip, but school personnel remain responsible for protecting them from foreseeable harm.

Intentional Torts

> School personnel can be liable for intentionally harming others through assault, battery, false imprisonment, or the intentional infliction of mental distress.

To be an intentional tort, the behavior must be purposeful. Qualifying behaviors do not include negligence, acts that occur through happenstance, or events that are due to an act of nature. Each of the more common types of intentional torts is discussed briefly here (see Figure 2.2).

31. *See, e.g.,* Papa v. Russo, 719 N.Y.S.2d 723 (App. Div. 2001) (holding that an experienced rider assumed the risks associated with horseback riding when her horse fell for reasons unrelated to the condition of the track).
32. *See, e.g.,* Bentley v. Cuyahoga Falls Bd. of Educ., 709 N.E.2d 1241 (Ohio Ct. App. 1998).

FIGURE 2.2 ***Intentional Torts: Types of Behavior***

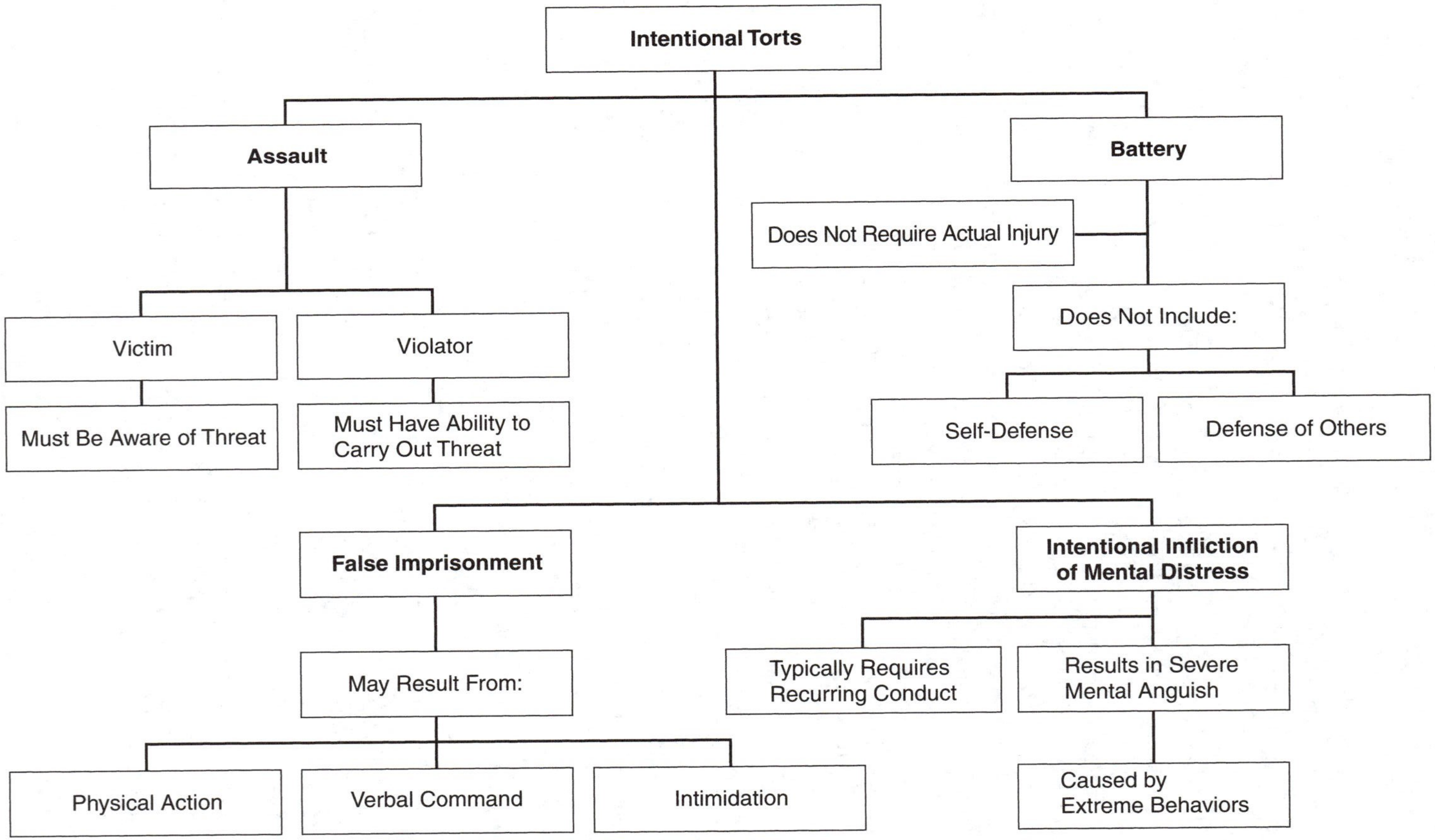

Assault and Battery

***Assault* consists of an overt attempt to place another in fear of bodily harm; no actual physical contact need take place.** Examples include threatening with words, pointing a gun, waving a knife, or shaking a fist. For there to be an assault, the plaintiff needs to be aware of the threat, and the person committing the assault needs to be perceived as having the ability to carry out the threat. In contrast, a ***battery* is committed when an assault is consummated.** Examples include being shot, stabbed, beaten, or struck.[33] However, actual injury need not result for a battery claim to succeed (e.g., the person could have been punched but not injured due to a comparatively weak blow).

Some school-based assault and battery cases have involved the administration of corporal punishment and other forms of discipline that require physical touching. Generally, courts have been reluctant to interfere with a teacher's authority to discipline students and have sanctioned the use of *reasonable* force to control pupil behavior. In Louisiana, the appeals court concluded that a substitute teacher was not guilty of battery when he grabbed a confrontational eighth-grade student by the arm and escorted him out of the room—the student had been talking during a test and was asked to leave.[34] In contrast, a second Louisiana student was successful in obtaining damages.[35] The pupil sustained a broken arm when a teacher shook him, lifted him against the bleachers in the gymnasium, and then let him fall to the floor. The court reasoned that the teacher's action was unnecessary either to discipline the student or to protect himself.

Although comparatively uncommon, school personnel may initiate battery suits against students who injure them.[36] Suits are not barred simply because the person committing the tort is a minor, although the amount of the award may be capped by state statute. A Wisconsin appeals court awarded damages to a teacher when he was physically attacked outside the school building while attempting to escort a student to the office for violating a smoking ban. The court held that the student, who had five previous fighting violations, acted with malicious intent in striking the teacher numerous times and in pushing his face into the corner of a building. Both actual and punitive damages were awarded, notwithstanding the fact that the student was a minor at the time of the battery or that the student's psychiatrist purported that a punitive award would not be a deterrent for the defendant's impulsive conduct.[37] The court also was unpersuaded by the argument that the defendant's violence and anger were due to his poor self-control and that it would be inappropriate to

33. Students may sue the school district when they are battered by a fellow student while at school. As a general rule, districts will not be liable unless it can be shown that officials had specific knowledge or notice of the dangerous conduct and failed to act responsibly. *See, e.g.,* Sanzo v. Solvay Union Free Sch. Dist., 750 N.Y.S.2d 252 (App. Div. 2002).
34. Frame v. Comeaux, 735 So. 2d 753 (La. Ct. App. 1999).
35. Frank v. Orleans Parish Sch. Bd., 195 So. 2d 451 (La. Ct. App. 1967).
36. In addition, some negligence suits are filed by school personnel against their districts when they have been battered at work. In most cases, however, courts have found that the incidents were unforeseen and that no special duty existed on the part of the district to prevent the battery. *See, e.g.,* Genao v. Bd. of Educ., 888 F. Supp. 501 (S.D.N.Y. 1995).
37. Anello v. Savignac, 342 N.W.2d 440 (Wis. Ct. App. 1983).

award punitive damages given that the defendant had a learning disability. In conclusion, the court noted that if the defendant expected to continue to live freely in society, he would have to learn to control his assaultive behavior, or "appreciate" the consequences.

Self-defense often has been used to shield an individual from liability for alleged battery. **An individual need not wait to be struck to engage in defensive acts, although reasonable grounds must exist to substantiate that harm was imminent.** The "test" in such cases is to determine whether the defendant's conduct was that in which a reasonable person may have engaged given the circumstances. Consideration should be given to the magnitude of the existing threat, possible alternatives to physical contact, and the time frame available to make a decision (i.e., whether the defendant had to act instantaneously without time for deliberation).[38] Even where contact is justified, the defendant must use only force that is reasonably necessary for self-protection. Furthermore, if the alleged aggressor is disarmed, rendered helpless, or no longer capable of aggressive behavior, the defendant may not take the opportunity to engage in revenge or to punish.

In addition to self-defense, individuals accused of battery also may claim that they were acting in the defense of others. This type of tort defense is of particular importance in a school setting where educators often are called on to separate students who are fighting or to come to the aid of someone being attacked. Most jurisdictions not only permit such action on behalf of others but also consider it to be a responsibility or duty of educators, assuming good faith and the use of reasonable and necessary force.

False Imprisonment

Obviously, all restrictions on the freedom of movement or the effort to enter or exit will not qualify as false imprisonment[39] (e.g., temporarily detaining a student after school as a form of reasonable school discipline, being assigned to Saturday school to compensate for tardiness). Interestingly, to be falsely imprisoned, one need not be incarcerated; walls, locks, and iron bars are not required. Rather, imprisonment can result from being placed in a closet, room, corner, automobile, or even a circle in the middle of a football field; it can occur when confined to an entire building or when forced to accompany another on a walk or trip. The taking of a purse, car keys, or other property with the intent to force the person to remain also may qualify as imprisonment. ***Imprisonment* results when physical action, verbal command, or intimidation is used to restrain and/or detain persons against their will.** Tone of voice, body language, and what was reasonably understood or even implied from the defendant's conduct will be considered.

In imprisonment cases, the plaintiff need not show that physical force was used; it will suffice that the plaintiff submitted given the apprehension of force. The plaintiff must be aware of the restraint, but need not show damages beyond the confinement itself to prevail

38. The American Law Institute, *A Concise Restatement of Torts* (St. Paul, MN: American Law Institute, 2000), p. 9.
39. *See, e.g.*, Harris *ex rel.* Tucker v. County of Forsyth, 921 F. Supp. 325 (M.D.N.C. 1996) (finding no false imprisonment when a student was placed for seven minutes in a holding cell in a county detention facility for disrupting a tour of the building; the student's behavior jeopardized the safety of the children and disrupted an otherwise orderly environment).

at trial. Accordingly, any time children are unjustifiably restrained against their will, tied or taped to chairs, or bound and gagged, false imprisonment (as well as other possible violations) may be claimed.[40] Although there are times when the use of physical restraints may be necessary, educators need to document the circumstances requiring such actions and provide a narrative explaining why restraint is an appropriate and reasoned response to the behavior. Also, when behavioral management techniques such as "time-out" are used, any resulting isolation needs to be for reasonable periods of time, and the confinement area needs to be both safe and clean.[41]

Intentional Infliction of Mental Distress

This area of tort law is comparatively new because of the historical resistance to awarding damages for a mental injury when it was not accompanied by a physical injury (e.g., pain and suffering associated with a broken leg). Such reluctance purportedly was due to the difficulty of generating proof of both injury and proximate cause and then determining the appropriate amount of damages to be awarded. Nevertheless, a tort claim of intentional infliction of mental distress now is available to individuals who have experienced *severe* mental anguish. This claim, however, does not provide a remedy for every trivial indignity, insult, bad manners, annoyance, or sexist or racist comment.

Some forms of communication can result in an assault claim (e.g., a threat to strike) or defamation suit (e.g., an unfounded claim that a teacher has been sexually involved with students); other communications might provide a basis for discrimination suits under federal laws (e.g., sexual or racial harassment). However, **for the conduct to result in intentional infliction of mental distress under tort laws, it must be flagrant, extreme, or outrageous; it must go beyond all possible bounds of decency and be regarded as atrocious and utterly intolerable in civilized society.**[42] No reasonable person should be expected to endure such conduct (e.g., severe and extreme acts of stalking or harassment). Moreover, in most instances the conduct needs to be prolonged and recurring, since single acts seldom meet the necessary threshold.

Given the difficulty of meeting this stringent standard, it is not surprising that few school-based claims succeed. Numerous claims have involved injured feelings or reputations, appearing trivial at best. In one such claim that bordered on the disingenuous, a sixth-grade Oregon student claimed intentional infliction of mental distress when two of her teachers refused to use her nickname, Boo. "Boo" also is the street name for marijuana and was recognized as such by other students. Neither teacher had ever stated that the plaintiff used or condoned the use of drugs. In granting summary judgment for the teachers, the court

40. Gerks v. Deathe, 832 F. Supp. 1450 (W.D. Okla. 1993) (denying summary judgment for the district when a child with disabilities was locked in the bathroom for three hours by her teacher for creating a "mess" on the floor).

41. Peters v. Rome City Sch. Dist., 747 N.Y.S.2d 867 (App. Div. 2002) (upholding a jury verdict awarding the parents $75,000; their second-grade son had been placed in a small, poorly ventilated time-out room, reportedly smelling like "dirty feet" and urine, on 75 occasions for periods at times in excess of one hour).

42. Keeton et al., *Prosser and Keeton on Torts,* pp. 54–66.

concluded that no juror could reasonably find that the conduct of the teachers was an "extraordinary transgression of the bounds of socially tolerable conduct."[43]

In contrast, a Florida teacher was found to have supported a claim of intentional infliction of mental distress against two students. The youths had planned, edited, written, printed, copied, and distributed a newsletter that referred to the plaintiff in racially derogatory and sexually vulgar ways; threatened to rape her, her children, and their cousins; and threatened to kill her. The court distinguished the present case from those that involved mere name-calling, embarrassing photos, or harassment, and concluded that the conduct here was extreme and went beyond all possible bounds of decency.[44]

Defamation

> Individuals can receive damages for written or spoken injury to their reputations.

Most tort actions have involved claims for damages that were due to physical or mental injuries, but plaintiffs also have claimed injury to their reputations in the form of defamation. ***Slander* is the term generally associated with spoken defamation (but also includes sign language), whereas *libel* often is used to refer to written defamation (but also includes pictures, statues, motion pictures, and conduct carrying a defamatory imputation—e.g., hanging a person in effigy).**[45] In determining whether defamation has occurred, courts will consider whether:

- The targeted individual was a private or public person,
- The communication was false,
- The expression qualified as opinion or fact, and
- The comment was privileged (see Figure 2.3).

Private and Public Persons

To prevail in a defamation case, private individuals need to prove only that a false publication by the defendant was received and understood by a third party *and* that injury resulted. Individuals considered public figures or officials additionally must show that the publication was made with either malice or a reckless disregard for the truth. Although definitions vary considerably by state, public figures generally are those who are known or recognized by the public (e.g., professional athletes, actors), and public officials

43. Phillips v. Lincoln County Sch. Dist., 984 P.2d 947, 951 (Or. Ct. App. 1999).

44. Nims v. Harrison, 768 So. 2d 1198 (Fla. Dist. Ct. App. 2000).

45. Keeton et al., *Prosser and Keeton on Torts,* p. 786.

FIGURE 2.3 *Types of Defamation*

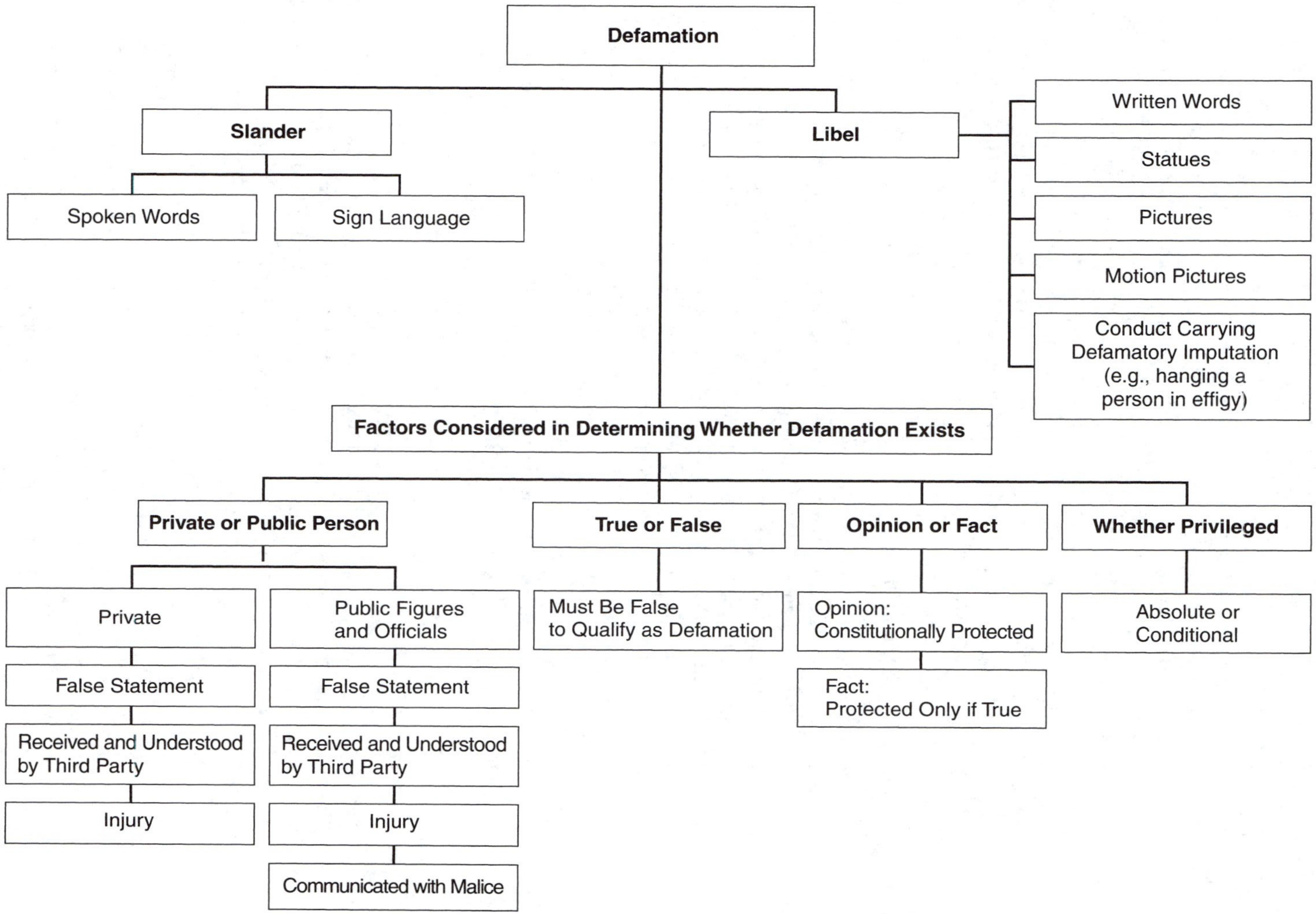

are those who have substantial control over governmental affairs (e.g., politicians, school board members).

The trend in recent years has been to broaden the class of public officials and figures, but it is fortunate for teachers that the vast majority of courts have not found them to be "public," in large part because their authority typically is limited to school children.[46] Some courts, however, have found school board members, administrators, and coaches to be either public officials or figures.[47] This does not mean that all board members, administrators, or coaches even within the same jurisdiction will qualify as public persons; such a determination is made on an individual basis and is dependent on the role, responsibility, degree of notoriety, and authority of the specific individual.

Veracity of Statements

In assessing defamation claims, courts also consider whether a statement is true or false. If the statement is found to be true, or at least substantially true, judgment will generally be for the defendant, assuming that critical facts have not been omitted, taken out of context, or otherwise artificially juxtaposed to misrepresent. Educators should be particularly careful, however, when discussing students and must avoid making comments in bad faith that will result in liability. For example, if a teacher were to comment in class that a particular female student is a "slut," his comments would qualify as defamation per se.[48] In such cases no proof of actual harm to reputation is required.

In addition to proving a communication to be false, the individual must show that he or she was the subject addressed. Interestingly, the individual's identity need not be clear to all third parties (i.e., readers, viewers, or hearers of the defamation). As long as "some" third parties can identify the individual, the claim is actionable even though the individual is not mentioned by name. Furthermore, the defamatory content need not be explicit; it may be implied or may be understood only by third parties with additional information.

Fact versus Opinion

Most opinions receive constitutional protection, particularly when public figures or officials are involved or the issue is one of public concern. **To qualify as *opinion,* the communication must not lend itself to being realistically proven as true or false, and must be communicated in such a way as to be considered a personal perspective on the matter.** Parents may express critical opinions about a teacher (verbally or in writing) and may sub-

46. McCutcheon v. Moran, 425 N.E.2d 1130 (Ill. App. Ct. 1981). *But see* Elstrom v. Indep. Sch. Dist. No. 270, 533 N.W.2d 51 (Minn. Ct. App. 1995) (concluding that a teacher was a public official).

47. *See, e.g.,* Garcia v. Bd. of Educ., 777 F.2d 1403 (10th Cir. 1985) (school board members); Jordan v. World Publ'g Co., 872 P.2d 946 (Okla. Ct. App. 1994) (principal); Johnson v. Southwestern Newspapers Corp., 855 S.W.2d 182 (Tex. Ct. App. 1993) (football coach).

48. *See, e.g.,* Smith v. Atkins, 622 So. 2d 795 (La. Ct. App. 1993).

mit such opinions to a principal or school board.[49] Moreover, parents even have the constitutionally protected right to express negative views directly to the teacher, assuming that the expression does not amount to "fighting words"[50] or qualify as an assault.

Notwithstanding the above, allegations that "the teacher sold drugs to a student" or that "the superintendent stole school funds" are factual statements that are capable of being substantiated, and therefore may qualify as defamation unless proven true. In an Oregon case, an appeals court affirmed a damage award against parents who accused a school bus driver of sexual abuse. Even though there were no facts or evidence that supported the claim, the parents persisted in making accusations over an extended period of time by writing letters, uniting parents in protest, and attending board meetings. Their unsupported claims injured the driver's reputation, adversely affected his employability, and caused him to suffer emotional distress.[51]

Privilege

Whether a communication qualifies as "privileged" also may affect whether defamation is supported. Statements that are considered *absolutely privileged* cannot serve as a basis for defamation under any circumstance, even if they are false and result in injury.[52] Although less common in education than qualified privilege, an absolute privilege defense has been selectively applied in statements made by superintendents and school board members.[53]

Communication between parties with *conditional privilege* also may be immune from liability if made in good faith with appropriate motives and content. For example, teacher notations in student records generally are considered conditionally privileged. This privilege may be lost, however, where actual malice exists (i.e., where a person made a defamatory statement that he or she knew to be false, acted with a high degree of awareness of probable falsity, or entertained serious doubts as to whether the statement was true).[54]

49. *See, e.g.,* Nodar v. Galbreath, 462 So. 2d 803 (Fla. 1984) (holding that a parent's statement before the school board concerning the teacher was conditionally privileged).

50. "Fighting words" are by their nature likely to result in an immediate breach of the peace and do not qualify as First Amendment protected speech. *See* text accompanying note 14, Chapter 5.

51. Kraemer v. Harding, 976 P.2d 1160 (Or. Ct. App. 1999).

52. Gallegos v. Escalon, 993 S.W.2d 422 (Tex. App. 1999) (finding the superintendent absolutely immune in answering questions posed by the school board in regard to the use of a district credit card by two other district employees).

53. Rykowsky v. Dickinson Pub. Sch. Dist. # 1, 508 N.W.2d 348 (N.D. 1993).

54. *But see* Rocci v. Ecole Secondaire MacDonald-Cartier, 755 A.2d 583 (N.J. 2000) (finding no malice, defamation, or emotional distress when a teacher sent a letter to a principal alleging that the plaintiff, another teacher, had acted unprofessionally on a trip because she drank wine excessively on the flight and kept the students out late despite their early-morning responsibilities).

Damages

> Tort suits for damages may be filed against school districts and the individuals responsible for the injury.

Damages in tort suits can be either compensatory or punitive, and many include attorneys' fees that are typically calculated as a percent of the total award (often 33⅓ to 40 percent). ***Compensatory damages*** **include past and future economic loss, medical expenses, and pain and suffering.** These awards are intended to make the plaintiff whole, at least to the degree that money is capable of doing so. If a plaintiff's previous injury has been aggravated, the defendant is generally liable only for the additional loss.

Although damages vary by state, it is common to cap damages for intangibles (e.g., pain, suffering, mental anguish) but not to cap those for actual loss. When plaintiffs prevail, it is important to note that school district assets are not subject to execution, sale, garnishment, or attachment to satisfy the judgment. Instead, judgments are paid from funds appropriated specifically for that purpose or are acquired through revenue bonds. If sufficient funds are not available, it is common for states to require fiscal officers to certify the amount of unpaid judgment to the taxing authority for inclusion in the next budget. When the amounts are significant, many states permit districts to pay installments (at times up to 10 years) for payment of damages that do not represent actual loss.[55]

Furthermore, in most states, educators can be sued individually. When they are not "save harmlessed"[56] by their school district and do not have personal insurance coverage, their personal assets (e.g., cars, boats, bank accounts) may be attached, their wages may be garnished, and a lien may be placed on their property. If a lien is filed, the property may not be sold until the debt is satisfied. Moreover, debtors are not permitted to transfer ownership to avoid attachment (i.e., this would represent *fraudulent conveyance*).

Punitive damages are awarded to punish particularly wanton or reckless acts and are in addition to actual damages. The amount is discretionary with the jury and is based on the circumstances, behaviors, and acts. Unlike the calculation of actual damages, the debtor's financial worth may be a factor in determining punitive amounts. When jury verdicts are seemingly out of line, the court may reduce *(remittitur)* or increase *(additur)* the amount where either passion or prejudice is a factor.

55. Jonathan E. Buchter, Susan C. Hastings, Timothy J. Sheeran, and Gregory W. Stype, *Ohio School Law* (Cleveland, OH: West, 2001), p. 862.
56. "Save harmless" means that the school district provides counsel for the employee and pays any resulting liability and court costs.

Conclusion

All individuals, including educators, are responsible for their actions and can be liable for damages if they intentionally or negligently cause injury to others. Educators have a responsibility to act reasonably, but some negligent conduct is likely to occur. Consequently, educators should be knowledgeable about their potential liability under applicable state laws and should ensure that they are either protected by their school districts or have adequate insurance coverage for any damages that might be assessed against them.

Moreover, school personnel should refrain from intentionally injuring others, engaging in assaultive behaviors, detaining students for inappropriate reasons, or participating in conduct that ultimately may result in the emotional distress of another. Educators also should be cautious when sharing information about colleagues or students, as the dissemination of incorrect or confidential information may result in liability.

Points to Ponder

1. During a faculty meeting, a high school principal mentioned that one of the teachers in the building had been arrested for shoplifting and that extra precautions should be taken to safeguard personal belongings. However, the principal failed to mention that although the teacher had been arrested, evidence was inadequate to support her guilt or conviction and that she was released soon after her arrest. Other than the fact that she was arrested, there was no reason to believe she was guilty. The principal did not mention the teacher by name, but his comments about her gender and teaching area left no doubt as to her identity. Her reputation was tarnished and her personal relationships were adversely affected. She sued the principal, claiming defamation of character. Is she likely to win? Why or why not?

2. A secondary school principal directed a student teacher in social studies to supervise a chemistry class, because the regular science teacher was ill. During lab, a student was injured in an explosion. The parents of the injured child sued the principal (even though he was not present during the explosion, nor had he instructed the class in regard to the chemicals) and the school district. Are the parents likely to prevail in this suit? Explain your reasoning.

3. A physical education instructor requires a student to climb a 30-foot rope in physical education class even though the student informed the teacher that he was afraid of heights (a fact that also is part of his school record). After the instructor threatened the student with corporal punishment, he climbed the rope, but fell when about half way up. He is not injured, but sued the instructor and the district, claiming negligence. Is he likely to win? Why or why not?

4. While on the school bus, two students got into an altercation over a loud radio. The zydeco music (a type of cajun music) emanating from the boombox was more than the second student could tolerate. The owner of the boombox refused to turn off or even turn down the music. As a result, the one student informed the other that if the music was not turned off, the radio would be destroyed and the owner would be struck. Numerous passengers overheard the conversation. The boombox owner was a large, athletic, 18-year-old male; the confronting student was a small, frail, 12-year-old female. She had no special martial arts skill and did not give the impression of being capable of carrying out the threat. The male student sued the female, claiming assault. Will he succeed in his claim? Why or why not?

3

Church/State Relations

Efforts to identify the appropriate relationship between government and religion have generated substantial controversy in our nation, and since the mid-twentieth century, schools have provided the battleground for some of the most volatile disputes. This chapter provides an overview of the constitutional framework, the evolution of legal activity, and the current status of church/state relations involving education.

Constitutional Framework

> The Establishment Clause is used primarily to challenge government *advancement* of religion, whereas claims under the Free Exercise Clause usually focus on secular government regulations alleged to impair the *practice* of religious beliefs.

The First Amendment to the United States Constitution stipulates in part that "Congress shall make no law respecting an establishment of religion or prohibiting the free exercise thereof." Although this amendment was directed toward the *federal* government, the Fourteenth Amendment specifically placed restrictions on *state* action impairing personal rights. **In the twentieth century, the Supreme Court recognized that the fundamental concept of "liberty" embodied in the Fourteenth Amendment incorporates First Amendment guarantees and safeguards them against state interference.**[1] Education is primarily a state function, so church/state controversies involving schools usually have been initiated through the Fourteenth Amendment. Most constitutional law governing church/state relations has developed since World War II, and judicial standards to assess claims under the

1. *See* Cantwell v. Connecticut, 310 U.S. 296, 303 (1940); Gitlow v. New York, 268 U.S. 652, 666 (1925).

Establishment and Free Exercise Clauses and their interaction with free speech guarantees are still evolving.

In the first major Establishment Clause decision, *Everson v. Board of Education*, the Supreme Court in 1947 reviewed the history of the First Amendment and concluded that the Establishment Clause (and its Fourteenth Amendment application to states) means:

> Neither a state nor the Federal Government can set up a church. Neither can pass laws which aid one religion, aid all religions, or prefer one religion over another.... In the words of Jefferson, the clause against establishment of religion by law was intended to erect "a wall of separation between church and state."[2]

Whether this "wall of separation" should be the guiding standard has evoked substantial debate. Jefferson's metaphor was used widely by the federal judiciary for more than 30 years following *Everson,* even though this phrase does not appear in the First Amendment. During this period, the Establishment Clause seemed to be given greater weight than the Free Exercise Clause, with courts often supporting the notion that church/state separation "must be complete and unequivocal."[3]

In a 1971 case, *Lemon v. Kurtzman,* the Supreme Court first applied a tripartite test to assess Establishment Clause claims.[4] **To withstand scrutiny under this test, usually referred to as the *Lemon* test, government action must (1) have a secular purpose, (2) have a primary effect that neither advances nor impedes religion, and (3) avoid excessive government entanglement with religion**. This three-part test was used consistently in Establishment Clause cases involving school issues until 1992. However, a majority of the current justices has voiced dissatisfaction with the test, and reliance on *Lemon* has been noticeably absent in the Supreme Court's recent Establishment Clause rulings. Support for church/state separation seems to be waning, even in school cases where separationist doctrine traditionally has been the strongest.

Some of the current Supreme Court justices favor an *endorsement standard* under which government action would be struck down if an objective observer would view it as having the purpose or effect of endorsing or disapproving religion. The endorsement principle is not as strict as separationism. But it is easier to substantiate an Establishment Clause violation using this standard than the *coercion test,* which is supported by some justices. The latter test requires direct or indirect government coercion on individuals to profess a faith. **Instead of replacing the *Lemon* test with another standard or a combination, the current Supreme Court seems likely to continue to draw on various tests depending on the specific circumstances of each case.** Some lower courts are attempting to cover all bases by reviewing challenged government action under the three-part *Lemon* test, the endorsement standard, and the coercion test[5] (see Figure 3.1).

2. 330 U.S. 1, 15-16 (1947).
3. Zorach v. Clauson, 343 U.S. 306, 312 (1952).
4. 403 U.S. 602 (1971).
5. *See, e.g.,* Doe v. Beaumont Indep. Sch. Dist., 240 F.3d 462 (5th Cir. 2001); Stark v. Indep. Sch. Dist. No. 640, 123 F.3d 1068 (8th Cir. 1997).

FIGURE 3.1 ***Judicial Standards to Evaluate Challenged Government Action under the Establishment Clause***

The government actions or practices will violate the Establishment Clause if they:	
• Have a religious (sectarian) purpose • Advance or impede religion • Create excessive government entanglement with religion	**Lemon Test**
• Have a purpose or effect of endorsing or disapproving religion	**Endorsement Test**
• Place direct or indirect government coercion on individuals to profess a faith	**Coercion Test**

Whereas in establishment cases the legality of the government action itself is at issue, in free exercise claims, individuals often accept the secular nature of the government regulation but assert that it burdens their religious exercise. To evaluate free exercise claims, the judiciary traditionally applied a balancing test that includes an assessment of whether practices dictated by a sincere and legitimate religious belief have been impeded by the government, and if so, to what extent. If such an impairment is found, the court then evaluates whether the government action serves a compelling interest that justifies the burden imposed on the exercise of religious beliefs. Even if such a compelling interest is shown, the government is expected to attain its objectives through means that are the least burdensome on free exercise rights.

In the most significant school case involving a free exercise claim, *Wisconsin v. Yoder,* the Supreme Court exempted Amish children from compulsory school attendance upon successful completion of eighth grade.[6] Although noting that the assurance of an educated citizenry ranks at the "apex" of state functions, the Court nonetheless concluded that parents' rights to practice their legitimate religious beliefs outweighed the state's interest in mandating two additional years of formal schooling for Amish youth. The Court cautioned, however, that its ruling was limited to the Amish who offer a structured vocational program to prepare their youth for a cloistered agrarian community rather than mainstream American society.

In a 1990 decision, the Supreme Court modified this balancing test, ruling that the government does not have to demonstrate a compelling interest to defend a criminal law that burdens the free exercise of religious beliefs.[7] The case was initiated by two employees who had been fired for misconduct and subsequently denied unemployment benefits because they ingested peyote at a religious ceremony of the Native American Church. Distinguishing this case from *Yoder,* which involved a combination of free exercise rights and parental

6. 406 U.S. 205 (1972).

7. Employment Div. v. Smith, 494 U.S. 872 (1990).

rights, the Court majority concluded that without such a "hybrid" situation, individuals cannot rely on the Free Exercise Clause to be excused from complying with a valid criminal law prohibiting specific conduct.

Courts not only apply different criteria to assess claims under the Free Exercise and Establishment Clauses, they also impose different remedies for violations of the two clauses. **If an Establishment Clause violation is found, the unconstitutional government activity must cease. If government action is found to impair the Free Exercise Clause, accommodations to enable individuals to practice their beliefs may be required, but the secular policy or program would not have to be eliminated.**

Troublesome church/state controversies involve competing claims under the Free Exercise and Establishment Clauses because there is an inherent tension between the two provisions. The controversies become even more complex when Free Speech Clause protections are involved as has been prevalent in recent cases. Accommodations to free exercise and free speech rights can be interpreted as advancing religion in violation of the Establishment Clause, but overzealous efforts to guard against state sponsorship of religion can impinge on protections under the Free Exercise and Free Speech Clauses. This tension among First Amendment guarantees has complicated the judiciary's task in assessing claims regarding the role of religion in public schools and government relations with sectarian schools.

Religious Influences in Public Schools

> Devotionals sponsored by public schools violate the Establishment Clause, whereas private religious expression is protected by the Free Exercise and Free Speech Clauses.

From colonial days until the mid-twentieth century, religious (primarily Protestant) materials and observances were prevalent in many public schools. In two precedent-setting decisions in the early 1960s, the Supreme Court prohibited public schools from sponsoring daily prayer and Bible reading, concluding that such activities advance religion in violation of the Establishment Clause.[8] The Court reasoned that the students' voluntary participation in the religious activities was irrelevant to the constitutional impairment. The fact that daily devotional activities were sponsored by the public school was sufficient to abridge the First Amendment. In a number of subsequent decisions, federal appellate courts have struck down various legislative attempts to return state-condoned religious activities to public schools.[9]

8. Sch. Dist. of Abington Township v. Schempp, 374 U.S. 203 (1963); Engel v. Vitale, 370 U.S. 421 (1962).
9. *See, e.g.,* Doe v. Sch. Bd., 274 F.3d 289 (5th Cir. 2001); Ingebretsen v. Jackson Pub. Sch. Dist., 88 F.3d 274 (5th Cir. 1996); Doe v. Duncanville Indep. Sch. Dist., 70 F.3d 402 (5th Cir. 1995).

However, these rulings have not resolved many issues pertaining to religious influences in public education. Is the constitutional violation lessened if students, rather than teachers, initiate the devotional activities? If religious observances are occasional rather than daily, is the threat of an Establishment Clause impairment reduced? Can religious speech be distinguished from other types of speech in applying restrictions? To date, only partial answers have been provided to these and related questions in the public school context.

Silent Prayer Statutes

Students have a free exercise right to engage in *private* devotional activities in public schools as long as they do not interfere with regular school activities. Indeed, it would be difficult to monitor whether students were engaging in silent prayer. Controversies have focused on state laws or school board policies that condone silent devotionals, thus placing the stamp of public school approval on such activities.

In 1985, the Supreme Court rendered its first and only opinion to date on this issue in *Wallace v. Jaffree,* invalidating a 1981 Alabama silent prayer law under the Establishment Clause.[10] Since a 1978 Alabama law already authorized a period of silent meditation in public schools, the Court majority concluded that the only logical reason for adding the phrase "or voluntary prayer" in the 1981 amendment was to encourage students to pray. But the Court indicated that such laws without a legislative intent to impose prayer might withstand scrutiny under the Establishment Clause.

The constitutionality of laws calling for a moment of silence for prayer or meditation in public schools, which currently are on the books in almost half the states, remains to be resolved on a case-by-case basis, and courts have rejected most recent challenges to such laws. For example, a high school teacher who was fired for refusing to comply with Georgia's law challenged the constitutionality of the law that requires each public school teacher to conduct a minute of quiet reflection at the opening of the school day. In upholding the statute, the appeals court concluded that the provision had the secular purpose of providing an opportunity for pupils to reflect on the upcoming day.[11] The Fourth Circuit also upheld a Virginia statute authorizing a daily minute of silence for meditation or prayer in public schools, finding it neutral toward religion since students were not encouraged to pray during the moment of silence.[12] The appeals court reasoned that the law provides a neutral medium—silence—during which students can be involved in sectarian or secular activities. Unlike the Alabama law struck down in *Jaffree,* which the Supreme Court held was intended to return prayer to public schools, the appeals court reasoned that Virginia's law was enacted to provide time for quiet reflection, which is a good management strategy to settle students.

10. 472 U.S. 38 (1985).
11. Bown v. Gwinnett County Sch. Dist., 112 F.3d 1464 (11th Cir. 1997).
12. Brown v. Gilmore, 258 F.3d 265 (4th Cir. 2001), *cert. denied,* 533 U.S. 1301 (2001). *See also* the No Child Left Behind Act, 20 U.S.C.§ 6061 (2003) (specifying that no federal funds can be appropriated under the act for policies that prevent voluntary prayer and meditation in public schools); *infra* note 24.

School-Sponsored versus Private Devotionals

The most controversial issues currently revolve around whether the Establishment Clause concerns are eliminated if students initiate and lead devotionals in public schools. In short, what constitutes protected *private* religious expression in the public school context? There are some mixed signals from the federal courts regarding student-led graduation devotionals and prayers in other school events.

Weisman *and Its Progeny.* The impetus for the recent wave of legislative activity pressing the limits of the Establishment Clause was the seminal 1992 decision, *Lee v. Weisman.* The Supreme Court in *Weisman* struck down a Rhode Island school district's policy that permitted principals to invite clergy members to deliver invocations and benedictions at middle and high school graduation ceremonies.[13] In a five-to-four decision, the Court affirmed the appellate court's conclusion that such clergy-led devotionals at public school graduations violate the Establishment Clause. The Court majority reasoned that the policy had a coercive effect; students felt peer pressure to participate in the devotionals that were conducted at the school-sponsored graduation ceremony. The Court was not persuaded that the voluntary nature of graduation exercises eliminated the constitutional infraction. According to the majority, students should not have to make a choice between attending their graduation ceremony, a milestone event in their lives, and respecting their religious convictions.

Rather than reducing devotional activities in public school graduations, the Supreme Court's decision had the opposite impact. Negative reactions to this ruling resulted in school authorities and students finding creative strategies to include prayers in graduation ceremonies. In some districts, baccalaureate services were reinstated that had not been held for many years. To pass constitutional scrutiny, such baccalaureates cannot be sponsored by the public school, but students, churches, or other groups can rent space from the school district to conduct the religious services. In a Wyoming case, the federal district court ruled that students could rent the high school gym for a baccalaureate program because the event was not school sponsored, even though the school band performed and the district's graduation announcements mentioned the baccalaureate program.[14]

Because of the prohibition on school-sponsored religious activities, most post-*Weisman* controversies have involved student-led devotionals. Some school districts have given students discretion to include religious messages in their graduation speeches, designating the graduation ceremony a forum for student expression. Accordingly, students' messages (including any religious references) are not subject to review and do not bear the stamp of school approval. The Ninth Circuit upheld an Idaho school district's policy that prohibited school authorities from censoring students' graduation speeches and allowed student speakers (chosen by academic standing) to select "an address, poem, reading, song, musical presentation, prayer, or any other pronouncement of their choosing."[15] Finding the ceremony a forum for student expression, the court reasoned that the student speakers were selected based on secular criteria and were not advised to include devotionals in their remarks.

13. 505 U.S. 577 (1992).

14. Shumway v. Albany County Sch. Dist. No. One, 826 F. Supp. 1320 (D. Wyo. 1993).

However, in two other Ninth Circuit cases, the appeals court upheld school districts in not allowing students to deliver proselytizing graduation speeches that had been submitted to their principals for review in accordance with school policy. Unlike the first case, school authorities in these districts clearly maintained control of the graduation ceremony. Thus, the court found censorship of the proposed religious speeches appropriate to avoid an Establishment Clause violation.[16] **The central consideration seems to be whether the school has explicitly created a forum for student expression in the graduation ceremony or has retained control over students' graduation speeches.**

Student Elections to Authorize Prayers. Especially volatile controversies have focused on having students decide by election to include student-led devotionals in graduation ceremonies and other school activities, and courts are split on this issue. The Fifth Circuit upheld the practice of allowing students to vote on whether to have nonsectarian graduation prayers selected and delivered by students, reasoning that the student election removed school sponsorship.[17] But, the Third and Ninth Circuit appellate courts were not convinced that the Establishment Clause could be satisfied simply by giving students control of devotional activities at school-sponsored events. These courts reasoned that school authorities could not delegate decisions to students that the Establishment Clause forbids school districts from making.

In 2000, the Supreme Court in *Santa Fe Independent School District v. Doe* found an Establishment Clause violation in a Texas school district's policy authorizing student-led devotionals before public school football games.[18] The controversial policy and an identical graduation prayer policy authorized two elections—one to determine whether to have invocations and the second to select the student to deliver them. **The Supreme Court limited its ruling to the policy authorizing student-led prayers before football games and declared that student-led expression at a school event on school property and representing the student body under the supervision of school personnel could not be considered private speech.**[19] Even though the ultimate choice of speakers and content was made by the students, the school authorized the election in the first place. The degree of school involvement gave the impression that the devotionals at issue represented the school, leading the Court majority to conclude that the practice entailed both perceived and actual endorsement of religion. The majority reasoned that the current policy had a sham secular purpose and was intended to promote Christian religious observances in school-related events. Noting that the purpose of the Bill of Rights is to shield certain subjects from the political process, the Court held that the use of student elections intensifies the lack of rep-

15. Doe v. Madison Sch. Dist. No 321, 147 F.3d 832 (9th Cir. 1998), *vacated and remanded en banc* (because the student had graduated), 177 F.3d 789, 792 (9th Cir. 1999). For a discussion of students' free expression rights, *see* Chapter 5.
16. Lassonde v. Pleasanton Unified Sch. Dist., 320 F.3d 979 (9th Cir. 2003); Cole v. Oroville Union High Sch. Dist., 228 F.3d 1092 (9th Cir. 2000).
17. Jones v. Clear Creek Indep. Sch. Dist., 930 F.2d 416 (5th Cir. 1991), *vacated and remanded,* 505 U.S. 1215 (1992), *on remand,* 977 F.2d 963 (5th Cir. 1992).
18. 530 U.S. 290 (2000).
19. *Id.* at 310.

resentation of minority views, ensuring that they will never be heard. While rejecting the argument that Establishment Clause concerns can be eliminated by delegating decisions to students, **the majority emphasized that only state sponsorship of devotionals violates the Establishment Clause; nothing in the Constitution prohibits public school students from voluntarily praying at school.**

Post*-Santa Fe *Rulings. The *Santa Fe* decision has not settled what distinguishes protected private religious expression from unconstitutional school-sponsored devotionals. Indeed, some post-*Santa Fe* federal appellate rulings represent an expansive stance regarding the reach of the Free Speech Clause in protecting students' private religious expression in public schools. For example, after a lengthy series of court orders, the Eleventh Circuit upheld a Florida school district's policy that authorizes public school seniors to select classmates to give graduation messages and allows the speakers to choose the content, which could be religious.[20] Even though the school district's memo outlining the policy was entitled "Graduation Prayer," the court emphasized that the student elections are not to identify classmates to deliver prayers—the graduation messages are of unspecified content, which may or may not include sectarian material.

In a second Eleventh Circuit ruling, the court lifted the part of an injunction imposed by the lower court that had prohibited students from publicly expressing religious views in most public school settings in Dekalb County, Alabama.[21] The appeals court declared that the Establishment Clause does not *require* and the Free Speech Clause does not *permit* suppression of student-initiated religious expression in public schools or relegating it to whispers or closets.

Although the Supreme Court vacated these appellate decisions and remanded the cases for further consideration in light of *Santa Fe,* the appeals court subsequently reaffirmed both rulings. Distinguishing the Supreme Court's condemnation of school-sponsored student prayer in *Santa Fe,* the Eleventh Circuit reasoned that school censorship of *private* student religious expression is also unconstitutional.[22] The appeals court emphasized that all student religious speech in public schools cannot be equated with expression *representing* the public school.

Even more recently, the Ninth Circuit found a school district guilty of viewpoint discrimination against a student religious club that was not treated like other student clubs in access to school facilities, supplies, and equipment. The court concluded that equal treatment is required by the Free Speech Clause and does not abridge the Establishment Clause.[23] Furthermore, recent federal guidelines to implement the No Child Left Behind Act expansively interpret what constitutes protected religious expression in public schools, and the

20. Adler v. Duval County Sch. Bd., 206 F.3d 1070 (11th Cir. 2000), *vacated and remanded,* 531 U.S. 801 (2000), *reinstated on remand,* 250 F.3d 1330 (11th Cir. 2001), *cert. denied,* 534 U.S. 1065 (2001).

21. Chandler v. James, 180 F.3d 1254 (11th Cir. 1999), *vacated and remanded,* 530 U.S. 1256 (2000), *reinstated on remand sub nom.* Chandler v. Siegelman, 230 F.3d 1313 (11th Cir. 2000), *cert. denied,* 533 U.S. 916 (2001).

22. *Id.,* 230 F.3d at 1315.

23. Prince v. Jacoby, 303 F.3d 1074 (9th Cir. 2002); *infra* text accompanying note 55.

law conditions federal aid on school districts certifying that they have no policies preventing constitutionally protected prayer.[24]

The Supreme Court undoubtedly will be asked to provide additional clarification regarding the scope of permissible student-initiated religious activities in public schools and how to distinguish protected private religious expression from prohibited school-sponsored devotionals. **Student religious expression may be considered private if truly student initiated, but the *Santa Fe* decision casts doubt on the legality of holding student elections to determine that student-led devotionals will be included in school-sponsored activities.**

Religious Displays and Holiday Observances

The display of religious documents and the observance of religious holidays in public schools also remain controversial. In 1980, the Supreme Court declined to hear an appeal of a decision allowing religious holiday observances and the temporary display of religious symbols in public education,[25] but a week later, the divided Court struck down a Kentucky law calling for the posting of the Ten Commandments in public school classrooms.[26] In the first case, the historical and cultural significance of Christmas convinced the Eighth Circuit that the prudent and objective observance of this holiday in public schools does not serve to advance religion, even though songs such as *Silent Night* are sung and the nativity scene is displayed.[27] The appeals court held that the school board's policy, allowing the observance of holidays with both a religious and secular basis, had the nonreligious purpose of improving the overall instructional program.

In contrast, the five-member Supreme Court majority in the second case was not persuaded that the Ten Commandments' cultural significance justified posting this religious document in public schools. Distinguishing the display of religious texts from the permissible use of religious literature in academic courses, the majority held that the Kentucky law's purpose was to advance a particular religious faith, which violates the Establishment Clause. The majority rejected the state judiciary's conclusion that the constitutional impairment was neutralized because the copies were purchased with private donations and carried the disclaimer that "the secular application of the Ten Commandments is clearly seen in its adoption as the fundamental legal code of Western Civilization and the common law of the United States."[28] In spite of the Supreme Court ruling, state efforts to authorize the posting

24. Secretary Roderick Paige, *Guidance on Constitutionally Protected Prayer in Public Elementary and Secondary Schools* (Washington, DC: United States Department of Education, 2003), interpreting the No Child Left Behind Act, 20 U.S.C. § 6061 (2003).
25. Florey v. Sioux Falls Sch. Dist. 49-5, 619 F.2d 1311 (8th Cir.1980).
26. Stone v. Graham, 449 U.S. 39 (1980).
27. *Florey,* 619 F.2d at 1314. *See also* Sechler v. State Coll. Area Sch. Dist., 121 F. Supp. 2d 439 (M.D. Pa. 2000) (rejecting an Establishment Clause challenge to holiday observance that allegedly was not "Christian enough"; the program included the Menorah and Kwanzaa candelabra as well as a Christmas tree and carols and was designed to celebrate diversity).
28. *Stone,* 449 U.S. at 41.

of the Ten Commandments with other historic documents in public buildings, including schools, continue to generate litigation.[29]

Other religious displays also have been controversial. The Sixth Circuit held that the display of a portrait of Jesus in a public secondary school failed all three prongs of the *Lemon* test.[30] Also, a New York federal district court enjoined the display of a religious painting in the high school auditorium because it conveyed government endorsement of religion.[31] However, a federal district court in New Jersey found that inclusion of religious holidays, such as Christmas and Hanukkah, on school district calendars was designed to broaden students' sensitivity toward religious diversity and their knowledge of the role of religion in the development of civilization and satisfied all prongs of the *Lemon* test.[32]

Some parents have alleged that public schools promote the religion of Wicca by observing Halloween with pictures of witches and goblins. A Florida appeals court held that the display of witches does not promote a nontheistic religion or give any perception of public school endorsement of Wicca.[33] Similarly, an Establishment Clause challenge to using a devil as a public school's mascot has been rejected.[34]

The Supreme Court has condoned the use of public funds or property for certain religious displays in several decisions outside the school domain,[35] but courts nonetheless seem likely to continue to strike down the display of sectarian documents in public schools. **However, the objective recognition of religious holidays will presumably withstand judicial scrutiny as long as particular faiths are not compromised.**

Proselytization in the Classroom

Public schools must abide by Establishment Clause restrictions on government promotion of religious creeds. Because teachers and other school personnel are working with a vulnerable captive audience in public schools, their actions have been scrutinized to ensure that classrooms are not used as a forum to indoctrinate sectarian beliefs. To illustrate, the Tenth Circuit held that school officials could order the removal of religiously oriented books from a teacher's classroom library and require the teacher to keep his Bible out of sight and to

29. *See, e.g.,* Baker v. Adams County/Ohio Valley Sch. Bd., 310 F.3d 927 (6th Cir. 2002); ICLU v. O'Bannon, 259 F.3d 766 (7th Cir. 2001), *cert. denied,* 534 U.S. 1162 (2002).

30. Washegesic v. Bloomingdale Pub. Schs., 33 F.3d 679 (6th Cir. 1994). *See also* Fleming v. Jefferson County Sch. Dist., 298 F.3d 918 (10th Cir. 2002) (finding no Establishment or Free Speech Clause violation in not allowing persons connected with the Columbine shootings to paint religious messages on tiles hung in the school).

31. Joki v. Bd. of Educ., 745 F. Supp. 823 (N.D.N.Y. 1990). *See also* Gernetzke v. Kenosha Unified Sch. Dist. No. 1, 274 F.3d 464 (7th Cir. 2001), *cert. denied,* 535 U.S. 1017 (2002); *infra* text accompanying note 57.

32. Clever v. Cherry Hill Township Bd. of Educ., 838 F. Supp. 929 (D.N.J. 1993).

33. Guyer v. Sch. Bd., 634 So. 2d 806 (Fla. Dist. Ct. App. 1994).

34. *See* Kunselman v. W. Reserve Local Sch. Dist., 70 F.3d 931 (6th Cir. 1995).

35. For citations to these cases, *see* Nelda Cambron-McCabe, Martha McCarthy, and Stephen Thomas, *Public School Law: Teachers' and Students' Rights,* 5th ed. (Boston: Allyn and Bacon, 2004), Chapter 2.

refrain from silently reading it during school hours.[36] More recently, the Second Circuit found no free exercise impairment in a New York school board's directive for a teacher to stop using religious references in delivering his instructional program,[37] and a federal district court held that school authorities properly instructed a Connecticut teacher to cover a proselytizing shirt at school.[38] The judiciary has recognized that the Establishment Clause bars public school teachers' use of the "power, prestige, and influence" of their position to lead devotional activities.[39]

In several cases, teachers have been discharged for proselytizing students or disregarding selected aspects of the curriculum that conflict with their religious values. For example, the Seventh Circuit upheld a school board's dismissal of a kindergarten teacher who literally interpreted the biblical prohibition against worshiping graven images, and thus refused to teach about the American flag, the observance of patriotic holidays, and the importance of historical figures such as Abraham Lincoln. The appellate court noted that the teacher enjoys the freedom to hold such beliefs but has "no constitutional right to require others to submit to her views and to forego a portion of their education they would otherwise be entitled to enjoy."[40] A New York appeals court also upheld the dismissal of a tenured teacher based on evidence that she had tried to recruit students to join her religious organization, conducted prayer sessions in her office, and used her classroom to promote her religious faith.[41] In addition, courts have supported disciplinary action against teachers who have continued to teach the biblical account of creation in their classes after repeated warnings to conform to school board guidelines regarding the biology course content.[42]

Although proselytization of students by public school teachers violates the Establishment Clause, the Supreme Court has emphasized that it is permissible, even desirable, to teach the Bible and other religious documents from a literary, cultural, or historical perspective.[43] The insufficient treatment in textbooks of the role of religion in the development of Western civilization has been partially due to fears of violating the Establishment Clause. Several coalitions of national education, civic, and religious groups as well as the Department of Education have distributed materials addressing permissible methods to teach about the role of religion in society and attempting to clarify the legal status of various church/state issues in public schools.[44]

36. Roberts v. Madigan, 921 F.2d 1047 (10th Cir. 1990). However, the court enjoined the school board from removing the Bible from the school library, noting that the Bible has significant literary and historical significance.
37. Marchi v. Bd. of Coop. Educ. Servs., 173 F.3d 469 (2d Cir. 1999).
38. Downing v. W. Haven Bd. of Educ., 162 F. Supp. 2d 19 (D. Conn. 2001). The shirt read "Jesus 2000, J2K."
39. Fink v. Bd. of Educ., 442 A.2d 837, 842 (Pa. Commw. Ct. 1982) (upholding a teacher's dismissal for refusing to comply with the superintendent's directives to cease opening classes with devotional activities). *See also* Jaffree v. Bd. of Sch. Comm'rs, 705 F.2d 1526 (11th Cir. 1983) (enjoining teacher-initiated devotional activities in an Alabama school district).
40. Palmer v. Bd. of Educ., 603 F.2d 1271, 1274 (7th Cir. 1979). For a discussion of teachers' wearing religious attire in public schools, *see* text accompanying note 50, Chapter 11.
41. La Rocca v. Bd. of Educ., 406 N.Y.S.2d 348 (App. Div. 1978).
42. *See, e.g.,* LeVake v. Indep. Sch. Dist. No. 656, 625 N.W.2d 502 (Minn. Ct. App. 2001), *cert. denied,* 534 U.S. 1081 (2002); Dale v. Bd. of Educ., 316 N.W.2d 108 (S.D. 1982).
43. *See* Sch. Dist. of Abington Township v. Schempp, 374 U.S. 203, 225 (1963).

Comparative religion courses in high schools have seldom been controversial, but the line is not always clear between teaching about religion and instilling religious tenets in other courses. Numerous Bible study courses, particularly at the elementary school level, have been challenged as a ploy to advance sectarian beliefs. Courts have carefully evaluated curricular materials and even reviewed videotapes of lessons in determining whether such instruction fosters a particular creed. The judiciary has struck down programs designed to inculcate religious tenets rather than to study about religion or where private groups have controlled the personnel or curriculum.[45]

Performances of school choirs often have evoked controversies over alleged proselytization. A Utah choir director agreed to exempt a student from singing religious songs, but the student sought an injunction against the choir performing the songs and against holding two performances at religious sites. The Tenth Circuit accepted the school district's justification that the music promoted friendship, noting that a substantial amount of choral music is religious in nature, and also accepted that the religious sites had superior facilities.[46] The Fifth Circuit similarly ruled that forbidding the school choir to sing religious songs would disqualify appropriate choral music, so the use of religious songs does not constitute an endorsement of religion.[47]

Some controversies over proselytization in the classroom have not challenged teachers' activities but have entailed requests for students to include sectarian materials in their presentations, artwork, or other assignments. In most of these cases, the schools have prevailed in denying the students' requests. For example, the Sixth Circuit upheld a school district's prohibition on an elementary school student showing in class a videotape of herself singing a proselytizing religious song.[48] Recognizing that the public school curriculum is

44. *See, e.g.,* Paige, *Guidance on Constitutionally Protected Prayer in Public Elementary and Secondary Schools; Religion in the Public Schools: A Joint Statement of Current Law,* American Jewish Congress, Chair Drafting Committee (New York: American Jewish Congress, 1995).

45. *See, e.g.,* Hall v. Bd. of Sch. Comm'rs, 707 F.2d 464 (11th Cir. 1983); Doe v. Porter, 188 F. Supp. 2d 904 (E.D. Tenn. 2002). *But see* Doe v. Beaumont Indep. Sch. Dist., 240 F.3d 462 (5th Cir. 2001) (*en banc*) (remanding for a trial to determine if use of volunteer clergy counselors in public schools violates the Establishment Clause).

46. Bauchman v. W. High Sch., 132 F.3d 542 (10th Cir. 1997).

47. Doe v. Duncanville Indep. Sch. Dist., 70 F.3d 402 (5th Cir. 1995). However, the court struck down the basketball team's policy of praying before games, practices, and pep rallies with the encouragement of school employees.

48. DeNooyer v. Merinelli, 12 F.3d 211 (6th Cir. 1993). *See also* C.H. v. Oliva, 226 F.3d 198 (3d Cir. 2000), *cert. denied,* 533 U.S. 915 (2001) (upholding a teacher in denying an elementary child's request to read a Bible story to the class and removing his poster temporarily because it depicted a religious theme); Settle v. Dickson County Sch. Bd., 53 F.3d 152 (6th Cir. 1995) (upholding a junior high school teacher who gave a student a zero on a report because the student had cleared a different topic with the teacher but then wrote her report on the life of Jesus Christ); Walz v. Egg Harbor Township Bd. of Educ., 187 F. Supp. 2d 232 (D.N.J. 2002) (rejecting contention that a student had a First Amendment right to distribute religious gifts in the classroom; reasonable accommodations were made in that religious materials could be distributed before and after school and during recess). *But see* Paige, *Guidance on Constitutionally Protected Prayer in Public Elementary and Secondary Schools,* which stipulates that students should not be disadvantaged if they express their religious beliefs in their class assignments; *supra* note 24.

supervised by faculty and designed to impart knowledge, the appeals court held that student projects can be censored to ensure that the school is not viewed as endorsing religious content.

Equal Access for Religious Expression and Groups

In the 1960s and 1970s, it often was assumed that the Establishment Clause prohibited religious speech in government forums. More recently, however, the Supreme Court has reasoned that **singling out religious views for differential treatment compared with other private expression would be unconstitutional viewpoint discrimination, which abridges the Free Speech Clause.** The Court started this trend in education cases in its 1981 decision, *Widmar v. Vincent,* finding no Establishment Clause violation in allowing student religious groups to have access to a forum created for student expression on state-supported college campuses.[49]

The Equal Access Act. Free Speech Clause protections were augmented in public secondary schools by passage of the Equal Access Act (EAA) in 1984 (see Figure 3.2).[50] In 1990, the Supreme Court in *Board of Education of Westside Community Schools v. Mergens* rejected the contention that the EAA abridges the Establishment Clause because student religious groups are allowed to meet, recognizing the law's clear secular purpose of preventing discrimination against religious and other types of private expression.[51] The Court dis-

FIGURE 3.2 ***The Equal Access Act***

20 U.S. C. §§ 4071- 4074 (2003)

Sec. 801(a) It shall be unlawful for any public secondary school which receives federal financial assistance and which has a limited open forum to deny equal access or a fair opportunity to, or discriminate against, any students who wish to conduct a meeting within that limited open forum on the basis of the religious, political, philosophical, or other content of the speech at such meetings.

(b) A public secondary school has a limited open forum whenever such school grants an offering to or opportunity for one or more noncurriculum-related student groups to meet on school premises during noninstructional time.

(c) Schools shall be deemed to offer a fair opportunity to students who wish to conduct a meeting within its limited open forum if such school uniformly provides that

(1) The meeting is voluntary and student initiated;
(2) There is no sponsorship of the meeting by the school, the government, or its agents or employees;
(3) Employees or agents of the school or government are present at religious meetings only in a nonparticipatory capacity;
(4) The meeting does not materially and substantially interfere with the orderly conduct of educational activities within the school; and
(5) Nonschool persons may not direct, conduct, control, or regularly attend activities of student groups.

49. 454 U.S. 263 (1981).

50. 20 U.S.C. §§ 4071- 4074 (2003).

51. 496 U.S. 226, 249 (1990).

tinguished government speech promoting religion that is prohibited by the Establishment Clause from private religious expression protected by the Free Speech and Free Exercise Clauses. In subsequent cases, federal appellate courts have ruled that the EAA:

- Prevails over state constitutional provisions requiring greater separation of church and state than demanded by the Establishment Clause;[52]
- Authorizes student religious meetings during lunch if that is considered noninstructional time;[53]
- Authorizes student religious groups to require certain officers to be Christians to preserve the spiritual content of their meetings;[54] and
- Requires student religious groups to be provided equal access to fund-raising activities, school bulletin boards, and other resources available for student clubs.[55]

A California appeals court further noted that the religious club itself would not have to be student initiated to be protected under the EAA—only its on-campus meetings would have to be initiated by students.[56]

Although there are limits on the reach of the EAA,[57] this federal law has provided substantial protection to student religious meetings in secondary schools during noninstructional time. **The EAA has codified the concept of equal access and equal treatment of religious expression that is currently guiding First Amendment litigation as well.**

School Access for Community Groups. The EAA applies *only* to secondary students, so community religious groups desiring public school access during noninstructional time must rely on First Amendment protections. Since the early 1990s, the Supreme Court has made some definitive pronouncements about protecting private religious expression from viewpoint discrimination. In *Lamb's Chapel v. Center Moriches Union Free School District,* the Court held that if secular community groups are allowed to use the public school after school hours to address particular topics (i.e., family life, child rearing), a sectarian group desiring to show a film series addressing these topics from religious perspectives cannot be denied public school access.[58] **In essence, school districts cannot enforce policies governing facility use during nonschool time that entail viewpoint discrimination against a religious group's message.**

52. Ceniceros v. Bd. of Trs., 106 F.3d 878 (9th Cir. 1997); Garnett v. Renton Sch. Dist. No. 403, 987 F.2d 641 (9th Cir. 1993).
53. *Ceniceros,* 106 F.3d 878.
54. Hsu v. Roslyn Union Free Sch. Dist., 85 F.3d 839 (2d Cir. 1996).
55. Prince v. Jacoby, 303 F.3d 1074 (9th Cir. 2002).
56. Schoick v. Saddleback Valley Unified Sch. Dist., 104 Cal. Rptr. 2d 562 (Ct. App. 2001). *See* Chapter 5 for a discussion of criteria used in determining what student clubs are curriculum related.
57. *See, e.g.,* Gernetzke v. Kenosha Unified Sch. Dist. No. 1, 274 F.3d 464 (7th Cir. 2001), *cert. denied,* 535 U.S. 1017 (2002) (finding no EAA violation when a principal barred a student religious group from including a large cross in the group's school hallway mural).
58. 508 U.S. 384 (1993).

In 2001, the Supreme Court delivered a seminal decision, *Good News Club v. Milford Central School,* allowing a private Christian organization to hold its meetings in a New York public school after school hours.[59] The Milford School District had denied the Good News Club's request under its community-use policy that allows civic and recreational groups to use the school but not for religious purposes. The district contended that the club was engaging in religious worship and instruction that must be barred from public school facilities.

Disagreeing with the school district and the lower courts, the Supreme Court in *Milford* relied heavily on *Lamb's Chapel* and held that the school district's policy discriminated against religious viewpoints in violation of the Free Speech Clause. Milford school authorities attempted to distinguish meetings of the Good News Club, which targets children under age 12 and involves religious instruction and prayer, from a religious group using the school to show films primarily to adults, which was upheld in *Lamb's Chapel.* However, the Supreme Court did not find the distinction significant, noting that whether moral lessons are taught through live storytelling and prayers or through films is inconsequential from a constitutional standpoint.[60] The majority reasoned that the Good News Club was merely seeking access to school facilities like other community groups and that the Free Speech Clause protected the religious viewpoints expressed during the club's devotional meetings, even though elementary children would be present.

Under the *Milford* ruling, if a public school establishes a limited forum for community meetings, it cannot bar religious groups, even those involved in worship activities that target students attending the school. The Court did not find a danger that the community would perceive the Good News Club's access as school district endorsement of religion.

Distribution of Religious Literature. The Supreme Court has not directly addressed the distribution of religious literature in public schools, and lower courts have rendered a range of opinions. Courts consistently have ruled that school personnel cannot give students Bibles or other religious materials,[61] and most courts have prohibited religious sects, such as the Gideon Society, from visiting public schools to distribute materials to captive student audiences.[62]

Departing from this trend, the Fourth Circuit upheld a West Virginia school district's policy allowing sectarian organizations along with political groups to distribute materials,

59. 533 U.S. 98 (2001). *See also* Culbertson v. Oakridge Sch. Dist. No. 76, 258 F.3d 1061 (9th Cir. 2001) (upholding the Good News Club's right to meet in the public school after school hours, but enjoining teachers from distributing permission slips for the meetings as encouraging the club in violation of the Establishment Clause).

60. *Good News Club,* 533 U.S. at 108-110. *See also* Bronx Household of Faith v. Bd. of Educ., 226 F. Supp. 2d 401 (S.D.N.Y. 2002) (applying *Good News* and finding substantial likelihood that the denial of a request to use the public school for a group's religious worship services violated the First Amendment).

61. *See, e.g.,* Jabr v. Rapides Parish Sch. Bd., 171 F. Supp. 2d 653 (W.D. La. 2001) (finding that the school principal violated the Establishment Clause by distributing New Testament Bibles to public school students).

62. *See, e.g.,* Doe v. Duncanville Indep. Sch. Dist., 70 F.3d 402 (5th Cir. 1995); Berger v. Rensselaer Cent. Sch. Corp., 982 F.2d 1160 (7th Cir. 1993).

such as Bibles, in public secondary schools on a designated day because the organizations were considered private entities that do not represent the school.[63] However, the policy was invalidated at the elementary school level because of the impressionability of younger children and their greater difficulty in distinguishing private from school-sponsored speech.

Recent controversies usually have focused on student requests to distribute religious publications. **Most courts have applied the "equal access" concept in concluding that the same legal principles govern students' distribution of religious and nonreligious literature.**[64] In a higher education case, the Supreme Court reasoned that not only is the government's equal treatment of religious and secular private expression permitted by the Establishment Clause, but in some circumstances it is required by the Free Speech Clause.[65] Yet, even personal expression is subject to reasonable time, place, and manner regulations. For example, an Indiana federal district court supported a school policy requiring students to give the principal advance notice of the distribution and to submit a copy of the literature to the superintendent, but not for approval purposes.[66] Whereas reasonable restrictions on how material is distributed have been upheld, school districts cannot place a blanket ban on students' distribution of religious literature.

Accommodations for Religious Beliefs

> Religious exemptions from school observances and assignments will be upheld as long as they do not interfere with the management of the school or the student's academic progress.

In addition to challenging sectarian influences in public schools, some students have asserted a right to accommodations so they can practice their religious beliefs. These disputes often pit free exercise and free speech protections against prohibitions on religious establishment. Conflicts have arisen over release-time programs for religious education, excusal from public schools for religious observances, and religious exemptions from secular school activities.

63. Peck v. Upshur County Bd. of Educ., 155 F.3d 274 (4th Cir. 1998).
64. *See, e.g.,* Muller v. Jefferson Lighthouse Sch., 98 F.3d 1530 (7th Cir. 1996); Hedges v. Wauconda Cmty. Unit Sch. Dist., 9 F.3d 1295 (7th Cir. 1993).
65. Rosenberger v. Rector & Visitors, 515 U.S. 819 (1995) (holding that a public university could not withhold support from a student group wanting to use student activity funds to distribute sectarian materials).
66. Harless v. Darr, 937 F. Supp. 1351 (S.D. Ind. 1996).

Release-Time Programs

Although the Supreme Court has struck down the practice of using public school classrooms to provide religious training to public school students during the instructional day,[67] the Court has recognized that the school must not be hostile toward religion and thus can release students to receive such religious training off public school grounds.[68] A release-time program was even upheld in a school district where students received an hour of religious instruction each week in a mobile unit parked at the edge of school property.[69] Courts have not been persuaded that nonparticipating students are denied their state-created right to an education because academic instruction ceases during the time that their classmates are released for religious instruction. Confining students to a single choice of attending religious classes or remaining in the public school has not been found to advance religion.

While upholding a release-time program in Utah, the Tenth Circuit enjoined the school's practice of awarding course credit in the public high school for the secular aspects of daily instruction received at a Mormon seminary.[70] Nevertheless, the court reasoned that time spent by students in the seminary program could be counted in satisfying compulsory school attendance and in calculating the school's eligibility for state aid. More recently, an Indiana federal district court enjoined several features of a release-time program that was held in trailers brought on public school property, with utilities supported by the school district. Nonparticipating students were required to read silently when their classmates attended the religious instruction to discourage students from remaining in the classroom during the release-time program.[71] Recognizing the legality of release-time programs, the federal court nonetheless found Establishment Clause violations in this school district's effort to encourage participation in the program and in the use of school property for the religious classes.

Excusal for Religious Observances

Requests for students and teachers to be excused from public schools to observe religious holidays raise particularly delicate issues. Such requests usually are made by members of minority sects, since schools are closed when the majority of teachers and students are observing their religious holidays. Courts have been asked to determine how far public school authorities must go in accommodating religious holidays and how far they can go before such accommodations abridge the Establishment Clause. **Courts have required school districts to accommodate reasonable religious absences, but not excessive absences for religious reasons (e.g., one day a week).** Also, courts have *not* been receptive

67. McCollum v. Bd. of Educ., 333 U.S. 203 (1948).
68. Zorach v. Clauson, 343 U.S. 306, 313-314 (1952).
69. Smith v. Smith, 523 F.2d 121 (4th Cir. 1975). A program in which all students are released early one day a week might be easier to defend constitutionally, because students would not be restricted to either remaining at the public school or attending sectarian classes.
70. Lanner v. Wimmer, 662 F.2d 1349 (10th Cir. 1981).
71. Moore v. Metro. Sch. Dist., No. IP 00-1859-C-M/S, 2001 U.S. Dist. LEXIS 2722 (S.D. Ind. Feb. 7, 2001).

to attempts to avoid school attendance altogether on religious grounds, although parents can select private education or home schooling for their children. As discussed previously, the one judicially endorsed exception to compulsory school attendance involves Amish children after completion of the eighth grade, because of the uniqueness of the Amish lifestyle.[72]

Religious Exemptions from Secular Activities

Teachers and other school employees have requested exemptions from public school activities that offend their religious beliefs, but most exemptions have been sought for students, because particular school requirements allegedly impair the practice of their religious tenets. In evaluating whether school authorities must honor such requests, courts have attempted to balance parents' interests in directing the religious upbringing of their children against the state's interest in ensuring an educated citizenry.

Courts have relied on the First Amendment in striking down required student participation in certain public school activities and observances. In the landmark case, *West Virginia State Board of Education v. Barnette,* the Supreme Court in 1943 ruled that students could not be required to salute the American flag in contravention of their religious beliefs, overturning a precedent established by the Court only three years earlier.[73] In *Barnette,* the Court held that refusal to participate in the flag salute and Pledge of Allegiance does not interfere with the rights of others to do so or threaten any type of disruption. Courts subsequently have protected students' rights not only to decline to participate for religious or philosophical reasons in the flag-salute ceremony but also to register a silent protest by remaining seated during the observance.[74] Of course, if students should carry the silent protest to the point that it disrupts the classroom, such conduct could be curtailed.

The Supreme Court has not directly addressed teachers' free exercise rights in connection with patriotic observances in public schools, but several lower courts have adopted the *Barnette* rationale in concluding that teachers, like students, have a First Amendment right to refuse to pledge allegiance as a matter of personal conscience.[75] Teachers, however, cannot use their religious beliefs to deny students the opportunity to engage in this observance. If a school district requires the pledge to be recited daily, which is more prevalent since the terrorist attacks on September 11, 2001, teachers must make provisions for this observance in their classrooms.

Although individuals are entitled to be excused, it has generally been assumed that saying the Pledge of Allegiance in public schools is not vulnerable to a First Amendment challenge. The Seventh Circuit ruled that the phrase, "under God," which was added to the pledge in 1954, does not convert this patriotic observance into a religious exercise that would abridge the Establishment Clause.[76] The Ninth Circuit reached an opposite

72. *See* Wisconsin v. Yoder, 406 U.S. 205 (1972); *supra* text accompanying note 6.

73. 319 U.S. 624 (1943), overturning Minersville Sch. Dist. v. Gobitis, 310 U.S. 586 (1940).

74. *See, e.g.,* Lipp v. Morris, 579 F.2d 834 (3d Cir. 1978).

75. *See, e.g.,* Russo v. Cent. Sch. Dist. No. 1, 469 F.2d 623, 634 (2d Cir. 1972).

76. Sherman v. Cmty. Consol. Sch. Dist. 21, 980 F.2d 437 (7th Cir. 1992). The court reasoned that through rote repetition, some phrases have lost their sectarian meaning and can be characterized as "ceremonial deism." *Id.,* 980 F.2d at 447.

conclusion, holding that public school children saying the phrase "under God" in the Pledge violates the Establishment Clause.[77] Given the volatile political response to the Ninth Circuit ruling, the Supreme Court likely will be called on to resolve the conflict between federal appellate courts.

Patriotic observances have not been the only source of controversy; religious exemptions also have been sought from components of the curriculum. Whereas teachers cannot assert a free exercise right to disregard aspects of the state-prescribed curriculum, the judiciary has been more receptive to students' requests for exemptions from instructional requirements. Students, unlike teachers, are compelled to attend school, and for many this means a public school. Accordingly, the judiciary has been sensitive to the fact that certain public school policies may have a coercive effect on religious practices. In balancing the interests involved, courts consider:

- The extent the school requirement burdens the exercise of sincere religious beliefs,
- The government justification for the requirement, and
- Alternative means available to meet the state's objectives.

School authorities must have a compelling justification to deny students an exemption from a requirement that impairs the exercise of sincere religious beliefs.

Most requests for religious exemptions are handled at the classroom or school level, but a few have generated legal controversies. Students have been successful in securing religious exemptions from various instructional activities, such as drug education, sex education, coeducational physical education, dancing instruction, officers' training programs, and specific course assignments if alternatives can satisfy the instructional objectives.[78] The relief ordered in these cases has entailed the excusal of specific children, but the secular activities themselves have not been disturbed.

Religious exemptions have not been honored if considered unnecessary to accommodate the practice of religious tenets or if the exemptions would substantially disrupt the school or students' academic progress or pose a safety hazard.[79] In a widely publicized 1987 case, the Sixth Circuit rejected the request of fundamentalist Christian parents for their children to be excused from exposure to the basal reading series used in elementary grades in a Tennessee school district.[80] Reversing the lower court's grant of the exemption, the Sixth Circuit reasoned that the readers did not burden the students' exercise of their fundamentalist religious beliefs, because the students were not required to profess a creed or perform religious exercises. More recently, a federal court rejected a parent's request for his son to be exempted from a Connecticut school district's mandatory health

77. Newdow v. U.S. Congress, 292 F.3d 597 (9th Cir. 2002), *amended and rehearing en banc denied,* 321 F.3d 772 (9th Cir. 2003).

78. *See* Cambron-McCabe et al., *Public School Law,* Chapter 2.

79. *See, e.g.,* Menora v. Ill. High Sch. Ass'n, 683 F.2d 1030 (7th Cir. 1982); Keller v. Gardner Cmty. Consol. Grade Sch. Dist. 72C, 552 F. Supp. 512 (N.D. Ill. 1982).

80. Mozert v. Hawkins County Bd. of Educ., 827 F.2d 1058 (6th Cir. 1987).

curriculum.[81] The student was allowed to be excused from certain lessons, but his father argued that state law entitled him to be exempt from the entire health course because the subject matter conflicted with his religious beliefs. Ruling that the health curriculum served the legitimate interest of providing important information, the Court was not persuaded that the state law entitling students to religious exemptions from a family life education program could be used to secure exemptions from the entire health curriculum.

As discussed in Chapter 4, conservative parents' organizations have secured federal and state laws allowing students to be excused from public school activities and components of the curriculum for religious and other reasons. Thus, parents may be able to use legislation to secure exemptions for their children,[82] even if they cannot substantiate that particular instructional activities impair free exercise rights.

Religious Challenges to the Secular Curriculum

> Most lawsuits claiming that components of the public school curriculum (e.g., evolution) advance an antitheistic religious belief have not been successful.

Some parents have not been content with securing religious exemptions for their own children and have pressed for elimination of various courses, activities, and instructional materials from public schools. Although courts often have been receptive to requests for individual exemptions from specific public school activities, the judiciary has not been inclined to allow the restriction of the secular curriculum to satisfy parents' religious preferences. The Supreme Court has recognized that "the state has no legitimate interest in protecting any or all religions from views distasteful to them."[83]

Defining What Is "Religious"

Challenges to the curriculum raise complex questions involving what constitutes religious beliefs and practices that are subject to First Amendment protections and restrictions. **In several cases protecting the free exercise of beliefs, the Supreme Court has expansively interpreted "religion" as any belief of ultimate concern,[84] but it has not yet found an Establishment Clause violation in connection with a nontheistic creed.** The Third Cir-

81. Leebaert v. Harrington, 193 F. Supp. 2d 491 (D. Conn. 2002).
82. *See* Protection of Pupil Rights Amendment, No Child Left Behind Act of 2001, 20 U.S.C. § 1232h (2003); text accompanying note 110, Chapter 4.
83. Epperson v. Arkansas, 393 U.S. 97, 107 (1968) (quoting Joseph Burstyn, Inc. v. Wilson, 343 U.S. 495, 505 (1952)).
84. *See, e.g.*, Thomas v. Review Bd., 450 U.S. 707, 714 (1981); United States v. Seeger, 380 U.S. 163, 175 (1965).

cuit, however, ruled that a public school curricular offering (instruction in transcendental meditation) unconstitutionally advanced a nontraditional religious belief (the Science of Creative Intelligence).[85] Also, the Ninth Circuit held that taxpayers had standing to raise an Establishment Clause challenge to a school district's magnet school that used the Waldorf approach (emphasizing the arts and alternative teaching methods), which is based on the spiritual science known as "anthroposophy."[86] Other courts have suggested that secular religions should be subjected to the same standards that are applied to theistic religions in determining whether the Establishment Clause has been breached.[87]

Even courts that have considered nontheistic creeds to be "religions" for First Amendment purposes have not ruled that challenged public school courses and materials advance such creeds, often referred to as *secular humanism* or *New Age theology*. In a 1987 case that attracted substantial media attention, the Eleventh Circuit reversed an Alabama federal judge's conclusion that secular humanism was being unconstitutionally advanced in the Mobile County schools.[88] The judge had enjoined the school district's use of several dozen home economics, history, and social studies books found to advance secular humanism. Disagreeing, the appellate court held that the books did not promote an antitheistic creed and rejected the contention that the mere omission of religious facts in the curriculum represented unconstitutional hostility toward theistic beliefs.

Challenged Curriculum Components

Sex education classes have been particularly susceptible to charges that an antitheistic faith is being advanced, but courts consistently have found that the challenged courses present public health information that furthers legitimate educational objectives and do not denounce Christianity.[89] **However, students have a free exercise right to be excused from sex education classes if such instruction conflicts with their sectarian beliefs.**

Because conservative citizen groups have not been successful in getting sex education barred from the public school curriculum, they have lobbied for the adoption of programs that stress abstinence between unmarried people. Courts have struck down use of programs that include erroneous information or deal with the spiritual implications of premarital sex, contraceptives, and sexually transmitted diseases.[90]

85. Malnak v. Yogi, 592 F.2d 197 (3d Cir. 1979).

86. Plans, Inc. v. Sacramento City Unified Sch. Dist., 319 F.3d 504 (9th Cir. 2003).

87. *See, e.g.,* Sch. Dist. of Abington Township v. Schempp, 374 U.S. 203, 225 (1963) (noting that "the state may not establish a 'religion of secularism' in the sense of affirmatively opposing or showing hostility to religion, thus 'preferring those who believe in no religion'").

88. Smith v. Bd. of Sch. Comm'rs, 655 F. Supp. 939 (S.D. Ala. 1987), *rev'd,* 827 F.2d 684 (11th Cir. 1987). *See also* Cowan v. Strafford R-VI Sch. Dist., 140 F.3d 1153 (8th Cir. 1998) (sending a "magic rock" home with each student did not advance New Ageism in violation of the Establishment Clause), text accompanying note 51, Chapter 4; Grove v. Mead Sch. Dist. No. 354, 753 F.2d 1528 (9th Cir. 1985) (reasoning that *The Learning Tree* does not advance an antitheistic faith).

89. *See, e.g.,* Smith v. Ricci, 446 A.2d 501 (N.J. 1982).

90. *See, e.g.,* ACLU v. Foster, No. 02-1440, 2002 U.S. Dist. LEXIS 13778 (E.D. La. July 24, 2002).

Instruction pertaining to the origin of humanity also has generated continuing legal disputes. Historically, some states by law barred evolution from the curriculum, because it conflicted with the biblical account of creation. In the famous Scopes "monkey trial" in the 1920s, the Tennessee Supreme Court upheld such a law, prohibiting the teaching of any theory that denies the Genesis version of creation or suggests "that man has descended from a lower order of animals."[91] In 1968, however, the United States Supreme Court struck down an Arkansas anti-evolution statute under the Establishment Clause, reasoning that evolution is science (not a secular religion), and a state cannot restrict student access to such information simply to satisfy religious preferences.[92]

After creationists were unable to convince the judiciary that evolution unconstitutionally advances an antitheistic faith, they focused on securing laws that require equal emphasis on the biblical account of creation whenever evolution is taught in public schools. In 1987, the Supreme Court invalidated a Louisiana statute that mandated "equal time" for creation science and evolution and required school boards to make available curriculum guides, teaching aids, and resource materials on creation science.[93] Reasoning that creationism is not science, the Court concluded that the law was intended to discredit scientific information and advance religious beliefs in violation of the Establishment Clause. More recently, the Fifth Circuit struck down a Louisiana school board's resolution, specifying that teachers must tell students that the presentation of evolutionary theory is not intended to dissuade students from the biblical version of creation.[94] Teaching about the origin of humanity remains a volatile topic, with states considering anti-evolution measures despite the judicial posture supporting such instruction.

Reading texts and supplementary materials also have been faulted for allegedly advancing antitheistic doctrine. For example, the Impressions reading series, published by Harcourt Brace Jovanovich, generated numerous challenges in the late 1980s and early 1990s. The series, employing the whole-language approach to reading instruction, was challenged as being morbid and depressing and promoting witchcraft based on the Wicca religion. Federal appellate courts, however, have ruled that reading stories about witches or even creating poetic chants does not entail the practice of witchcraft or advance a pagan cult.[95] Recently, books in the *Harry Potter* series have been attacked because they deal with wizardry and magic, which allegedly advances Satanism.[96]

Some New York parents asserted that specific components of the curriculum offended their Catholic faith.[97] The Second Circuit agreed with the parents that one teacher's assign-

91. Scopes v. State, 289 S.W. 363, 364 (Tenn. 1927).

92. Epperson v. Arkansas, 393 U.S. 97 (1968).

93. Edwards v. Aguillard, 482 U.S. 578 (1987). *See also* Peloza v. Capistrano Unified Sch. Dist., 37 F.3d 517 (9th Cir. 1994).

94. Freiler v. Tangipahoa Parish Bd. of Educ., 185 F.3d 337 (5th Cir. 1999).

95. *See, e.g.,* Brown v. Woodland Joint Unified Sch. Dist., 27 F.3d 1373 (9th Cir. 1994); Fleischfresser v. Dirs. of Sch. Dist. 200, 15 F.3d 680 (7th Cir. 1994). This series was discontinued in 1994 in part because of the controversies generated.

96. *See* Kathy Ishizuka, "'Harry Potter' Tops Most Challenged Books—Again," *School Library Journal,* vol. 48, no. 3 (2002), p. 29.

97. Altman v. Bedford Cent. Sch. Dist., 245 F.3d 49 (2d Cir. 2001), *cert. denied,* 534 U.S. 827 (2001).

ment for students to construct images of a Hindu deity abridged the First Amendment. Also, the court reasoned that making worry dolls amounted to preference of superstition over religion in violation of the Establishment Clause. But the court did not find constitutional violations in celebrating Earth Day or in role playing as part of a drug prevention program using peer facilitators.

Although courts have not usually condoned parental attacks on various aspects of the public school curriculum that allegedly conflict with their religious values, more difficult legal questions are raised when policymakers support curriculum restrictions for religious reasons. Since courts show considerable deference to legislatures and school boards in educational matters, conservative parent organizations have worked to elect board members and legislators who are sympathetic to their claims and have pressed for state and federal legislation and school board policies barring certain content from public schools. There is concern among educators that neutral, nonreligious instruction is threatened by such efforts.

State Aid to Private Schools

> The Supreme Court is likely to uphold government aid to religious schools that primarily benefits the child, rather than the religious institution, or that goes to sectarian schools because parents have chosen such schools.

In addition to disputes over the place of religion in public schools, government relations with private—primarily religious—schools have generated a substantial amount of First Amendment litigation. Unquestionably, parents have a legitimate interest in directing the upbringing of their children, including their education. **In 1925, the Supreme Court afforded constitutional protection to private schools' rights to exist and to parents' rights to select private education as an alternative to public schooling.**[98] Yet, the Court also recognized that the state has a general welfare interest in mandating school attendance and regulating private education to ensure an educated citizenry, considered essential in a democracy. Some disputes have resulted from conflicts between the state's exercise of its *parens patriae* authority to protect the well-being of children and parental interests in having their children educated in settings that reinforce their religious and philosophical beliefs. If the government interferes with parents' child-rearing decisions, it must show that the intervention is necessary to protect the child or the state. Although courts have upheld minimum state requirements for private schools (e.g., prescribed courses, personnel requirements), the recent trend has been toward imposing outcome measures, such as requiring private school students to participate in statewide testing programs.

98. Pierce v. Soc'y of the Sisters, 268 U.S. 510 (1925).

About 12 percent of all K–12 students are enrolled in private schools or home education, but this ratio could change if additional government aid flows to private education. Despite the fact that more than three-fifths of the states specifically prohibit the use of public funds for sectarian purposes, about three-fourths of the states provide public aid to private school students, including those attending sectarian schools. The primary types of aid are for transportation services, the loan of textbooks, state-required testing programs, special education for children with disabilities, and counseling services. Some of the most significant Supreme Court decisions interpreting the Establishment Clause have pertained to the use of public funds for private, primarily sectarian, education. The following discussion focuses on the legality of government aid for student services in parochial schools and to encourage family choice in education.

Aid for Student Services

The Supreme Court's stance of allowing government support for parochial school students has been consistent since 1993, with some evidence of the accommodationist trend much earlier. Indeed, the "child benefit" doctrine has been used to justify government aid for transportation and secular textbooks for parochial school students since the mid-twentieth century.[99] Also, the Supreme Court in 1980 upheld government support for state-required testing programs in private schools.[100]

In 1993, the Supreme Court in *Zobrest v. Catalina Foothills School District* found no Establishment Clause violation in publicly supporting sign-language interpreters in parochial schools, reasoning that the aid is going to the child as part of a federal government program that distributes benefits neutrally to qualifying children with disabilities under federal law.[101] The child is the primary recipient of the aid, and the school receives only an incidental benefit. The Court abandoned the presumption that public employees in sectarian schools would be tempted to inculcate religion. Four years later, the Court in *Agostini v. Felton* removed the ban on public school personnel providing remedial instruction in religious schools that it had announced 12 years earlier.[102] The controversy focused on Title I of the Elementary and Secondary Education Act (ESEA) of 1965, which targets educationally and economically disadvantaged students and requires comparable services to be provided for eligible students attending nonpublic schools.[103] For the first time, the Court in

99. *See* Bd. of Educ. v. Allen, 392 U.S. 236 (1968) (finding no Establishment Clause violation in a state law requiring public school districts to loan secular textbooks to all secondary students, including those attending parochial schools); Everson v. Bd. of Educ., 330 U.S. 1 (1947) (rejecting an Establishment Clause challenge to the use of public funds to provide transportation services for nonpublic school students).

100. Comm. for Pub. Educ. & Religious Liberty v. Regan, 444 U.S. 646 (1980).

101. 509 U.S. 1 (1993).

102. 521 U.S. 203 (1997) (overturning its ruling that barred the use of public school personnel to provide Title I remedial services on sectarian school premises, Aguilar v. Felton, 473 U.S. 402 (1985), and the portion of its decision that invalidated a shared-time program under which public school classes were provided for parochial school students on parochial school premises, Sch. Dist. v. Ball, 473 U.S. 373 (1985)).

Agostini held that comparability can be achieved by allowing public school personnel to provide *instructional* services in sectarian schools.

The Supreme Court in *Mitchell v. Helms* subsequently found no Establishment Clause violation in using federal aid to purchase instructional materials and equipment for student use in sectarian schools.[104] Specifically, the ruling allows the use of public funds for computers, other instructional equipment, and library books in religious schools under Title II of the ESEA federal aid program. Those challenging the program argued that the aid could be diverted for religious purposes, was direct and nonincidental, and supplanted rather than supplemented private school funds. Finding none of these contentions persuasive, the Court reasoned that religious indoctrination could not be attributed to the government when aid, even direct aid:

- Is distributed based on secular criteria and would be appropriate for public schools,
- Is allocated in a nondiscriminatory manner to religious and secular beneficiaries, and
- Flows to religious schools only because of private choices of parents.

Six justices agreed that prior Supreme Court rulings barring state aid in the form of providing maps, slide projectors, and other instructional materials and equipment to sectarian schools were no longer good law.[105]

Very few rulings remain that reflect the Supreme Court's separationist stance regarding state aid to nonpublic schools. In fact, the Supreme Court seems to have dismantled most of the decisions rendered during the heyday of applying the stringent *Lemon* test in the 1970s to strike down various types of public assistance to parochial schools. The only separationist decisions of this period that have not been eroded at least in part by subsequent Supreme Court opinions involved government aid made available *solely* to private schools or their patrons.[106] And in the only separationist decision in this domain since 1990, *Board of Education v. Grumet,* the Supreme Court invalidated a legislative attempt to create a separate school district along religious lines to serve Satmar Hasidic children with special needs whose strict form of Judaism does not allow them to be educated with non-Satmars.[107]

However, because courts have interpreted the Establishment Clause as allowing various types of public aid for nonpublic school students does not mean that states must use public funds for these purposes. States still can invalidate the aid under state constitutional provisions prohibiting the use of public funds for sectarian purposes.

103. As discussed in Chapter 1, the most recent reauthorization of the ESEA is the No Child Left Behind Act of 2001, 20 U.S.C. § 6301 *et seq.* (2003).

104. 530 U.S. 793 (2000), *on remand sub nom.* Helms v. Picard, 229 F.3d 467 (5th Cir. 2000).

105. *Id.,* overturning Wolman v. Walter, 433 U.S. 229 (1977) and Meek v. Pittenger, 421 U.S. 349 (1975). These six justices also supported a modification of the *Lemon test,* making it explicit that excessive entanglement is simply part of consideration of the policy's primary effect.

106. *See, e.g.,* Sloan v. Lemon, 413 U.S. 825 (1973); Comm. for Pub. Educ. & Religious Liberty v. Nyquist, 413 U.S. 756 (1973); Lemon v. Kurtzman, 403 U.S. 602 (1971).

107. 512 U.S. 687 (1994). *But see* Stark v. Indep. Sch. Dist. No. 640, 123 F.3d 1068 (8th Cir. 1997) (upholding a school district's decision to reopen a one-class school with a modified curriculum in response to a request from the Brethren sect).

Aid to Encourage Educational Choice

There also has been legislation to provide indirect aid to make private schooling a viable choice for more families. Tax-relief measures for private school tuition and educational vouchers have received considerable attention in legislative forums. The primary justification for such measures is that the aid flows to religious schools only because of private choices of parents.

Tax-Relief Measures. Tax benefits in the form of deductions or credits for private school expenses have been proposed at both state and federal levels. Although Congress has not yet endorsed any proposals for federal income tax credits for private school tuition, a few states have enacted tax-relief provisions for educational expenses. The central constitutional question is whether such measures advance religion in violation of the Establishment Clause because the primary beneficiaries are parents of parochial school children and ultimately religious institutions.

In 1983, the Supreme Court upheld a Minnesota tax-benefit program allowing parents of public or private school students to claim a limited state income tax deduction for tuition, transportation, and secular textbook expenses incurred for each elementary or secondary school dependent. The Court majority in *Mueller v. Allen* found the Minnesota law "vitally different" from an earlier New York provision, which violated the Establishment Clause by bestowing tax benefits only on private school patrons.[108] The majority declared that Minnesota's "decision to defray the cost of some educational expenses incurred by parents—regardless of the type of schools their children attend—evidences a purpose that is both secular and understandable."[109] The Court opined that such state assistance differs significantly from the direct transmission of public funds to parochial schools. Notwithstanding this ruling, only a few states provide such tax benefits. Most efforts to provide state tax relief for educational expenses have been defeated when placed before the voters, possibly because of their significant impact on state revenues.

Vouchers. For years, a number of New England states have had de facto voucher plans under which school districts without high schools provide a designated amount for high school tuition in neighboring public school districts or in private schools that the families select. However, very few other plans were adopted until the mid-1990s, and no statewide program existed until 1999 when Florida enacted a plan targeting students attending failing public schools. Under the Florida program, students attending schools that are rated as deficient (based on test scores, attendance, graduation rates, and other factors) are entitled to government vouchers that can be used in qualified public or private schools of their choice.[110] Also, a few urban districts have adopted state-funded voucher plans for disadvan-

108. 463 U.S. 388, 398 (1983), distinguishing Comm. for Pub. Educ. & Religious Liberty v. Nyquist, 413 U.S. 756 (1973) (striking down the provision of tax benefits only for private school patrons as violating the Establishment Clause).

109. *Id.*, 463 U.S. at 395. *See also* Kotterman v. Killian, 972 P.2d 606 (Ariz. 1999) (rejecting an Establishment Clause challenge to a state tax credit of up to $500 for contributions to school tuition organizations to support private school tuition).

taged youth, and privately funded scholarships are available for students to attend private schools in many major cities nationally.

In 2002, the Supreme Court rendered a significant decision, *Zelman v. Simmons-Harris,* resolving the conflict among lower courts regarding the participation of religious schools in state-funded voucher programs.[111] In this five-to-four ruling, the Court upheld a scholarship program that gives choices to economically disadvantaged families in the Cleveland City School District through various programs including vouchers that can be used for up to $2,250 of the tuition at participating public or private schools. No public school has elected to be involved in this voucher program, and the vast majority of the participating private schools are church related.

The Supreme Court in *Zelman* relied heavily on the fact that parents—not the government—make the decision for the scholarship funds to flow to private schools. The Court emphasized that the aid is completely neutral with respect to religion because the government benefits are provided to a broad group of individuals defined only by their financial need and residence in the Cleveland School District. Considering the program to be one of "true private choice" among public and private options, the Court found no Establishment Clause violation. Even though 96 percent of participating students attend religious schools, the Court reasoned that the program does not provide incentives for parents to choose sectarian schooling for their children, since they must still contribute a small portion of the tuition. Similar to its reasoning in *Mueller,* the Court emphasized that the neutral program does not become unconstitutional simply because most recipients decide to use the aid in religious schools.

Immediately following *Zelman,* a number of states indicated that they were seriously considering voucher programs to provide additional choices to disadvantaged students. Such programs still face state constitutional hurdles, despite the Supreme Court's conclusion that the use of state vouchers in religious schools does not abridge the Establishment Clause. Many state constitutions contain explicit prohibitions on the use of public funds for religious purposes.[112] And even where voucher programs that include sectarian schools satisfy state constitutions, fiscal concerns may influence whether large-scale voucher initiatives are implemented, because states currently are not supporting students attending private schools.

Conclusion

For almost a half century, church/state controversies have generated a steady stream of education litigation, and there are no signs of diminishing legal activity in this domain. The prin-

110. In 2002, a circuit court struck down the voucher plan under the explicit state constitutional prohibition on using public funds for religious purposes. Holmes v. Bush, No. CV 99-3370, 2002 WL 1809079 (Fla. Cir. Ct. Aug. 5, 2002).

111. 536 U.S. 639 (2002). *See also* Witters v. Wash. Dep't of Servs. for the Blind, 474 U.S. 481 (1986) (upholding use of federal vocational rehabilitation aid to support ministerial training).

112. *See Holmes,* 2002 WL 1809079, rendered a few months after the *Zelman* decision; *supra* note 110.

ciple that the First Amendment demands wholesome government neutrality toward religion has been easier to assert than to apply. Although some lawsuits have involved claims under the Free Exercise Clause, most school cases have focused on interpretations of Establishment Clause prohibitions.

From the 1960s through the mid-1980s, the federal judiciary seemed more committed to enforcing Establishment Clause restrictions in elementary and secondary school settings than elsewhere. Recently, however, there seems to be greater government accommodation of religion, especially in terms of public funds flowing to religious schools. Also, the "bright line rule that public schools could never be a home for religious activity" is no longer very bright.[113] The Free Speech Clause increasingly seems to prevail over Establishment Clause restrictions in protecting religious expression in public schools. The concepts of equal access and equal treatment for religious groups and expression seem to have replaced the principle of church/state separation in assessing religious influences in public schools and government aid to religious schools.

Points to Ponder

1. Some courts have emphasized that for student-initiated devotional activities in public schools to be upheld, prayers must be *nonsectarian.* Can a prayer be nonsectarian, or is the term "nonsectarian prayer" an oxymoron?
2. A student who attended the middle school where you teach was killed in an automobile accident. The next day, a classmate asks you if she can lead the class in saying a prayer for the deceased student. What would be your response and why?
3. The majority of the senior class engaged in a recitation of the Lord's Prayer five minutes before the high school graduation ceremony. School authorities did not lead the prayer, and although they had heard rumors that the student-initiated recitation was planned, they had not been officially informed. Did this activity represent the school? Did it violate an injunction prohibiting school personnel from authorizing, conducting, sponsoring, or intentionally permitting prayers during the graduation ceremony? *See* Goluba v. Sch. Dist., 45 F.3d 1035 (7th Cir. 1995).
4. High school students have requested that their religious club be allowed to hold meetings in the public school during lunch when other student groups meet. They also have asked for access to student activity funds to promote their meetings and distribute religious materials, because other student groups can use such funds to support their activities. How would you respond and why? *See* Prince v. Jacoby, 303 F.3d 1074 (9th Cir. 2002).
5. The "wall of separation" has been the dominant metaphor in church/state litigation for almost half a century. How viable is this metaphor today?

113. Ira C. Lupu, "The Lingering Death of Separationism," *George Washington Law Review*, vol. 62 (1994), p. 246.

4

Instructional Issues

Although U.S. citizens have no federal constitutional right to a public education, each state constitution places a duty on its legislature to provide for free public schooling, thus creating a state entitlement (property right) for all children to be educated at public expense.[1] Substantial litigation has resulted from the collision of state interests in guaranteeing the general welfare with individual interests in exercising constitutional and statutory rights. This chapter focuses on legal mandates pertaining to various requirements and rights associated with the instructional program.

The School Curriculum

> States and local school boards control the public school curriculum, but they must respect federal constitutional guarantees.

The federal government influences the curriculum through funds it provides for particular initiatives, such as reading instruction in early grades,[2] but such influence is quite limited. In contrast, state legislatures have plenary or complete power over education and thus broad authority to impose curriculum mandates. This section addresses legal developments involving curriculum requirements and restrictions, instructional censorship, and teachers' academic freedom interests.

1. *See* Goss v. Lopez, 419 U.S. 565 (1975); text accompanying note 25, Chapter 8. For a discussion of compulsory education requirements and exceptions, residency requirements, and related issues, *see* Nelda Cambron-McCabe, Martha McCarthy, and Stephen Thomas, *Public School Law: Teachers' and Students' Rights,* 5th ed. (Boston: Allyn and Bacon, 2004), Chapter 3.
2. *See* No Child Left Behind Act of 2001 (Reading First), 20 U.S.C. § 6362 (2003).

Requirements and Restrictions

A few state constitutions include specific curriculum mandates, but more typically, the legislature is given responsibility for curricular determinations. Most states require instruction pertaining to the Federal Constitution, American history, English, mathematics, drug education, health, and physical education. Some state statutes specify what subjects will be taught in which grades, and many states have detailed legislation pertaining to vocational education, bilingual education, and special services for children with disabilities. State laws usually stipulate that local school boards must offer the state-mandated minimum curriculum, which they may supplement unless there is a statutory prohibition.[3] In about half of the states, local school boards (and in some instances, school-based councils) are empowered to adopt courses of study, but often they must secure approval from the state board of education.

Despite states' substantial latitude in curricular matters, some legislative attempts to impose curriculum restrictions have impaired federal constitutional rights. The first curriculum case to reach the Supreme Court involved a 1923 challenge to a Nebraska law that prohibited instruction in a foreign language to any public or private school students who had not successfully completed the eighth grade.[4] The state high court had upheld the dismissal of a private school teacher for teaching reading in German to elementary school students. In striking down the statute, the Supreme Court reasoned that the teacher's right to teach, the parents' right to engage him to instruct their children, and the children's right to acquire useful knowledge were protected liberties under the Due Process Clause of the Fourteenth Amendment.

The Supreme Court on occasion has ruled that other curriculum decisions violate constitutional rights. The Court held in 1968 that the First Amendment precludes states from barring public school instruction, such as teaching about evolution, simply because it conflicts with certain religious views.[5] Almost two decades later, the Supreme Court invalidated a Louisiana law requiring instruction in the Biblical account of creation whenever evolution was introduced in the curriculum, concluding that the law unconstitutionally advanced religion.[6]

Yet, **courts will not interfere with instructional decisions made by state and local education agencies, unless the decisions are clearly arbitrary or impair constitutional rights.** For example, federal appellate courts have rejected allegations that mandatory community service requirements for students represent involuntary servitude prohibited by the Thirteenth Amendment, forced expression of altruistic values in violation of the First Amendment, or impairments of parents' Fourteenth Amendment rights to direct the upbringing of their children.[7] School authorities also have discretion in establishing stan-

3. *See, e.g.,* Triplett v. Livingston County Bd. of Educ., 967 S.W.2d 25 (Ky. Ct. App. 1997) (holding that local boards can go beyond state minimums in setting graduation requirements).
4. Meyer v. Nebraska, 262 U.S. 390 (1923).
5. Epperson v. Arkansas, 393 U.S. 97 (1968).
6. Edwards v. Aguillard, 482 U.S. 578 (1987). *See* text accompanying note 93, Chapter 3.
7. *See, e.g.,* Herndon v. Chapel Hill-Carrboro City Bd. of Educ., 89 F.3d 174 (4th Cir. 1996); Immediato v. Rye Neck Sch. Dist., 73 F.3d 454 (2d Cir. 1996).

dards for pupil performance and imposing other instructional requirements, such as prerequisites and admission criteria for particular courses, as long as the criteria are not arbitrary and do not disadvantage certain groups of students.

In addition to having authority over the content of the public school curriculum, states also have the power to specify textbooks and to regulate the method by which such books are obtained and distributed. In most states, textbooks are prescribed by the state board of education or a textbook commission. A list of acceptable books typically is developed at the state level, and local school boards then adopt specific texts for their course offerings. However, in some states, such as Colorado, almost complete authority is delegated to local boards to make textbook selections. Courts will not interfere with textbook decisions unless the established procedures are not followed or overtly biased materials are adopted.[8]

Censorship of Instructional Materials

Attempts to remove books from classrooms and libraries and to tailor curricular offerings and methodologies to particular religious and philosophical values have led to substantial litigation. Few aspects of the public school program remain untouched by censorship activities. Although most people agree that schools transmit values, there is little consensus regarding *which* values should be transmitted or *who* should make this determination.

Challenges to the Curriculum. Some challenges to public school materials and programs emanate from civil rights and consumer groups, contesting materials that allegedly promote racism, sexism, or bad health habits for students. But most of the challenges come from conservative parent groups, alleging that the use of instructional activities and materials considered immoral and anti-Christian impairs parents' rights to control their children's course of study in public schools.[9] As discussed in Chapter 3, courts have endorsed requests for specific children to be excused from selected course offerings (e.g., sex education) that offend their religious beliefs, as long as the exemptions do not impede the students' academic progress or the management of the school. Challenges to the courses themselves, however, have not found a receptive judicial forum.

To date, courts have not allowed mere parental disapproval of instructional materials to dictate the public school curriculum. Federal appellate courts have been unsympathetic to claims that reading series or individual novels used in public schools conflict with Christian doctrine and advance an antitheistic creed, finding the challenged materials to be religiously neutral and related to legitimate educational objectives.[10]

8. *See* Loewen v. Turnipseed, 488 F. Supp. 1138 (N.D. Miss. 1980) (finding evidence of unlawful racial bias by a state textbook-rating committee that barred a history textbook from the approved list because of its controversial treatment of racial matters, particularly the reconstruction period and civil rights movement). *But see* Grimes v. Sobol, 832 F. Supp. 704 (S.D.N.Y. 1993) (rejecting damages suit claiming that city's public school curriculum was biased against African Americans by failing to incorporate their important contributions).
9. Some of the best-known conservative groups are the American Coalition for Traditional Values, the Christian Coalition, Citizens for Excellence in Education, Concerned Women for America, the Eagle Forum, and Focus on the Family.

Many challenges have religious overtones,[11] but some simply assert parents' rights to determine their children's education. The Supreme Court declined to review a case in which the First Circuit rejected parents' claim that the school district was liable for subjecting their children to a mandatory AIDS-awareness assembly that featured a streetwise, comedic approach to the topic. The appeals court observed that "if all parents had a fundamental constitutional right to dictate individually what the schools teach their children, the schools would be forced to cater a curriculum for each student whose parents had genuine moral disagreements with the school's choice of subject matter."[12] The Ninth Circuit subsequently held that the Oregon law restructuring public schools to impose a rigorous academic program and student assessments did not abridge speech rights or "freedom of mind," as nothing in the law compelled students to adopt state-approved views.[13] And the same court dismissed African American parents' complaint that their daughter suffered psychological injuries due to being required to read two literary works that contained repeated use of the term "nigger."[14]

School Board Censorship. Although courts have not been receptive to challenges to school boards' curricular decisions simply because some materials or course content offend the sensibilities of specific students or parents, the legal issues are more complicated when policymakers themselves (e.g., legislators, school board members) support the censorship activity. Bills calling for instructional censorship have been introduced in Congress and numerous state legislatures, and policies have been proposed at the school board level to eliminate "objectionable" materials from public school classrooms and libraries.

The Supreme Court has recognized the broad discretion of school boards to make decisions that reflect the "legitimate and substantial community interest in promoting respect for authority and traditional values, be they social, moral, or political."[15] Thus, the judiciary has been reluctant to interfere with school boards' prerogatives in selecting and eliminating instructional materials. The Second Circuit on two occasions upheld a school board's right to remove particular books from public school libraries, noting that a book does not acquire tenure and can therefore be removed by the same authority that

10. *See, e.g.,* Monteiro v. Tempe Union High Sch. Dist., 158 F.3d 1022 (9th Cir. 1998); Fleischfresser v. Dirs. of Sch. Dist. 200, 15 F.3d 680 (7th Cir. 1994); Smith v. Sch. Comm'rs, 827 F.2d 684 (11th Cir. 1987); text accompanying note 95, Chapter 3.
11. *See, e.g.,* Altman v. Bedford Cent. Sch. Dist., 245 F.3d 49 (2d Cir. 2001), *cert. denied,* 534 U.S. 827 (2001) (finding that the celebration of Earth Day in public schools did not constitute a religious ceremony, but concluding that having students construct worry dolls and images of a Hindu deity advanced nontraditional faiths in violation of the Establishment Clause); text accompanying note 97, Chapter 3.
12. Brown v. Hot, Sexy and Safer Productions, 68 F.3d 525, 534 (1st Cir. 1995).
13. Tennison v. Paulus, 144 F.3d 1285, 1287 (9th Cir. 1998).
14. *Monteiro,* 158 F.3d 1022 (remanding for further proceedings, however, regarding allegations that school personnel failed to respond to complaints of a racially hostile environment in violation of Title VI of the Civil Rights Act of 1964).
15. Bd. of Educ. v. Pico, 457 U.S. 853, 864 (1982).

made the initial selection.[16] The court reasoned that a school board's decision to remove books considered vulgar and obscene and to screen future library acquisitions does not threaten to suppress ideas. Similarly, the Seventh Circuit endorsed a lower court's conclusion that school officials can "prohibit the use of texts, remove library books, and delete courses from the curriculum as a part of the effort to shape students into good citizens," unless the board flagrantly abuses that discretion.[17]

Although the judiciary has generally upheld school boards' authority in determining curricular materials and offerings, some specific censorship activities have been invalidated. For example, the Sixth Circuit upheld the school board's right to override faculty judgments regarding the selection of books for academic courses and the school library.[18] The court, however, concluded that the board failed to demonstrate any compelling reason for removing books that had already been placed in the library. Other courts have intervened if the censorship of specific library selections has clearly been motivated by a desire to suppress particular viewpoints or controversial ideas in violation of the First Amendment.[19] To illustrate, the Fifth Circuit held that there were material factual issues regarding a Louisiana school board's motivation in removing all copies of *Voodoo & Hoodoo* from public school libraries. This book traces the development of African tribal religion and its evolution in African American communities in the United States. The appeals court remanded the case for a trial to determine whether removal of the book was substantially based on unconstitutional motivation to suppress ideas.[20]

Despite substantial activity in lower courts, the Supreme Court has rendered only one decision involving censorship in public schools. This case, *Board of Education v. Pico,*[21] unfortunately, did not provide significant clarification regarding the scope of school boards' authority to restrict student access to particular materials. In fact, seven of the nine Supreme Court justices wrote separate opinions, conveying a range of viewpoints as to the governing legal principles. At issue in *Pico* was the school board's removal of certain books from junior high and high school libraries, in spite of the contrary recommendation of a committee appointed to review the books. The Supreme Court narrowly affirmed the appellate court's remand of the case for a trial because of irregularities in the removal procedures and unresolved factual questions regarding the school board's motivation. But, even the three justices endorsing the notion that students have a protected right to receive information recognized the broad authority of school boards to remove materials that are vulgar or educationally unsuitable. They indicated that a trial might have been unnecessary if the school board had employed regular and unbiased procedures in reviewing the controversial materials. The *Pico* plurality also emphasized that the controversy involved *library* books, which

16. Bicknell v. Vergennes Union High Sch. Bd. of Dirs., 638 F.2d 438 (2d Cir. 1980); Presidents Council v. Cmty. Sch. Bd. No. 25, 457 F.2d 289 (2d Cir. 1972).

17. Zykan v. Warsaw Cmty. Sch. Corp., 631 F.2d 1300, 1303 (7th Cir. 1980).

18. Minarcini v. Strongsville City Sch. Dist., 541 F.2d 577 (6th Cir. 1976).

19. *See, e.g.,* Case v. Unified Sch. Dist. No. 233, 908 F. Supp. 864 (D. Kan. 1995) (*Annie on My Mind*); Salvail v. Nashua Bd. of Educ., 469 F. Supp. 1269 (D.N.H. 1979) (*Ms.* magazine).

20. Campbell v. St. Tammany Parish Sch. Bd., 64 F.3d 184 (5th Cir. 1995).

21. 474 F. Supp. 387 (E.D.N.Y. 1979), *rev'd and remanded,* 638 F.2d 404 (2d Cir. 1980), *aff'd,* 457 U.S. 853 (1982).

are not required reading for students, noting that school boards "might well defend their claim of absolute discretion in matters of *curriculum* by reliance upon their duty to inculcate community values."[22]

Further strengthening the broad discretion of school authorities in curriculum-related censorship was the landmark 1988 Supreme Court decision involving students' free speech rights, *Hazelwood School District v. Kuhlmeier.*[23] The Court declared that public school authorities can censor student expression in school-sponsored activities to ensure that the expression is consistent with educational objectives. Relying on *Hazelwood,* the Eleventh Circuit upheld a Florida school board's decision to ban a humanities book because it included Aristophanes' *Lysistrata* and Chaucer's *The Miller's Tale,* which board members considered vulgar and immoral. Although not addressing the wisdom of the board's decision, the court deferred to the board's broad discretion in curricular matters.[24] A California appeals court similarly acknowledged that school boards can censor instructional materials based on educational concerns. However, the court noted that this authority does have limits; motives of board members must be assessed to ensure that they are not banning materials for religious reasons.[25]

Specific issues may change, but controversies surrounding the selection of materials for the public school library and curriculum will likely persist, reflecting the "inherent tension" between the school board's two essential functions of "exposing young minds to the clash of ideologies in the free marketplace of ideas" and instilling basic community values in our youth.[26] School boards would be wise to establish procedures for reviewing objections to course content and library materials, and to do so *before* a controversy arises. Criteria used to acquire and eliminate instructional materials should be clearly articulated and educationally defensible. **Once a process is in place to evaluate complaints relating to the instructional program, school boards should follow it carefully, as courts will show little sympathy when a school board ignores its own established procedures.**

Electronic Censorship. The next wave of censorship activity is likely to focus on the electronic frontier. It was estimated in 2001 that approximately 176.5 million Americans had Internet access.[27] With schools increasingly making on-line services accessible to students, concerns are being raised about the possible transmission of sexually explicit material to minors. Several states have enacted laws or are considering measures that would prohibit sending obscene materials over the Internet. Also, the federal Child Online Protection Act (COPA) prohibits materials harmful to minors from being distributed for commercial pur-

22. *Id.,* 457 U.S. at 869. Following the Supreme Court's decision, the school board voted to return the controversial books to the school libraries, thus averting the need for a trial regarding the board's motivation for the original censorship.
23. 484 U.S. 260 (1988). *See* text accompanying note 29, Chapter 5.
24. Virgil v. Sch. Bd., 862 F.2d 1517 (11th Cir. 1989).
25. McCarthy v. Fletcher, 254 Cal. Rptr. 714 (Ct. App. 1989).
26. Seyfried v. Walton, 668 F.2d 214, 219 (3d Cir. 1981) (Rosenn, J., concurring).
27. "More Americans Online," *The New York Times* (November 19, 2001), p. C7.

poses through the World Wide Web.[28] However, the Third Circuit recently ruled that the law's content-based restriction on speech was not narrowly tailored or the least restrictive means to accomplish the legitimate goal of protecting children.[29]

Controversy also surrounds the federal Children's Internet Protection Act (CIPA) that requires public libraries and school districts receiving technology funds to monitor Internet use and to implement measures to protect children from access to harmful content.[30] In implementing the required Internet safety plans, most school districts are relying on filtering software and thus delegating to companies the decisions as to what materials are appropriate for their students. The Supreme Court recently upheld CIPA as placing valid conditions on the use of federal funds.[31] The Court reasoned that the use of filtering software does not violate library patrons' constitutional rights. There are some fears that measures such as CIPA and COPA could have a chilling effect on schools using computer networks to enhance instructional experiences for students.

Academic Freedom

From its origin in German universities, the concept of academic freedom historically was applied to postsecondary education and embodied the principle that faculty members should be free from governmental controls in conducting research and imparting knowledge to students. Public school teachers have asserted a similar right to academic freedom, but courts have not extended the protections found in higher education to public elementary and secondary schools.[32] Although reasoning that teachers possess academic interests, courts have refrained from establishing precise legal principles in this domain. Instead, courts have balanced teachers' interests in academic freedom against school boards' interests in assuring an appropriate instructional program and efficient school operations.

Curriculum Content. **Public school teachers do not have a right to determine the content of the instructional program.** Recognizing that the state, as employer, controls the curriculum, the Ninth Circuit rejected a vagueness challenge to California legislation holding teachers personally liable for actual damages if they willfully refuse to teach predominantly in English.[33] The court concluded that in the vast majority of instances, it would be clear to teachers when they were dispensing instruction that would be subject to the lan-

28. 47 U.S.C. § 231 (2003). An affirmative defense can be offered that reasonable steps have been taken to restrict access by minors.

29. ACLU v. Reno, 217 F.3d 162 (3d Cir. 2000), *vacated and remanded sub nom.* Ashcroft v. ACLU, 535 U.S. 564 (2002), *on remand,* 322 F.3d 240 (3d Cir. 2003).

30. H.R. 5666 § 1721; 20 U.S.C..§ 9134(f) (2003); 47 U.S.C. § 254(h)(5) (2003).

31. United States v. Am. Library Ass'n, No. 02-361, 2003 U.S. LEXIS 4799 (June 23, 2003).

32. *See, e.g.,* Bates v. Dallas Indep. Sch. Dist., 952 S.W.2d 543 (Tex. Ct. App. 1997) (holding that a teacher's refusal to assign a grade to a student, as instructed by his supervisor, is not shielded by academic freedom). But school boards must follow their adopted grading procedures and cannot single out specific students for differential treatment. *See, e.g.,* Vermilion Teachers' Ass'n v. Vermilion Local Sch. Dist., 648 N.E.2d 1384 (Ohio Ct. App. 1994).

33. Cal. Teachers Ass'n v. State Bd. of Educ., 271 F.3d 1141 (9th Cir. 2001).

guage restriction. Despite the state's legal authority to impose such curricular restrictions, state law often delegates to local school boards considerable authority to make instructional decisions.

Several courts have declared that school boards are not legally obligated to accept teachers' curricular recommendations in the absence of a board policy to that effect. For example, the Fifth Circuit held that teachers cannot assert a First Amendment right to substitute their own supplemental reading list for the officially adopted list without securing administrative approval.[34] And the Fourth Circuit ruled that a high school teacher did not have complete discretion to select the plays performed by her acting class students, recognizing school officials' legitimate pedagogical interests in regulating the curriculum.[35]

Teachers are not permitted to ignore or omit prescribed course content under the guise of academic freedom. To illustrate, the Seventh Circuit upheld a school board's dismissal of a kindergarten teacher who, for religious reasons, refused to teach patriotic topics.[36] The Supreme Court of Washington similarly found no First Amendment impairment in a school board prohibiting two teachers from team-teaching a history course. The court reasoned that "course content is manifestly a matter within the board's discretion," and requiring teachers to cover this content in a conventional manner does not violate their academic freedom.[37] Also, the Colorado Supreme Court upheld a school district's policy requiring administrative review of "controversial learning resources," noting the district's legitimate pedagogical interest in shaping its secondary school curriculum.[38] Finding the policy neither vague nor overbroad, the court upheld termination of a teacher for showing his high school class portions of a movie that included nudity, profanity, and graphic violence.

The Supreme Court of Alaska endorsed a school board's rule requiring the superintendent's approval of supplementary materials used in the classroom.[39] A teacher refused to comply with this rule in selecting materials to teach about homosexual rights in a unit on American minorities. Acknowledging that the issue was not whether the materials selected by the teacher were appropriate, but rather where the authority to make curriculum determinations resides, the court concluded that the school board has such authority.

Teaching Strategies. **State laws and school board policies establish the basic contours of the curriculum, but teachers retain some discretion in choosing *strategies* to convey prescribed content.** In reviewing school board restrictions on teachers' classroom activities, the judiciary considers a number of factors, such as:

34. Kirkland v. Northside Indep. Sch. Dist., 890 F.2d 794 (5th Cir. 1989).
35. Boring v. Buncombe County Bd. of Educ., 136 F.3d 364 (4th Cir. 1998).
36. Palmer v. Bd. of Educ., 603 F.2d 1271, 1274 (7th Cir. 1979).
37. Millikan v. Bd. of Dirs., 611 P.2d 414, 418 (Wash. 1980). *See also* Murray v. Pittsburgh Bd. of Educ., 919 F. Supp. 838 (W.D. Pa. 1996), *aff'd mem.,* 141 F.3d 1154 (3d Cir. 1998) (holding that a teacher could not assert a First Amendment right to disregard school board instructions and continue to use a classroom management technique, Learnball, that gave students responsibility for establishing class rules and grading procedures).
38. Bd. of Educ. v. Wilder, 960 P.2d 695, 712 (Colo. 1998) (rejecting also the teacher's due process claim, finding that sufficient notice of the policy had been provided).
39. Fisher v. Fairbanks N. Star Borough Sch. Dist., 704 P.2d 213 (Alaska 1985).

- Whether teachers have been provided adequate notice that use of specific teaching methodologies or materials will result in disciplinary action,
- The relevance of the method to the course of study and age and maturity of the students,
- Support of the method by the profession,
- The threat of disruption posed by the method, and
- The impact of the strategy on community norms.

Courts in general have recognized teachers' latitude to select appropriate teaching methods that serve a demonstrated educational purpose and are supported by the profession. Although teachers enjoy some discretion in this regard, classroom conduct may be restricted by the school board as long as teachers are given proper notice of proscribed methods. The First Circuit recently ruled that the Massachusetts law permitting termination for "conduct unbecoming a teacher" furnishes sufficient notice that indecent speech directed toward students is impermissible.[40] Accordingly, the court upheld a teacher's suspension for giving a student a document containing indecent content.

A primary consideration in reviewing the legitimacy of classroom activities is whether instructional strategies are related to course objectives. In the absence of such a relationship, the teacher's behavior is not constitutionally protected. Relevancy applies not only to objectives but also to the age and maturity of the students. A controversial topic appropriate for high school students would not necessarily be suitable for elementary and junior high pupils. Even though a certain method may be considered relevant, if it lacks the general support of the profession, a school board still may prevail in barring its use. Relevance to course objectives has been found lacking in several cases in which teachers have shown R-rated movies to public school students.[41] Also, the Eighth Circuit upheld termination of a teacher who willfully violated board policy by permitting her students to use profanity in their creative writing assignments.[42] The Second Circuit similarly allowed a state college to dismiss a teacher for a classroom "clustering" exercise in which students uttered sexually profane comments in a word-association exercise.[43]

However, teachers cannot be forced to discontinue instructionally relevant activities solely because of parental displeasure. The Fifth Circuit ruled that a teacher's use of a simulation to teach about post–Civil War American history was related to legitimate educational objectives, and therefore dismissal for refusing to stop using the simulation impaired the teacher's academic rights.[44] The Sixth Circuit ordered reinstatement of a teacher who

40. Conward v. Cambridge Sch. Comm., 171 F.3d 12 (1st Cir. 1999).

41. *See, e.g.,* Fowler v. Bd. of Educ., 819 F.2d 657 (6th Cir. 1987); Bd. of Educ. v. Wilder, 960 P.2d 695, 702 (Colo. 1998). *See also* Borger v. Bisciglia, 888 F. Supp. 97 (E.D. Wis. 1995) (upholding a school district's ban on showing R-rated films as related to legitimate pedagogical concerns).

42. Lacks v. Ferguson Reorganized Sch. Dist. R-2, 147 F.3d 718 (8th Cir. 1998). *See also* Oleske v. Hilliard City Sch. Dist., 764 N.E.2d 1110 (Ohio Ct. App. 2001) (upholding dismissal of a teacher who told dirty jokes to middle school students and referred to another teacher by a derogatory name).

43. Vega v. Miller, 273 F.3d 460 (2d Cir. 2001), *cert. denied,* 535 U.S. 1097 (2002).

44. Kingsville Indep. Sch. Dist. v. Cooper, 611 F.2d 1109 (5th Cir. 1980).

had been effectively discharged when citizens complained to the school board regarding his instruction in a life science course. The teacher was suspended and told that he would be terminated after he refused to accept a letter of reprimand. The court found the teacher's classroom behavior appropriate and relevant to the course objectives, noting that the films and text had been approved by the school board and used for several years.[45]

Among the factors courts examine in assessing restrictions on classroom instruction is whether a teacher's action poses a threat of disruption to the operation of the school.[46] To illustrate, an Oregon federal district court found a school board's policy, banning all political speakers from the high school, unreasonable on several grounds, including the fact that no disruptions had occurred or could be anticipated from political discussions.[47] However, an Illinois federal district court recognized that a school board does not necessarily have to show that instructional materials actually caused a disruption to justify nonrenewal of a teacher's contract. Materials may be considered inappropriate for classroom use (e.g., an R-rated film with vulgarity and sexually explicit scenes), even though students "quietly acquiesce" to their use.[48] Also, the Supreme Court of Maine held that a school board's decision to cancel a "Tolerance Day" program did not impair First Amendment rights, as the decision was based on a legitimate concern for safety, order, and security due to bomb threats that had been received.[49]

Courts have been protective of school boards' authority to design the curriculum to reflect community values. A New York appeals court held that a teacher who defied warnings that use of certain materials and sexual words in classroom discussions offended community mores had no First Amendment grounds to challenge his reprimand.[50] Yet, if a particular strategy is instructionally relevant and supported by the profession, it likely will survive judicial review even though it might disturb some school patrons. For example, the Eighth Circuit found sufficient evidence that a teacher's contract was not renewed for impermissible religious reasons after parents complained that she was promoting New Age doctrine by sending a letter and "magic" rock home with her second-graders.[51] The letter indicated that the rocks are unique, like the students, and that if the students rub their magic rocks and think good things about themselves, they can achieve their goals. The teacher was

45. Stachura v. Memphis Cmty. Sch. Dist., 763 F.2d 211 (6th Cir. 1985), *rev'd and remanded* (regarding award of compensatory damages), 477 U.S. 299 (1986). For a discussion of the damages issue, *see* text accompanying note 97, Chapter 12.

46. *See, e.g.,* Bauer v. Sampson, 261 F.3d 775 (9th Cir. 2001) (finding that a professor's right to express insulting and uncivil views on a matter of public concern outweighed the college's interests in curtailing the expression to deter potential disruption).

47. Wilson v. Chancellor, 418 F. Supp. 1358 (D. Or. 1976). *See also Kingsville,* 611 F.2d 1109 (holding that complaints from parents and students about use of a simulation to teach history did not constitute a sufficient disruption to destroy the teacher's effectiveness).

48. Krizek v. Bd. of Educ., 713 F. Supp. 1131, 1141 (N.D. Ill. 1989).

49. Solmitz v. Me. Sch. Admin. Dist. No. 59, 495 A.2d 812 (Me. 1985).

50. *In re* Arbitration Between Bernstein and Norwich City Sch. Dist., 726 N.Y.S.2d 474 (App. Div. 2001).

51. Cowan v. Strafford R-VI Sch. Dist., 140 F.3d 1153 (8th Cir. 1998).

awarded two years of pay, but the court did not order reinstatement because of the damaged relationship between the teacher and school principal.

Copyright Compliance

Educators must comply with the federal copyright law; some copyrighted materials may be used for instructional purposes without the publisher's permission if fair use guidelines are followed.

Another instructional concern pertains to the use of copyrighted materials. Educators extensively use published materials and various other media in the classroom, and all school personnel are expected to comply with the federal copyright law. Although the law grants the owner of a copyright exclusive control over the protected material, courts have long recognized exceptions to this control under the doctrine of "fair use." The fair use doctrine cannot be precisely defined, but a definition frequently used by the judiciary is the privilege for those other than the copyright owner to use the copyrighted material in a reasonable manner without the owner's consent.[52]

Congress incorporated the judicially created fair use concept into the 1976 revisions of the Copyright Act. In identifying the purposes of the fair use exception, Congress specifically noted teaching. **The exception provides needed flexibility for teachers but does *not* exempt them from copyright infringements**. The following factors are used in assessing whether copying specific material constitutes fair use or an infringement:

- The purpose and character of the use, including whether such use is of a commercial nature or is for nonprofit educational purposes;
- The nature of the copyrighted work;
- The amount and substantiality of the portion used in relation to the copyrighted work as a whole; and
- The effect of the use upon the potential market for or value of the copyrighted work.[53]

To clarify fair use pertaining to photocopying from books and periodicals, the House and Senate conferees incorporated into their conference report a set of classroom guidelines developed by a group representing educators, authors, and publishers. These guidelines are only part of the legislative history of the Copyright Act and do not have the force of law, but they have been widely used as persuasive authority in assessing the legality of reproducing printed materials in the educational environment. The guidelines permit making single copies of copyrighted material for teaching or research but are quite restrictive on the use of multiple copies. **To use multiple copies of a work, the tests of brevity, spontaneity, and cumulative effect must be met** (see Figure 4.1). Furthermore, the guidelines do not permit

52. Marcus v. Rowley, 695 F.2d 1171, 1174 (9th Cir. 1983).

53. 17 U.S.C. § 107 (2003).

FIGURE 4.1 ***Copyright Guidelines for Not-for-Profit Educational Institutions: Multiple Copies***

Each copy must include the copyright notice and meet the following criteria:

Brevity
- For poems, not more than 250 words can be copied.
- For prose, a complete article of less than 2,500 words or an excerpt of not more than 1,000 words or 10 percent of the work, whichever is less, can be copied.
- Copies of illustrations can be one chart, graph, diagram, drawing, cartoon, or picture per book or periodical.

Spontaneity
- The copying is initiated by the individual teacher (not an administrator or supervisor).
- The inspiration to use the material occurs in such a manner that does not reasonably permit a timely request for permission.

Cumulative effect
- The copies are for use in one course.
- Not more than one short poem, article, or two excerpts can be copied from a given source or author during one class term.
- Multiple copying in a term is limited to nine instances.

The following practices are prohibited:

- Copying cannot substitute for compilations or collective works.
- Consumable works cannot be copied (e.g., workbooks, standardized tests).
- The same items cannot be copied from term to term.
- Copying cannot replace the purchase of books or periodicals.

---

copying to substitute for anthologies or collective works or to replace consumable materials such as workbooks.

Publishers have taken legal action to ensure compliance with these guidelines. The Sixth Circuit held that a commercial copy shop violated the fair use doctrine in the reproduction of course packets for faculty at the University of Michigan. Three publishers (Macmillan, Princeton University Press, and St. Martin's Press) challenged the duplication of copyrighted material for commercial sale by a for-profit corporation. The copy shop owner argued that such reproduction of multiple copies for classroom use is a recognized statutory exemption. The appellate court disagreed, reasoning that the sale of multiple copies for commercial, not educational, purposes destroyed the publishers' potential licensing revenue from photocopying, contained creative material, and involved substantial portions of the copyrighted publications (as much as 30 percent of one work).[54] This ruling does not prevent faculty use of course packets or anthologies in the classroom, but it does require permission from publishers and the possible payment of fees prior to photocopying.

54. Princeton Univ. Press v. Mich. Document Servs., 99 F.3d 1381 (6th Cir. 1996).

The fair use doctrine and congressional guidelines have been strictly construed in educational settings. Although materials reproduced for the classroom meet the first factor in determining fair use—educational purpose—the remaining factors must be met. The Ninth Circuit held that a teacher's use of a copyrighted booklet to make a learning activity packet abridged the copyright law.[55] The court concluded that fair use was not met in this case because the learning packet was used for the same purpose as the protected booklet, the nature of the work reproduced was a "creative" effort rather than "information," and one-half of the packet was verbatim copy of the copyrighted material. Furthermore, the copying was found to violate the guideline of spontaneity in that it was reproduced several times over two school years. The appeals court was not persuaded that the absence of personal profit on the part of the teacher lessened the violation.

Rapid developments in instructional technology pose a new set of legal questions regarding use of videotapes and computer software. Recognizing the need for guidance related to videotaping, Congress issued guidelines for educational use in 1981.[56] These guidelines specify that taping must be made at the request of the teacher. The taped material must be used for relevant classroom activities only once within the first 10 days of taping. Additional use is limited to instructional reinforcement or evaluation. After 45 calendar days, the tape must be erased.

Taping television broadcasts on home video recorders for later classroom use may constitute copyright infringement if the off-the-air taping guidelines above are not followed. The Supreme Court ruled that personal video recording for the purpose of "time shifting" is a legitimate, unobjectionable purpose, posing minimal harm to marketability.[57] However, **home taping for broader viewing by students in the classroom would be beyond the purposes envisioned by the Supreme Court and would necessitate careful adherence to the guidelines for limited use**.

Under 1980 amendments to the copyright law, software was included as protected intellectual property.[58] Established copyright principles provide guidance in analyzing fair use. It is clear from the amended law that only one duplicate or backup copy can be made of the master computer program by the owner. This is to ensure a working copy of the program if the master copy is damaged. Application of the fair use exception does not alter this restriction for educators. Although duplicating multiple copies would be clearly for educational purposes, other factors of fair use would be violated: The software is readily accessible for purchase (not impossible to obtain), programs may be duplicated only in their entirety, and copying substantially reduces the potential market.

In spite of the amendments, publishers continue to be concerned about illegal copying of computer software in the school environment. Limited school budgets and high costs have led to abuse of copyrighted software. In 1999, the Los Angeles Board of Education settled what might be the worst case of software piracy discovered in public schools.[59] An

55. *Marcus,* 695 F.2d 1171.

56. Guidelines for Off-the-Air Recording of Broadcast Programming for Educational Purposes, Cong. Rec. § E4751, October 14, 1981.

57. Sony Corp. v. Universal City Studios, 464 U.S. 417 (1984).

58. 17 U.S.C. § 117 (2003).

investigation by a group of software companies discovered more than 1,400 copies of software, such as Microsoft Word and Adobe Photoshop, allegedly being used without authorization. The school district denied the violation but settled to avoid the costs of a trial.

A question not answered by the copyright law but plaguing schools is the legality of multiple use of a master program. That is, can a program be loaded in a number of computers in a laboratory for simultaneous use, or can a program be modified for use in a network of microcomputers? Again, application of the fair use concept would indicate that multiple use is not permissible. The most significant factor is that the market for the educational software would be greatly diminished. A number of students using the master program one at a time (serial use), however, would appear not to violate the copyright law. To acquire broad use of particular software, school systems must either purchase multiple copies or negotiate site license agreements with the publishers.

As schools are developing their capacity to take advantage of the Internet, copyright law also is evolving. Congress amended the law in 1998, passing the Digital Millennium Copyright Act.[60] The "White Paper" produced by President Clinton's Working Group on Intellectual Property Issues identified numerous and complex issues that influenced the law.[61] Questions were raised about what constitutes *distribution* (traditionally interpreted as a hard copy being transferred to another individual as opposed to transmission over data lines) and *publication* (current definition limits protection to physical copies). **The 1998 law reinforces that an individual's copyright is secured when the work is created and "fixed in any tangible medium of expression."**[62] Although critics find many ambiguities in the law, they agree that it includes a clear commitment to extend fair use to digital technology for educators.

Extraordinary technological advances have given teachers and their school systems the means to access a wide range of instructional materials and products, but many of them are protected by the federal copyright law that restricts unauthorized reproduction. Because violation of the law can result in school district and educator liability, school boards should

59. "L.A. School Board Settles Software Copyright Suit," *School Law News* (March 5, 1999), p. 2. The case was settled for $300,000 plus an additional $1.5 million for a task force to monitor software usage over a three-year period.

60. 112 Stat. 2860 § 1 (2003).

61. Bruce A. Lehman, Chair, Working Group on Intellectual Property Rights, "Report on Intellectual Property and the National Information Infrastructure," Washington, DC: Information Infrastructure Task Force (1995).

62. 17 U.S.C. § 102 (2003). Recent litigation indicates that material published and distributed on the Internet will be fully protected by the basic principles of copyright law. For example, the Ninth Circuit imposed an injunction against Napster Corporation and its distribution of a file-sharing program that allowed individuals to download music files. A&M Records v. Napster, 239 F.3d 1004 (9th Cir. 2001). But the 2002 Technology, Education, and Copyright Harmonization (TEACH) Act, 17 U.S.C. § 110 (2003), provides increased flexibility for accredited, nonprofit education institutions to use the Internet to provide copyrighted materials under limited circumstances to students enrolled in distance education programs.

adopt policies or guidelines to prohibit infringement and to alert individuals of unlawful practices.[63]

Student Proficiency Testing

> Courts have recognized that assurance of an educated citizenry is an appropriate government goal and that the establishment of minimum performance standards to give value to a high school diploma is a rational means to attain that goal.

The concept of performance assessment is not new, but the use of proficiency tests as a condition of grade promotion or the receipt of a high school diploma has a relatively brief history. In 1976, only four states had enacted student proficiency testing legislation. Now all states have laws or administrative regulations pertaining to statewide performance testing programs, and more than half of the states condition receipt of a high school diploma on test passage. Given a state's authority to establish academic standards, including mandatory examinations, the judiciary traditionally has been reluctant to interfere with assessments of pupil performance.

Recently, other forms of performance assessment, such as portfolios, have received attention, but standardized tests continue to be used in most school districts. Annual student testing is strongly supported by the federal government. Indeed, the No Child Left Behind Act:

- Mandates annual testing in grades 3 through 8 in reading and math by 2006 and in science by 2007 at certain grade intervals,
- Requires high school students to take a general test in core subjects at least once, and
- Ties federal assistance and sanctions for schools to student test scores.[64]

High-stakes assessments shape the instructional program, and states increasingly are evaluating educators' performance based on their students' test scores. Not surprisingly, claims are being made that teachers are limiting classroom activities to material covered on the tests and/or unfairly coaching students for the exams.[65]

Although the state's authority to evaluate student performance has not been questioned, specific high-stakes assessment programs have been legally challenged as impairing students' rights to fair and nondiscriminatory treatment. In a case still widely cited as estab-

63. In response to several appellate court decisions holding that under the Eleventh Amendment states and their agents were not subject to suit in federal courts for the infringement of copyrights, Congress amended the copyright law (Copyright Remedy Clarification), 17 U.S.C. § 511(a) (2003), specifically abrogating immunity. *See also* BV Engineering v. UCLA, 858 F.2d 1394 (9th Cir. 1988); Richard Anderson Photography v. Brown, 852 F.2d 114 (4th Cir. 1988).
64. No Child Left Behind Act of 2001, 20 U.S.C. § 6301 *et seq.* (2003).

lishing the legal standards, *Debra P. v. Turlington,* the Fifth Circuit in 1981 recognized that by making schooling mandatory, Florida created a property interest—a valid expectation that students would receive diplomas if they passed required courses.[66] **This property right requires sufficient notice of conditions attached to high school graduation and a fair opportunity to satisfy them before a diploma can be withheld.** The court found that 13 months was insufficient notice of the test requirement and further held that the state may have administered a fundamentally unfair test covering material that had not been taught in Florida schools. The appeals court also enjoined the state from using the test as a diploma prerequisite for four years to provide time for the vestiges of prior school segregation to be removed and to ensure that all minority students subjected to the requirement started first grade under desegregated conditions. However, the court held that continued use of the test to determine remediation needs was constitutionally permissible, noting that the disproportionate placement of minority students in remedial programs *per se* does not abridge the Equal Protection Clause without evidence of intentional discrimination.

On remand, the district court ruled that the injunction should be lifted, and the appeals court affirmed this decision in 1984.[67] By presenting substantial evidence, including curriculum guides and survey data, the state convinced the judiciary that the test was instructionally valid in that it covered material taught to Florida students. Also, data showed that only students who entered school under desegregated conditions would be subjected to the diploma sanction. Furthermore, there was significant improvement among African American students during the six years the test had been administered.

Other courts have reiterated the principles established in *Debra P.*[68] A Texas federal district court in 2000 rejected challenges to the Texas Assessment of Academic Skills (TAAS) that has been administered to all Texas students since 1990.[69] Despite evidence of higher minority failure rates, the court noted that the passing-rate gap was narrowing and that the testing and remediation programs were addressing the effects of prior discrimination. The court also held that the test met curricular validity standards in that students were given a fair opportunity to learn the material on the test and they had received adequate notice of the test requirement. Courts have not resolved whether students should be allowed

65. *See* Buck v. Lowndes County Sch. Dist., 761 So. 2d 144 (Miss. 2000) (upholding nonrenewal of teachers' contracts for noncompliance with testing procedures that resulted in a reduction in the district's accreditation level). The American Evaluation Association joined a number of other professional associations when it issued a statement in 2002 opposing "the use of tests as the sole or primary criterion for making decisions with serious negative consequences for students, educators, and the schools." *American Evaluation Association Position Statement on High Stakes Testing in Pre-K–12 Education,* Fairhaven, MA (February, 2002), p. 1.

66. 474 F. Supp. 244 (M.D. Fla. 1979), *aff'd in part, vacated in part,* 644 F.2d 397 (5th Cir. Fla. 1981).

67. Debra P. v. Turlington, 564 F. Supp. 177 (M.D. Fla. 1983), *aff'd,* 730 F.2d 1405 (11th Cir. 1984). The Fifth Circuit was divided into the Fifth and Eleventh Circuits while this case was in progress.

68. *See, e.g.,* Anderson v. Banks, 540 F. Supp. 761 (S.D. Ga. 1982); Rankins v. La. State Bd. of Elementary and Secondary Educ., 637 So. 2d 548 (La. Ct. App. 1994).

69. GI Forum v. Tex. Educ. Agency, 87 F. Supp. 2d 667 (W.D. Tex. 2000).

to participate in graduation exercises if they have failed the statewide proficiency examination.[70]

In addition to graduation tests, grade promotion increasingly is being conditioned on passing proficiency tests. The Supreme Court in 2002 declined to review a decision in which the lower courts rejected a challenge to a Louisiana school district's policy that tied fourth- and eighth-grade promotion to test passage. The court found no property or liberty interest in grade promotion.[71]

Given the high stakes attached to some exams, parents have requested access to questions on previously administered tests. The Ohio Supreme Court ruled that the statewide proficiency test fell under the definition of a public record, so previously administered exams must be disclosed to parents, except for portions owned and developed by a private nonprofit corporation.[72] But, a Kentucky appeals court held that parents were not entitled to view the statewide proficiency exam because indiscriminate viewing by the public could jeopardize the test's reliability.[73]

Administering proficiency tests to children with disabilities has been controversial. Courts in general have ruled that the state does not have to alter its academic standards for students with disabilities; they can be denied grade promotion or a diploma if they do not meet the specified standards.[74] A child with mental disabilities may be given the option of not taking a proficiency examination if the team charged with planning the individualized education program (IEP) concludes that there is little likelihood of the child mastering the material covered on the test. Children excused from the test requirement usually are awarded certificates of school attendance instead of diplomas. Such children, however, cannot be denied the *opportunity* to satisfy requirements (including tests) for promotion or a diploma.

The Seventh Circuit has suggested that children with disabilities may need earlier notice of a proficiency test requirement than other students to ensure an adequate opportunity for the material on the test to be incorporated into their IEPs.[75] However, an Indiana appeals court subsequently reasoned that three years' notice of the test requirement as a prerequisite to a diploma was sufficient for children with disabilities.[76] In upholding the state-

70. *Compare* Williams v. Austin Indep. Sch. Dist., 796 F. Supp. 251 (W.D. Tex. 1992) (finding no right to participate in the ceremony) *with* Crump v. Gilmer Indep. Sch. Dist., 797 F. Supp. 552 (E.D. Tex. 1992) (requiring school district to allow students who satisfied other graduation requirements to participate in the ceremony).

71. Parents Against Testing Before Teaching v. Orleans Parish Sch. Bd., 273 F.3d 1107 (5th Cir. 2001), *cert. denied,* 534 U.S. 1162 (2002). Other courts have upheld the practice of conditioning grade promotion on test scores. *See, e.g.,* Bester v. Tuscaloosa City Bd. of Educ., 722 F.2d 1514 (11th Cir. 1984); Sandlin v. Johnson, 643 F.2d 1027 (4th Cir. 1981); Erik V. v. Causby, 977 F. Supp. 384 (E.D.N.C. 1997).

72. Rea v. Ohio Dep't of Educ., 692 N.E.2d 596 (Ohio 1998).

73. Triplett v. Livingston County Bd. of Educ., 967 S.W.2d 25 (Ky. Ct. App. 1997).

74. *See, e.g.,* Brookhart v. Ill. State Bd. of Educ., 697 F.2d 179 (7th Cir. 1983); Anderson v. Banks, 540 F. Supp. 761 (S.D. Ga. 1982); Bd. of Educ. v. Ambach, 457 N.E.2d 775 (N.Y. 1983).

75. *Brookhart,* 697 F.2d at 187. *See* Chapter 7 for a discussion of federal and state protections of children with disabilities.

76. Rene v. Reed, 751 N.E.2d 736 (Ind. Ct. App. 2001), *transfer denied,* 774 N.E.2d 506 (Ind. 2002).

FIGURE 4.2 ***High-Stakes Proficiency Testing Programs***

Proficiency tests used as a prerequisite to high school graduation will survive legal challenges if:

- Students are advised upon entrance into high school of test requirements as a prerequisite to graduation,
- Students have the opportunity to be adequately prepared for the tests,
- Tests are not intentionally discriminatory and do not perpetuate the effects of past school segregation,
- Students who fail are provided remedial opportunities and the chance to retake the examinations, and
- Children with disabilities receive appropriate accommodations.

wide testing requirement, the court also noted that there were ample opportunities to receive remediation and retake the exam and that the plaintiff student's IEP sufficiently covered material on the test.

Students with disabilities are entitled to special accommodations in the administration of examinations to ensure that their knowledge, rather than their disability, is being assessed (e.g., braille tests). They are not entitled to accommodations that would jeopardize the validity of the graduation test, such as reading to the student a test measuring reading comprehension.[77] The types of accommodations required for graduation tests remain controversial, especially when accommodations that are part of the student's IEP for classroom instruction are denied for high-stakes tests.[78] Specific proficiency testing programs will likely continue to be challenged on constitutional and statutory grounds (see Figure 4.2).

Educational Malpractice/Instructional Negligence

Students have not yet secured damages from school districts for instructional negligence, but detailed proficiency standards and special education requirements may strengthen the grounds for such claims.

A topic prompting litigation since the mid-1970s is instructional negligence, commonly referred to as *educational malpractice.* Initial suits focused on whether students have a right to attain a predetermined level of achievement in return for state-mandated school atten-

77. *Id.* The Office for Civil Rights in the U.S. Department of Education has also reasoned that states can deny use of reading devices to accommodate children with disabilities on graduation exams, even though their IEPs allow use of such devices. *See* Ala. Dep't of Educ., 29 IDELR 249 (1998).

78. *See* Smiley v. Cal. Dep't of Educ., 53 Fed. Appx. 474 (9th Cir. 2002) (dissolving the parts of the lower court's injunction pertaining to required test waivers and alternative assessments for children with disabilities as not ripe for adjudication).

dance; parents asserted a right to expect their children to be functionally literate upon high school graduation. More recent cases have involved allegations that school authorities have breached their duty to diagnose students' deficiencies and place them in appropriate instructional programs. This section includes an overview of claims in which parents have sought damages from school districts for instructional negligence.

In the first educational malpractice suit to receive substantial attention, a student asserted that the school district was negligent in teaching, promoting, and graduating him from high school with the ability to read only at the fifth-grade level.[79] He also claimed that his performance and progress had been misrepresented to his parents, who testified that they were unaware of his deficiencies until he was tested by a private agency after high school graduation. Concluding that the school district was not negligent, a California appeals court reasoned that the complexities of the teaching/learning process made it impossible to place the entire burden on the school to ensure that all students, with their varying abilities to learn, attain a specified reading level before high school graduation.

The New York high court in 1979 dismissed what had appeared to be a successful educational malpractice suit. A state appellate court had awarded a former public school student $500,000 in damages after concluding that the New York City Board of Education had negligently diagnosed his needs and erroneously instructed him for 12 years in a program for the mentally retarded.[80] The thrust of the negligence claim was that the school psychologist's report, recommending reassessment of the child within two years of the original evaluation, was ignored for over a decade—even though the student scored in the 90th percentile on reading readiness tests at ages 8 and 9. Distinguishing this case from previous educational malpractice suits, the state appeals court noted that school personnel committed affirmative acts of negligence (i.e., ignoring the psychologist's report) that placed crippling burdens on the student. Nonetheless, the New York high court reversed the lower court's ruling and held that it was not the role of the judiciary to make such educational policy determinations. The same court subsequently ruled that a student who was incorrectly diagnosed at age 10, after having been tested in English although he understood only Spanish, was not entitled to damages from the child-care agency for its alleged failure to obtain suitable instruction for him to learn to read.[81] The court determined that the issue involved educational policy matters regarding which instructional programs might have been preferable and was not actionable in a negligence suit.

Other courts also have rejected instructional malpractice claims, voicing reluctance to intervene in such educational policy decisions.[82] **Although educational malpractice suits have not yet been successful, some courts have recognized circumstances under which plaintiffs possibly could recover damages in an instructional tort action for intentional**

79. Peter W. v. S.F. Unified Sch. Dist., 131 Cal. Rptr. 854 (Ct. App. 1976). *See* Chapter 2 for an overview of tort law pertaining to negligence suits.

80. Hoffman v. Bd. of Educ., 410 N.Y.S.2d 99 (App. Div. 1978), *rev'd*, 424 N.Y.S.2d 376 (1979). *See also* Donohue v. Copiague Union Free Schs., 391 N.E.2d 1352 (N.Y. 1979) (dismissing an educational malpractice suit brought by a learning-disabled high school graduate who claimed that because of the school district's negligence he was unable to complete job applications and cope with the problems of everyday life).

81. Torres v. Little Flower Children's Servs., 485 N.Y.S.2d 15 (1984).

acts that injure a child.[83] The Third Circuit, though not awarding monetary damages, held that a student with severe disabilities who had not progressed over the past decade was entitled to compensatory services from a New Jersey school district, because school authorities should have known that the child's individualized education program was inadequate.[84]

The increasing specificity of legislation pertaining to student proficiency standards and special education placements may strengthen the grounds for tort suits involving *placement negligence.* Also, state and federal legislation making school districts accountable for ensuring student mastery of state standards may increase school districts' potential liability. Even though it seems unlikely that public schools in the near future will be held responsible for a specified quantum of student achievement, it is conceivable that schools will be held legally accountable for:

- Diagnosing students' needs,
- Placing them in appropriate instructional programs,
- Reporting their progress to parents, and
- Providing other educational options if students are not progressing in their current placements.

Instructional Privacy Rights

> Parents are entitled to review their children's records and instructional materials and to have personal information kept confidential.

The protection of students' privacy rights has become an increasingly volatile issue in political forums. State and federal laws place dual duties on the government—to protect the public's First Amendment right to be informed about government activities and to protect the personal privacy of individuals. In addition, laws have been enacted to protect students from mandatory participation in research projects or instructional activities designed to reveal personal information in sensitive areas. This section provides an overview of legal developments pertaining to students' privacy rights in instructional matters.

Student Records

The Supreme Court has recognized that the Constitution protects a zone of personal privacy.[85] Thus, there must be a compelling justification for governmental action that impairs

82. *See, e.g.,* Denver Parents Ass'n v. Denver Bd. of Educ., 10 P.3d 662 (Colo. Ct. App. 2000); Vogel v. Maimonides Acad., 754 A.2d 824 (Conn. App. Ct. 2000). For additional cases, *see* Cambron-McCabe et al., *Public School Law,* Chapter 3.
83. *See, e.g.,* Hunter v. Bd. of Educ., 439 A.2d 582 (Md. 1982).
84. M.C. v. Cent. Reg'l Sch. Dist., 81 F.3d 389 (3d Cir. 1996).
85. *See* Griswold v. Connecticut, 381 U.S. 479 (1965); text accompanying note 72, Chapter 10.

privacy rights, including the right to have personal information kept confidential. Because of this right, questions about who has access to public school students' permanent files and the contents of such files have been the source of controversy. Legal challenges to school record-keeping procedures have resulted in courts ordering school officials to expunge irrelevant information from students' permanent folders. In some situations, students have brought successful libel suits for damages against school authorities who allegedly recorded and communicated defamatory information about them.[86]

Because of widespread dissatisfaction with educators' efforts to ameliorate abuses associated with student record-keeping practices, Congress enacted the Family Educational Rights and Privacy Act (FERPA) in 1974.[87] **This law stipulates that federal funds may be withdrawn from any educational agency or institution that (1) fails to provide parents access to their child's educational records or (2) disseminates such information (with some exceptions) to third parties without parental permission.** Upon reaching age 18, students may exercise the rights guaranteed to parents under this law.[88] Education officials may assume that a parent is entitled to exercise rights under FERPA unless state law or a court order bars a parent's access to his or her child's records under specific circumstances and the education agency has been instructed accordingly.[89] The Second Circuit recognized that joint custodial parents must have equal access to education information about their child.[90]

After reviewing a student's permanent file, the parent or eligible student can request amendments in any information thought to be inaccurate, misleading, or in violation of the student's protected rights. If school authorities decide that an amendment is not warranted, the parent or eligible student must be advised of the right to a hearing. The hearing officer may be an employee of the school district, but may not be an individual with a direct interest in the outcome of the hearing. Either party may be represented by counsel at the hearing, and the hearing officer must issue a written decision summarizing the evidence presented and the rationale for the ruling. If the hearing officer concludes that the records should not be amended, the parent or eligible student has the right to place in the file a personal statement specifying objections.

Individuals can file a complaint with the U.S. Department of Education if they believe a school district displays a custom or practice of violating FERPA provisions. The remedy for FERPA violations is the withdrawal of federal funds, and the Department of Education has enforcement authority. Some school districts have been advised to change their practices to conform to FERPA, but no district to date has lost federal funds for noncompliance.

86. *See, e.g.,* Elder v. Anderson, 23 Cal. Rptr. 48 (Ct. App. 1962). *See also* Chapter 2 for a discussion of tort law.

87. 20 U.S.C. § 1232g (2003); 34 C.F.R. § 99 *et seq.* (2003).

88. The Family Policy Compliance Office was created to investigate alleged FERPA violations, 20 U.S.C. § 1232g(g) (2003). This office reviews complaints and responses from accused agencies and submits written findings with steps the agency must take to comply, 34 C.F.R. §§ 99.65(a)(2), 99.66(b), 99.66(c)(1) (2003).

89. *See, e.g.,* Cherry v. LeDeoni, No. 99 CV 6860 (SJ), 2002 U.S. Dist. LEXIS 6701 (E.D.N.Y. April 8, 2002).

90. Fay v. S. Colonie Cent. Sch. Dist., 802 F.2d 21 (2d Cir. 1986).

In *Gonzaga University v. Doe,* the Supreme Court in 2002 held that individuals cannot bring damages suits for FERPA violations, because the law does not create privately enforceable rights.[91] Resolving the conflict among lower courts, the Supreme Court further held that since FERPA contains no rights-creating language, the law cannot be enforced through suits under 42 U.S.C. Section 1983, which provides individuals a damages remedy for the deprivation of federal rights.[92] Accordingly, the Supreme Court overturned the Washington Supreme Court's award of damages to a student for a FERPA violation in connection with a private university's release of an unsubstantiated allegation of sexual misconduct to the state education department. The allegation resulted in the student being denied an affidavit of good moral character required for a teaching license. The Court reiterated that the remedy for FERPA violations is the denial of federal funds to schools that exhibit a policy or practice of noncompliance. School personnel were relieved that the Court did not authorize private suits for damages to enforce FERPA, as such a ruling would have provided a significant incentive for parents to challenge student record-keeping practices in court.

Also in 2002, the Supreme Court ruled in *Owasso Independent School District v. Falvo* that peer grading practices do not violate FERPA.[93] **The Supreme Court concluded that peer graders are not *maintaining* student records under FERPA, and even though they may call out the scores in class, they are not acting for the educational institution.** There may be educational reasons for not having students grade each others' work, but given the *Falvo* ruling, there is no legal barrier under FERPA. The Court also hinted that teachers' grade books may not be subject to FERPA, mentioning that records covered by the act are usually kept in a central repository, but the court specifically declined to resolve the legal status of grade books.

A student's records can be released to officials of a school where the student is transferring if the parents or eligible student are notified, or the sending institution has given prior notice that it routinely transfers such records. Similarly, students' privacy rights do not preclude federal and state authorities from having access to data needed to audit and evaluate federally supported education programs. These data, however, are to be collected in a way that prevents the disclosure of personally identifiable information. Identifiable information can be disclosed to appropriate authorities, however, if necessary to protect the health or safety of the student or others.[94]

91. 536 U.S. 273 (2002).

92. Civil Rights Act of 1871, § 1, codified as 42 U.S.C. § 1983 (2003). For a discussion of this law, *see* text accompanying note 82, Chapter 12.

93. 233 F.3d 1203 (10th Cir. 2000), *rev'd and remanded,* 534 U.S. 426 (2002), *on remand,* 288 F.3d 1236 (10th Cir. 2002) (granting summary judgment in favor of defendant school district and administrators). Although peers can call out scores, students' grades cannot be posted or disseminated in any manner that allows individual students to be identified (e.g., by name or alphabetical order). LeRoy S. Rooker, Director, Family Policy Compliance Office, letter dated July 15, 1993.

94. *See, e.g.,* Doe v. Woodford County Bd. of Educ., 213 F.3d 921 (6th Cir. 2000) (upholding disclosure to coach of information that student was a hemophiliac and carrier of hepatitis B); 34 C.F.R. § 99.36 (2003).

Under FERPA, certain public directory information—such as students' names, addresses, dates and places of birth, major fields of study, e-mail addresses, pictures, and degrees and awards received—can be released without parental consent.[95] Any education agency releasing such data must give public notice of the specific categories it has designated as "directory" and must allow a reasonable period of time for parents to inform the agency that any or all of this information on their child should not be released without their prior consent. Directory data about a student cannot be released if accompanied by other personally identifiable information unless it is among the specified exceptions to the general rule against nonconsensual disclosure.[96]

There are exceptions to FERPA's "access and disclosure" provisions. For example, a teacher's daily notes pertaining to pupil progress are not considered educational records under the law. Private notes become education records once they are shared (except with a substitute teacher), even among educators who have a legitimate need for access to such information.

Most FERPA controversies have involved the dissemination of information about students, but a few have focused on parental rights to review such records. A Pennsylvania court held that parents of elementary students were entitled under FERPA to have access to notes taken by the school psychologist during interviews with the students. The interviews pertained to allegations that a teacher had physically and emotionally abused the students.[97] However, FERPA cannot be used by parents to assert a right to review faculty evaluations used to determine which students will be given academic honors, such as membership in the National Honor Society.[98] Also, students cannot rely on FERPA to challenge teachers' grading procedures, other than whether grades were accurately recorded.[99] The Fourth Circuit ruled that FERPA does not entitle students to see an answer key to exams to check the accuracy of their grades, because the key is not part of students' educational records.[100]

Other federal laws provide additional protections regarding the confidentiality and accessibility of student records. For example, the Individuals with Disabilities Education Act stipulates that records of children with disabilities must be accessible to their parents or guardians.[101] Furthermore, the school must hire interpreters, if necessary to translate the

95. For a complete list of directory items, *see* 34 C.F.R. § 99.3(b) (2003). *See also* the provision of the U.S.A. Patriot Act of 2001 that amends FERPA to authorize federal officers designated by the Attorney General to seek a court order requiring educational institutions to reveal to the Attorney General's designee any educational records that are relevant to authorized investigations of terrorism. 29 U.S.C. § 1232g(j) (2003).

96. *See, e.g.,* Codell v. D.F., No. 1998-CA-002895-MR, 2001 Ky. App. LEXIS 71 (Ky. Ct. App. June 22, 2001), *rev. granted,* 2002 Ky. LEXIS 205 (Ky. Oct. 9, 2002).

97. Parents Against Abuse in Schs. v. Williamsport Area Sch. Dist., 594 A.2d 796 (Pa. Commonw. Ct. 1991).

98. *See, e,g.,* Moore v. Hyche, 761 F. Supp. 112 (N.D. Ala. 1991); Becky v. Butte-Silver Bow Sch. Dist. 1, 906 P.2d 193 (Mont. 1995).

99. *See, e.g.,* Tarka v. Cunningham, 917 F.2d 890 (5th Cir. 1990).

100. Lewin v. Cooke, 28 Fed. Appx. 186 (4th Cir. 2002).

101. 20 U.S.C. § 1415(b)(1) (2003).

contents of students' files for parents, and must obtain parental consent before such records can be disclosed to third parties.

Many states also have enacted legislation addressing the maintenance and disclosure of student records, such as *freedom of information* laws. Under such laws, composite information on pupil achievement can be released to the public as long as individual students are not personally identified. In a typical case, a Louisiana appeals court found that the release of composite achievement data did not violate students' privacy rights, declaring that the public had the right to examine the rankings of schools participating in a school effectiveness study conducted by the state department of education.[102]

At times there are conflicts between *freedom of information* or *right to know* provisions and federal and state laws protecting privacy rights. The Virginia Supreme Court denied a student editor's request for individual vote totals in a student election, reasoning that such information was exempt from public disclosure by the law granting custodians discretion concerning disclosure of identifiable scholastic records.[103]

Courts have ruled that student disciplinary records can be released to school employees authorized to review such information[104] and to law-enforcement agencies under certain circumstances. The Supreme Court declined to review a decision in which the Massachusetts high court held that a school district did not violate a student's rights under state privacy law when it shared samples of the student's school work with police to compare his handwriting with graffiti on school property in connection with criminal charges.[105] Also, an institution's general disciplinary information (number of occurrences and when) must be released to the media under some state *open records* laws. However, such information remains an education record under FERPA, so personally identifiable data cannot be released.[106]

Students' records must be disclosed if subpoenaed by a court. In compelling a school district to reveal records of individual pupils, a New York federal district court held that FERPA does not preclude the disclosure of student records where a genuine need for the information outweighs the students' privacy interests. In this case, data on the performance of individual students were needed to substantiate charges that inadequate instructional programs were being provided for children with English language deficiencies.[107]

Since Congress, state legislatures, and the judiciary have indicated a continuing interest in safeguarding students' privacy rights in connection with school records, school boards would be wise to reassess their policies to ensure that they are adhering to federal and state laws. School personnel should use some restraint, however, before purging information from student files. Pertinent material that is necessary to provide continuity in a student's

102. Laplante v. Stewart, 470 So. 2d 1018 (La. Ct. App. 1985). *See also* Bowie v. Evanston Cmty. Consol. Dist. 65, 538 N.E.2d 557 (Ill. 1989).

103. Wall v. Fairfax County Sch. Bd., 475 S.E.2d 803 (Va. 1996).

104. See, e.g., Achman v. Chisago Lakes Indep. Sch. Dist. No. 2144, 45 F. Supp. 2d 664 (D. Minn. 1999).

105. Commonwealth v. Buccella, 751 N.E.2d 373 (Mass. 2001), *cert. denied,* 534 U.S. 1079 (2002).

106. *See, e.g.,* United States v. Miami Univ., 294 F.3d 797 (6th Cir. 2002); Hardin County Schs. v. Foster, 40 S.W.3d 865 (Ky. 2001); Burlington Free Press v. Univ. of Vt., 779 A.2d 60 (Vt. 2001).

107. Rios v. Read, 480 F. Supp. 14 (E.D.N.Y. 1978).

instructional program *should* be included in a permanent record and be available for use by authorized personnel. It is unfortunate that school personnel, fearing federal sanctions under FERPA, have deleted useful information—along with material that should be removed—from student records. Also, the mere fact that information in a student's file is negative does not imply that the material is inappropriate. School authorities have an obligation to record relevant data pertaining to students' activities, including disciplinary actions, as long as such information is accurate.

Pupil Protection Laws

Congress and state legislatures have enacted laws to protect family privacy in connection with school research activities and treatment programs. Under federal law, human subjects are protected in research projects supported by federal grants and contracts in any private or public institution or agency.[108] **Informed consent must be obtained before placing subjects at risk of being exposed to physical, psychological, or social injury as a result of participating in research, development, or related activities.** All education agencies are required to establish review committees to ensure that the rights and welfare of all subjects are adequately protected.

Several amendments to the General Education Provisions Act, most notably the 1978 Hatch Amendment, require all instructional materials in federally assisted research or experimentation projects to be made available for inspection by parents of participating students. The most recent Protection of Pupil Rights Amendment has extended federal privacy protections for students and their families (see Figure 4.3). Parents must be allowed to review in advance all instructional materials in programs administered by the Department of Education, and such federally assisted programs cannot require students, without prior written parental consent, to be subjected to surveys or evaluations that reveal information pertaining to personal beliefs, behaviors, and family relationships.[109] The department is

FIGURE 4.3 ***Protection of Pupil Rights Amendment, 20 U.S.C. § 1232h (2003)***

No federal funds will be given to schools that provide a survey, analysis, or evaluation to a student without prior, informed, written consent of the parent or guardian, concerning:

- Political affiliations of the student or parents;
- Mental or psychological problems of student or families;
- Sexual behavior or attitudes;
- Illegal, antisocial, self-incriminating, and demeaning behavior;
- Critical appraisals of individuals with whom respondents have close family relationships;
- Legally recognized privileged relationships;
- Religious practices, affiliations, or beliefs of the student or parents; or
- Income (other than that required to determine eligibility for financial assistance programs).

108. 42 U.S.C. § 201 *et seq.* (2003); 45 C.F.R. § 46.101 *et seq.* (2003).

109. 20 U.S.C. § 1232h (2003). Parents must be notified at least annually of their rights under this law.

charged with reviewing complaints under this law; if an educational institution is found in violation and does not comply within a reasonable period, federal funds can be withheld.

Some conservative citizen groups have pressed for a broad interpretation of the Protection of Pupil Rights Amendment as allowing students to be excused from a broad array of instructional activities. Courts, however, have not generally supported parental attempts to use this law to challenge items in student assessments or their children's participation in voluntary surveys and other school activities.[110] Nonetheless, there is some concern that federal requirements and similar provisions being enacted or considered by many states will cause certain instructional activities to be dropped even before they are legally challenged. Although these measures are couched in terms of protecting students' privacy rights by granting them exemptions from particular instructional activities, if a substantial number of exemptions are requested, the instructional activity itself may be eliminated from the curriculum.

Conclusion

The state and its agents enjoy considerable latitude in regulating various aspects of public education, but any requirements that restrict students' activities must be reasonable and necessary to carry out legitimate educational objectives. When students' or parents' protected rights are impaired, school authorities must be able to substantiate that there is an overriding public interest to be served. But, parents on behalf of their children or teachers asserting academic freedom do not have a right to determine the public school curriculum. The state and its agencies have the authority to determine public school course offerings and instructional materials, and such curricular determinations will be upheld by courts unless clearly arbitrary or in violation of constitutional or statutory provisions. For example, school personnel cannot censor instructional materials for religious reasons or disregard federal copyright requirements.

Courts defer to school authorities in assessing student performance in the absence of evidence of arbitrary or discriminatory academic decisions. Accordingly, proficiency examinations can be used to determine pupil remedial needs and as a prerequisite to high school graduation if students are given sufficient notice prior to implementation of the test requirements and are provided adequate preparation for the examinations.

Public schools do not have a legal duty to ensure that students attain a specified level of achievement. But they do have a duty to provide parents information on their child's progress and to ensure that the confidentiality of such records is maintained. Also, parents have the right to inspect materials used in federally funded experimental projects or surveys,

110. *See, e.g.,* Newkirk v. E. Lansing Pub. Schs., No. 1:91:CV:563, 1993 U.S. Dist. LEXIS 13194 (W.D. Mich. Aug. 19, 1993), *aff'd mem.,* 57 F.3d 1070 (6th Cir. 1995); Triplett v. Livingston County Bd. of Educ., 967 S.W.2d 25 (Ky. Ct. App. 1997). *But see* C.N. v. Ridgewood Bd. of Educ., 281 F.3d 219 (3d Cir. 2001) (reversing the lower court's summary judgment for the school board and remanding the case for consideration of whether the survey asking students about their attitudes and behaviors was purchased with federal funds and whether students knew that participation was voluntary).

and students have a right to be excused from participation in such programs or activities involving psychiatric or psychological testing or treatment designed to reveal sensitive information about them or their families.

Points to Ponder

1. A school board decided to eliminate several books from the English curriculum, including *The Learning Tree, The Adventures of Huckleberry Finn,* and *The Catcher in the Rye,* because of parental complaints. Several teachers contend that they have a right to use these books in their classes, because the books relate to course objectives and their use is supported by the profession. How would the court rule and why?

2. A school district has a policy stipulating that students cannot be promoted from third to fourth grade or from seventh to eighth grade until they demonstrate on proficiency tests that they have mastered specified skills. Parents of children who were promoted at both grade levels based on test passage have brought an instructional negligence suit against the school district. They claim that their children do not have the specified academic skills based on an external evaluation by a licensed psychometrist. Is the testing program vulnerable? Will the parents prevail in their educational malpractice suit? Why or why not?

3. A school secretary's daughter gained access to a classmate's file without permission and divulged that he was adopted. Should the school be liable for a FERPA violation? *See* Appelberg v. Devilbiss, No. 00-0202 BH-C, 2001 U.S. Dist. LEXIS 1456 (S.D. Ala. Jan. 30, 2001).

4. A school distributed an anonymous survey asking students about their attitudes and behaviors. The students and their parents were informed that participation was completely voluntary and that no student's responses could be identified, but parents were not asked to give written permission for their children to participate. Parents claimed that the survey violated the federal Protection of Pupil Rights Amendment. How should the court rule? *See* C.N. v. Ridgewood Bd. of Educ., 281 F.3d 219 (3d Cir. 2001).

5

Student Expression, Association, and Appearance

Students continue to test the limits of their personal freedoms in public schools, frequently colliding with educators' efforts to maintain an appropriate school environment. This chapter addresses students' substantive rights regarding First Amendment freedoms of speech and press and closely related association rights.

Freedom of Speech and Press

> Students have the right to express nondisruptive ideological views at school, but restrictions can be placed on their expression if it is viewed as representing the school.

The First Amendment, as applied to the states through the Fourteenth Amendment, restricts *government* (not private) interference with citizens' free expression rights. The government, including public school boards, must have a compelling justification to curtail citizens' freedom of expression. The First Amendment also shields the individual's right to remain silent when confronted with an illegitimate government demand for expression, such as mandatory participation in the salute to the American flag in public schools.[1] In short, the First Amendment protects decisions regarding what to say and what not to say.

In our nation, free expression rights are perhaps the most preciously guarded individual liberties.[2] And these rights extend to unpopular viewpoints, such as political protesters'

1. *See* W. Va. State Bd. of Educ. v. Barnette, 319 U.S. 624 (1943); text with note 73, Chapter 3.
2. Despite their fundamental significance, free expression rights can be restricted. As Justice Holmes noted, freedom of speech does not allow an individual to yell "fire" in a crowded theater when there is no fire. Schenck v. United States, 249 U.S. 47, 52 (1919).

burning of the American flag[3] and the Ku Klux Klan's placement of a cross on public property.[4] In 2002, the Ninth Circuit observed:

> The First Amendment judicial scrutiny should now be at its height, whether the individual before us is a troubled schoolboy, a right-to-life-activist, an outraged environmentalist, a Taliban sympathizer, or any other person who disapproves of one or more of our nation's officials or policies for any reason whatsoever.[5]

The Supreme Court has recognized since the mid-twentieth century that students do not shed their constitutional rights as a condition of public school attendance and that public education is an appropriate setting in which to instill a respect for these rights. The Court has acknowledged that schools function as "a marketplace of ideas"[6] and First Amendment freedoms must receive "scrupulous protection" in schools "if we are not to strangle the free mind at its source and teach youth to discount important principles of our government as mere platitudes."[7]

However, the Supreme Court also has stated that "the constitutional rights of students in public school are not automatically coextensive with the rights of adults in other settings" and may be limited by reasonable policies designed to take into account the special circumstances of the educational environment.[8] Particularly sensitive constitutional issues are being raised in connection with the national surge of patriotism following the terrorist attacks on September 11, 2001. Many school districts have reinstated the daily Pledge of Allegiance to the American flag, and some schools are displaying banners with "God Bless America" or "In God We Trust." These activities have placed new strains on individuals exercising their First Amendment rights to abstain from patriotic observances, to criticize government policies, or to raise church/state questions in connection with patriotic displays in public schools.

Unprotected Conduct and Expression

A threshold question before applying First Amendment standards is whether the behavior at issue constitutes expression *at all.* **Only if conduct is meant to communicate an idea that is likely to be understood by the intended audience is it considered expression for First Amendment purposes.**[9] Even if specific conduct qualifies as expression, it is not assured

3. Texas v. Johnson, 491 U.S. 397 (1989).
4. Capitol Square Rev. & Advisory Bd. v. Pinette, 515 U.S. 753 (1995). *But see* Virginia v. Black, 123 S. Ct. 1536 (2003) (upholding a statutory prohibition on cross burning with the intent to intimidate).
5. Lavine v. Blaine Sch. Dist., 279 F.3d 719, 720 (9th Cir. 2002), *cert. denied,* 536 U.S. 959 (2002).
6. Keyishian v. Bd. of Regents, 385 U.S. 589, 603 (1967).
7. W. Va. State Bd. of Educ. v. Barnette, 319 U.S. 624, 637 (1943).
8. Bethel Sch. Dist. No. 403 v. Fraser, 478 U.S. 675, 682 (1986). *See also* Tinker v. Des Moines Indep. Sch. Dist., 393 U.S. 503, 506-507 (1969).
9. *See, e.g.,* Jarman v. Williams, 753 F.2d 76 (8th Cir. 1985) (holding that social and recreational dancing in public schools does not enjoy First Amendment protection).

constitutional protection; the judiciary has recognized that defamatory, obscene, and inflammatory communications are outside the protective arm of the First Amendment. In addition, lewd and vulgar expression is not protected in the public school context.

Defamatory Expression. Defamation includes spoken (slander) and written (libel) statements that are false, expose another to public shame or ridicule, and are communicated to someone other than the person defamed. Courts have upheld school authorities in banning libelous content from publications distributed at school and imposing sanctions on students responsible for such material, but regulations cannot be vague or grant school officials complete discretion to censor potentially libelous materials.[10]

Obscene, Lewd, or Vulgar Expression. The judiciary has held that individuals cannot claim a First Amendment right to voice or publish obscenities,[11] but school authorities do not have to prove that student expression is obscene for it to be curtailed. In a significant 1986 decision, *Bethel School District No. 403 v. Fraser,* the Supreme Court granted school authorities considerable latitude in censoring lewd, vulgar, and indecent student expression. Overturning the lower courts, the Supreme Court upheld disciplinary action against a student for using a sexual metaphor in a nominating speech during a student government assembly.[12] **Concluding that the sexual innuendos were offensive to both teachers and students, the *Fraser* majority held that the school's legitimate interest in protecting the captive student audience from exposure to lewd, vulgar, and offensive speech justified the disciplinary action.** The Court reiterated that speech protected by the First Amendment for adults is not necessarily protected for children, reasoning that in the public school context the sensibilities of fellow students must be considered. The majority recognized that an important objective of public schools is the inculcation of fundamental values of civility and that the school board has the authority to determine what manner of speech is appropriate in classes or assemblies. The majority further reasoned that the school rule barring obscene and disruptive expression and teachers' admonitions that the student's planned speech was inappropriate provided adequate notice of the consequences of the expression.

More recently, the South Dakota federal district court upheld punishment of a student for saying the word "shit" within earshot of the school secretary in the school's office.[13] Under the school's zero tolerance rule prohibiting profane or inappropriate language on school property, the student received an in-school suspension resulting in a grade reduction

10. *See* Chapter 2 for a discussion of the principles of tort law governing defamation suits for damages and how these apply to public figures and officials.
11. *See* Miller v. California, 413 U.S. 15, 24 (1973) (distinguishing obscene material from constitutionally protected material based on whether the work as a whole appeals to prurient interests based on community standards; depicts sexual activity as defined by state law in a patently offensive way; or lacks serious literary, artistic, political or scientific value). On several occasions, the Supreme Court has recognized the government's authority to adjust the definition of obscenity as applied to minors. *See, e.g.,* Ginsberg v. New York, 390 U.S. 629 (1968) (upholding a state law prohibiting the sale to minors of magazines depicting female nudity).
12. 478 U.S. 675 (1986). Fraser was suspended for two days and disqualified as a candidate for commencement speaker. However, he did eventually deliver a commencement speech, so his claim that the disqualification violated due process rights was not reviewed by the appellate court.

for classes missed. The court recognized that promoting proper decorum and complying with school rules are legitimate educational concerns justifying such a rule.

Inflammatory Expression. The judiciary also has supported regulations banning the use of inflammatory expression in public schools. **Expression that agitates, threatens, or incites an immediate breach of peace (fighting words) has been distinguished from speech that represents ideological views and leaves an opportunity for calm and reasonable discussion.** Although inflammatory student expression at school is not constitutionally protected, questions remain regarding whether such expression off school grounds can be the basis for school sanctions.[14]

A growing body of First Amendment litigation involves alleged threats made by students toward classmates or school personnel. For example, the Ninth Circuit upheld suspension of a student for threatening a teacher, despite conflicting testimony regarding what was actually said.[15] The appeals court emphasized that threats of physical violence are not shielded by the First Amendment. In determining if a true threat has been made, courts consider a number of factors, such as:

- Reactions of the recipient and other listeners,
- Whether the maker of the alleged threat had made similar statements to the victim in the past,
- Whether the utterance was conditional and communicated directly to the victim, and
- Whether the victim had reason to believe that the speaker would engage in violence.[16]

In an illustrative case, the Arkansas Supreme Court held that a rap song did not entail fighting words but was a true threat, as it contained an unconditional threat to the life of a classmate and was delivered to the targeted student who perceived it as unequivocally threatening.[17] Also finding a true threat, the Eighth Circuit reversed the court below and upheld expulsion of a student for writing a letter threatening to rape and murder his former girlfriend. The Court was convinced that the writer intended to communicate the threat, as he shared the letter with a friend whom he assumed would give it to his former girlfriend.[18]

Utterances can be considered inflammatory, and thus unprotected, even if not found to be true threats or fighting words. A Ninth Circuit panel ruled that a student could be subject to emergency expulsion, with a hearing occurring afterwards, for writing a poem about someone who committed multiple murders two years earlier and decided to kill himself for

13. Anderson v. Milbank Sch. Dist., 197 F.R.D. 682 (D.S.D. 2000). *See also* Pangle v. Bend-Lapine Sch. Dist., 10 P.3d 275 (Or. App. 2000), *review denied,* 34 P.3d 1176 (Or. 2001) (upholding punishment of a student who distributed an underground newspaper that used vulgar and threatening language).
14. *See* text with note 8, Chapter 8.
15. Lovell v. Poway Unified Sch. Dist., 90 F.3d 367 (9th Cir. 1996).
16. *See* United States v. Dinwiddie, 76 F.3d 913 (8th Cir. 1996).
17. Jones v. State, 347 Ark. 409 (2002). *See also* United States v. Morales, 272 F.3d 284 (5th Cir. 2001), *cert. denied,* 536 U.S. 941 (2002); *infra* text accompanying note 67.
18. Doe v. Pulaski County Special Sch. Dist., 306 F.3d 616 (8th Cir. 2002).

fear of murdering others.[19] The disciplinary action was upheld, even though the poem was not considered a true threat or fighting words. The Wisconsin Supreme Court also held that school authorities had more than enough reason to suspend a student for his creative writing assignment. He described a student who was removed from class for being disruptive (as the writer had been) and then returned the next day to behead his teacher.[20] But, the court held that there was no true threat that would justify prosecution as disorderly conduct. The Supreme Court of New Hampshire similarly overruled a disorderly conduct conviction of a student who said he might "shoot up the school" if a teacher did not give him a hug. The court found no evidence that the expression caused a school disruption to justify the conviction.[21] Courts seem more inclined to uphold school disciplinary action, in contrast to criminal prosecution, for students' alleged threats.

Commercial Expression

Unlike obscene, lewd, inflammatory, or defamatory expression, commercial speech enjoys some measure of constitutional protection. However, **expression with economic motives has not been afforded the same level of First Amendment protection as has speech intended to convey a particular point of view.**[22] The Supreme Court has recognized that government restrictions on commercial speech do not have to be the least restrictive means to achieve the desired end; rather, there only needs to be a reasonable "fit" between the restrictions and the government goal.[23] In several cases involving school newspapers, courts have upheld school authorities in rejecting advertisements that conflict with educational objectives.[24] In general, sales and fund-raising activities can be prohibited to preserve public schools for their educational function and to prevent commercial exploitation of students.

19. Lavine v. Blaine Sch. Dist., 279 F.3d 719 (9th Cir. 2002), *cert. denied,* 536 U.S. 959 (2002). The school board wanted the student's file to note that the action was for safety rather than disciplinary reasons, and the student was readmitted to school after three psychiatric visits. *See also* Cuesta v. Miami-Dade County Sch. Bd., 285 F.3d 962 (11th Cir. 2002) (upholding the principal's compliance with the school's zero tolerance policy by reporting to the police a student's distribution of a threatening pamphlet).
20. *In re* Douglas D., 626 N.W.2d 725 (Wis. 2001). *See also* C.C.H., 651 N.W.2d 702 (S.D. 2002) (finding a student's threat against a classmate that was conveyed privately to the teacher could not be considered a true threat).
21. State v. McCooey, 802 A.2d 1216 (N.H. 2002). *See also* Shoemaker v. State, 343 Ark. 727 (2001) (finding a state law unconstitutionally vague that criminalized student conduct or expression abusing or insulting a teacher; a student could not be charged with a misdemeanor for calling her teacher "a bitch" because this utterance did not entail fighting words). *But see In re* A.S., 626 N.W.2d 712 (Wis. 2001) (finding a student's comments that he intended to kill everyone at his middle school to represent an intent to inflict harm in violation of the disorderly conduct law).
22. *See, e.g.,* Bolger v. Youngs Drug Prods. Corp., 463 U.S. 60, 64-75 (1983).
23. Bd. of Trs. v. Fox, 492 U.S. 469 (1989).
24. See, *e.g.,* Planned Parenthood v. Clark County Sch. Dist., 887 F.2d 935 (9th Cir. 1989), *infra* text accompanying note 34; Williams v. Spencer, 622 F.2d 1200 (4th Cir. 1980), *infra* text accompanying note 51.

Some controversies focus on students' rights *not* to be exposed to commercial expression in public schools, rather than on their rights to engage in commercial activity. For example, a number of school districts nationwide subscribe to Channel One. In return for students watching a 10-minute news program and 2 minutes of commercials each day, the schools receive free equipment. Although the judiciary has recognized the legal authority of school boards to enter into contracts for supplementary instructional materials that include commercials,[25] some courts have required school boards to excuse students whose parents do not want them exposed to the commercial activities.[26] With an increasing number of companies offering monetary enticements for school boards to air commercials over public address systems and to display advertisements on scoreboards, such commercial activities in public schools seem destined to generate additional legal challenges.

School-Sponsored (Governmental) Expression

In contrast to defamatory, obscene, vulgar, and inflammatory expression, students' airing of political or ideological views in public schools *is* protected by the First Amendment. **Since the mid-1980s, the Supreme Court has emphasized the distinction between student expression that appears to represent the school and *private* student expression of ideological views that merely occurs at school. The latter commands substantial constitutional protection, but student expression appearing to bear the school's imprimatur can be restricted to ensure that it is consistent with educational objectives.** The Court's expansive interpretation of what constitutes school-sponsored expression has narrowed the circumstances under which students can prevail in First Amendment claims.

Type of Forum. In recent Free Speech Clause litigation, an assessment of the type of forum the government has created for expressive activities has been important in determining whether expression can be restricted. The Supreme Court has recognized that public places, such as streets and parks, are traditional public forums for assembly and communication where content-based restrictions cannot be imposed unless justified by a compelling government interest.[27] In contrast, expression can be confined to the government purpose of the property in a nonpublic forum, such as a public school. Content-based restrictions are permissible in a nonpublic forum to assure that expression is compatible with the intended government purpose, provided that regulations are reasonable and do not entail viewpoint discrimination.

The government, however, can create a limited public forum for expression on public property that otherwise would be considered a nonpublic forum and reserved for its government function.[28] For example, a student activities program held after school might be estab-

25. *See, e.g.,* Wallace v. Knox County Bd. of Educ., No. 92-6195, 1993 U.S. App. LEXIS 20477 (6th Cir. Aug. 10, 1993); State v. Whittle Communications, 402 S.E.2d 556 (N.C. 1991).

26. *See, e.g.,* Dawson v. E. Side Union High Sch. Dist., 34 Cal. Rptr.2d 108 (Ct. App. 1994).

27. *See, e.g.,* Cornelius v. NAACP Legal Def. & Educ. Fund, 473 U.S. 788 (1985).

28. *See, e.g.,* Kincaid v. Gibson, 236 F.3d 342 (6th Cir. 2001) (holding that a university's yearbook was created as a limited public forum for student expression; the university's actions in confiscating copies because of objections violated the editors' First Amendment rights).

lished as a limited forum for student expression. A limited forum can be restricted to a certain class of speakers (e.g., students) and/or to specific categories of expression (e.g., noncommercial speech). Otherwise, expression in a limited forum is subject to the same protections that govern a traditional public forum.

Hazelwood *and Its Progeny.* In 1988, the Supreme Court delivered a significant decision, *Hazelwood School District v. Kuhlmeier,* holding that **school authorities can censor student expression in school publications and other school-related activities as long as the censorship decisions are based on legitimate pedagogical concerns.**[29] At issue in *Hazelwood* was a high school principal's deletion of two pages from the school newspaper because of the content of articles on divorce and teenage pregnancy and fears that individuals could be identified in the articles. The Court ruled that the principal's actions were based on legitimate educational concerns. Rejecting the assertion that the school newspaper had been established as a public forum for student expression, the Court declared that only with school authorities' clear *intent* do school activities become a public forum.[30] The Court distinguished a public school's *toleration* of private student expression, which is constitutionally required under some circumstances, from its *promotion* of student speech that represents the school. Reasoning that student expression appearing to bear the school's imprimatur can be censored, the Court acknowledged school authorities' broad discretion to ensure that such expression occurring in school publications and all school-sponsored activities (including extracurricular) is consistent with educational objectives.[31] The Court reiterated the sentiment voiced in *Fraser* two years earlier that school boards can determine for themselves what expression is consistent with the school's mission.[32]

Relying on *Hazelwood,* the Sixth Circuit in 1989 held that a student could be disqualified from running for student council president because his candidacy speech at a school-sponsored assembly was discourteous. Noting that civility is a legitimate pedagogical concern, the court emphasized that limitations can be placed on speech in schools that would not be allowed elsewhere. The court acknowledged that decisions regarding whether specific comments are rude are "best left to the locally elected school board, not to a distant, life-tenured judiciary."[33]

Also echoing the *Hazelwood* rationale, the Ninth Circuit rejected Planned Parenthood's claim that a school district's denial of its request to advertise in school newspapers, yearbooks, and programs for athletic events violated free speech rights. The court concluded that the district could reject advertisements that were inconsistent with its educational mis-

29. 484 U.S. 260 (1988), *on remand,* 840 F.2d 596 (8th Cir. 1988).

30. *Id.,* 484 U.S. at 267.

31. In response to this decision, several state legislatures have enacted laws granting student editors of school-sponsored papers specific rights in determining the content of those publications. *See, e.g.,* Cal. Ed. Code § 48907 (2003); Colo. Rev. Stat. Ann. § 22-1-120 (2002); Iowa Code § 280.22 (2003); Kan. Stat. Ann. § 72-1506 (2002); Mass. Gen. Laws Ann. ch. 71, § 82 (2003).

32. 484 U.S. at 267. The Court in *Fraser* noted that school authorities' broad discretion to curtail lewd and vulgar student expression is not confined to school-sponsored events. Bethel Sch. Dist. No. 403 v. Fraser, 478 U.S. 675 (1986); *supra* text accompanying note 12.

33. Poling v. Murphy, 872 F.2d 757, 761 (6th Cir. 1989).

sion.[34] Similarly reflecting the broad discretion granted to school authorities, the Fourth Circuit upheld a high school principal's decision to bar the school's use of the Johnny Reb symbol following complaints that it offended African American students.[35] The court reasoned that the school can disassociate itself from controversial expression that conflicts with its objectives.

In 1999, the Eighth Circuit again relied on *Hazelwood* in upholding a principal's decision to disqualify a student council candidate who handed out condoms with stickers bearing his campaign slogan.[36] The court noted that *Hazelwood* grants school authorities considerable discretion to control student expression in school-sponsored activities, including administrative approval of materials students distribute. Also, a Missouri federal district court upheld school authorities in prohibiting the marching band's performance of a song they feared would be construed as advocating drug use.[37] The court found band performances to be school-sponsored expression over which the school exercises broad control.

There are limits, however, on school authorities' wide latitude to censor student expression that bears the public school's imprimatur. **Blatant viewpoint discrimination, even in a nonpublic forum, abridges the First Amendment.** For example, the Ninth Circuit held that a school board violated students' First Amendment rights, because it failed to produce a compelling justification for excluding an antidraft organization's advertisement from the school newspaper, while allowing military recruitment advertisements.[38] Similarly, the Eleventh Circuit placed the burden on school authorities to justify viewpoint discrimination against a peace activist group that was excluded from the public school's career day and not allowed to display its literature on school bulletin boards and in counselors' offices, whereas military recruiters were allowed such access.[39] The court found no compelling justification for censoring specific views that the board found distasteful.

Even if viewpoint discrimination is not involved, censorship actions in a nonpublic forum still must be based on legitimate pedagogical concerns. Recognizing that the junior high school newspaper was not a public forum, the New Jersey Supreme Court nonetheless found no legitimate educational reason to exclude a student's reviews of R-rated movies when such movies were discussed in class and available in the school library.[40]

34. Planned Parenthood v. Clark County Sch. Dist., 887 F.2d 935 (9th Cir. 1989), *rehearing en banc,* 941 F.2d 817 (9th Cir. 1991).
35. Crosby v. Holsinger, 852 F.2d 801 (4th Cir. 1988) (noting also that the one-day delay in posting students' notices of the upcoming board meeting constituted a minimal impairment of expression rights).
36. Henerey v. City of St. Charles Sch. Dist., 200 F.3d 1128 (8th Cir. 1999).
37. McCann v. Ft. Zumwalt Sch. Dist., 50 F. Supp. 2d 918 (E.D. Mo. 1999).
38. San Diego Comm. Against Registration & the Draft v. Governing Bd., 790 F.2d 1471 (9th Cir. 1986).
39. Searcey v. Harris, 888 F.2d 1314 (11th Cir. 1989).
40. Desilets v. Clearview Reg'l Bd. of Educ., 647 A.2d 150 (N.J. 1994).

Protected Private Expression

Student expression that does not fall within one of the categories of unprotected expression or bear the school's imprimatur is governed by the landmark Supreme Court decision, *Tinker v. Des Moines Independent School District,* rendered in 1969. In *Tinker,* three students were suspended from school for wearing armbands to protest the Vietnam War. School officials did not attempt to prohibit the wearing of all symbols, but instead prohibited the expression of one particular opinion. Concluding that school authorities punished the students for expression that was not accompanied by any disorder or disturbance, the Supreme Court ruled that "undifferentiated fear or apprehension of disturbance is not enough to overcome the right to freedom of expression."[41] Student expression cannot be curtailed merely because it causes school officials some discomfort. The Court emphasized that "students in school as well as out of school are 'persons' under our Constitution. They are possessed of fundamental rights which the state must respect."[42]

In *Tinker,* the Supreme Court echoed statements made in an earlier federal appellate ruling: A student may express opinions on controversial issues in the classroom, cafeteria, playing field, or any other place, as long as the exercise of such rights does not "materially and substantially interfere with the requirements of appropriate discipline in the operation of the school" or collide with the rights of others.[43] The Supreme Court emphasized that educators have the authority and duty to maintain discipline in schools, but they must consider students' constitutional rights as they exert control.

Because school authorities can censor school-sponsored student expression for educational reasons, the *Tinker* standard now applies *only* to protected expression that does not give the appearance of representing the school. Although subsequent decisions have narrowed the reach of *Tinker,* private expression of ideological views still enjoys First Amendment protection. Ironically, since *Hazelwood,* student expression in underground student papers distributed at school enjoys greater constitutional protection than does expression in school-sponsored publications.[44] The former is considered private expression governed by the *Tinker* principle, whereas the latter is subject to censorship under *Hazelwood.* Figure 5.1 displays the questions that should guide school personnel in determining when they can regulate student expression.

Prior Restraints. If determined that protected private expression is at issue, courts then are faced with the difficult task of assessing whether restrictions are justified in particular circumstances. Under the *Tinker* principle, private expression can be curtailed if it is likely to disrupt the educational process. The Sixth Circuit concluded that a rule banning the wearing of freedom buttons was lawful in a situation where the learning environment would be disrupted if pupils were allowed to wear such symbols of their disagreements.[45]

41. 393 U.S. 503, 508 (1969).

42. *Id.* at 511.

43. *Id.* at 513 (quoting Burnside v. Byars, 363 F.2d 744, 749 (5th Cir. 1966)).

44. Most courts have treated students' distribution of religious literature like the distribution of other material that is not sponsored by the school. *See* text accompanying note 64, Chapter 3.

45. Guzick v. Drebus, 431 F.2d 594 (6th Cir. 1970).

FIGURE 5.1 ***Assessing Student Expression***

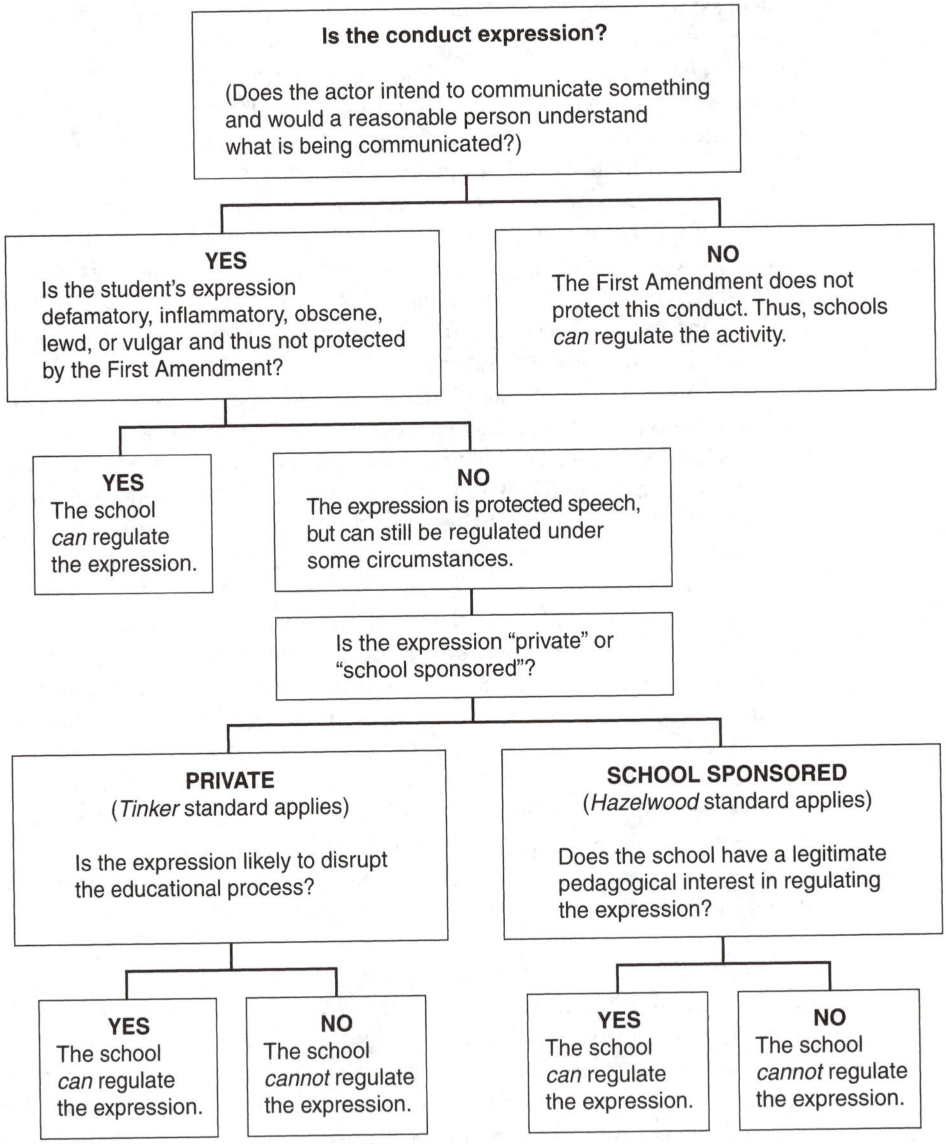

Developed by Amy Steketee, Associate Instructor, Indiana University.

The law clearly allows students to be punished after the fact if they cause a disruption, but school authorities have a greater burden of justification when they impose prior restraints on such expression. The Supreme Court has recognized that "a free society prefers to punish the few who abuse rights of speech after they break the law [rather] than to throttle them and all others beforehand."[46] The imposition of prior restraints on student speech must bear a substantial relationship to an important government interest and contain narrow, objective, and unambiguous criteria for determining what material is prohibited. It also must include procedures that allow a speedy determination of whether materials meet those criteria.[47]

The burden is on school authorities to justify policies requiring administrative approval of unofficial (underground) student publications, but such prior review is not unconstitutional *per se.* In 1987, the Eighth Circuit rejected a vagueness challenge to a school board's policy requiring administrative review of unofficial student papers distributed at school and barring the distribution of material that advertises anything unlawful, disruptive, obscene, libelous, or pervasively indecent.[48] However, the court invalidated the part of the policy proscribing material that invades others' privacy, reasoning that such expression could not be curtailed unless it would subject the school to a libel suit under state law.

Several other courts have approved the *concept* of prior review of nonschool publications, but have found challenged policies constitutionally defective because they lacked criteria to assess the materials and explicit review procedures.[49] In decisions rendered after *Hazelwood,* courts have continued to scrutinize prior review regulations applied to unofficial student publications, recognizing that the Constitution requires a high degree of specificity when imposing restraints on *private* expression. For example, the Ninth Circuit held that school authorities in a Washington school district could not bar distribution of a student paper produced off campus and could not subject the paper's content to prior review. The appeals court considered the policy subjecting *all* nonschool publications to prior review for the purpose of censorship to be overbroad, and ruled that suspending students for distributing the unauthorized paper at a school function impaired the First Amendment.[50]

Postexpression Discipline. Although prior restraints on private expression may be legally vulnerable, courts are inclined to support disciplinary action and confiscation of materials *after* the expression has occurred, if it:

- Is considered unprotected (e.g., libelous or vulgar comments),
- Fosters a disruption of the educational process, or
- Encourages others to engage in dangerous or unlawful activity.

46. Southeastern Promotions v. Conrad, 420 U.S. 546, 559 (1975).
47. *See, e.g.,* Muller v. Jefferson Lighthouse Sch., 98 F.3d 1530 (7th Cir. 1996).
48. Bystrom v. Fridley High Sch. Indep. Sch. Dist. No. 14, 822 F.2d 747 (8th Cir. 1987). *See also* Bystrom v. Fridley High Sch., 686 F. Supp. 1387 (D. Minn. 1987), *aff'd mem.,* 855 F.2d 855 (8th Cir. 1988).
49. *See, e.g.,* Quarterman v. Byrd, 453 F.2d 54 (4th Cir. 1971); Eisner v. Stamford Bd. of Educ., 440 F.2d 803 (2d Cir. 1971).
50. Burch v. Barker, 861 F.2d 1149 (9th Cir. 1988).

For example, the Fourth Circuit upheld school administrators in impounding copies of a student publication that contained an advertisement for drug paraphernalia and in banning further distribution on school property.[51] The court emphasized that the literature was not subjected to predistribution approval; copies were impounded only after distribution began. The court held that school officials were not required to demonstrate that a publication encouraging actions that endanger students' health or safety would lead to a substantial disruption.

Students often have been disciplined after the fact for distributing material that is abusive toward classmates or teachers.[52] To illustrate, the Eighth Circuit found no impairment of speech rights in requiring a student, who distributed a letter that criticized the girl's varsity basketball coach, to apologize to the coach and teammates as a condition of returning to the team.[53] The student's comments violated provisions of the student conduct handbook and the basketball handbook prohibiting disrespectful and insubordinate behavior.

Students also can be disciplined for advocating the destruction of school property in publications they distribute at school. The Seventh Circuit recognized that a "reason to believe" or "reasonable forecast" standard can be applied to punish a student for such expression, even though the anticipated destruction of school property never materializes.[54] In this case, the student was expelled for one year for distributing at school an article in an underground paper that contained information about how to disable the school's computer system.

Courts consistently have condoned disciplinary action against students who have engaged in walkouts, boycotts, sit-ins, or other protests involving conduct that blocks hallways, damages property, causes students to miss class, or in other ways interferes with essential school activities. For example, an Indiana federal district court upheld disciplinary action against several students who staged a student walkout to protest the school's disciplinary procedures.[55] However, the Ninth Circuit relied on *Tinker* in ruling that students could not be suspended for nondisruptive, private expression in the form of wearing buttons containing the word *scab* in connection with a teachers' strike.[56] The court nonetheless acknowledged that vulgar, lewd, obscene, or plainly offensive buttons could be banned *even if* considered private expression.

Antiharassment Policies. A number of school districts have adopted policies prohibiting expression that constitutes verbal or physical harassment based on race, religion, color, national origin, gender, sexual orientation, disability, or other personal characteristics.[57] Until recently, these public school policies have not appeared vulnerable to First Amend-

51. Williams v. Spencer, 622 F.2d 1200 (4th Cir. 1980).
52. *See, e.g.,* Kicklighter v. Evans County Sch. Dist., 968 F. Supp. 712 (S.D. Ga. 1997), *aff'd mem.,* 140 F.3d 1043 (11th Cir. 1998); Donovan v. Ritchie, 68 F.3d 14 (1st Cir. 1995).
53. Wildman v. Marshalltown Sch. Dist., 249 F.3d 768 (8th Cir. 2001).
54. Boucher v. Sch. Bd., 134 F.3d 821, 828 (7th Cir. 1997). *See also* Bd. of Educ. v. Comm'r of Educ., 690 N.E.2d 480 (N.Y. 1997).
55. Dodd v. Rambis, 535 F. Supp. 23 (S.D. Ind. 1981). *See also* Walker-Serrano v. Leonard, 168 F. Supp. 2d 332 (M.D. Penn. 2001).
56. Chandler v. McNinnville Sch. Dist., 978 F.2d 524 (9th Cir. 1992).

ment challenges, whereas "hate speech" policies have been struck down in municipalities and public higher education.[58] Public schools have been considered a special environment in terms of government restrictions on private expression, because of their purpose in educating America's youth and inculcating basic values, such as civility and respect for others with different backgrounds and beliefs.

To illustrate, the Tenth Circuit upheld disciplinary action against a Kansas middle-school student for drawing a Confederate flag during math class in violation of the school district's antiharassment policy.[59] The student had been disciplined numerous times during the school year and had been accused of using racial slurs. The court was persuaded that the school district had reason to believe that the display of the Confederate flag might cause a disruption and interfere with the rights of others, as the school district had experienced some racial incidents related to the Confederate flag. In another case involving an incident with a Confederate flag, the Eleventh Circuit applied a "flexible reasonableness standard," instead of the *Tinker* disruption standard, to assess student expression that intruded on the school's legitimate function of inculcating manners and habits of civility.[60] Holding that school authorities were not liable for disciplining a student who displayed a small Confederate flag to a group of friends during an outdoor lunch break, the court observed: "Racist and other hateful views can be expressed in a public forum. But an elementary school under its custodial responsibilities may restrict such speech that could crush a child's sense of self-worth."[61]

However, the Third Circuit in 2001 struck down a Pennsylvania school district's anti-harassment policy.[62] The controversy arose because the plaintiffs feared reprisals under the policy for voicing their religious views about moral issues, including the harmful effects of homosexuality. The policy defined the term *harassment,* provided specific examples of what would be considered unacceptable behavior (e.g., demeaning comments, graffiti, gestures), and set forth punishments for any member of the school community who violated the policy. Holding that the policy was unconstitutionally overbroad, the Third Circuit found no evidence that the policy was necessary to advance the government's compelling interests in maintaining an orderly, nondisruptive school environment and protecting the rights of others. The court concluded that the overbroad policy went beyond expression that could be curtailed under the *Tinker* disruption standard.

57. *See, e.g.,* Fister v. Minn. New Country Sch., 149 F.3d 1187 (8th Cir. 1998) (upholding a policy specifying that fighting, threatening language, other endangerment, or harassment would be grounds for suspension or expulsion).
58. *See, e.g.,* R.A.V. v. St. Paul, 505 U.S. 377 (1992) (invalidating a St. Paul ordinance barring expression that could arouse anger or resentment on the basis of race, color, creed, religion, or gender); Dambrot v. Cent. Mich. Univ., 55 F.3d 1177 (6th Cir. 1995) (striking down the university's policy prohibiting harassing speech as overbroad and vague, but holding that the coach's use of the term "nigger" during locker room talk was not protected by the First Amendment).
59. West v. Derby Unified Sch. Dist., 206 F.3d 1358 (10th Cir. 2000).
60. Denno v. Sch. Bd., 218 F.3d 1267, 1272 (11th Cir. 2000).
61. *Id.* at 1273.
62. Saxe v. State Coll. Area Sch. Dist., 240 F.3d 200 (3d Cir. 2001). Since the policy was found to be overbroad, the court did not have to evaluate whether it was unconstitutionally vague. *Id.* at 214.

The same court in 2002 upheld a district's antiharassment policy that was enacted to respond to incidents of race-based conflicts and narrowly designed to reduce racially divisive expression. Yet, the court ordered elimination of the phrase banning speech that "creates ill will or hatred," as it would allow some protected expression to be curtailed.[63] The Third Circuit rulings have highlighted the tension between the school's duty to instill civil behavior and students' rights to express their opinions at school. **Questions remain regarding the legality of school districts' antiharassment policies, especially those adopted in the absence of disruptive incidents.**

Electronic Expression. Another topic generating volatile controversies pertains to students' expression rights involving the Internet. These cases are particularly troublesome because students often prepare and disseminate the materials from their homes, but their expression is immediately available to the entire school population and beyond. Courts have not spoken with a single voice on the First Amendment issues raised in these cases.

Students have prevailed in several instances when they were disciplined for web pages they created at home. For example, a high school senior developed a web site where he posted mock obituaries of students and allowed visitors to the site to vote as to who would "die" next.[64] After a television news story called it a "hit list" of people who would be killed at the school, the student removed the web site. The next day, the student was placed on emergency expulsion, which was modified to a five-day suspension. The student challenged the disciplinary action, and the federal district court granted a preliminary injunction to halt the suspension, reasoning that the student was likely to succeed on the merits of his claim. The court noted that the student's web site was not produced in connection with any class or school activity, and school personnel failed to substantiate that the material threatened or intended harm to anyone. Another student received a preliminary injunction blocking his suspension for using his home computer to create a home page criticizing school administrators, given the lack of evidence of any interference with school discipline.[65] And a Pennsylvania federal district court invalidated the suspension of a student for sending an e-mail message to friends that included a discourteous and rude "top 10 list" about the school's athletic director.[66] The student did not print the list or bring copies to school, although a friend who received his e-mail message did so.

In contrast, the Fifth Circuit upheld a student's conviction for his Internet communication threatening to shoot and kill students at his high school. Finding that only general intent was required to constitute a threat in violation of federal law, the court upheld the student's conviction of knowingly and intentionally transmitting in interstate commerce a threat to injure another.[67] Also, the Pennsylvania Supreme Court upheld a student's expul-

63. Sypniewski v. Warren Hills Reg'l Bd. of Educ., 307 F.3d 243 (3d Cir. 2002). *See infra* text accompanying note 96.

64. Emmett v. Kent Sch. Dist. No. 415, 92 F. Supp. 2d 1088 (W.D. Wa. 2000).

65. Beussink v. Woodland R-IV Sch. Dist., 30 F. Supp. 2d 1175 (E.D. Mo. 1998).

66. Killion v. Franklin Reg'l Sch. Dist., 136 F. Supp. 2d 446 (W.D. Pa. 2001).

67. United States v. Morales, 272 F.3d 284 (5th Cir. 2001), *cert. denied,* 536 U.S. 941 (2002), interpreting 18 U.S.C. § 875(c) (2003).

sion because he created a web site ("Teacher Sux") on his home computer that contained derogatory comments about teachers and administrators and a graphic depiction of the algebra teacher's death. In this case, the court reasoned that the off-campus activities substantially disrupted the school, noting that the algebra teacher was so upset by the material that she had to take a leave of absence.[68] **The key determinant in these cases appears to be whether the material created off campus has a direct and detrimental impact on the school.**

Time, Place, and Manner Regulations. Although private expression enjoys greater constitutional protection than does school-sponsored expression, the judiciary consistently has upheld reasonable policies regulating the time, place, and manner of private expression. For example, students can be prohibited from voicing political and ideological views and distributing literature during instructional time. Also, to ensure that the distribution of student publications does not impinge on other school activities, distribution can be barred near the doors of classrooms while class is in session, near building exits during fire drills, and on stairways when classes are changing.

Time, place, and manner regulations, however, must be reasonable, content neutral, and uniformly applied to expressive activities. School officials must provide students with specific guidelines as to when and where they can express their ideas and distribute materials. Moreover, literature distribution cannot be relegated to remote times or places either inside or outside the school building, and regulations must not inhibit any person's right to accept or reject literature that is distributed in accordance with the rules. Policies governing demonstrations should convey to students that they have the right to gather, distribute petitions, and express their ideas under nondisruptive circumstances.[69] If regulations do not precisely inform demonstrators of what behavior is prohibited, the judiciary may conclude that punishment cannot be imposed.

Student-Initiated Clubs

> Public schools can deny access to all noncurriculum student clubs but cannot discriminate against specific groups based on the content of their meetings.

Association and related free expression rights have arisen in connection with the formation and recognition of student clubs. Freedom of association is not specifically included among First Amendment protections, but the Supreme Court has held that associational rights are "implicit in the freedoms of speech, assembly, and petition."[70] The term *association* refers

68. J.S. v. Bethlehem Area Sch. Dist., 807 A.2d 847 (Pa. 2002).
69. *See, e.g.,* Orin v. Barclay, 272 F.3d 1207 (9th Cir. 2001).
70. Healy v. James, 408 U.S. 169, 181 (1972).

to the medium through which individuals seek to join with others to make the expression of their own views more meaningful.[71]

Public school pupils have not prevailed in asserting that free expression and association rights protect student-initiated social organizations or secret societies that determine their exclusive membership by a vote of the clubs' members. Courts have upheld public school officials in denying recognition of and prohibiting student membership in such secret societies.[72]

In contrast, prohibitions on student-initiated organizations with *open* membership are vulnerable to First Amendment challenge. Even before Congress enacted the Equal Access Act (EAA), courts recognized that public school access policies for student meetings must be content neutral.[73] **The EAA, enacted in 1984, codified these rulings by stipulating that if federally assisted secondary schools provide a limited open forum for noncurricular student groups to meet during noninstructional time, access cannot be denied based on the religious, political, philosophical, or other content of the groups' meetings.**[74] The EAA was championed by the Religious Right, but its protection encompasses far more than student-initiated religious expression.

As discussed in Chapter 3, the Supreme Court in 1990 rejected an Establishment Clause challenge to the EAA in *Board of Education of the Westside Community Schools v. Mergens.*[75] The Court reasoned that religious expression initiated by students during noninstructional time does not give the impression that the school endorses religion. The Court further held that if a federally assisted high school allows even one noncurricular group to use school facilities during noninstructional time, such as a chess club or scuba-diving club, the EAA guarantees equal access for other noncurricular student groups. Of course, meetings that threaten a disruption can be barred.

Moreover, school authorities can decline to establish a limited forum for student-initiated meetings and thus confine school access to student organizations that are an extension of the curriculum, such as drama groups, language clubs, and athletic teams. Controversies have surfaced over what constitutes a curriculum-related group since the EAA is triggered only if noncurriculum student groups are allowed school access during noninstructional time. For example, a California federal district court ruled that a school board had established a limited forum by allowing some noncurriculum student groups (e.g., Mountain Bike Club, Eighties Club) to meet during noninstructional time and thus could not discriminate against the Gay/Straight Alliance. The board raised a novel argument, claiming that the Alliance was not protected under the EAA because it was related to the sex education curriculum, which is governed by district instructional guidelines. Rejecting this argument, the

71. *See* Griswold v. Connecticut, 381 U.S. 479, 483 (1965).

72. *See, e.g.,* Passel v. Fort Worth Indep. Sch. Dist., 453 S.W.2d 888 (Tex. Civ. App. 1970).

73. *See, e.g.,* Dixon v. Beresh, 361 F. Supp. 253 (E.D. Mich. 1973).

74. 20 U.S.C. § 4071 (2003). *See* text accompanying note 50 and Figure 3.2, Chapter 3.

75. 96 U.S. 226 (1990). The Court rejected the contention that only noncurricular, *advocacy* groups are protected under the EAA. *See also* Student Coalition for Peace v. Lower Merion Sch. Dist., 776 F.2d 431 (3d Cir. 1985), *on remand,* 633 F. Supp. 1040 (E.D. Pa. 1986) (finding that the Student Coalition for Peace had to be granted access to the school's limited forum during noninstructional time to hold its peace exposition; also recognizing students' private right to initiate suits to compel EAA compliance).

court held that the board cannot foreclose access to its limited forum "merely by labeling a group curriculum-related."[76]

Even if agreed that a secondary school has *not* established a limited forum, it still cannot exert viewpoint discrimination against particular curriculum-related groups. After the Salt Lake City schools eliminated any forum for noncurriculum student groups to meet, a federal district court held that there were genuine issues regarding whether the school board had an unwritten policy excluding all gay-positive viewpoints from curriculum-related student club meetings.[77] The court subsequently enjoined school authorities from denying access to a student club designed to address issues related to the school's history and sociology courses, even though the club's major focus was on the rights of gay, lesbian, bisexual, and transgendered persons.[78]

Controversies over school access for community groups focus on the Free Speech Clause since the EAA pertains only to student groups in secondary schools. If schools create a limited forum for community groups to meet, they cannot deny access because of the content of the meetings, even if the groups, such as Good News Clubs, target students attending the school.[79] School access for the Boy Scouts has been controversial following the Supreme Court's decision that allows this organization to deny homosexuals the opportunity to be group leaders,[80] which conflicts with some school districts' antidiscrimination policies. A Florida federal district court struck down a school board's prohibition on the Boy Scouts using school facilities since other groups were allowed school access.[81] The court reasoned that the school's antidiscrimination policy applied to members of the school community and not to private organizations using the school during a limited forum for expression after school hours. The scope of constitutional and statutory protections afforded to student and community groups seeking school access seems likely to remain contentious.

Student Appearance

> Restrictions can be placed on student grooming and attire if based on legitimate educational and safety objectives and not intended to suppress expression.

Fads and fashions in hairstyles and clothing have regularly evoked litigation as educators have attempted to exert some control over pupil appearance. Courts have been called on to

76. Colin v. Orange Unified Sch. Dist., 83 F. Supp. 2d 1135, 1146 (C.D. Cal. 2000).
77. E. High Gay/Straight Alliance v. Bd. of Educ., 81 F. Supp. 2d 1166 (D. Utah 1999).
78. E. High Sch. Prism Club v. Seidel, 95 F. Supp. 2d 1239 (D. Utah 2000).
79. *See, e.g.,* Good News Club v. Milford Cent. Sch., 533 U.S. 98 (2001); Lamb's Chapel v. Ctr. Moriches Union Free Sch. Dist., 508 U.S. 384 (1993); text accompanying note 58, Chapter 3.
80. Boy Scouts of Am. v. Dale, 530 U.S. 640 (2000).
81. Boy Scouts of Am. v. Till, 136 F. Supp. 2d 1295 (S.D. Fla. 2001). *See supra* text accompanying note 57 for a discussion of controversies over school districts' antiharassment policies.

weigh students' interests in selecting their attire and hairstyle against school authorities' interests in preventing disruptions and promoting school objectives.

Hairstyle

Substantial judicial activity in the 1970s focused on school regulations governing the length of male students' hair. The Supreme Court, however, refused to review these cases, and federal circuit courts of appeal reached different conclusions in determining the legality of policies governing student hairstyle.[82] If school officials have offered health or safety reasons for grooming regulations, such as requiring hair nets, shower caps, and other hair restraints intended to protect students from injury or to promote sanitation, the policies typically have been upheld. Furthermore, restrictions on male students' hairstyles at vocational schools have been upheld to create a positive image for potential employers visiting the school for recruitment purposes. Special grooming regulations have been endorsed as conditions of participation in extracurricular activities for legitimate health or safety reasons, and in some instances, to enhance the school's image.[83] Of course, students can be disciplined for hairstyles that cause a disruption, such as hair groomed or dyed in a manner that distracts classmates from educational activities.

But hairstyle regulations cannot be arbitrary or devoid of an educational rationale. For example, the Fifth Circuit affirmed a lower court's ruling that enjoined a school district's restriction on male students' hair length because school officials failed to show that the restriction was a valid means to maintain discipline, foster respect for authority, or project an appropriate public image.[84] The court concluded that long hair worn by Native American students was protected expression that did not disrupt the educational process. Whether different hair-length restrictions can be applied to male and female students has not been judicially clarified.[85]

Attire

Although public school students' hair length has subsided as a major subject of litigation, other appearance fads have become controversial as students have asserted a First Amendment right to express themselves through their attire at school. Some courts have distinguished attire restrictions from hair regulations because clothes, unlike hair length, can be changed after school. Even in situations where students' rights to govern their appearance have been recognized, the judiciary has noted that attire can be regulated if immodest, disruptive, unsanitary, or contrary to the school's objectives.

82. For a discussion of these cases, *see* Nelda Cambron-McCabe, Martha McCarthy, and Stephen Thomas, *Public School Law: Teachers' and Students' Rights,* 5th ed. (Boston: Allyn and Bacon, 2004), Chapter 4.

83. *See, e.g.,* Davenport v. Randolph County Bd. of Educ., 730 F.2d 1395 (11th Cir. 1984); Menora v. Ill. High Sch. Ass'n, 683 F.2d 1030 (7th Cir. 1982).

84. Ala. and Coushatta Tribes v. Trs., 817 F. Supp. 1319 (E.D. Tex. 1993), *remanded,* 20 F.3d 469 (5th Cir. 1994).

85. For a discussion of these cases, see Cambron-McCabe et al., *Public School Law,* Chapter 4.

Dress Codes. Under the principle established in *Fraser,* lewd and vulgar expression is outside the protective arm of the First Amendment. Thus, **indecent attire can be curtailed applying *Fraser,* regardless of whether the attire would meet the *Tinker* test of threatening a disruption.** For example, an Idaho federal district court held that a school could prevent a student from wearing a t-shirt that depicted three high school administrators drunk on school grounds.[86] Finding the shirt intolerable, the court noted that the student had no free expression right to portray administrators in a fashion that would undermine their authority and compromise the school's efforts to educate students about the harmful effects of alcohol.

A Virginia middle school student was unsuccessful in challenging her one-day suspension for refusing to change her shirt printed with the words "Drugs Suck." The court reasoned that regardless of whether *suck* has a sexual meaning, its use is offensive and vulgar to many people, including some middle school students. Citing *Fraser,* the court found the disciplinary action permissible "to regulate middle school children's language and channel their expression into socially appropriate speech."[87] More recently, a Georgia federal district court upheld the suspension of a student who wore a t-shirt with the phrases "kids have civil rights too" and "even adults lie."[88] The court ruled that wearing the shirt was the last incident in a series of disruptions justifying the student's suspension. Several courts also have upheld dress codes that prohibit male students from wearing earrings to inhibit gang influences and promote community values, rejecting the assertion that jewelry restrictions must be applied equally to male and female students.[89]

In a New Mexico case, the federal district court upheld a student's suspension for wearing "sagging" pants in violation of the school's dress code.[90] The student did not convince the court that his attire conveyed an African American cultural message. Instead, the court noted that "sagging" pants could as easily be associated with gang affiliation or gang "wannabes," or it simply could reflect a fashion trend among adolescents. Also, an Ohio federal court upheld the removal of two students from the high school prom for dressing in clothing of the opposite sex. The court reasoned that the school board's dress regulations were "reasonably related to the valid educational purposes of teaching community values and maintaining school discipline."[91]

More recently, the Sixth Circuit upheld a school district's decision to prohibit students from wearing Marilyn Manson t-shirts. The appeals court agreed with school authorities that the shirts were offensive, promoted destructive conduct, and were counter to the school's

86. Gano v. Sch. Dist. 411, 674 F. Supp. 796 (D. Idaho 1987).

87. Broussard v. Sch. Bd., 801 F. Supp. 1526, 1537 (E.D. Va. 1992) (rejecting also the student's due process claim, because sufficient notice was given that wearing inappropriate attire would result in suspension).

88. Smith v. Greene County Sch. Dist., 100 F. Supp. 2d 1354 (M.D. Ga. 2000).

89. *See, e.g.,* Olesen v. Bd. of Educ., 676 F. Supp. 820 (N.D. Ill. 1987); Jones v. W.T. Henning Elem. Sch., 721 So. 2d 530 (La. App. 1998); Barber v. Colo. Indep. Sch. Dist., 901 S.W.2d 447 (Tex. 1995).

90. Bivens *ex rel.* Green v. Albuquerque Pub. Schs., 899 F. Supp. 556 (D.N.M. 1995), *aff'd mem.,* 131 F.3d 151 (10th Cir. 1997).

91. Harper v. Edgewood Bd. of Educ., 655 F. Supp. 1353, 1355 (S.D. Ohio 1987).

efforts to denounce drugs and promote human dignity and democratic ideals.[92] The court reiterated that **a school can prohibit student expression that is inconsistent with its basic educational mission even though such speech might be protected by the First Amendment outside the school environment.**

The same court in 2001 upheld a restrictive student dress code devised by a Kentucky school-based council. The code limited the colors, materials, and type of clothing that could be worn, and barred logos, shorts, cargo pants, jeans, and other specific items. The council justified the restrictions based on evidence of gang symbols in the school and student conflicts over clothing. Finding no intent to suppress free speech, the Sixth Circuit affirmed the lower court's acceptance of the school's safety justifications for the dress code.[93] An Illinois court also upheld a restrictive dress code that confined student clothing to all black, all white, or a combination of the two, and prohibited logos, patches, imprinted words, and designs on clothing.[94] Noting the opportunity to opt out of the dress code for religious reasons, the court held that the restriction on student expression in the school's nonpublic forum is justified by pedagogical concerns that include maintaining an orderly environment and inculcating civility and traditional moral, social, and political norms.

However, as with hairstyle regulations, school authorities must have an educational rationale for attire restrictions, such as preventing class disruptions, curtailing gang behavior, and/or advancing educational objectives. For example, a Texas federal district court found overly broad a dress code prohibiting students from wearing gang-related apparel. Two students who wore rosaries outside their shirts were advised that they were in violation of the policy, and the court held that wearing rosaries was a well-recognized form of religious expression protected by the First Amendment. Since the term *gang related* was ambiguous and not defined, the policy also was held to be void for vagueness.[95] The Third Circuit similarly struck down a prohibition on wearing t-shirts with the comedian Jeff Foxworthy's "red-neck sayings," as not sufficiently linked to racial harassment or other disruptive activity.[96]

In addition, **dress codes must not discriminate on the content of students' messages or be discriminatorily enforced.** The Sixth Circuit ordered a school district to reconsider suspensions of two students who wore t-shirts with a country singer on the front and the Confederate flag on the back and who refused to turn the shirts inside out or to go home and change.[97] School authorities asserted that the shirts violated the school's dress code pro-

92. Boroff v. Van Wert City Bd. of Educ., 220 F.3d 465 (6th Cir. 2000), *cert. denied,* 532 U.S. 920 (2001).

93. Long v. Bd. of Educ., 121 F. Supp. 2d 621 (W.D. Ky. 2000), *aff'd mem.,* 21 Fed. Appx. 252 (6th Cir. 2001).

94. Vines v. Zion Sch. Dist., No. 01 C 7455, 2002 U.S. Dist. LEXIS 382 (N.D. Ill. Jan. 10, 2002).

95. Chalifoux v. New Caney Indep. Sch. Dist., 976 F. Supp. 659 (S.D. Tex. 1997).

96. Sypniewski v. Warren Hills Reg'l Bd. of Educ., 307 F.3d 243 (3d Cir. 2002); *supra* text accompanying note 63.

97. Castorina v. Madison County Sch. Bd., 246 F.3d 536 (6th Cir. 2001). *See also* Chambers v. Babbitt, 145 F. Supp. 2d 1068 (D. Minn. 2001) (granting a temporary order allowing a student to wear a sweatshirt bearing the message "straight pride" in the absence of any disruption). For a discussion of challenges to antiharassment policies, *see supra* text accompanying note 57.

hibiting clothing or emblems that contain slogans or words depicting alcohol or tobacco or have illegal, immoral, or racist implications. Finding evidence that the dress code had been selectively enforced, the court reasoned that any restriction on private expression cannot be enforced in a content-specific manner. Thus, the case was remanded to determine if the students' First Amendment rights had been violated.

Student Uniforms. Some student attire controversies since the 1990s have focused on school board policies specifying uniforms for students, and the line is not always clear between restrictive dress codes and student uniforms. Voluntary as well as mandatory student uniforms are gaining popularity in many urban school districts. Advocates assert that student uniforms eliminate gang-related attire, reduce violence and socioeconomic distinctions, and improve school climate by placing the emphasis on academics rather than fashion fads.

The Fifth Circuit has rejected challenges to uniform policies in Louisiana and Texas school districts. In both cases the court recognized that attire can communicate a message and thus may be entitled to First Amendment protection. Nonetheless, the appellate court reasoned that the student uniform policies were justified by substantial government interests unrelated to suppressing expression. In the Louisiana case, evidence was presented that test scores increased and disciplinary problems decreased after the uniform policy was adopted. The court rejected the parents' claim that the uniforms posed a financial burden, noting that the uniforms were inexpensive and a donation program was available for those who could not afford them.[98] In the Texas case, the school district required students to wear specified types and colors of shirts or blouses with blue or khaki pants, shorts, skirts, or jumpers.[99] Parents could apply for their children to be exempt from wearing the uniform based on philosophical or religious objections or medical necessity. **The court found only a minimal intrusion on students' rights and concluded that the uniform policy served the legitimate educational purposes of improving safety, decreasing socioeconomic tensions, increasing attendance, and reducing dropout rates.** The court rejected the parents' assertion that the policy violates their Fourteenth Amendment right to direct the upbringing of their children and found no impairment of the religion clauses as the policy includes a process to grant religious exemptions.

After the New York City school board adopted a citywide uniform policy for children in elementary schools, a father brought suit claiming that if his child took advantage of the opt-out provision, the child would "stick out," which would violate the child's rights.[100] But, the Second Circuit affirmed the federal district court's conclusion that the opt-out provision adequately addressed parents' rights to direct the upbringing of their children. Courts have not been persuaded that any rights are violated because a stigma is associated with exercising the First Amendment right to be exempt from certain requirements.

Although federal appellate courts have differed in their interpretations of constitutional protections regarding appearance regulations, school officials would be wise to

98. Canady v. Bossier Parish Sch. Bd., 240 F.3d 437 (5th Cir. 2001).

99. Littlefield v. Forney Indep. Sch. Dist., 268 F.3d 275 (5th Cir. 2001) (prohibiting clothing made of specific materials, certain types of shoes, and any clothing suggesting gang affiliation).

100. Lipsman v. N.Y. City Bd. of Educ., 13 Fed. Appx. 13 (2d Cir. 2000).

ensure that they have a legitimate educational justification for any grooming or dress code. **Policies designed to protect students' health and safety, reduce violence and discipline problems, and enhance learning usually will be endorsed.** Given the current student interest in tatoos, body piercing, and other fashion fads and school authorities' concerns about attire linked to gangs and violence, continued legal controversies over student appearance in public schools seem assured.

Conclusion

Courts will continue to be called on to balance students' rights to express views and receive information with educators' duty to maintain an appropriate educational environment. In the latter 1960s and early 1970s, the federal judiciary expanded constitutional protections afforded to students in noninstructional matters. Since the mid-1980s, however, courts have emphasized that school officials can restrict student conduct and expression in school-related activities for educational reasons. Concerns over student violence, coupled with restrictions imposed on expression in response to terrorism, have placed new strains on First Amendment freedoms in public schools. Tensions are exacerbated by students' ability to distribute materials to broad audiences through the Internet.

It appeared that the reach of *Tinker* was narrowing after the Supreme Court ruled that lewd and vulgar student speech and attire are not protected by the First Amendment and that public school authorities can censor school-sponsored expression. Nonetheless, courts still rely on the *Tinker* disruption standard in evaluating student expression rights in connection with underground publications, antiharassment policies, and postings on personal web pages. Moreover, students do not need to base claims solely on constitutional protections, as federal and state laws, most notably the Equal Access Act, also protect students' expression and association rights. Judicial criteria applied in weighing the significant competing interests of students and school authorities continue to be refined.

Points to Ponder

1. Students opposed to the United States' military involvement in the Middle East organized several activities to protest the government's policy. The students:
   a. Distributed flyers condemning the war to classmates at school,
   b. Posted flyers on school bulletin boards that announced an antiwar rally to be held after school,
   c. Led students in walking out of a school assembly to meet with protesting adults who were holding a rally across from the school, and
   d. Held a rally in front of the county courthouse after school.
   Can school authorities legally curtail any of these activities? Which activities implicate students' First Amendment rights?

2. Students developed a newspaper in their homes and distributed it at a local store. The articles were critical of school administrators and contained vulgar language. Can school authorities discipline the students for their expression? Would your conclusion be different if the paper were distributed over the Internet?

3. A high school allows a chess club to meet in a classroom after school. Three other student clubs have asked for similar privileges: the Gay/Straight Alliance, the Fellowship of Christian Athletes, and the Young Neo-Nazis. Must these groups be provided school access?

4. A school-based council has decided to adopt a policy requiring students to wear uniforms. What features should the policy include to survive a legal challenge?

6

Student Classifications

It might appear from a literal translation of *equality* that once a state establishes an educational system, all students must be treated in the same manner. Courts, however, have recognized that individuals are different and that equal treatment of unequals can have negative consequences. Accordingly, valid classification practices, designed to enhance the educational experiences of children by recognizing their unique needs, generally have been accepted as a legitimate prerogative of educators. Indeed, all schools classify students in some fashion, and state laws often specifically authorize or even require school boards to group students by academic levels, gender, age, and other distinguishing traits.

Although educators' authority to classify students has not been contested, the bases for certain classifications and the procedures used to make distinctions among students have been the focus of substantial litigation. To the extent that school classifications determine a student's access to educational resources, courts and legislatures have looked closely at the practices. Under no circumstances is it permissible for public schools to impose student classifications based on race. Under certain circumstances, however, other student classifications have been upheld. This chapter explores differential treatment of students based on race, native language, age, and gender. Classifications based on disability are discussed in Chapter 7.

Classifications Based on Race

> In regard to the racial segregation of children in public schools, the Supreme Court has declared that separate facilities are inherently unequal and has ordered local school districts and states to integrate with all deliberate speed.

The most prevalent reason for classifying students according to race has been to establish or perpetuate racially segregated schools. Widespread racial segregation in educational institutions existed by law in this country from the colonial period well into the twentieth century. Even after the adoption of the Fourteenth Amendment in 1868, most schools remained segregated either by state constitution or statute, local ordinance, district policy or practice, or court interpretation, but seldom were they equal. When such practices were challenged, courts generally mandated only that minority children be provided access to public education. They did not require equal access to integrated schools or to equal school facilities, the provision of equal curricular or extracurricular opportunities, instruction by equally trained professionals, or an equivalent school year.

Today, most former de jure segregated schools (i.e., those where the separation of the races was required by law or the result of other action by the state or its agents) are already, or are in the process of becoming, integrated. In some instances, costs have exceeded $200 million, and court supervision has lasted 20 to 30 years and more. No other area of school law has involved such volatile debate, obligated such a high percentage of a school district's budget, or resulted in greater political and social turmoil than desegregation.

Lawsuits challenging school segregation often claim a violation of the Fourteenth Amendment, which provides in pertinent part that no state shall "deny to any person within its jurisdiction the equal protection of the laws." **Because race qualifies as a suspect class, the state or local school district must demonstrate a compelling interest in its use of any facially discriminatory racial classifications and must show that its procedures are narrowly tailored if it uses race to advantage one student over another.** This rigorous standard is almost impossible to satisfy.

The Brown *Mandate*

Perhaps the most infamous case supporting the "separate but equal" concept was *Plessy v. Ferguson* in 1896, where the Supreme Court upheld racial segregation of passengers in railroad coaches as required by Louisiana law.[1] Three years following *Plessy,* the Supreme Court was asked to review its first school case dealing with the "equal" treatment of school children. In *Cumming v. Richmond County Board of Education* in 1899, the Court held that the temporary cessation of services at a high school reserved for minority children did not violate equal protection, even though services continued at the high school for Caucasian students.[2] Following *Plessy* and *Cumming,* the separate but equal standard thrived, notwithstanding challenges in both state and federal courts.[3] Individuals, groups, and organizations wishing to equalize educational opportunities or to integrate schools made little progress during the nineteenth and early twentieth centuries. Then, in the late 1930s and 1940s, courts began looking more closely at segregated educational programs. Four key higher education appeals reached the Supreme Court between 1938 and 1950. These cases included claims from minority students alleging that there were no separate but equal programs available

1. 163 U.S. 537 (1896).
2. 175 U.S. 528 (1899).
3. *See, e.g.,* Gong Lum v. Rice, 275 U.S. 78 (1927) (finding that a 9-year-old Chinese student was not entitled to attend the school reserved for Caucasian students and that she was properly assigned to the school for minorities; it was irrelevant that there was no school for her particular group as all nonmajority children could be grouped together).

(two cases),[4] that the separate program was inferior,[5] or that the education received within a previously all-Caucasian institution was unequal due to the student's segregation from the rest of the student body.[6] The plaintiffs in each case prevailed.

Given the success of the higher education plaintiffs, the time appeared ripe to attack the K–12 "separate but equal" standard directly. This occurred in 1954 when the Supreme Court combined cases from four states—Kansas, South Carolina, Virginia, and Delaware.[7] Minority children in each state sought the assistance of the courts under the Fourteenth Amendment to obtain admission to public schools on a nonsegregated basis. **In the landmark decision, collectively called *Brown v. Board of Education,* Chief Justice Warren, writing for a unanimous Court, declared that education is "perhaps the most important function of state and local governments."[8] The Court repudiated the separate but equal doctrine, stipulating that racially segregated public schools were "inherently unequal."[9]**

Because of the significant impact of this decision and the difficulty in fashioning an immediate remedy, the Supreme Court delayed an implementation decree for one year to consider alternative strategies to convert de jure segregated dual school districts into integrated unitary districts. **Then, in 1955, in *Brown II,* the Court concluded that the conversion from dual to unitary must occur "with all deliberate speed,"[10]** although it gave little guidance as to what specific time frame was required or to what extent integration was mandated. As a result, states varied widely in their efforts to comply.

De Jure Segregation in the South

Despite the *Brown* mandate to end segregation, during the next decade the Supreme Court was forced to react to a number of blatant violations, such as state officials' efforts to physically block the desegregation of schools in Little Rock,[11] and an attempt to avoid integration by closing public schools in one Virginia county, while maintaining public schools in other counties in the state.[12] Even where violations were found, however, many courts hesitated to require anything more than the removal of barriers to integration, given the dearth of guidance regarding compliance.[13]

4. Missouri *ex rel.* Gaines v. Canada, 305 U.S. 337 (1938); Sipuel v. Bd. of Regents, 332 U.S. 631 (1948) (per curiam).
5. Sweatt v. Painter, 339 U.S. 629 (1950).
6. McLaurin v. Okla. State Regents for Higher Educ., 339 U.S. 637 (1950).
7. Brown v. Bd. of Educ., 98 F. Supp. 797 (D. Kan. 1951); Briggs v. Elliott, 98 F. Supp. 529 (E.D.S.C. 1951), *vacated and remanded,* 342 U.S. 350 (1952), *on remand,* 103 F. Supp. 920 (E.D.S.C. 1952); Davis v. County Sch. Bd., 103 F. Supp. 337 (E.D. Va. 1952); Gebhart v. Belton, 87 A.2d 862, *aff'd,* 91 A.2d 137 (Del. 1952).
8. Brown v. Bd. of Educ. (Brown I), 347 U.S. 483, 493 (1954).
9. *Id.* at 495.
10. Brown v. Bd. of Educ. (Brown II), 349 U.S. 294, 301 (1955).
11. Cooper v. Aaron, 358 U.S. 1 (1958).
12. Griffin v. County Sch. Bd., 377 U.S. 218 (1964).
13. *See, e.g.,* Briggs v. Elliott, 132 F. Supp. 776, 777 (E.D.S.C. 1955) (declaring that the Constitution "does not require integration" but "merely forbids discrimination").

Then, in a trilogy of cases in 1968, the Supreme Court announced that school officials in systems that were segregated by law in 1954 had an affirmative duty to take whatever steps were necessary to convert to unitary school systems and to eliminate the effects of past discrimination.[14] Furthermore, the Court declared that desegregation remedies would be evaluated based on their effectiveness in dismantling dual school systems. Thus, the notion of state neutrality was transformed into a requirement of affirmative state action to desegregate; the mere removal of barriers to school integration was not sufficient.

In one of these 1968 cases, *Green v. County School Board,* the Court reviewed a freedom-of-choice plan adopted by a small district in Virginia. The district historically operated only two schools, both kindergarten through twelfth grade: one for African Americans, the other for Caucasians. To eliminate race-based assignments within the district, the local board implemented a plan to allow children to attend the school of their choice. During the three-year period immediately following implementation, no Caucasian children enrolled in the historically African American school, and only a few African American children enrolled in the historically Caucasian school. The district contended that any resulting segregation was due to the choices of individuals, not to government action, and was therefore permissible; but the Supreme Court disagreed. The problem with this plan was simply that it was not achieving school integration. As a result, the district was ordered to come forward with a new plan that promised "realistically to work and to work now."[15] In addition, **the Court ruled that school authorities must eliminate the racial identification of schools in terms of the composition of the student body, faculty, and staff; transportation; extracurricular activities; and facilities**. These six elements still are used today and are referred to in the aggregate as the *Green criteria.*

In 1971, additional direction was provided when the Supreme Court ruled in *Swann v. Charlotte-Mecklenburg Board of Education* that the elimination of invidious racial distinctions may be sufficient in connection with transportation, support personnel, and extracurricular activities, but that more was necessary in terms of constructing facilities and making faculty and student assignments.[16] The Court endorsed the practice of assigning teachers on the basis of race until faculties were integrated and declared that new schools must be located so that the dual school system would not be perpetuated or reestablished.

Correcting racial imbalance among student populations, however, was more difficult. For the vestiges of segregation to be eliminated, the school district had to achieve racial balance in a sufficient number of schools. Every school, however, did not have to reflect the racial composition of the school district as a whole. The continued presence of a small number of predominantly one-race schools did not necessarily mean that the district continued to practice state-imposed segregation. But, the burden of proof was placed on school officials to establish that such schools were not the result of present or past discriminatory action. To achieve the desired racial balance, the Court suggested pairing or consolidating schools, altering attendance zones, and using racial quotas, but rejected the practice of assigning students to the schools nearest their homes if it failed to eliminate de jure segre-

14. Green v. County Sch. Bd., 391 U.S. 430 (1968); Raney v. Bd. of Educ., 391 U.S. 443 (1968); Monroe v. Bd. of Comm'rs, 391 U.S. 450 (1968).
15. *Green,* 391 U.S. at 439.
16. 402 U.S. 1 (1971).

gation. The Court also endorsed the use of reasonable busing as a means to integrate schools, yet qualified that endorsement by noting that the soundness of any transportation plan must be evaluated based on the time involved, distance traveled, and age of students.

By applying the criteria established in *Green* and *Swann,* substantial desegregation was attained in southern states during the 1970s. Where unconstitutional segregation was found, federal courts exercised broad power in ordering remedies affecting student and staff assignments, curriculum, school construction, personnel practices, and budgetary allocations. Judicial activity was augmented by threats from the former Department of Health, Education, and Welfare to terminate federal funds to school districts not complying with Title VI of the Civil Rights Act of 1964.[17] Title VI, like the Fourteenth Amendment, requires the integration only of de jure segregated school districts.

Distinguishing De Jure from De Facto Segregation

Since the Supreme Court carefully limited its early decisions to states and school districts with a long history of school segregation by official policy, questions remained regarding what type of evidence—other than explicit legislation requiring school segregation—was necessary to establish unconstitutional de jure segregation. That is, **what factors would distinguish de jure segregation (e.g., intentional acts of the school board in the selection of a new school location) from permissible de facto segregation (e.g., community segregation caused by the choices of families in the selection and location of homes)**? The answer to this question began to evolve in *Keyes v. School District No. 1, Denver* when the Supreme Court in 1973 held that if "no statutory dual system has ever existed, plaintiffs must prove not only that segregated schooling exists but also that it was brought about or maintained by intentional state action."[18] Some federal courts have assumed that a presumption of unlawful purpose can be established if the natural, probable, and foreseeable result of public officials' acts perpetuate segregated conditions,[19] whereas others have required evidence that policymakers actually harbored a desire to segregate.[20]

Although courts vary in the processes they use to determine whether school districts are guilty of discriminatory intent, they often consider:

- The impact of the disputed governmental act,
- The history of discriminatory official action,
- Procedural and substantive departures from norms generally followed, and
- Discriminatory statements made publicly or in legislative or administrative sessions.

If discriminatory intent is proven, courts then are responsible for fashioning appropriate remedies, but, when allegations of discriminatory intent are not supported, no action on the part of the district is required.[21] Moreover, **school districts that either have no history of**

17. 42 U.S.C. §§ 2000d-2000d-7 (2003).
18. 413 U.S. 189, 198 (1973).
19. *See, e.g.,* Arthur v. Nyquist, 573 F.2d 134 (2d Cir. 1978).
20. *See, e.g.,* Vill. of Arlington Heights v. Metro. Hous. Dev. Corp., 429 U.S. 252 (1977).
21. *See, e.g.,* Price v. Austin Indep. Sch. Dist., 945 F.2d 1307 (5th Cir. 1991).

unlawful segregation or have become unitary while under court supervision, will not be responsible for correcting any future racial imbalance they have not created.[22]

Fashioning Appropriate Remedies

Because each desegregation case involves a combination of unique circumstances and violations, it is not surprising that each remedy also is unique and at times requires:

- Rezoning and redistricting;[23]
- Providing thematic magnet schools;[24]
- Developing new curricular offerings;[25]
- Providing specialized learning centers; [26]
- Closing, reopening, renovation, or construction of schools;
- Busing students;[27] and
- Hiring, transferring, or retraining current staff.[28]

Basically, courts can require nearly anything of districts and states that would result in fulfillment of the primary objective—the integration of public schools. "All deliberate speed" in many instances took decades, and cost often seemed irrelevant.

One approach to achieving integration that has been closely scrutinized by courts is the use of interdistrict remedies. Many city school districts have experienced both real and percentage increases in minority populations due to a variety of reasons, including "white flight" and "zone jumping."[29] Integration in these areas then becomes problematic, given the presence of primarily one race. As a result, several courts have reasoned that if racial integration in a predominantly one-race district is to be achieved, adjacent districts must be involved in student transfer and busing provisions. The Supreme Court has not accepted this approach, however, and has concluded that each district involved in a desegregation remedy must have been involved in purposeful discrimination and has reasoned that a remedy must not be broader in scope than warranted by the constitutional violation.[30] Furthermore, the Court has articulated a three-part framework to guide district courts in the exercise of their authority. This framework requires that the nature and scope of the desegregation remedy:

22. *See, e.g.,* Pasadena City Bd. of Educ. v. Spangler, 427 U.S. 424 (1976).
23. *See, e.g.,* Newburg Area Council v. Bd. of Educ., 510 F.2d 1358 (6th Cir. 1974).
24. *See, e.g.,* Bradley v. Pinellas County Sch. Bd., 165 F.R.D. 676 (M.D. Fla. 1994).
25. *See, e.g.,* Keyes v. Sch. Dist. No. 1, 895 F.2d 659 (10th Cir. 1990).
26. *See, e.g.,* Tasby v. Black Coalition to Maximize Educ., 771 F.2d 849 (5th Cir. 1985).
27. *See, e.g.,* N.C. State Bd. of Educ. v. Swann, 402 U.S. 43 (1971).
28. *See, e.g.,* Swann v. Charlotte-Mecklenburg Bd. of Educ., 402 U.S. 1, 19 (1971). *See also* Lee v. Lee County Bd. of Educ., No. 70-T-845-E, 2002 U.S. Dist. LEXIS 10277 (M.D. Ala., May 29, 2002) (declaring the district unitary except for faculty assignments in two schools).
29. *See, e.g.,* Elston v. Talladega County Bd. of Educ., 997 F.2d 1394 (11th Cir. 1993). Zone jumping is transferring from the assigned attendance zone to an adjacent zone.
30. Milliken v. Bradley, 418 U.S. 717 (1974) (Milliken I).

- Be determined by the nature and scope of the constitutional violation,
- Be remedial so as to restore the victims of discriminatory conduct to the position they would have occupied in the absence of such conduct, and
- Take into account the interests of state and local authorities in managing their own affairs.[31]

Accordingly, an interdistrict remedy can include only those districts that were involved in de jure segregation; courts are not authorized to include districts that were not segregated or were segregated only due to de facto circumstances.

In a 1995 decision involving interdistrict remedies, *Missouri v. Jenkins,* the Supreme Court evaluated Kansas City's 18-year history of desegregation orders. Over this period, the district court ordered approximately $1.5 billion in program improvements, comprehensive magnet schools, transportation, extensive capital improvements, and salary assistance.[32] The Supreme Court noted that racial imbalance within a school district, without more, did not violate the Constitution and that the lower court's plan to attract nonresident nonminority students represented an interdistrict remedy and was therefore beyond the court's authority. The Supreme Court further admonished that the lower court should have determined whether the lower achievement of minority students was attributable to prior de jure segregation and, if so, whether it had been remedied to the extent practicable. Once this had been accomplished, the court then was required to return control of the schools to state and local school officials. Notwithstanding the limitations on courts to order interdistrict remedies, unitary districts have at times voluntarily entered into such agreements.

Achieving Unitary Status

Federal courts have found numerous school systems guilty of having engaged in de jure segregation and have fashioned a variety of remedies. Some orders continue to exist today, even though the original decisions may have been rendered in the 1950s, 1960s, or 1970s. Such lengthy supervision has usurped the traditional roles of trained and licensed school administrators, elected school boards, and state legislatures regarding funding, facilities, personnel, and curriculum. Furthermore, judicial oversight continued in many states when compliance seemingly had occurred. With key decisions in 1991 and 1992, however, the Supreme Court provided complying districts with a means to an end.

In *Board of Education v. Dowell,* the school district had been operating since 1972 under a court-ordered plan that entailed substantial student busing to achieve integration. Five years after the initial decision, the federal district court ruled that the board had complied with the order in good faith and was entitled to pursue its legitimate policies without further court supervision. At that time, judicial monitoring was removed, but the 1972 decree was not dissolved. However, the appeals court reasoned that the district's circum-

31. Milliken v. Bradley, 433 U.S. 267, 280-281 (1977) (Milliken II).

32. 515 U.S. 70 (1995).

stances had not changed enough to justify modifying the 1972 decree.[33] The court concluded that compliance alone could not be the basis for dissolving an injunction and observed that the school board failed to meet its burden of proof.

On appeal, the Supreme Court held that the appellate court's standard for dissolving the original decree was too stringent and emphasized that federal supervision of local school systems was intended only as a temporary measure to remedy past discrimination. The Court reasoned that the intent of a desegregation plan is met upon finding—as the district court had done—that the school system was operating in compliance with the Equal Protection Clause and was not likely to return to its former ways. Furthermore, the Court concluded that **the federal judiciary should terminate supervision of school districts where school boards have complied with desegregation mandates in good faith and have eliminated vestiges of past discrimination "to the extent practicable."**[34] In making this determination, the district court on remand was directed to assess the six factors identified 23 years earlier in *Green.*[35] The lower court also was instructed to reconsider whether current residential segregation in Oklahoma City was the result of private decision making and economics or a vestige of prior school segregation.

Although the *Dowell* decision gave districts the means to eventually end judicial supervision, many have had difficulty proving that they were unitary.[36] In 1992, the Supreme Court clarified several related issues in a Georgia case, *Freeman v. Pitts.* The Court held that a district court must relinquish its supervision and control over those aspects of a school system in which there has been compliance with a desegregation decree even if other aspects of the decree have not been met. Through this approach, the Court sought to restore to state and local authorities control over public schools at the earliest possible date and noted that "**partial relinquishment of judicial control . . . can be an important and significant step in fulfilling the district court's duty to return the operations and control of schools to local authorities.**"[37] To guide the lower courts in determining whether supervision should be removed, the Court identified three questions:

- Has there been full and satisfactory compliance with the decree in those aspects of the system where supervision is to be withdrawn?
- Is the retention of judicial control necessary or practicable to achieve compliance with the decree in other facets of the school system?
- Has the district demonstrated good faith commitment to the court's entire decree and relevant provisions of federal law?

33. 890 F.2d 1483 (10th Cir. 1989).

34. Bd. of Educ. v. Dowell, 498 U.S. 237, 249-250 (1991).

35. See *supra* text accompanying note 15.

36. *See, e.g.,* Lee v. Talladega County Bd. of Educ., 963 F.2d 1426 (11th Cir. 1992) (ending judicial supervision). *But see* Lee v. Etowah County Bd. of Educ., 963 F.2d 1416 (11th Cir. 1992) (continuing judicial supervision).

37. 503 U.S. 467, 489 (1992).

With this guidance, numerous districts have been able to show that they have achieved a unitary operation.[38]

Postunitary Transfer and School Assignment

Litigation will not necessarily end simply because the school district has achieved unitary status and has initially been relieved of judicial control and supervision. Any decision that may even potentially result in racial imbalance, whether de jure or de facto, is likely to be challenged.

Parents also have questioned presumably good faith district policies that were designed and administered to maintain racial balance or to achieve the goal of a diverse student body.[39] In such instances, students generally have been permitted to enroll in or transfer to schools where their race was a minority or otherwise underrepresented (e.g., a Caucasian student would be permitted to transfer from a predominantly Caucasian school to a predominantly African American school, but not vice versa). In a Fourth Circuit case, a Caucasian student was denied the right to transfer to a magnet school with an enriched curriculum. His transfer would have adversely affected the racial diversity of the district and was therefore denied. The transfer policy applied equally to all races and was administered uniformly, unless the student could demonstrate "unique hardship circumstances." The court noted that the practice was voluntary on the part of the district, rather than court ordered, and that the district had never been found guilty of segregation. In ruling for the student, the court observed that even if majority and nonmajority students were treated the same, they still were subjected to racial classification and discriminated against solely because of their race. Since race was used as the primary qualifying criterion, strict judicial scrutiny was applied. The court argued that even if it were to assume that diversity qualified as a compelling state interest (which it did not decide), the action of the board was not narrowly tailored to achieve that objective and was therefore unconstitutional.[40]

38. People Who Care v. Rockford Bd. of Educ., 246 F.3d 1073 (7th Cir. 2001); Manning v. Sch. Bd., 244 F.3d 927 (11th Cir. 2001), *cert. denied,* 534 U.S. 824 (2001); NAACP, Jacksonville Branch v. Duval County Sch., 273 F.3d 960 (11th Cir. 2001); Belk v. Charlotte-Mecklenburg Bd. of Educ., 269 F.3d 305 (4th Cir. 2001). Other judicial rulings, however, have not released school districts from judicial supervision. *See, e.g.,* Jenkins v. Missouri, 216 F.3d 720 (8th Cir. 2000); Liddell v. Special Sch. Louis County, 149 F.3d 862 (8th Cir. 1998).

39. *See, e.g.,* Parents Involved in Cmty. Schs. v. Seattle Sch. Dist. No. 1, 285 F.3d 1236 (9th Cir. 2002) (concluding that under state law race may not be used as a factor in determining school assignment in an open enrollment district); Tuttle v. Arlington County Sch. Bd., 195 F.3d 698 (4th Cir. 1999) (concluding that it was unconstitutional for a board to use a weighted lottery for admission to its schools that promotes racial and ethnic diversity; the goal was not to remedy past discrimination but to promote racial, ethnic, and socioeconomic diversity and was not narrowly tailored). *But see* Brewer v. W. Irondequoit Cent. Sch. Dist., 212 F.3d 738 (2d Cir. 2000) (denying a Caucasian student the right to transfer from a district where she was a minority to a district where she would be among the majority).

40. Eisenberg v. Montgomery County Pub. Schs., 197 F.3d 123 (4th Cir. 1999).

A similar ruling was provided by the First Circuit in a Boston case where the assignment of students to its three renowned "examination schools," including the prestigious Boston Latin School (BLS), was based in part on race.[41] Unlike the Fourth Circuit case, Boston had been found guilty of operating a dual school system.[42] At that time, the district court required that at least 35 percent of the enrollment at BLS be composed of African American and Hispanic students. In 1987, the district was declared unitary in regard to student assignment, but the consideration of race in admitting students to the "examination" schools continued to be used with the intent of providing racial balance and diversity. The court reasoned that although the district may have achieved balance in regard to some racial groups, it had failed to achieve the goal of diversity, as a far greater array of qualifications and characteristics needed to be considered.

Moreover, the efforts to address past discrimination at BLS were ineffectual in that the use of racial preference advantaged some individuals who were not previously or currently victims of discrimination (e.g., African American students who had previously attended private schools; Asian American students who were preferred over Caucasian students but were not considered part of the class that had been injured) to the disadvantage of others. Accordingly, the practice of admitting students in part based on race neither served a purported compelling interest nor was sufficiently narrowly tailored and was therefore unconstitutional.

In contrast, the Supreme Court in 2003 upheld the use of race in a university's admissions practices that were found to have met the compelling interest of obtaining the educational benefits derived from a diverse student body. Creating a critical mass of minority representation was viewed as essential in preparing all students for today's increasingly global marketplace. To achieve this goal, the Court encouraged the holistic review of each applicant and the use of race-neutral alternatives when feasible. Any "plus" given to underrepresented students was not to be without reasonable time limits or to unduly harm the educational opportunity of nonminority applicants. The Court will not, however, permit the assignment of additional admissions points to minority candidates or the use of quotas or different race-based standards.[43]

The next decade should continue to provide ample desegregation case law as districts continue to request to be relieved from judicial supervision. The stage appears set for a significant reduction in judicial control and a long-awaited return of school operations to school administrators, teachers, and boards.

41. Wessmann v. Gittens, 160 F.3d 790 (1st Cir. 1998).
42. Morgan v. Hennigan, 379 F. Supp. 410 (D. Mass. 1974).
43. Grutter v. Bollinger, No. 02-241, 2003 U.S. LEXIS 4800 (Sup. Ct. June 23, 2003); Gratz v. Bollinger, No. 02-516, 2003 U.S. LEXIS 4801 (Sup. Ct. June 23, 2003).

Classifications Based on Native Language

> School districts have the responsibility to remove English language barriers that impede equal participation of non-English-speaking students; educators may use bilingual education or other appropriate methods that prepare recipient children for classrooms where English is the prominent language of instruction.

Among the numerous identifiable "classes" of students in American schools are "linguistic minorities," some of whom have been denied an adequate education due to the failure of the school district to address their language barriers through appropriate instruction. Although programs that are designed to meet the educational needs of linguistic minorities are largely financed through state and local funds, the federal government provides modest funding for research regarding how students learn a second language, how to train instructors, and the effectiveness of alternative teaching methodologies and programs.[44] The Office of English Language Acquisition, Language Enhancement, and Academic Achievement for Limited English Proficient Students administers the grant programs, provides leadership and technical assistance, coordinates services, promotes best practices, and assesses outcomes. Through efforts such as these, many students today are provided with English language instruction that allows them to benefit from the public school curriculum.

However, when access to school is denied or when language barriers are not removed, students often turn to federal courts for protection. The rights of linguistic minorities are protected by the Fourteenth Amendment, Title VI of the Civil Rights Act of 1964, and the Equal Educational Opportunities Act of 1974 (EEOA).

Title VI stipulates that "no person in the United States shall, on the ground of race, color, or national origin, be excluded from participation in, be denied the benefits of, or be subjected to discrimination under any program or activity receiving federal financial assistance from the Department of Education."[45] Moreover, this statute requires compliance throughout a school district if *any* activity is supported by federal funds (e.g., the federal lunch program). Discrimination against linguistic minorities is considered a form of national origin discrimination and is therefore prohibited by Title VI.

In addition, the EEOA requires *public* school systems to develop appropriate programs for limited English proficient (LEP) students.[46] The act mandates in part that "no state shall deny equal educational opportunity to an individual on account of his or her race, color, sex, or national origin, by . . . the failure by an educational agency to take appropriate action to overcome language barriers that impede equal participation by its students in its instructional program."[47] The EEOA does not impose any specific type of instruction or teaching methodology on education agencies but rather requires "appropriate action."

44. 20 U.S.C. §§ 3420, 3423d, 6931, 6932 (2003).

45. 42 U.S.C. § 2000d *et seq.* (2003). Regulations may be found at 34 C.F.R. § 100 *et seq.* (2003).

46. 20 U.S.C. § 1701 *et seq.* (2003).

In the only United States Supreme Court decision involving the rights of LEP students, *Lau v. Nichols,* Chinese children asserted that the San Francisco public schools failed to provide for the needs of non-English-speaking students. The Supreme Court agreed with the students and held that the lack of sufficient remedial English instruction violated Title VI. The Court reasoned that equality of treatment was not realized merely by providing students with the same facilities, textbooks, teachers, and curriculum, and that requiring children to acquire English skills on their own before they could hope to make any progress in school made "a mockery of public education."[48] The Court emphasized that "basic English skills are at the very core of what these public schools teach," and therefore "students who do not understand English are effectively foreclosed from any meaningful education."[49]

As a rule, courts acknowledge that there are numerous legitimate educational theories and practices that may be used to eliminate language barriers and do not typically require one method (e.g., bilingual education) over another. In fact, they tend to order the use of bilingual education (often the method preferred by plaintiffs) only when less expensive and less cumbersome options have proven ineffective.[50] In making such determinations, courts will examine:

- The level of resources committed to the various programs,
- The competency and training of the instructors,
- The methods of classifying students for instruction, and
- The procedures for evaluating student progress.

A Colorado federal district court, in assessing compliance of the Denver Public Schools, concluded that the law does not require a full bilingual education program for every LEP student but does place a duty on the district to take action to eliminate barriers that prevent LEP children from participating in the educational program. According to the court, **good faith effort is inadequate; what is required is an effort that "will be reasonably effective in producing intended results."**[51] Such an effort was not found in the Denver public schools. Although district personnel selected a transitional bilingual program, it was not being implemented effectively, primarily due to poor teacher training, selection, and assignment. Accordingly, an EEOA violation was found. Likewise, the Seventh Circuit, in examining Illinois's compliance, reasoned that "appropriate action" under the law certainly means more than "no action."[52] Once again, the court found that the selection of transitional bilingual education was appropriate, but that it had not been effectively implemented. The court identified violations of both the EEOA and Title VI regulations.

In contrast, a California school district's Spanish bilingual program and three forms of English as a Second Language were judicially endorsed. District teachers were found to

47. 20 U.S.C. § 1703(f) (2003).

48. Lau v. Nichols, 414 U.S. 563, 566 (1974).

49. *Id.*

50. *See, e.g.,* Castaneda v. Pickard, 648 F.2d 989 (5th Cir. 1981).

51. Keyes v. Sch. Dist. No. 1, Denver, Colo., 576 F. Supp. 1503, 1520 (D. Colo. 1983).

52. Gomez v. Ill. State Bd. of Educ., 811 F.2d 1030, 1043 (7th Cir. 1987).

be proficient, qualified, and experienced; native-language academic support was available for 38 languages in all subjects; and a cultural enrichment program was operating for grades K–3. Plaintiffs claimed a violation of the EEOA and Title VI and requested instruction in the students' native tongue. The court disagreed and found that the program was based on sound theory, implemented consistent with that theory, and produced satisfactory results (i.e., area LEP students were learning at rates equal to or higher than their English-speaking counterparts.)[53]

In recent years, California has generated a significant amount of case law involving the instruction of non- and limited-English-speaking students. Most suits attack Proposition 227, which requires that all children within public schools be taught English through "sheltered English immersion" (SEI) (i.e., specially designed materials and procedures where "nearly all" classroom instruction is in English). In most instances, the law requires school districts to abandon their use of bilingual education. Notwithstanding the prior use of bilingual programming, immigrant children within the state had experienced a high dropout rate and were low in English literacy. Only those children who already possess good English language skills or those for whom an alternate course of study would be better suited may be excused from the SEI initiative. Even then, 20 or more exempted students per grade level are required before an alternative program such as bilingual education needs to be provided.

To ensure that the SEI approach is used, the state legislature included a parental enforcement provision in the law that gives parents the right to sue to receive SEI instruction, as well as for actual damages and attorneys' fees. Any educator who willfully and repeatedly refuses to teach "overwhelmingly" in English may be held personally liable. The state teachers' association attacked this provision as being unconstitutionally vague. But, the Ninth Circuit found terms such as *nearly all* and *overwhelmingly* to be no more vague than other descriptive terms used in the writing of statutes and reasoned that such language was likely to chill only a negligible amount of non-English speech, if any.[54]

For decades, educators have disagreed as to which method is best for instructing LEP students. **The "best," however, is not legally required. What is required is the elimination of language barriers that will allow LEP students the opportunity to participate in the programs and activities offered in public school.**

Classifications Based on Age

> Generally, age may be used in determining eligibility for school programs.

Age is one of the factors most commonly used to classify individuals, not only in schools but also in society (e.g., obtaining a driver's license, buying alcoholic beverages, viewing

53. Teresa P. v. Berkeley Unified Sch. Dist., 724 F. Supp. 698 (N.D. Cal. 1989).
54. Cal. Teachers Ass'n v. State Bd. of Educ., 271 F.3d 1141 (9th Cir. 2001).

certain movies). The two primary federal grounds used by students when they claim age-based violations are the Fourteenth Amendment and the Age Discrimination Act of 1975.[55] The Age Discrimination Act applies to recipients of federal financial assistance, but is seldom used today (e.g., in regard to early school admission or to eligibility for particular programs, activities, or athletic competition).

Ranges vary, but within most states students *must* attend school between the ages of 6 and 16 and *may* attend between ages 3 and 21. Students below or above state-established age limits do not have a state property right to public school attendance. Nevertheless, parents have challenged state and local decisions denying admission or services. In a Texas case, a policy was challenged that excluded children under the age of 6 as of September 1 of the current year from admission to the first grade.[56] The plaintiff had completed kindergarten in a private accredited school and had scored well on a standardized test, but was two months too young to qualify. The district had uniformly adhered to the state statute and local policy, refusing all requests for early admission. Noting this uniform application, the Texas appeals court upheld the school district's action. Similar decisions have been reached by other courts in denying students' admission to kindergarten and other programs. Rationales used to justify age limitations include:

- The state's right to limit the benefit of public education and related curricular and extracurricular opportunities to children between specific ages;
- The administrative need to project enrollment;
- The costs of assessing learning readiness and meeting a wide range of individual needs; and
- The desire for children to develop emotionally, socially, and physiologically prior to admission.

In addition to admissions decisions, age also is permissibly used as one of several criteria to determine eligibility for special courses or programs (e.g., college credit courses, gifted programs), selected activities (e.g., interscholastic sports[57]), or specialized services (e.g., those available under the Individuals with Disabilities Education Act). With few exceptions (e.g., when interscholastic sports participation has been written into an overage student's individualized educational program), it is unlikely that schools will be restricted in their uniform application of legitimate age requirements. Where exceptions are made, school personnel must document a permissible basis.

55. 42 U.S.C. §§ 6101 *et seq.* (2003).

56. Wright v. Ector County Indep. Sch. Dist., 867 S.W.2d 863 (Tex. Ct. App. 1993).

57. *See, e.g.,* Cruz v. Pa. Interscholastic Athletic Ass'n, 157 F. Supp. 2d 485 (E.D. Pa. 2001).

Classifications Based on Gender

> Students are protected against discrimination based on gender, including sexual harassment by educators or peers.

Gender classifications and discriminatory treatment based on gender in public education are as old as public education itself, as the first public schools and colleges primarily served males. When women were eventually allowed to enroll, programs were typically segregated and inferior. Over the years, gender equality in public schools has improved, but at times gender classifications have limited both academic as well as extracurricular activities for females.

Aggrieved parties often have turned to federal courts to vindicate their rights. In most cases, plaintiffs allege a violation of either the Fourteenth Amendment or Title IX of the Education Amendments of 1972.[58] Under Title IX, educational recipients of federal financial assistance are prohibited from discriminating against, excluding from participation, or denying benefits to individuals because of gender.

Interscholastic Sports

Gender discrimination litigation involving interscholastic sports has focused on two primary themes:

- The integration of single-gender teams; and
- The unequal treatment of males and females (e.g., the number of athletic opportunities available for males and females, the use of facilities, the selection of "seasons," and the development of different rules for competition).

Although courts will issue injunctions to correct discriminatory conduct where it is found, they will not award monetary damages unless the school had knowledge of the violation and then was deliberately indifferent to the claim.[59]

Single-Gender Teams. One of the more controversial issues involving high school athletics is the participation of males and females together in contact sports (e.g., boxing, wrestling, rugby, ice hockey, football, basketball, and other sports that involve bodily contact). Title IX allows recipients to:

> operate or sponsor separate teams for members of each sex where selection for such teams is based upon competitive skill or the activity involved is a contact sport. However, where a

58. 20 U.S.C. § 1681 (2003).
59. Grandson v. Univ. of Minn., 272 F.3d 568 (8th Cir. 2001), *cert. denied,* 535 U.S. 1054 (2002).

> recipient operates or sponsors a team in a particular sport for members of one sex but operates or sponsors no such team for members of the other sex, and athletic opportunities for members of that sex have previously been limited, members of the excluded sex must be allowed to try out for the team offered unless the sport involved is a contact sport.[60]

Accordingly, Title IX permits, but does not require, gender segregation in contact sports. Because Title IX does not explicitly proscribe female participation on contact teams, it has been interpreted to allow each school the flexibility of determining whether to meet the goal of equal athletic opportunity through single-gender or coeducational teams. However, in many instances athletic association rules have limited the options available to school districts by prohibiting coeducational competition.

The Sixth Circuit reviewed an Ohio High School Athletic Association rule that prohibited coeducational participation in all contact sports in grades 7 through 12.[61] In this case, the school system wanted to establish coeducational interscholastic basketball teams at the middle school level. The appeals court, noting that compliance with Title IX rests with individual schools and not with athletic associations, concluded that the rule impermissibly restricted the discretion of school systems to provide equal athletic opportunities for female students. The court emphasized, however, that its ruling did not mean that all teams must be coeducational or that Title IX's regulations were unconstitutional because they permitted separate teams.[62]

In a Fourteenth Amendment case, a federal district court in New York reviewed a female student's request to try out for the junior varsity football squad.[63] The school district was unable to show that its policy of prohibiting mixed competition served an important governmental objective. In rejecting the district's assertion that its policy was necessary to ensure the health and safety of female students, the court noted that no female student was given the opportunity to show that she was as fit, or more fit, than the weakest male member of the team.

A Wisconsin federal district court similarly ruled that female students have the right to compete for positions on traditionally male contact teams, declaring that once a state provides interscholastic competition, such opportunities must be provided to all students on equal terms.[64] The court reasoned that the objective of preventing injury to female athletes was not sufficient to justify the prohibition of coeducational teams in contact sports. In prohibiting the school district from denying female students the opportunity to participate in varsity interscholastic competition in certain contact sports, the court noted that school officials had options available other than establishing coeducational teams. For example, inter-

60. 34 C.F.R. § 106.41(b) (2003).

61. Yellow Springs Exempted Vill. Sch. Dist. Bd. of Educ. v. Ohio High Sch. Athletic Ass'n, 647 F.2d 651 (6th Cir. 1981).

62. It is unlikely that state athletic associations will be subjected to Title IX suits in the future as the Supreme Court has ruled that the receipt of dues from member institutions that are recipients of federal aid does not make the association an indirect recipient. NCAA v. Smith, 525 U.S. 459 (1999).

63. Lantz v. Ambach, 620 F. Supp. 663 (S.D.N.Y. 1985).

64. Leffel v. Wis. Interscholastic Athletic Ass'n, 444 F. Supp. 1117 (E.D. Wis. 1978).

scholastic competition in these sports could be eliminated for all students or separate teams for females could be established. The court also recognized that if comparable gender-segregated programs were provided, female athletes could not assert the right to try out for the male team simply because of its higher level of competition.

In addition to the controversies regarding coeducational participation in contact sports, there have been numerous challenges to policies denying gender integration of noncontact sports. Females filed the majority of these suits and prevailed in nearly every instance. As noted, **Title IX regulations explicitly require recipient districts to allow coeducational participation in those noncontact sports that are available only to one gender, presuming that athletic opportunities for that gender have been historically limited.** Thus, females tend to succeed in their claims, whereas males tend to fail,[65] notwithstanding the fact that the same laws apply to both genders. As a rule, school districts have been able to show an important governmental interest (e.g., redressing disparate athletic opportunities for females) in support of their decisions to exclude males from participating on teams traditionally reserved for females, whereas males have had difficulty supporting the claim that their athletic opportunities have been historically limited.

Fewer Sports Opportunities for Females. Although athletic opportunities for females have significantly increased since passage of Title IX in 1972, equal opportunity has not been achieved within all school districts. State efforts to provide a greater number of opportunities for girls have been weakened significantly by public education budgetary problems. Expenditures for special education, literacy, the elimination of language barriers, school safety, and the like have been given priority when dividing a shrinking public purse. As a result, in recent years equality of athletic opportunities for males and females often has been achieved either by reducing the number of sports traditionally available for males,[66] or by lowering the number of participants on boys' teams (e.g., football) to provide generally equal opportunities for boys and girls.[67]

Additionally, at times female athletes have expressed an insufficient interest in a given sport to have it approved by the state athletic association. In a Kentucky case, female high school athletes claimed a Title IX violation when the state athletic association refused to approve females' interscholastic fast-pitch softball. The association's decision was based on its policy of not sanctioning a sport unless at least 25 percent of its member institutions demonstrated an interest in participation. Since only 17 percent indicated an interest, approval was denied. In its review of the controversy, the Sixth Circuit in two separate opinions held that the 25 percent requirement violated neither Title IX[68] nor the Equal Protection Clause (i.e., the facially neutral policy was not proven to entail intentional discrimination).[69] It also observed that grouping sports by gender did not violate federal law.

65. *See, e.g.,* Williams v. Sch. Dist., 998 F.2d 168 (3d Cir. 1993) (remanding to determine whether the "real" opportunities for females exceeded those for males and whether the opportunities available to males were limited).

66. *See, e.g.,* Chalenor v. Univ. of N.D., 291 F.3d 1042 (8th Cir. 2002); Boulahanis v. Bd. of Regents, Ill. State Univ., 198 F.3d 633 (7th Cir. 1999).

67. Neal v. Bd. of Trs., 198 F.3d 763 (9th Cir. 1999).

68. Horner v. Ky. High Sch. Athletic Ass'n, 206 F.3d 685 (6th Cir. 2000).

In a higher education case, Brown University responded to budget cuts in 1991 by eliminating two interscholastic teams for men and two for women. At the time of the reductions, only 37 percent of the participants in varsity sports, compared to 48 percent of the institution's students, were women. By 1994, the ratio had not improved. The First Circuit found a Title IX violation, concurring with the Office for Civil Rights' policy interpretation that for schools to be in compliance they should:

- Provide interscholastic sports opportunities for both genders in terms of numbers of participants that are substantially proportionate to the respective enrollments of male and female students,
- Show a history of expanding sports programs for the underrepresented gender, and
- Provide enough opportunities to match the sports interests and abilities of the underrepresented gender.[70]

The court rejected the university's unproven assertion that female students were less interested in sports and viewed the comment as being based on a stereotypical view of women.

Modified Sports and Separate Seasons for Females. Among the equity claims initiated by female athletes are those contesting the use of gender-based modifications in sports. Although federal courts historically have permitted different rules for boys and girls (e.g., split-court rules for women's basketball), unfounded and unsupported stereotypes about either gender regarding strength, endurance, or ability will no longer justify differential treatment of male and female athletes.[71]

Also, maintaining separate playing seasons for female and male teams has been challenged as a violation of the equal protection clauses of both federal and state constitutions. In some instances, separate seasons have been upheld due to a lack of adequate facilities and general comparability of programs;[72] in other instances, separate playing seasons have been found to violate equal protection rights. This was the case in Michigan in 2001 when a federal district court ruled that the difficulty in finding facilities, coaches, and officials did not justify the use of separate seasons for boys and girls where the girls bore the burden of off-season participation.[73] The court opined that if single-sexed seasons were in fact necessary, the burden must be shared. The court suggested that junior varsity teams of both genders could be placed into the disadvantageous season and that the varsity teams then could compete during the preferred season.

69. Horner v. Ky. High Sch. Athletic Ass'n, 43 F.3d 265 (6th Cir. 1994).
70. Cohen v. Brown Univ., 101 F.3d 155 (1st Cir. 1996).
71. *See, e.g.,* Cape v. Tenn. Secondary Sch. Athletic Ass'n, 563 F.2d 793 (6th Cir. 1977) (permitting the use of split-court rules as they reflected physical differences between males and females).
72. *See, e.g.,* Ridgeway v. Mont. High Sch. Ass'n, 749 F. Supp. 1544 (D. Mont. 1990); Striebel v. Minn. State High Sch. League, 321 N.W.2d 400 (Minn. 1982).
73. Cmtys. for Equity v. Mich. High Sch. Athletic Ass'n, 178 F. Supp. 2d 805 (W.D. Mich. 2001).

Academic Programs

Allegations of gender bias in public schools have not been confined to athletic programs. Differential treatment of males and females in academic courses and schools also has generated litigation.[74] **Although the "separate but equal" principle has been applied in this area, as it has in athletics, rulings indicate that public school officials must bear the burden of showing a substantial justification for classifications based on gender in academic programs. Moreover, where the programs are separate, they must be proven equal.**

Single-Gender Schools. In a Third Circuit case, the court held that the operation of gender-segregated public high schools, in which enrollment is voluntary and educational offerings are essentially equal, is permissible under the Equal Protection Clause and the Equal Educational Opportunities Act of 1974.[75] Noting that Philadelphia's gender-segregated college preparatory schools offered functionally equivalent programs, the court concluded that the separation of males and females was justified because adolescents might study more effectively in gender-segregated high schools. The court emphasized that the female plaintiff was not compelled to attend the gender-segregated academic school; she had the option of enrolling in a coeducational school within her attendance zone. Furthermore, the court stated that her petition to attend the male academic high school was based on personal preference rather than on an objective evaluation of the offerings available in the two schools.

In contrast, Detroit school officials did not prevail in their attempt to segregate inner-city, African American male students to address more effectively these students' unique educational needs. Three African American male academies (preschool to grade 5, grades 6 to 8, and high school) were proposed. The three-year experimental academies were to offer an Afrocentric, pluralistic curriculum, including a futuristic course on preparation for the twenty-first century. The programs were to emphasize male responsibility, provide mentors, offer Saturday classes and extended classroom hours, provide individual counseling, and require student uniforms. No comparable program existed for females, although school authorities indicated that one would be forthcoming. The district court issued a preliminary injunction prohibiting the board from opening the academies, given the likelihood that the practice violated the Equal Protection Clause, Title IX, and state law. Additionally, the court reasoned that failing to provide the injunction could result in irreparable injury to the female students and cause great disruption if the schools were allowed to open and then were forced to close.[76] The court noted that Title IX does not permit the opening of new public single-gender schools, and that the district failed to show a substantial justification for its actions, as is required under the Fourteenth Amendment for facially discriminatory acts involving gender.

74. *See, e.g.,* Gossett v. Oklahoma, 245 F.3d 1172 (10th Cir. 2001) (remanding for a factual determination of whether a male nursing student was discriminated against by female instructors by failing to provide help, counseling, and opportunities to improve his performance).

75. Vorchheimer v. Sch. Dist., 532 F.2d 880 (3d Cir. 1976), *aff'd by equally divided court,* 430 U.S. 703 (1977).

76. Garrett v. Bd. of Educ., 775 F. Supp. 1004 (E.D. Mich. 1991).

In a higher education case, the Fourth Circuit addressed male-only admissions policies in Virginia.[77] The court found such a policy at the Virginia Military Institute (VMI) to be in violation of the Equal Protection Clause[78] because there were no comparable opportunities for women.[79] The appellate court held that VMI's claims that its male-only program provided needed diversity in higher education did not justify exclusion of women. The state was given three options: admit women, establish a parallel institution for women, or abandon state support for VMI. The state chose to establish a parallel program for women at Mary Baldwin College, a small private women-only institution; that decision was initially upheld.[80] On appeal in *United States v. Virginia,* however, the Supreme Court reversed the lower courts and held that the state had violated the Fourteenth Amendment by its failure to provide equal opportunities for women in the area of military training.[81] The Court refuted the reasons given by VMI for its refusal to admit women. The exclusion of women from VMI failed to further the institution's purported purpose of providing diversity in higher education. VMI's distinctive teaching methods and techniques could be used unchanged or slightly modified in the instruction of women, and privacy issues were resolvable.

Gender-Segregated Courses and Programs. Courts will not permit unequal educational opportunities for males and females. Although most cases challenging the exclusion of one gender from specific curricular offerings have been settled on constitutional grounds, Title IX regulations prohibit gender-segregated health, industrial arts, business, vocational-technical, home economics, music (although requirements based on vocal range that result in disparate impact are permissible), and adult education classes. These regulations also prohibit gender discrimination in counseling and bar gender-based course requirements for graduation (e.g., home economics for females and industrial arts for males). Moreover, Title IX prohibits separate physical education classes, although students may be grouped by skill levels.[82]

77. *See also* Faulkner v. Jones, 51 F.3d 440 (4th Cir. 1995). In this South Carolina case, a woman sued for admission to the all-male cadet corps. With the state unable to show a substantial justification for the discrimination, the court found that the institution's admission policy violated the Fourteenth Amendment. The court also reasoned that establishing a comparable parallel all-female cadet corps (assuming that was even possible) would not address the female student's interest in a timely manner. Moreover, relinquishing state control was not feasible for both political and economic reasons. Accordingly, the court ordered that the female student be admitted to the existing male academy.
78. This case did not involve allegations of a Title IX violation. That law does not apply to education institutions whose primary purpose is the training of individuals for the military or to public undergraduate institutions that have admitted students of only one gender since they were established. *See* 20 U.S.C. § 1681(a)(4),(5) (2003).
79. United States v. Virginia, 976 F.2d 890 (4th Cir. 1992).
80. United States v. Virginia, 852 F. Supp. 471 (W.D. Va. 1994), *aff'd,* 44 F.3d 1229 (4th Cir. 1995).
81. 518 U.S. 515 (1996).
82. 34 C.F.R. § 106.34(b) (2003).

Gender-Based Admission Criteria. At times, two sets of admission standards have been used, one for males the other for females. Without a substantial justification, this facially discriminatory practice will not satisfy constitutional scrutiny or provisions of Title IX.[83] For example, the admission practices of two Boston schools were found to have discriminated against female applicants and were therefore invalidated.[84] Due to the different seating capacities of the two schools, the Latin School for males required a lower score on the entrance examination than did the school for females. Although permitting the operation of gender-segregated schools, the federal district court was unsympathetic to the school's alleged physical plant problems and ruled that the same entrance requirements had to be applied to both genders. Similarly, the Ninth Circuit concluded that a school district's plan to admit an equal number of male and female students to a high school with an advanced college preparatory curriculum violated equal protection guarantees because it resulted in unequal admission criteria.[85] The court found the district's admission policy to be an illegitimate means of reaching its goal of balancing the number of male and female students enrolled in the school.

If the district uses reliable, valid, and bias-free forms of assessment to admit students to special programs or to grant awards or scholarships, decisions will be upheld even if a disparate impact occurs. Moreover, it is recommended that multiple forms of assessment be used and that all personnel involved in assessment have appropriate credentials and training.

Sexual Harassment of Students

Title IX and the Fourteenth Amendment also have been applied in gender-based claims of sexual harassment and abuse of students. Title IX, however, does not apply when the harassment is due to sexual preference, transvestism, transsexualism, or other behaviors that are sexual in nature; it applies only when the harassment is due to gender (i.e., being male or being female). For example, in a Tenth Circuit case, Title IX was held not to apply where a male high school football player was hazed by his teammates, duct-taped while nude to a towel rack, and then subjected to viewing by his former girlfriend, who had been invited into the locker room. He reported the incident and it resulted in the eventual cancellation of the final game of the season. Following these events, he was subjected to verbal threats and harassment from numerous students until he eventually transferred schools. Because the plaintiff was unable to show that his harassment was gender related, however, the Title IX portion of his suit was dismissed.[86]

Historically, claims of sexual harassment against school districts generally were not successful. In 1992, however, the Supreme Court heard the appeal of a case in which a female student alleged that a coach initiated sexual conversations, engaged in inappropriate touching, and had coercive intercourse with her on school grounds on several occasions. In this case, *Franklin v. Gwinnett County Public Schools,* the Court held that Title IX prohib-

83. 5 C.F.R. § 86.35(b) (2003).

84. Bray v. Lee, 337 F. Supp. 934 (D. Mass. 1972).

85. Berkelman v. S.F. Unified Sch. Dist., 501 F.2d 1264 (9th Cir. 1974).

86. Seamons v. Snow, 84 F.3d 1226 (10th Cir. 1996).

ited the sexual harassment of students and that damages could be awarded.[87] Since *Gwinnett,* current and former students have filed numerous additional cases with mixed results. They have alleged student-to-student harassment,[88] sexual involvement and abuse of students by school staff,[89] off-campus harassment that resulted in an on-campus hostile environment,[90] harassment by a student teacher,[91] and same-sex and opposite-sex harassment.[92] With *Gwinnett* as a starting point, two similar but slightly different standards have evolved: one for employee-to-student harassment and the other for student-to-student harassment.

Employee-to-Student Harassment. In 1998, the Supreme Court provided further guidance regarding the liability of school districts when school employees harass students. In *Gebser v. Lago Vista Independent School District,* a high school student and a teacher had a relationship that had not been reported to the administration until the couple was discovered having sex and the teacher was arrested.[93] The district then terminated the teacher's employment and the parents sued under Title IX. On appeal, the Supreme Court rejected recovery of damages based on either respondeat superior[94] or *constructive notice* (i.e., notice that is inferred or implied) as inconsistent with the objective of Title IX, given that liability would attach even though the district had no actual knowledge of the conduct or an opportunity to take action to end the harassment.[95] **For there to be an award of damages, an official who has the authority to address the alleged discrimination must have actual knowledge of the inappropriate conduct and then fail to ameliorate the problem. Furthermore, the failure to respond must amount to deliberate indifference to the discrimination.** In the instant case, the plaintiff did not argue that she had notified anyone. Moreover, the district's failure to adopt a sexual harassment policy and grievance procedure did not establish deliberate indifference.

87. 503 U.S. 60 (1992).
88. *See, e.g.,* Doe v. Dallas Indep. Sch. Dist., No. 3:01-CV-1092-R, 2002 U.S. Dist. LEXIS 13014 (N.D. Tex. July 16, 2002).
89. *See, e.g.,* Canutillo Indep. Sch. Dist. v. Leija, 101 F.3d 393 (5th Cir. 1996).
90. *See, e.g.,* Patricia H. v. Berkeley Unified Sch. Dist., 830 F. Supp. 1288 (N.D. Cal. 1993).
91. *See, e.g.,* Oona R.-S. v. Santa Rosa City Schs., 890 F. Supp. 1452 (N.D. Cal. 1995).
92. *See, e.g.,* Shrum v. Kluck, 249 F.3d 773 (8th Cir. 2001) (male-to-male); M.H.D. v. Westminster Schs., 172 F.3d 797 (11th Cir. 1999) (male-to-female); Kinman v. Omaha Pub. Sch. Dist., 171 F.3d 607 (8th Cir. 1999) (female-to-female). *See also* Oncale v. Sundowner Offshore Servs., 523 U.S. 75 (1998) (permitting claims of same-sex sexual harassment under Title VII of the Civil Rights Act of 1964).
93. 524 U.S. 274 (1998).
94. This doctrine applies in cases where the master (e.g., school district) is held responsible for the acts of the servant (e.g., teacher or administrator).
95. *See also* Baynard v. Malone, 268 F.3d 228 (4th Cir. 2001) (noting that actual notice may be established where an appropriate person is notified that a teacher is abusing a student; the identity of the particular child is unnecessary), *cert. denied sub nom.,* Baynard v. Alexandria City Sch. Bd., 535 U.S. 954 (2002); Davis v. DeKalb County Sch. Dist., 233 F.3d 1367 (11th Cir. 2000) (finding no actual notice or deliberate indifference on the part of the board where a coach molested several school children).

Also of relevance in hostile environment cases involving school children is the fact that an educator's harassing behavior toward a student does not have to be "unwelcome," as it does in employment cases. The Seventh Circuit in 1997 reviewed a case where a 21-year-old male kitchen worker had a consensual sexual relationship with a 13-year-old middle school girl.[96] The court noted that, under Indiana criminal law, a person under the age of 16 cannot consent to sexual intercourse and that children may not even understand that they are being harassed. To rule that only unwelcome behavior is actionable would permit violators to take advantage of young, impressionable youth who voluntarily participate in requested conduct. Also, if welcomeness were an issue in court, the children bringing the suits would be subject to intense scrutiny regarding their degree of fault.

Student-to-Student Harassment. Educators must be in control of the school environment, including student conduct, and eliminate known dangers and harassment. Not all harassment will be known, however, and not all behavior that is offensive will be so severe as to violate Title IX. Furthermore, for student-to-student harassment to be actionable, the behavior must be unwelcome.

Clarification regarding liability associated with student-to-student harassment was provided in 1999 when the Supreme Court in *Davis v. Monroe County Board of Education*[97] proposed a two-part test:

- Whether the board acted with deliberate indifference to known acts of harassment;[98] and
- Whether the harassment was so severe, pervasive, and objectively offensive that it effectively barred the victim's access to an educational opportunity or benefit.

The Court remanded the case to determine whether these standards were met. The plaintiff's daughter had allegedly been subjected to unwelcome sexual touching and rubbing, as well as sexual talk. Ultimately, the youth was charged with and pled guilty to sexual battery for his misconduct. The student victim or her mother notified several teachers, the coach, and the principal of the harassment. No disciplinary action was ever taken other than to threaten the violating student with possible action.

Damage awards[99] are available under Title IX from educational institutions receiving federal funds, although not from those persons who were directly responsible for the harassment.[100] "Individuals" are not "recipients" and therefore cannot be held liable under this particular law. However, violators can be sued under state tort law for sexual battery or intentional infliction of emotional distress,[101] and criminal charges (e.g., rape, sodomy) may

96. Mary M. v. N. Lawrence Cmty. Sch. Corp., 131 F.3d 1220 (7th Cir. 1997).

97. 526 U.S. 629 (1999).

98. *See also* Oden v. N. Marianas Coll., 284 F.3d 1058 (9th Cir. 2002) (concluding that administrative sluggishness did not equate to deliberate indifference in a case where a student's initial hearing was slightly delayed).

99. However, it is unlikely that punitive awards are available under Title IX. *See* Schultzen v. Woodbury Cent. Cmty. Sch. Dist., 187 F. Supp. 2d 1099 (N.D. 2002).

100. *See, e.g.,* Hartley v. Parnell, 193 F.3d 1263 (11th Cir. 1999).

be filed against perpetrators where force is used or minors are involved. Additionally, being found guilty of sexual harassment can justify termination, even for tenured educators.

Conclusion

A basic purpose of public education is to enhance future opportunities for all students, regardless of their innate characteristics. Accordingly, courts and legislatures have become increasingly assertive in guaranteeing that students have the chance to realize their capabilities while in school. Arbitrary classification practices that disadvantage certain groups are not tolerated. On the other hand, valid classifications, applied in the best interests of students, are generally supported. Indeed, some legal mandates *require* the classification of certain students to ensure that they receive instruction appropriate to their needs.

For the future, gender-based classification schemes and discrimination should continue to be heavily litigated, particularly in the areas of harassment and sports opportunities. Also, the number of cases that claim native language or national origin discrimination will likely increase, given the significant number of non-English-speaking persons who immigrate yearly. Race discrimination cases will foreseeably focus on whether school districts have sufficiently complied with existing desegregation orders or whether current efforts to provide parental choice in the selection of schools violate the Constitution when integration is adversely affected. Age-based controversies should remain comparatively few in number and focus primarily on early admission to school.

Points to Ponder

1. A student and coach had a three-month affair that included sexual involvement. The student was 18 years old and voluntarily participated in all activities; the coach was tenured as a social studies teacher. The parents learned of the affair and informed the superintendent and principal. Both the student and coach admitted to their involvement. The coach was fired following an appropriate hearing; the parents nevertheless sued the district claiming a Title IX violation. How will the court respond?

2. An alternative school has been specially designed to address the unique needs of African American males; a comparable program has been developed for African American females. Both are to begin in the fall. Two suits are filed: one alleging a violation of Title IX, the other claiming a Title VI infraction. Who wins each suit and why?

3. A 4½-year-old child applies to kindergarten, but is denied admission as he is six months too young, given the cut-off date established in school district policy. Nevertheless, his parents want him admitted. He is reading at the second-grade level and is larger than his same-age peers. The parents sued the district under the Age Discrimination Act. Officials do not deny that the sole reason the child was denied early admission was his age. Will the parents be successful in this suit? Why or why not?

101. *See, e.g.,* Johnson v. Elk Lake Sch. Dist., 283 F.3d 138 (3d Cir. 2002).

4. There is only one non-English-speaking child in the school district. Officials refused her parent's request for a bilingual program. The parents then retained the services of three nationally known experts on bilingual education; each provided significant data that supported the use of bilingual education in the elimination of language barriers. Nonetheless, the district still refused to provide the requested program and, in the alternative, offered an English as a Second Language program. This program was successful in eliminating language barriers in the past (both in this district and throughout the state). School officials were unsure which of the two instructional methods was better, but claimed that they were not required to offer the best program. The parents sued the district under Title VI and the Equal Educational Opportunities Act. What will be the outcome of this legal challenge?

5. The local school district has been unitary for 10 years. Recently, however, the state implemented (1) a plan allowing students to enroll in private schools, (2) a program where students were permitted to transfer to any adjacent public school district, and (3) a transfer program where students may attend any public school in the state if their home school failed to meet state guidelines. Under these provisions, the district once again became racially segregated. A lawsuit was filed under the Fourteenth Amendment and Title VI challenging recent changes that have resulted in resegregation. Will the plaintiffs succeed in this suit?

7

Rights of Students with Disabilities

Since children with disabilities represent a vulnerable minority group, their treatment has aroused considerable judicial and legislative concern. Courts have addressed the constitutional rights of such children to attend school and to be classified accurately and instructed appropriately. Federal and state statutes have further delineated the rights of students with disabilities and have provided funds to assist school districts in meeting their special needs.

Legal Context

> Education must be made available to all school-aged children. Those with qualifying disabilities have additional rights guaranteeing them a free appropriate public education.

The first significant court case to impact children with disabilities dealt with racial segregation rather than special education, and was filed under the Fourteenth Amendment rather than under a narrowly tailored disability statute. Nevertheless, the Supreme Court's 1954 pronouncement in *Brown v. Board of Education* that "education must be made available to all on equal terms"[1] ultimately served as a basis for admission of a number of previously excluded populations (including those classified as disabled) to public schools. Court cases and changes in state laws eventually helped pave the way for the passage of federal laws specially designed to protect and enhance the rights of individuals with disabilities—the Rehabilitation Act, the Americans with Disabilities Act (ADA), and the Individuals with Disabilities Education Act (IDEA) (see Table 7.1).

1. 347 U.S. 483, 493 (1954).

TABLE 7.1 ***Applicability of Selected Federal Laws Affecting Students with Disabilities***

Federal Law	*Public Recipient of Federal Aid Required to Comply*	*Public Nonrecipient Required to Comply*	*Private Recipient of Federal Aid Required to Comply*	*Private Nonrecipient Required to Comply*
Fourteenth Amendment Equal Protection Clause	yes	yes	no	no
Fourteenth Amendment Due Process Clause	yes	yes	no	no
42 U.S.C. § 1983	yes	yes	no	no
Rehabilitation Act § 504	yes	no	yes	no
ADA Title II	yes	yes	no	no
ADA Title III	no	no	yes	yes
IDEA	yes, if state is recipient of IDEA funds	no	no, service contracts do not qualify	no

Rehabilitation Act

Section 504 of the Rehabilitation Act of 1973 applies to both public and private recipients of federal financial assistance. Under the Rehabilitation Act, an individual with a disability is one who has a *physical or mental impairment*[2] that substantially limits one or more major life activities, has a *record of impairment,* or is *regarded as having an impairment.*[3] These latter two definitions apply when a person has been subjected to discrimination (e.g., excluded from school for being HIV positive[4]). However, only those children who meet the first definition (i.e., have an impairment that is substantially limiting) will be eligible for individualized instruction and services. Students with only a record of impairment are not currently in need of accommodation, and students who are only regarded as having such an impairment have no actual limitation to accommodate.

2. 34 C.F.R. § 104.3(j)(2(i)) (2003) (defining physical or mental impairments as including "any physiological disorder or condition, cosmetic disfigurement, or anatomical loss affecting one or more of the following body systems: neurological; musculoskeletal; special sense organs; respiratory, including speech organs; cardiovascular; reproductive, digestive, genito-urinary; hemic and lymphatic; skin; and endocrine; or any mental or psychological disorder, such as mental retardation, organic brain syndrome, emotional or mental illness, and specific learning disorders").
3. 34 C.F.R. § 104.3(j)(1) (2003).
4. Ray v. Sch. Dist., 666 F. Supp. 1524 (M.D. Fla 1987).

To qualify as a disability, the limitation must *substantially limit* a *major life activity*.[5] In making this determination, courts compare the performance difficulties of the student with those of the theoretical "average person" (or in this discussion, "average student") in the general population. To qualify, the student will have to be either incapable of performing the designated activity or significantly restricted; functioning merely below average will be insufficient. This assessment requires a case-by-case evaluation, as impairments will vary in severity, affect people differently, and may or may not be restricting given the nature of the life activity. As a result, some students with physical or mental impairments will be substantially limited and others will not, with only the former qualifying for special instruction, services, and accommodations. **Failure to recognize the fact that Section 504 provides enhanced rights only for persons who have significant limitations of a life activity, but not for those who are merely impaired, can lead to the overclassification of students under Section 504**. This may result in increased instruction and services costs, additional hurdles and limitations in regard to discipline, greater parental expectations for programming, and the increased likelihood of litigation.

When a student's limitation qualifies as a disability, it still is necessary to determine whether he or she is *otherwise qualified.* For preK–12 education purposes, children may qualify if they are of school age, or if they are eligible for services for the disabled under either state law or the IDEA.[6] Students who qualify under Section 504, but not under the IDEA (e.g., regular education children who are wheelchair confined), need to be provided with accommodation plans that will include appropriate education, as well as any individualized aids and services that will allow participation in the educational program. The programs must be delivered in accessible facilities,[7] and programming must be designed and selected to meet the needs of students with disabilities as adequately as the needs of their nondisabled peers are met. Furthermore, children with disabilities should not be segregated from other children unless an appropriate program cannot otherwise be provided. Where such segregation exists, programs must be comparable in materials, facilities, teacher quality, length of school term, and daily hours of instruction.

When the school district and the parents disagree as to whether an appropriate education has been provided, the parents should have the opportunity to review records, participate in an impartial hearing, and be represented by counsel. Section 504 is not specific as to the procedures that must be followed, but it does acknowledge that providing notice and hearing rights comparable to those mandated under the IDEA would suffice. In addition, parents also have the right to file a complaint with the Office for Civil Rights within 180 days of the alleged discrimination.[8] If the recipient fails to correct its discriminatory practices, its federal funds may be terminated. Moreover, there is a private right of action under

5. Major life activities include caring for oneself, performing manual tasks, walking, seeing, hearing, speaking, breathing, *learning,* and working. 34 C.F.R. § 104.3(j)(2)(ii) (2003).

6. 34 C.F.R. § 104.3(l)(2) (2003).

7. 34 C.F.R. § 104.22 (2003). To comply, a recipient need not make each existing facility or every part of a facility accessible, but must operate its programs so that they are accessible to individuals with disabilities.

8. Section 504 does not have its own complaint procedures, but it has adopted those outlined in Title VI of the Civil Rights Act of 1964. 34 C.F.R. § 104.61 (2003).

Section 504, although IDEA administrative remedies must be exhausted if the relief sought also is available under the IDEA.

Americans with Disabilities Act

In addition to the Rehabilitation Act, in 1990 Congress passed the ADA.[9] Two titles of that act are of particular importance to students with disabilities: Title II applies to public schools and Title III applies to those that are private. Like Section 504, these titles prohibit discrimination against persons who are disabled. Unlike Section 504, however, the ADA requires compliance of schools that do not receive federal aid and were not heretofore federally regulated. Although this law will seldom apply in claims regarding the provision of an appropriate education, it is routinely used in suits contesting participation of children with disabilities in extracurricular activities and in alleging overt disability discrimination.

Individuals with Disabilities Education Act

Recipients of IDEA funds are required to provide qualifying children a free appropriate public education (FAPE) that is made available in the least restrictive environment.[10] States, but not local school districts, have the option of declining IDEA funds and thereby avoiding the myriad compliance requirements, but they still must address the needs of students with disabilities as stipulated in Section 504. All states, however, currently participate in the IDEA financial assistance program.

To qualify for services, a child must be mentally retarded, hard of hearing, deaf, speech or language impaired, visually impaired, blind, seriously emotionally disturbed, orthopedically impaired, autistic, other health impaired, or learning disabled, or suffer from traumatic brain injury, *and,* as a result, be in need of special education and related services.[11] Accordingly, it is possible to have a disability (e.g., quadriplegia) but not be in need of special education, and therefore not qualify for services under the IDEA. Although a child needs to qualify as "disabled" under one or more of these categories for the state and district to receive federal funding, it is not necessary to "label" the child in developing the individualized education program. It is important, however, for the child's needs to be correctly identified and for those needs to be properly addressed.

The IDEA remains the primary law under which a FAPE is challenged and as a result generates most of the student-disability case law. In the following sections, several of the most important and heavily litigated areas of the IDEA are reviewed.

9. 42 U.S.C. §§ 12101-12213 (2003).
10. 20 U.S.C. § 1400 *et seq.* (2003).
11. 20 U.S.C. § 1401(3)(A) (2003). Not all children with impairments will possess qualifying disabilities. *See, e.g.,* Bd. of Educ. v. J.D., No. 99-2180, 2000 U.S. App. LEXIS 26902 (4th Cir. Oct. 26, 2000) (upholding a district court ruling that the drug-using student was socially maladjusted and did not have a qualifying educational disability).

Free Appropriate Public Education

> The Individuals with Disabilities Education Act requires recipients of funds under the Act to provide all resident children with disabilities with a free appropriate public education in the least restrictive environment.

All children with disabilities ages 3 through 21[12] are entitled to a free appropriate public education (FAPE) that must:

- Be provided at public expense and under public supervision and direction (even if the school district selects a private school placement);
- Meet the standards of the state educational agency;
- Include an appropriate preschool, elementary school, or secondary school education; and
- Be provided in conformity with the individualized education program (IEP).

An "appropriate" education is one that is designed to meet the unique needs of each child and includes special education and related services that are necessary for a child to benefit from special education.[13]

As needed, students also must be provided:

- Supplementary aids and services (to enable the child with a disability to be educated with nondisabled children to the maximum extent appropriate);
- Transition services (to assist in transitioning from school to postschool activities such as postsecondary education, vocational training, integrated employment, continuing and adult education, adult services, independent living, or community participation); and
- Assistive technology devices and services (to enable the child to increase, maintain, or improve functional capabilities).[14]

When services are provided, they must be made available as close to the child's home as possible, and preferably in the school the child would have attended if not disabled. However, it is unrealistic to assume that all programs can be made available in every neighborhood school.

12. This is true unless students ages 3 to 5 and 18 through 21 are not served within the state. 34 C.F.R. § 300.300(b)(5)(i) (2003).
13. 20 U.S.C. § 1401(22) (2003).
14. 20 U.S.C. §1401(1), (2), (29), (30) (2003).

Even though IEPs must be "appropriate," they need not be "the best" available or represent "optimum" programs that will maximize learning potential.[15] This issue was addressed in *Board of Education v. Rowley,*[16] where parents had requested that the school district provide a sign-language interpreter for their daughter in her academic classes due to her minimal residual hearing. The child's IEP specified a first-grade regular education placement with special instruction from a tutor one hour per day and a speech therapist three hours per week, but did not include interpreter services. An interpreter had been provided during a two-week period when she was in kindergarten, but the practice was discontinued based on recommendations by the interpreter and other educators working with the child. Due to this omission, the parents were dissatisfied with the IEP and, after unsuccessful administrative review, filed suit.

On appeal, the Supreme Court rejected the standard proposed by the lower court (i.e., maximization of the potential of children with disabilities commensurate with the opportunity provided to other children[17]) and reasoned that "the intent of the act was more to open the door of public education to [children with disabilities] on appropriate terms than to guarantee any particular level of education once inside."[18] The act was found to guarantee a "basic floor of opportunity,"[19] consisting of access to specialized instruction and related services that are individually designed to provide educational benefit. Applying these principles, the Court held that the plaintiff was receiving an appropriate education—that is, she was incurring educational benefit from individualized instruction and related services, as evidenced by her better-than-average performance in class, promotion from grade to grade, and positive interpersonal relationships with educators and peers.

The Court also made clear that lower courts are not to define an "appropriate education." Rather, their review is limited to two questions:

- **Has the state complied with the procedures identified in the IDEA?**
- **Is the IEP, as developed through these procedures, reasonably calculated to enable the child to receive educational benefit**?

Lower courts have interpreted this latter requirement to mandate educational programs that provide more than "trivial advancement."[20]

Courts often defer to state and local educators regarding the nature of IEPs and matters of pedagogy, but still will not uphold proposed placements that are clearly inappropriate. In

15. *See, e.g.,* D.B. v. Craven County Bd. of Educ., No. 99-1326, 2000 U.S. App. LEXIS 6176 (4th Cir. April 3, 2000) (concluding that the district had provided the plaintiff with a FAPE and that even if his writing skills were not as good as his parents would have liked, the IDEA requires that schools provide educational opportunities, not that they guarantee that every child will attain full potential).
16. 458 U.S. 176 (1982).
17. 483 F. Supp. 528, 534 (S.D.N.Y. 1980).
18. 458 U.S. 176, 192 (1982).
19. *Id.* at 200.
20. *See, e.g.,* Ridgewood Bd. of Educ. v. N.E. *ex rel.* M.E., 172 F.3d 238 (3d Cir. 1999) (finding that the IDEA requires "something more than a trivial educational benefit").

such situations, courts have not been reluctant to approve a private placement or to direct the development of an appropriate public one. For example, the Ninth Circuit concluded that a California district failed to provide an appropriate education by placing an autistic child in a program for the "communicatively handicapped." The program was not individualized, the student's needs were not being met, and the teacher was not trained to work with autistic children.[21] The district was required to reimburse the parents for the costs of an out-of-district placement, including expenses associated with commuting, lodging, and tuition, as well as attorneys' fees.

Individualized Education Programs

> Individualized education programs must be designed to provide the child with some educational benefit and be made available in the neighborhood school when appropriate and feasible.

The process of preparing and delivering an appropriate program begins when a child with a disability is identified and ends only when the child withdraws or graduates from the school, fails to qualify for services, or reaches the age of 21. To begin this process, the child is identified and evaluated; then an individualized education program (IEP) is written and a placement is selected.

Initial Identification

Under the Individuals with Disabilities Education Act's (IDEA's) "child find" mandate, states and school districts are required to identify, locate, and evaluate *all* resident children with disabilities, regardless of the severity of their disability or whether they attend public or private schools. No child with a disability is to be denied an appropriate program ("zero reject"[22]). Although federal law requires that children with disabilities be identified, it does not dictate how this is to occur. Nevertheless, courts will give deference to districts when their efforts appear substantial and in good faith.[23]

21. Union Sch. Dist. v. Smith, 15 F.3d 1519 (9th Cir. 1994).
22. 34 C.F.R. § 300.304 (2003). There has been some debate as to whether children with severe disabilities (i.e., those who seemingly cannot benefit or can benefit only marginally from instruction) actually qualify for services. The First Circuit concluded that Congress intended for *all* children with disabilities to be educated and reasoned that there should be "zero rejects." Timothy W. v. Rochester, N.H., Sch. Dist., 875 F.2d 954 (1st Cir. 1989).
23. Doe v. Metro. Nashville Pub. Schs., 9 Fed. Appx. 453 (6th Cir. 2001) (holding that the district had effectively participated in "child-find," given its dissemination of information, public service announcements through the local media, participation in PTA meetings, and implementation of an outreach program).

The screening process may necessitate the use of tests that are administered to all children, not simply those suspected of having disabilities. Prior to testing, a notice that identifies the tests to be used and provides a general explanation of their intended purpose must be given to the parents. Educators, however, need not acquire consent at this time, unless consent for all children is required. When these initial referral and screening efforts have been completed, all children *potentially in need* of special education ideally will be identified.

Next, school districts are responsible for evaluating further those children residing in their respective service areas who are initially perceived to be in need of special education. Although state residency laws vary, generally children who physically live in the district's service area with a custodial parent, legal guardian, or foster parent; are emancipated minors; or have reached the age of majority and live apart from their parents will qualify as "residents."

Evaluation

Prior to placement of a child with disabilities, the IDEA requires a multifactored evaluation. School personnel must use a variety of technically sound assessment tools and strategies to gather information related to the child's health, vision, hearing, social and emotional status, general intelligence, academic performance, communicative status, and motor abilities. Educators cannot rely on a single criterion or procedure to determine a child's placement. Standardized tests must be:

- Validated for the purposes for which they are used,
- Administered by qualified personnel,
- Selected and administered in ways that neither racially nor culturally discriminate, and
- Available in the child's native language or other mode of communication.

Furthermore, assessments must accurately reflect aptitude or achievement rather than the child's impaired sensory, manual, or speaking skills, unless those skills are the ones being measured.[24]

Notice must be provided to the parents that the district intends to test the student. It must describe any assessments the district proposes to conduct (including each evaluation procedure, test, record, or report that will be used), as well as any other relevant information. Generally, informed parental consent must be acquired prior to individualized testing for either an initial evaluation or reevaluation.[25] However, consent is not required when the parents fail to respond to requests for reevaluation, assuming that the school district can dem-

24. 34 C.F.R. § 300.532(a)(1), (c)(1), (e), (f), (g) (2003).

25. However, all IDEA rights, including the right to provide consent, transfer to the student upon reaching the age of majority (generally age 18) as specified within state statute. Also, one year prior to reaching majority age, students' IEPs must include a statement that they have been informed of their pending rights. 34 C.F.R. § 300.347(c) (2003).

onstrate that it took reasonable measures to obtain consent and the child's parent failed to respond.

If the parents refuse consent, the district may seek authority to evaluate the student by initiating due process procedures. Assuming the school district succeeds, the parents then have three options: permit the child to be evaluated, seek a court order to prohibit the assessment, or remove the child from public schools. If the latter action is taken, the parent must comply with state compulsory attendance requirements by enrolling the child in another school or by providing home schooling. If the child is to remain in public schools, the parents may not impede the assessment process by failing to make the child available for testing or by temporarily removing the child from the state to evade school officials.

As part of an initial evaluation or as part of any reevaluation, the IEP team and other qualified professionals are responsible for reviewing existing evaluation data on the child, including evaluations and information provided by the parents, current classroom-based assessments, and observations by teachers and related services providers. The IEP team then can identify what additional data, if any, are needed. Once this is accomplished, the team must identify the child's educational needs and present level of performance; assess whether the child requires special education and related services; and determine whether any additions or modifications to the instruction or services are necessary to enable the child to meet measurable annual goals and to participate, as appropriate, in the regular curriculum.

Parents have the right to request an independent evaluation if they disagree with the district's evaluation or placement decision. The public school pays for the additional evaluation, unless officials contest the need for reassessment or the evaluation already obtained by the parent did not meet district criteria.[26] To challenge the request, school personnel would need to request an impartial hearing and then demonstrate that all procedures and appropriate professional practices were followed. If the impartial hearing officer rules in favor of the district, and that decision is not appealed, the parents still may acquire a second, independent evaluation but must pay for it themselves. School personnel are required to *consider* the results of the independent evaluation but are not required to *follow* them.[27]

IEP Preparation

The school district, through its IEP teams, is responsible for determining whether children qualify under the IDEA for services and, if so, for designing appropriate, least restrictive placements. Each team should include:

- The parents of the child with a disability,
- The child, when appropriate,
- At least one regular education teacher,
- At least one special education teacher,
- A representative of the district who is qualified to provide and/or supervise specially designed instruction to meet the unique needs of the child, and

26. 34 C.F.R. § 300.502(a)(1), (b) (2003).
27. 34 C.F.R. § 300.502(c)(1) (2003).

- Other individuals (including related services personnel) who have knowledge about the child's needs or have special expertise.

The team also must include an individual who can interpret the evaluation results and identify instructional implications, assuming that no existing member of the team has such abilities. If the team decides that the child will not be placed in the regular education classroom, the regular educator then may be dropped from the committee.

Parents must agree to the IEP meeting time and location, and the district must ensure that the parents have the opportunity to participate fully (e.g., by hiring foreign-language translators or sign-language interpreters).[28] If neither parent is available or willing to attend, school officials should document each of their efforts to encourage parental involvement. Where no parent can be identified or located, a surrogate parent must be appointed. The surrogate possesses all of the IDEA rights and responsibilities of the parent. The surrogate may not be an employee of the district or have interests that conflict with those of the child and must have the knowledge and skills needed to ensure adequate representation.

The IEP should identify:

- The child's current level of educational performance;
- Annual and short-term goals and objectives;
- Special education, related services, supplementary aids and services, and transition services to be provided;
- Program modifications or supports for school personnel that will be applied;
- The extent, if any, to which the child will not be included in regular education program activities;
- Any modifications that will be made in performing state or district assessments of student achievement;
- The date to initiate services;
- The projected frequency, location, and duration of services;
- Appropriate evaluation procedures;
- How the parents will be informed of their child's progress; and
- Interagency responsibilities and linkages.

The program must be reviewed annually, or more often as appropriate, and a reevaluation must be performed every three years if the IEP team determines that conditions warrant, or if requested by the child's parent or teacher.

Public and Private Placement

After agreement has been reached as to the elements of an IEP, an appropriate placement must be made available at public expense. Alternative placements may include:

28. However, this right to participate does not extend to preparatory meetings conducted by the local school district to generate proposals to be discussed with the parents at a later IEP meeting. *In re* D., 32 IDELR 103 (SEA CT, 2000).

- A regular education classroom with various support services,
- A regular classroom with or without itinerant teachers or resource rooms,
- Self-contained special classes,
- Special schools,
- Home instruction, and
- Instruction in hospitals or residential institutions.[29]

Least Restrictive Environment. Within this continuum of placements, the IDEA requires that the child be educated in the least restrictive environment (LRE). In fact, **children with disabilities are to be educated with children who are not disabled to the *maximum extent appropriate*.** Special classes, separate schooling, or other removal of a child from regular education may occur only if the nature or severity of the disability is such that education cannot be achieved satisfactorily.[30] In making LRE decisions, school districts should determine within which types of placements the IEP may be delivered (along the continuum of alternative placements) and then select the option that is least restrictive. Educational and noneducational benefits for each placement should be assessed. The LRE for most children will be regular education with supplemental aids and services, although some will require a more restrictive, even residential, setting.[31] First and foremost is the provision of an appropriate program; only then should consideration be given to identifying a placement that also is least restrictive. This is true for initial as well as subsequent placement decisions.

Importantly, children do not have to be placed experimentally in the regular classroom under the guise of full inclusion,[32] and then moved to appropriate placements only after they fail to meet short-term objectives or acquire educational benefit. Inappropriate placements may require the unnecessary expenditure of thousands of dollars and delay the provision of appropriate and beneficial education.

Public Placement of a Child in a Private School. Placements may be made in public schools or in private facilities, including those that are residential. Although the fiscal obligation placed on school systems can be substantial, the district will be held financially responsible for residential placements that are required to provide a free appropriate public education. In such instances, the district must cover all nonmedical costs, including room and board. The IDEA's provision for residential care, however, is not intended to compensate for a poor home environment or to serve as a means of delivering social, medical, or

29. 34 C.F.R. § 300.551(b) (2003).
30. 34 C.F.R. § 300.550(b) (2003).
31. *See, e.g.,* Beth B. v. Clay, 282 F.3d 493 (7th Cir. 2002) (supporting placement that was more restrictive than regular education as the child's academic progress was virtually nonexistent within regular education), *cert. denied,* 123 S. Ct. 412 (2002).
32. The term *full inclusion* is used here to refer to placement in regular education where the child's educational needs are appropriately addressed through the use of supplemental aides and services.

incarceration services.[33] Accordingly, if a residential placement is sought by the parents for reasons other than the education of the child with a disability (e.g., the risk the child poses in the home,[34] the inability to shelter or feed the youth, the student being the target of a parent's abuse), the request for support may be denied.

When the public school system selects a private placement, a representative of the private school should participate in IEP meetings. If attendance is not possible, participation must be acquired through individual or conference calls. Subsequent meetings to review and revise the IEP may be initiated and conducted by private school personnel, if approved by district officials. When this occurs, both the parents and a public school representative must be involved in any decision about the child's IEP, and the district must authorize any change prior to implementation. Notwithstanding the above, the state education agency and local school district remain responsible for compliance with the IDEA. Of note also is the fact that **private schools are not required to implement special programs or to lower their academic standards to permit placement of children with disabilities**.[35] Applicants who cannot participate effectively in the private school's regular education curriculum may be denied admission.

Unilateral Parental Placement of Child in a Private School. In some instances parents elect to place their children in private schools, either initially or when they perceive public programs to be inappropriate. **Parents always have the option of selecting an alternative program, but such placements will be at parental expense unless the parents can show that the public placement is inappropriate and that their preferred placement is appropriate**. Accordingly, if the public school placement is found to be proper, reimbursement will be denied, even if the parentally selected program is shown to be appropriate, better, or even cheaper.[36] Furthermore, reimbursement will be denied when both the public and private placements are shown to be inappropriate.

In *Florence County School District Four v. Carter,* the Supreme Court gave additional support to parents seeking reimbursement for private placements.[37] In that case, a child with a learning disability was removed by her parents from what was proven to be an inappropriate public placement and enrolled in an appropriate private program. Controversy devel-

33. *See, e.g.,* Dale M. v. Bd. of Educ., 237 F.3d 813 (7th Cir. 2001) (concluding that the district was not required to pay the cost of confinement of an incorrigible youth; his problems were not primarily educational—they were based on his lack of proper socialization), *cert. denied,* 534 U.S. 1020 (2002).

34. Gonzalez v. P.R. Dep't of Educ., 254 F.3d 350 (1st Cir. 2001) (determining that the child had been offered a FAPE, notwithstanding parental arguments to the contrary or their concern for their daughter's safety if their son were to return home), *cert. denied,* 525 U.S. 815 (2001).

35. St. Johnsbury Acad. v. D.H., 240 F.3d 163 (2d Cir. 2001).

36. *Compare* Walker County Sch. Dist. v. Bennett, 203 F.3d 1293 (11th Cir. 2000) (requiring reimbursement to parents for one year of private education; the public placement was found inappropriate) *with* Burilovich v. Bd. of Educ., 208 F.3d 560 (6th Cir. 2000) (upholding lower court judgment that reimbursement was unnecessary because the parents failed to show that the IEP was inappropriate).

37. 510 U.S. 7 (1993).

oped when the parents sought reimbursement but were denied because the private school was not included on the state-approved list—a list that was not made available to the public because the state preferred to evaluate each case individually. The Court held that reimbursement could not be denied simply because the school was not state approved. The touchstone was that the public program was inappropriate, and the unilaterally selected program was appropriate. As a result, the reimbursement of "reasonable costs" was required.

Parental requests are not always reasonable, however, and therefore are not always funded. For example, the Eleventh Circuit upheld a lower court decision denying reimbursement, as the student had been provided an IEP that was reasonably calculated to confer an appropriate education. The requested residential placement was found to be both unnecessary and not least restrictive. The court also rejected the opinion of an expert hired by the parents who had indicated that the family needed respite care (i.e., someone to take care of their son in their home) because family members had responsibilities other than caregiver and teacher.[38] In another case, the parents sued a school district for failure to provide a FAPE, notwithstanding the out-of-state placement of the child in a private residential facility and payment for three round trips home for the child to visit. The parents were demanding that the district also pay transportation costs (including air fare for both parents and two siblings), hotel, food, and rental car expenses so they could visit the child. The court acknowledged that the IEP encouraged the development of family relations, but ruled that the district was not required to "foot the bill for family gatherings."[39]

In an effort to limit district liability for private placements selected by parents, the IDEA permits reduction or denial of reimbursement if the parents fail to provide public officials with notification of their intent or if a court finds their conduct unreasonable. Proper notification can be accomplished either by discussing the matter with the IEP team during a formal meeting or by providing the district with written notice, including an explanation of the reasons for the decision, at least 10 days prior to the projected removal of the child. At that point, if the district elects to perform additional student evaluations, the parent needs to make the child available.[40]

Services Available to Children in Private Schools. Students enrolled by their parents in private schools have no *individual right* to receive special education and related services provided by the school district.[41] Instead, public officials are responsible for meeting with representatives of the children to decide who is to receive services; what, where, and how services are to be provided; and how services are to be evaluated. In selecting a site for the delivery of services, officials will consider available alternative delivery systems as well as whether provision at a religious school violates state law.[42] If off-campus delivery is

38. Devine v. Indian River County Sch. Bd., 249 F.3d 1289 (11th Cir. 2001).

39. Cohen v. Sch. Bd., 450 So. 2d 1238, 1240 (Fla. Dist. Ct. App. 1984).

40. *See, e.g.*, Patricia P. v. Bd. of Educ., 203 F.3d 462 (7th Cir. 2000) (denying reimbursement to parents who would not allow the school district a reasonable opportunity to evaluate their child).

41. 34 C.F.R. § 300.454(a)(1) (2003).

42. *See, e.g.*, KDM v. Reedsport Sch. Dist., 196 F.3d 1046 (9th Cir. 1999) (upholding Oregon regulation stipulating that if a district provides services to children in private schools, the services must be provided in a religiously neutral setting).

selected, eligible children must be transported from the school to the site and back (or to home). Funding for services for private school children is provided under the IDEA at a per-pupil prorated amount. This amount is modest, however, when compared to the dollars contributed by state and local governments. As a result, available services will tend to be fewer in number or of less duration compared to those available in IEPs provided by the local school district.[43]

Change of Placement. Following an appropriate initial placement in a public or private school, adjustments to a child's IEP may be necessary due to the results of an annual review or reevaluation; discontinuation of a school, program, or service; violent or disruptive behavior; or graduation. Before changing a substantive aspect of a student's program, written notice must be given to the parents of their right to review the proposed alteration, although consent is not required at this time. In the alternative, parents have the right to discuss the matter with the rest of the IEP team and, if dissatisfied, challenge the decision through either mediation or an impartial hearing.

Related Services

> When related services are found to be essential elements of a free appropriate public education under the Individuals with Disabilities Education Act, they must be provided regardless of cost.

As noted previously, a free appropriate public education may require the provision of related services in addition to special education. Related services include transportation and such developmental, corrective, and other supportive services (including speech pathology and audiology, psychological services, physical and occupational therapy, recreation, social work services, early identification and assessment, orientation and mobility services, school health services, counseling services, medical services for diagnostic and evaluation purposes, and parent counseling and training) that are necessary for a child with a disability to benefit from special education.[44] Physical, speech, and occupational forms of therapy also may qualify as related services. The areas of transportation, psychological, and health services have been subject to comparatively high levels of litigation and are summarized briefly here.

43. 34 C.F.R. § 300.455(a)(2), (3) (2003).
44. 20 U.S.C. § 1401(a)(17) (2003).

Transportation

Federal regulations require the provision of transportation as a related service for qualified children to and from school, within school buildings, and on school grounds, even if specialized equipment is needed in making programs and activities accessible. The child qualifies for transportation if such a service is provided for other children (e.g., all children residing more than two miles from school), or if it is included within an individualized education program (IEP) or Section 504 plan. Failure to provide the service to qualified students has resulted in courts requiring districts to reimburse parents for transportation costs, time, effort, baby-sitting services, and interest on their expenses.[45] However, other courts have concluded that where alternative transportation was provided, the district was not required to reimburse parents who wanted to transport their own child;[46] that a child's hearing impairment did not qualify her for special transportation;[47] and that transportation did not have to be provided following involvement in a privately funded after-school program unrelated to the IEP.[48]

Psychological Services

Psychological services are explicitly identified in federal statutes as related services to be included within IEPs, as appropriate. Such services include:

- The administration and interpretation of psychological and educational tests as well as other assessment procedures;
- Obtaining, integrating, and interpreting information about the child's behavior and condition;
- Consulting with staff in planning IEPs;
- Planning and managing a program of psychological services; and
- Assisting in the development of positive behavioral intervention strategies.[49]

When psychological services are needed to assist the child to benefit from instruction and are provided by a psychologist or other qualified individual, the services should be included within the IEP. However, if parents request psychiatric and other services provided by a physician, such requests may be denied.[50]

45. *See, e.g.,* Hurry v. Jones, 734 F.2d 879 (1st Cir. 1984); Taylor v. Bd. of Educ., 649 F. Supp. 1253 (N.D.N.Y. 1986).
46. DeLeon v. Susquehanna Cmty. Sch. Dist., 747 F.2d 149 (3d Cir. 1984).
47. McNair v. Oak Hills Local Sch. Dist., 872 F.2d 153 (6th Cir. 1989).
48. Roslyn Union Free Sch. Dist. v. Univ. of N.Y., 711 N.Y.S.2d 582 (App. Div. 2000).
49. 34 C.F.R. § 300.24(b)(9) (2003).
50. *See, e.g.,* Butler v. Evans, 225 F.3d 887 (7th Cir. 2000) (concluding that the district was not responsible for paying for psychiatric placement or related medical expenses; the child was schizo-affective, paranoid, suicidal, and satanical and represented a danger to self and others).

Health Services

Courts also have been asked to differentiate between medical and health services. As indicated, the Individuals with Disabilities Education Act excludes medical services except for diagnostic and evaluative purposes and defines both *medical services* (i.e., those provided by a licensed physician) and *health services* (i.e., those provided by a school nurse or other qualified person). Health services such as catheterization often are essential in that they enable the child to attend school and thereby benefit from instruction.[51] Nevertheless, the issue of health care has been a volatile one given the growing number of medically fragile children now in public schools and escalating costs. This growth is due in part to the number of seriously ill children who now live to school age (e.g., children who are HIV positive or have AIDS) and to the desire of many parents to have their children educated in regular education facilities whenever possible.

In 1999, the Supreme Court provided guidance to lower courts in *Cedar Rapids Community School District v. Garret F.,*[52] a case involving a child with paralysis from the neck down. To remain in school he required full-time nursing care. The district argued that the services collectively should be viewed as medical, even if individually they qualified as health services, and asserted that it would incur an undue financial burden if required to provide the services. The Court acknowledged the legitimate financial concerns of the district, but noted that the law required the court to reject the undue burden claim.[53] **Moreover, the Court applied the "bright-line" test requiring the provision of all health care services provided by anyone other than a physician, if required to enable the child to attend school.** Thus, the Court clarified that any health service that a student may need to participate in a school setting[54] had to be provided, regardless of cost.

Extended School Year

> Extended school year programs must be made available to children who do not incur educational benefit during the traditional school year, presuming that additional schooling or services would foreseeably result in such benefit.

Federal statutes require that programs be both appropriate and designed to provide educational benefit. In meeting these mandates, it may be necessary for a particular child to

51. *See, e.g.*, Irving Indep. Sch. Dist. v. Tatro, 468 U.S. 883 (1984).
52. 526 U.S. 66 (1999).
53. Although school districts cannot use the undue burden defense under the IDEA, they can assert it under both § 504 and the ADA.
54. Note, however, that some health care services do not have to be provided when the child is home bound. *See, e.g.*, Daniel O. v. Mo. State Bd. of Educ., No. 99-2792, 2000 U.S. App. LEXIS 7032 (8th Cir. April 19, 2000).

receive services beyond the traditional nine-month school year. Although school districts can prescribe a fixed number of instructional days for students without disabilities, such a determination must be made on an individual basis for children with disabilities. Nonetheless, when extended school year (ESY) services are found "beneficial" or even "maximizing," but are not "essential" to the provision of an appropriate program, they are not required under the Individuals with Disabilities Education Act.

When ESY services are provided, programs will vary widely with some mandating the extension of the full individualized education program (IEP) for one, two, or three additional months; others providing new or different services; and yet others utilizing all or some of the same services, but in different amounts. Furthermore, in fairly narrow circumstances an ESY program may include the delivery of only related services (e.g., when a child needs physical therapy during the summer to remain sufficiently flexible or mobile to participate within the IEP in the fall). The IEP team is responsible for making individualized decisions regarding eligibility for ESY services and for selecting appropriate services, including their amount and duration.

Eligibility decisions should be made annually during the IEP review and be based on information in addition to regression-recoupment.[55] Consideration also should be given to:

- Individual need,
- The nature and severity of the disability,
- Self-sufficiency and independence,
- Whether educational benefit can be incurred without such services,
- Whether short-term goals and objectives are being met, and
- Whether progress is being made toward the accomplishment of long-term goals.

In contrast, whether the child received ESY services in previous years is not a factor to consider in making the eligibility decision for the current year.

Participation in Sports

Athletic association rules that deny or limit the participation of students with disabilities must qualify as reasonable *and* reflect the essential elements of the sport.

Children with disabilities, like many children without disabilities, often are interested in participating in interscholastic sports. But, the requests of these students to participate at times have been denied because either they failed to meet eligibility requirements or their participation represented too great a risk to themselves or others. Although a few cases have been

55. In this context, *regression* refers to the loss of knowledge, ability, or skill a student may experience during a break in instruction, whereas *recoupment* refers to the time it takes to regain the knowledge, ability, or skill that was lost once instruction is resumed.

filed under the Individuals with Disabilities Education Act (IDEA), most disputes are based either on Section 504 of the Rehabilitation Act or the Americans with Disabilities Act (ADA).

The IDEA has been involved in two types of sports-related disability cases: (1) where parents wanted to include sports in the individualized education program (IEP) and (2) where the planning team included sports in the IEP and the state athletic association penalized the school for allowing an ineligible student to participate. **Because sports participation is seldom considered *essential* for students to incur educational benefit, it typically is not included in IEPs**. Furthermore, from the school district's perspective, it generally is not prudent to include sports, or any other extracurricular activity, in individualized programs. Such a practice establishes an entitlement to team membership (not to participation per se, however) and enables sports to become a right that can be withdrawn only through due process.

In the second scenario (i.e., where the team is disciplined), state athletic associations do not receive IDEA funds or any other type of federal financial assistance and consequently are not required to comply with either the IDEA or Section 504. Accordingly, if the IEP team were to include sports in the IEP and thereby allow an otherwise ineligible student to participate in an interscholastic contest, school officials may have created a situation that will result in rules violations and penalties. The Montana Supreme Court "strongly encouraged" educators to be prudent in including sports in IEPs and warned that they might be "making a promise [they] simply cannot keep."[56] Given this situation, the district will have to sue the athletic association possibly under the Fourteenth Amendment[57] or the ADA to terminate whatever remedial actions have been taken against it. In the end, even if the district were to prevail, it will have incurred substantial expense and dedicated considerable personnel time to a problem that could have easily been avoided by not including sports in IEPs and by uniformly applying eligibility regulations.

Unlike the IDEA, there are myriad related scenarios and cases regarding athletic participation under Section 504, and more recently under the ADA. Most claims have alleged discrimination due to facially neutral regulations that disproportionately affect students with disabilities, such as age limitations,[58] grade-point average restrictions,[59] one-year residency and transfer requirements,[60] and eight-semester/four-season limitations.[61]

Historically, all students were required to meet eligibility criteria and were allowed to play only when they were otherwise qualified to participate *and* if they made the team. Most courts still permit the uniform application of such rules, but that approach may be changing. A related issue reviewed by the Supreme Court in a professional sport context has applica-

56. J.M. v. Mont. High Sch. Ass'n, 875 P.2d 1026, 1032 (Mont. 1994).

57. Such suits are more likely today given the Supreme Court's ruling in Brentwood Acad. v. Tenn. Secondary Sch. Athletic Ass'n., 535 U.S. 971 (2002), in which the state athletic association was declared a state actor, notwithstanding the fact that it was a private corporation.

58. *See, e.g.,* Sandison v. Mich. High Sch. Athletic Ass'n, 64 F.3d 1026 (6th Cir. 1995); Reaves v. Mills, 904 F. Supp. 120 (W.D.N.Y. 1995).

59. *See, e.g.,* Hoot v. Milan Area Sch., 853 F. Supp. 243 (E.D. Mich. 1994).

60. *See, e.g.,* Crocker v. Tenn. Secondary Sch. Athletic Ass'n, 980 F.2d 382 (6th Cir. 1992).

61. *See, e.g.,* J.M. v. Mont. High Sch. Ass'n, 875 P.2d 1026 (Mont. 1994).

tion to interscholastic and all other organized sports. In *PGA Tour v. Martin,* the Court supported a professional golfer's effort to be permitted to ride a cart rather than walk the course, as the event rules required.[62] Walking caused him pain that resulted in fatigue and anxiety that could lead to hemorrhaging and the development of blood clots or fractures. The Court reasoned that "shot making" was the essence of golf and that walking was neither an essential attribute nor an indispensable feature of the sport, notwithstanding contradictory testimony from golf legends Arnold Palmer, Jack Nicklaus, and Ken Venturi. This decision will have implications for all sports, as it requires the evaluation of any rule that disqualifies an otherwise qualified participant with a disability. Review of such rules should reveal whether they qualify as essential features of the sport or are peripheral and therefore subject to alteration or elimination.

Given the Supreme Court majority opinion in *PGA Tour,* state athletic associations (and other organizations that coordinate sports) need to follow a four-step process in the development and application of their policies and rules:

- Identify those rules that have the potential of disqualifying students with disabilities due to the limitations posed by their disabilities;
- Determine whether each identified rule supports a necessary and valid purpose;
- Assess whether the requested modification or adjustment is reasonable and necessary for the individual to participate in the activity; and
- Ascertain whether provision of the modification or adjustment would fundamentally alter the nature of the competition, adversely affect the demonstrated valid purpose of the rule, or result in an unfair advantage.[63]

The Seventh Circuit examined such a case where a student with above-average intelligence had dropped out of school at least in part due to his poor performance related to a learning disability.[64] He later reentered school and participated in basketball. Eventually, he was declared ineligible under the rule limiting participation to the first eight semesters following commencement of the ninth grade. The student argued that the period he was not enrolled in school should not count against his eligibility, notwithstanding explicit wording in the bylaw to the contrary. The court reasoned that waiver of the rule in *this* instance involving *this* student would not represent a fundamental alteration to the rule or create an undue financial burden for the association.[65]

Another type of sports-related case involves athletes with physically limiting conditions but who are otherwise qualified to participate. In many of these situations, the athlete

62. 532 U.S. 661 (2001).

63. *See, e.g.,* Cruz v. Penn. Interscholastic Athletic Ass'n, 157 F. Supp. 2d 485 (E.D. Pa. 2001) (applying *PGA Tour* criteria and granting a preliminary injunction when a student with a disability was denied the opportunity to participate in sports due to being overage).

64. Washington v. Ind. High Sch. Athletic Ass'n, 181 F.3d 840 (7th Cir. 1999).

65. *But see* McPherson v. Mich. High Sch. Athletic Ass'n, 119 F.3d 453 (6th Cir. 1997) (upholding application of an eight-semester rule against a student with ADHD and seizure disorder and concluding that its waiver would represent a fundamental alteration of the sports program and create an immense and undue financial burden for the state association).

is willing to assume the risks of participation, to sign a waiver of liability if injured in the normal occurrence of the game, and to provide affidavits signed by physicians both indicating that participation is safe and identifying any necessary safety wear. Since the mid-to-late 1970s, the majority of courts has supported the right of student athletes to participate, even for students missing an organ, limb, eye, and the like.[66] More recently, however, two courts addressing claims of discrimination filed by college athletes have sided with the educational institutions.[67] Both courts indicated that they were not in a position to determine which "experts" were correct as to the degree of risk that would be present if the athlete were to participate. Instead, it was their view that deference should be given to the institution's experts as long as their professional judgment was reasonable, rational, and supported by substantial, competent evidence. This reasoning is consistent with recent trends in disability law and may signal a return to providing deference to school experts in such matters.

Discipline

> Students with disabilities may be expelled only when it can be shown that the behavior on which the disciplinary action is based is not a manifestation of the child's disability.

Students with disabilities are not exempt from reasonable disciplinary measures, although due process exceeding that provided regular education students is required at times, and penalties are capped on occasion. **In 1988, the Supreme Court in *Honig v. Doe* concluded that the suspension of two students pending the outcome of expulsion proceedings was a prohibited change in placement and violated the stay-put provision of the IDEA.**[68] The state superintendent of public instruction had urged the Supreme Court to recognize a "dangerousness" exception to the stay-put requirement. The superintendent also contended that Congress could not have intended that school officials return violent or dangerous students to the classroom during lengthy administrative proceedings. Disagreeing, the Supreme Court stated that Congress deliberately stripped schools of the unilateral authority to exclude students with disabilities. The history of exclusion of such students prior to passage of the Act and the early litigation that guided the development of the law convinced the Court that the conspicuous absence of an emergency exception was intentional.

66. *See, e.g.,* Grube v. Bethlehem Area Sch. Dist., 550 F. Supp. 418 (E.D. Penn. 1982) (loss of kidney); Suemnick v. Mich. High Sch. Athletic Ass'n, No. 4-70592 (E.D. Mich. 1974) (loss of leg); Kampmeier v. Harris, 411 N.Y.S.2d 744 (App. Div. 1978) (impaired vision).

67. Knapp v. Northwestern Univ., 101 F.3d 473 (7th Cir. 1996); Pahulu v. Univ. of Kan., 897 F. Supp. 1387 (D. Kan. 1995).

68. 484 U.S. 305 (1988). The "stay-put" requirement stipulates that the child must remain in his or her current educational placement throughout administrative proceedings, unless an alternative placement is agreed to by the parents.

The Supreme Court, however, emphasized that school officials are not without options when confronted with a dangerous student. They can use a range of normal procedures (e.g., suspension of up to 10 days, detention, time-out). In addition, the Court indicated that if other forms of discipline are not successful, and the student already has been suspended for the maximum 10-day period but continues to pose a threat, school officials may seek injunctive relief if the parents refuse to agree to a change in placement.

Among the disciplinary options available to school officials, suspension and expulsion have resulted in considerable judicial action. Each is reviewed here in greater detail.

Suspension

Suspension is the removal of a student from the educational setting for 10 days or less and may result in either an in-school placement (e.g., in-school suspension room) or complete removal from the school setting. **Students with disabilities generally may not be suspended for more than 10 consecutive days or receive repetitive brief suspensions that aggregate to more than 10 days during the school year**. Successive suspensions exceeding the 10-day limit are possible, but only when they do not represent a pattern of removal and are based on separate incidents of misconduct.[69] In the comparatively exceptional circumstance when removal justifiably exceeds the 10-day limit, services consistent with the individualized education program must be provided beginning the eleventh day.[70] The key in determining whether a day of suspension is to apply toward the total is to assess whether the child has been removed from the IEP, not whether the child has received an in-school or out-of-school suspension.

If a student is assigned to a time-out room, rather than an in-school suspension room, and instruction and/or services identified within the IEP continue to be delivered by a properly credentialed individual, it is unlikely that the time removed from the regular education classroom will contribute to the 10-day limit. To reduce the likelihood of litigation, however, it is recommended that assignment to time-out be included within the IEPs of students who are likely to require such assignments as a form of behavior modification or intervention. Once the parent has agreed to such a provision, assignment to time-out will be *consistent with* the IEP and not be viewed as *removal from* the IEP.

Expulsion

Expulsion is the removal of a student from the IEP for more than 10 consecutive days and qualifies as a change of placement. In such instances, the student will either be at home or assigned to an appropriate interim alternative educational setting. Assignment to an alternative setting is possible when the student carries a weapon or *knowingly* possesses, uses, sells, or solicits illegal drugs while at school or at a school function. When this occurs, the school district is responsible for conducting a functional behavioral assessment and for preparing a behavioral intervention plan, if one has not already been prepared. Interventions should be

69. For example, a pattern of removal would be present where a student receives three five-day suspensions for smoking cigarettes while on school grounds.

70. 34 C.F.R. § 300.520(a)(1)(ii) (2003).

appropriately implemented to address the conduct that resulted in the disciplinary action, and modified when needed.[71]

A hearing officer, in an expedited hearing, is authorized to assign a student to an alternative setting if the claims are supported by *substantial evidence* (i.e., something greater than preponderance of evidence, but less than proof beyond a reasonable doubt) that maintaining the student in the current placement is likely to result in injury to the student or to others. The hearing officer will consider the appropriateness of the student's current placement, whether supplementary aids and services were used to minimize the risks in the current placement, and whether the alternative setting will permit the student to make progress within the IEP.

No later than 10 days following a student's removal, a review must be conducted to assess the relationship between the student's disability and the behavior that is subject to the disciplinary action. This *manifestation determination* must be conducted by the IEP team and other qualified personnel and entails reviewing evaluations, diagnostic results, information supplied by the parents, the IEP, observations, and the like. The team must determine whether:

- At the time of the disruption, the student was being provided with a free appropriate public education in the least restrictive environment;
- Intervention strategies were provided consistent with the IEP; and
- The disability impaired the student's ability to understand the impact and consequences of the conduct or to control the behavior.

If the placement and services were improper or the student's disability impaired the ability to "understand" or "control," the conduct must be considered disability related.[72] When this occurs, the student cannot be expelled, although a change of placement to a more restrictive setting may be necessary if the student's prior conduct is likely to be repeated within the current placement, in spite of behavioral interventions and supervision.

In situations where the behavior is not found to be disability related, the student may be subjected to the same punishment that would have been administered had the student not been disabled, except that services consistent with the IEP must continue to be provided. At this time, officials need to transmit the records of the student to those making the final disciplinary decision. If removal for more than 10 days is supported, services consistent with the IEP need to be delivered in the home or other environment that will enable the student to make progress toward achieving the goals identified in the IEP.

When expulsion is permissible and appropriate, the parents have the right to challenge the manifestation determination and resulting decision. In such instances, federal law once again requires that an expedited hearing be conducted. During the appeals process, the

71. 34 C.F.R. § 300.519-300.520(a)(2), (b), (c) (2003).

72. *See, e.g.*, Doe v. Bd. of Educ., 115 F.3d 1273 (7th Cir. 1997) (noting that the committee unanimously determined that the plaintiff's drug use was not related to his learning disability); Randy M. v. Texas City ISD, 93 F. Supp. 2d 1310 (S.D. Tex. 2000) (concluding that ripping the breakaway pants off a female student thereby exposing her underwear was not related to the student's learning disability).

"then-current placement" is the alternative setting (e.g., home setting, special program, special school), not the former placement where the disruption occurred.

Interestingly, even students who are not yet identified as disabled may be protected by the Individuals with Disabilities Education Act (IDEA) if district officials had knowledge that such students *may be* disabled. "Knowledge" exists where a parent or educator either expresses concern that the student may be disabled given the behavior or performance *or* requests an evaluation. The student is not entitled to protection if found not to qualify following an evaluation, or if school officials determine that assessment is not necessary. Where an evaluation is requested and appears justified, it should be expedited. If the student does not qualify as both disabled and in need of special education and related services, instruction during the removal period need not be provided, unless available to regular education students who have been similarly withdrawn. In contrast, if the student does qualify as disabled, special education and related services need to be provided.

It should be recognized, however, that the IDEA does not prohibit personnel from reporting any crime a student may have committed to law enforcement authorities. Law-enforcement officials are not bound by the IDEA and may require an unruly or delinquent student to submit to treatment, home detention, or incarceration.

Procedural Safeguards

> Whenever parents disagree with the placement committee or an action taken by the district, they are entitled to procedural due process.

School officials generally make good faith efforts to meet the needs of children with disabilities, yet there will be times when the parents disagree with evaluation, placement, and program decisions. Disagreement may come about early in the process (e.g., failure to provide consent for initial evaluation) or later (e.g., termination of services allegedly due to graduation). Either party may initiate the due process procedures identified in the Individuals with Disabilities Education Act (IDEA)—that is, mediation and/or impartial hearing, state review where appropriate, and court of appropriate jurisdiction (see Figure 7.1).

As discussed in the discipline section, during IDEA administrative and judicial appeals, the student is assigned to the "then-current educational placement" or a placement agreed to by the parents and the public officials.[73] This "stay-put" provision applies in *all* cases where a change of placement is to occur,[74] including those where the content of the

73. 34 C.F.R. § 300.514(a) (2003).

74. However, where a child transitioned from an individualized family service plan (similar to an IEP for preschool children) to an IEP, changing the personnel to provide the services (e.g., tutors) was not found to be a violation of the stay-put provision. Johnson v. Special Educ. Hearing Office, 287 F.3d 1176 (9th Cir. 2002).

FIGURE 7.1 *IDEA Due Process*

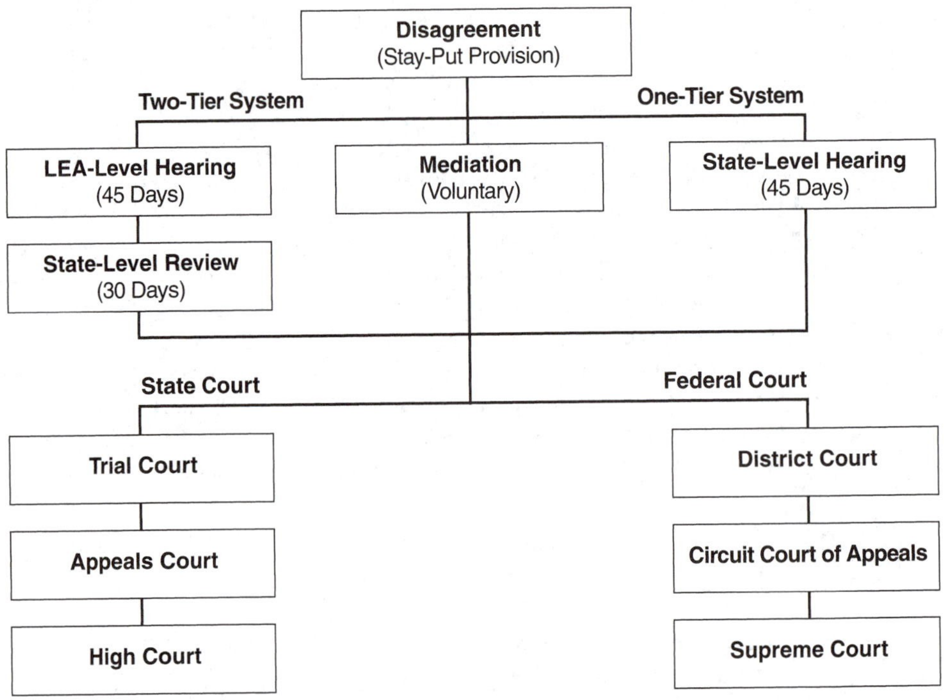

placement remains the same, but the least restrictive environment has been altered.[75] The current placement may be anywhere along the continuum of alternative public or private placements. If the complaint deals with the initial placement of the child, the regular classroom represents the current placement, although additional services may be agreed to by the parties. The placement remains the same until all administrative hearings have been completed, unless the child is unilaterally removed by the parent and placed in an alternative setting. Once administrative appeals have been exhausted, the current placement may change, depending on the position taken by the state hearing officer or state review official.

Also, according to the Office of Special Education Programs (OSEP), stay-put requirements apply even when a child changes school districts within the same state given that the placement has already been determined in accordance with state procedures and with the consent of the child's parents.[76] However, the OSEP does not expect public school systems to maintain the current placements of children moving into their service areas from

75. *See, e.g.,* Hale v. Poplar Bluff R-1 Sch. Dist., 280 F.3d 831 (8th Cir. 2002) (requiring the provision of compensatory education during the summer as the district violated the stay-put provision by changing the student's placement from home-bound to school without going through due process; the school had argued that it need not provide due process given that the services remained the same, only the location of service changed).

76. Inquiry of Rieser, OSEP Policy Letter, July 17, 1986 (U.S. Dep't Educ. 1986).

out of state,[77] or to maintain a private placement unilaterally selected by the parent, but not supported at the administrative hearings.[78]

Conclusion

The rights of students with disabilities have expanded significantly since 1975 and include rights to accessible facilities, appropriate programs, and least restrictive placements. Also, such students must be given the equal opportunity to participate in extracurricular activities, including sports, assuming that their participation does not represent a danger to themselves or others.

School districts are responsible for identifying, assessing, and placing all qualified students with disabilities. All placements must be both appropriate and least restrictive; most will require a public placement, although some placements will be in private schools. Also, students with disabilities may be disciplined in the same manner as other students, although there may be additional procedural requirements to meet. Moreover, where expulsion is merited, services consistent with the IEP must continue to be delivered. Understanding what federal laws both allow and require should help educators prepare legal and effective placements for children with disabilities.

Points to Ponder

1. The state provides limited support to children with special needs above that provided for all children ($7,000 per pupil). A family moves into a poor, rural community and requests appropriate programs for two children, ages 5 and 6, with severe physical and mental disabilities. The cost per child will be over $100,000, primarily due to health care. The services will have to be provided for several years, as neither child's health is likely to improve. The district refused to pay and claimed undue hardship. Following unsuccessful administrative review, the parents sued the district under the IDEA seeking a FAPE for their children. Are the parents likely to win the suit? Why or why not?

2. The school district considers itself to be a "full-inclusion" district. All children are initially placed in regular education with supplemental aids and services, as directed by the school administration. Parents, who recently moved into the district, contend that regular education is clearly not the appropriate placement for their child with severe disabilities. They request a more segregated placement, which is denied by school authorities. Following unsuccessful administrative appeals, the parents sued under the IDEA. Which party is likely to prevail?

77. OSEP Policy Memorandum 96-5. *See also* Michael C. *ex rel.* Stephen C. v. Radnor Township Sch. Dist., 202 F.3d 642 (3d Cir. 2000) (concluding that the stay-put provision did not apply when a child's family moved from one state to another).

78. *See, e.g.*, Tucker v. Calloway County Bd. of Educ., 136 F.3d 495 (6th Cir. 1998) (denying reimbursement and noting that the stay-put provision does not require the district to pay for a unilaterally selected private placement during the course of litigation).

3. A child in your homeroom has a mild learning disability. He lives one-half mile from school. His parents requested that transportation services be provided, but the request was denied. The district noted that the family lives less than a mile from the school (i.e., the distance established by the state to require the transportation of elementary school children), and that the nature of the student's disability does not necessitate the provision of transportation. The parents pointed out that the bus travels in front of their home each day and would merely need to stop to allow their son to board. The district would incur no additional cost. The parents sued under the IDEA and Section 504. Are they likely to win?

4. Your daughter wants to play softball for her school team, but was denied because of her low grade-point average. You sued the state athletic association under Section 504 when it denied her grade appeal. The association uniformly applies its academic, residency, and other requirements. You contend that the requirements should not apply to her, given that a learning disability is in large part responsible for her low GPA. Are you likely to win this suit? Explain.

8

Student Discipline

Student misconduct continues to be one of the most persistent and troublesome problems confronting educators. With the increased incidence of drug and alcohol abuse and violence among teenagers, greater public attention has focused on school disciplinary problems. Schools have devoted more attention to violence prevention strategies, including not only stringent security measures but also modification of the curricula to strengthen students' social skills and the training of teachers and administrators to monitor the school climate. Some states and local school districts have enacted restrictive laws or policies that call for "zero tolerance" of weapons, drugs, and violence on campus. The efficacy of legislating tougher approaches to create safe schools has evoked volatile debates, particularly in light of the higher rates of suspension and expulsion for African American and Hispanic students.[1] The range of strategies employed by educators to maintain a safe and secure learning environment is examined in this chapter from a legal perspective; no attempt is made to debate the merits of particular strategies. The analyses focus on the development of conduct regulations, the imposition of sanctions for noncompliance, and the procedures required in the administration of student punishments.

The law clearly authorizes the state and its agencies to establish and enforce reasonable conduct codes to protect the rights of students and school districts and to ensure that school environments are conducive to learning. Historically, courts exercised limited review of student disciplinary regulations, and pupils seldom were successful in challenging policies governing their behavior. Courts were reluctant to interfere with the judgment of school officials because public education was considered to be a privilege bestowed by the state.

There has been a quantum leap from this early judicial posture to the active protection of students' rights in the late 1960s and early 1970s, but judicial developments have not eroded educators' rights or their responsibilities. The Seventh Circuit noted that **the Supreme Court "has repeatedly emphasized the need for affirming the comprehensive authority of the states and of school officials, consistent with fundamental constitu-**

1. Robert C. Johnston, "Federal Data Highlight Disparities in Discipline," *Education Week* (June 21, 2000), p. 3.

tional safeguards, to prescribe and control conduct in the schools."[2] Reasonable disciplinary regulations, even those impairing students' protected liberties, have been upheld if justified by a legitimate educational interest. Educators not only have the authority but also the duty to maintain discipline in public schools. Although rules made at any level (e.g., classroom, building, school board) cannot conflict with higher authorities (e.g., constitutional and statutory provisions), building administrators and teachers retain substantial latitude in establishing and enforcing conduct codes that are necessary for instructional activities to take place. After a brief discussion of conduct regulations, subsequent sections of this chapter address legal issues related to expulsions and suspensions, corporal punishment, academic sanctions, search and seizure, and remedies for unlawful disciplinary actions.

Conduct Regulations

School boards are granted considerable latitude in establishing and interpreting their own disciplinary rules and regulations. The Supreme Court has held that the interpretation of a school regulation resides with the body that adopted it and is charged with its enforcement.[3] Disciplinary policies, however, have been struck down if unconstitutionally vague. Policies prohibiting "improper conduct" and behavior "inimical to the best interests of the school" have been invalidated because they have not specified the precise nature of the impermissible conduct.[4] A vague school district discipline policy prohibiting the consumption of alcohol prior to the school day or a school event was found to be overly broad in an Arkansas case; it could be arbitrarily interpreted as minutes, hours, or even days before attending a school activity.[5] Although policies should be precise, courts have recognized that disciplinary regulations do not have to satisfy the stringent criteria or level of specificity required in criminal statutes. The Eighth Circuit noted that the determining factor is whether a regulation's wording is precise enough to notify an individual that specific behavior is clearly unacceptable.[6]

In addition to reviewing the validity of the conduct regulation on which a specific punishment is based, courts evaluate the nature and extent of the penalty imposed in relation to the gravity of the offense. Courts also consider the age, gender, mental condition, and past behavior of the student in deciding whether a given punishment is appropriate. The judiciary has sanctioned punishments such as the denial of privileges, suspension, expulsion, corporal punishment, and detention after school. Any of these punishments, however, could be considered unreasonable under a specific set of circumstances. Consequently, courts examine

2. Boucher v. Sch. Bd., 134 F.2d 821, 827 (7th Cir. 1998).
3. *See* Bd. of Educ. v. McCluskey, 458 U.S. 966 (1982); Wood v. Strickland, 420 U.S. 308 (1975).
4. *See, e.g.*, Killion v. Franklin Reg'l Sch. Dist., 136 F. Supp. 2d 446, 459 (W.D. Pa. 2001) (finding school district's retaliatory policy against verbal or other abuse of teachers unconstitutionally vague—"devoid of any detail"); Wilson v. S. Cent. Local Sch. Dist., 669 N.E.2d 277 (Ohio Ct. App. 1995) (holding that a student could not be suspended for possession of tobacco under a conduct code specifying that suspension would be for "very serious offenses," because state law required the board of education to specify the type of misconduct for which a student may be suspended).
5. Caliborne v. Beebe Sch. Dist., 687 F. Supp. 1358 (E.D. Ark. 1988).
6. Woodis v. Westark Cmty. Coll., 160 F.3d 435 (8th Cir. 1998).

each unique factual situation; they do not evaluate the validity of student punishments in the abstract.

Litigation challenging disciplinary practices often has focused on the procedures followed in administering punishments rather than on the substance of disciplinary rules or the nature of the sanctions imposed. Implicit in all judicial declarations regarding school discipline is the notion that severe penalties require more formal procedures, whereas minor punishments necessitate only minimal due process (e.g., notice of the charges and an opportunity to refute them). Nonetheless, **any disciplinary action should be accompanied by some procedure to ensure the rudiments of fundamental fairness and to prevent mistakes in the disciplinary process.** The Fifth Circuit noted that "the quantum and quality of procedural due process to be afforded a student varies with the seriousness of the punishment to be imposed."[7]

The judiciary has recognized that punishment for student conduct off school grounds must be supported by evidence that the behavior has a detrimental impact on other pupils, teachers, or school activities.[8] In an early case, the Connecticut Supreme Court held that school officials could regulate student conduct outside school hours and off school property if such conduct affected the management of the school.[9] Courts have upheld sanctions imposed on students for engaging in assault or criminal acts off school grounds,[10] compiling a "shit list" of other students noting derogatory characteristics,[11] making threatening, harassing remarks on a web site created at home,[12] writing a threatening letter over the summer break to a former girlfriend,[13] and stealing automobile parts.[14] Courts, however, have prohibited school authorities from punishing students for misbehavior off school grounds if pupils had not been informed that such conduct would result in sanctions or if the misbehavior had no direct relationship to the welfare of the school.

School personnel must be careful not to place unnecessary constraints on student behavior. In developing disciplinary policies, all possible means of achieving the desired outcomes should be explored, and means that are least restrictive of students' personal freedoms should be selected (see Figure 8.1 for general guidelines). Once it is determined that a specific conduct regulation is necessary, the rule should be clearly written so that it is not open to multiple interpretations. Each regulation should include the rationale for enacting the rule as well as the penalties for infractions. Considerable discretion exists in determining

7. Pervis v. LaMarque Indep. Dist., 466 F.2d 1054, 1057 (5th Cir. 1972).

8. For a synthesis of applicable case law on conduct off school grounds, *see* Perry A. Zirkel, "Disciplining Students for Off-Campus Misconduct," *Education Law Reporter,* vol. 163 (2002), pp. 551-553.

9. O'Rourke v. Walker, 102 Conn. 130 (1925).

10. Pollnow v. Glennon, 757 F.2d 496 (2d Cir. 1985); Nicholas v. Sch. Comm., 587 N.E.2d 211 (Mass. 1992).

11. Donovan v. Ritchie, 68 F.3d 14 (1st Cir. 1995).

12. J.S. v. Bethlehem Area Sch. Dist., 807 A.2d 847 (Pa. 2002). *But see* Beussink v. Woodland R-IV Sch. Dist., 30 F. Supp. 2d 1175 (E.D. Mo. 1998) (concluding that a web site created off campus did not materially and substantially interfere with the educational process). *See also* text accompanying note 65, Chapter 5.

13. Howard v. Colonial Sch. Dist., 621 A.2d 362 (Del. Super. Ct. 1992).

14. Felton v. Fayette Sch. Dist., 875 F.2d 191 (8th Cir. 1989).

FIGURE 8.1 ***Guidelines for the Development of a Student Conduct Code***

- Rules must have an explicit purpose and be clearly written to accomplish that purpose.
- Any conduct regulation adopted should be necessary in order to carry out the school's educational mission; rules should not be designed merely to satisfy the preferences of school board members, administrators, or teachers.
- Rules should be publicized to students and their parents.
- Rules should be specific and clearly stated so students know what behaviors are expected and what behaviors are prohibited.
- Student handbooks that incorporate references to specific state laws should also include the law or paraphrase the statutory language.
- Regulations should not impair constitutionally protected rights unless there is an overriding public interest, such as a threat to the safety of others.
- A rule should not be "ex post facto"; it should not be adopted to prevent a specific activity that school officials know is being planned or has already occurred.
- Punishments should be appropriate to the offense, taking into consideration the child's age, gender, disability, and past behavior.
- Some procedural safeguards should accompany the administration of all punishments; the formality of the procedures should be in accord with the severity of the punishment.
- A process for periodic review of the student handbook should be established that involves students and school staff members in the revisions and refinement.

that certain actions deserve harsher penalties (i.e., imposing a more severe punishment for the sale of drugs as opposed to the possession or use of drugs). **To ensure that students are knowledgeable of the conduct rules, it is advisable to require students to sign a form indicating that they have read the conduct regulations.** With such documentation, pupils would be unable to plead ignorance of the rules as a defense for their misconduct.

In designing and enforcing pupil conduct codes, it is important that school personnel bear in mind the distinction between students' substantive and procedural rights. If a disciplinary regulation or the administration of punishment violates substantive rights (e.g., restricts protected speech), the regulation cannot be enforced nor the punishment imposed. When only procedural rights are impaired, however, the punishment generally can be administered if determined at an appropriate hearing that the punishment is warranted.

Expulsions and Suspensions

> Some type of procedural due process should be afforded to students prior to the imposition of expulsions or suspensions.

Expulsions and suspensions are among the most widely used disciplinary measures. Courts uniformly have upheld educators' authority to use such measures as punishments, but due process is required to ensure that students are afforded fair and impartial treatment.

Although most states have recognized that students have a property right to an education, they may be deprived of this right if they violate school rules. This section focuses on disciplinary action in which students are removed from the regular instructional program.

Expulsions

State laws and school board regulations are usually quite specific regarding the grounds for *expulsions*—that is, the removal of students from school for a lengthy period of time (usually in excess of 10 days). Such grounds are not limited to occurrences during school hours and can include infractions on school property immediately before or after school, at school-sponsored activities on or off school grounds, or en route to or from school. Although specific grounds vary from state to state, infractions typically considered legitimate grounds for expulsion include:

- Engaging in violence,
- Stealing or vandalizing school or private property,
- Causing or attempting to cause physical injury to others,
- Possessing a weapon,
- Possessing or using drugs or alcohol, and
- Engaging in criminal activity or other behavior forbidden by state laws.

Procedural Requirements. State statutes specify procedures for expulsion and the limitations on their length. Except for the possession of weapons, a student generally cannot be expelled beyond the end of the current academic year unless the expulsion takes place near the close of the term. A teacher or administrator may initiate expulsion proceedings, but usually only the school board can expel a student. **Prior to expulsion, students must be provided procedural protections guaranteed by the U.S. Constitution; however, school officials can remove students immediately if they pose a danger or threat to themselves or others.**[15] No duty exists to provide an educational alternative for a properly expelled student unless the school board policies or state mandates specify that alternative programs must be provided or the student is receiving special education services.[16]

Although the details of required procedures must be gleaned from state statutes and school board regulations, courts have held that students facing expulsion from public school are guaranteed at least minimum due process under the Fourteenth Amendment (see Figure 8.2 for a listing of elements). Procedural safeguards required may vary depending on the circumstances of a particular situation. In a Mississippi case, a student and his parents claimed that prior to an expulsion hearing they should have been given a list of the witnesses and a summary of their testimony.[17] Recognizing that such procedural protections generally

15. *See, e.g.,* Lavine v. Blaine Sch. Dist., 257 F.3d 981 (9th Cir. 2001), *cert. denied,* 536 U.S. 959 (2002).

16. *See* Gun-Free Schools Act, 20 U.S.C. § 7151 (2003) (allows school officials to place students' expelled for gun possession in alternative instructional programs). *See also* text accompanying note 67, Chapter 7, for a discussion of the expulsion of children with disabilities.

17. Keough v. Tate County Bd. of Educ., 748 F.2d 1077 (5th Cir. 1984).

FIGURE 8.2 ***Procedural Due Process for Student Expulsions***

- Written notice of the charges; the intention to expel; the place, time, and circumstances of the hearing; and sufficient time for a defense to be prepared;
- A full and fair hearing before an impartial adjudicator;
- The right to legal counsel or some other adult representatio;
- The right to be fully apprised of the proof or evidence;
- The opportunity to present witnesses or evidence;
- The opportunity to cross-examine opposing witnesses; and
- Some type of written record demonstrating that the decision was based on the evidence presented at the hearing.

should be afforded prior to a long-term expulsion, the Fifth Circuit nonetheless held that they were not requisite in this case. The parents had been fully apprised of the charges, the facts supporting the charges, and the nature of the hearing. Consequently, the court concluded that the student suffered no material prejudice from the school board's failure to supply a list of witnesses; the witnesses provided no surprises or interference with the student's ability to present his case. In a later case involving expulsion for possession of drugs, the same court found no impairment of a student's rights when he was denied an opportunity to confront and rebut witnesses who accused him of selling drugs.[18] The names of student witnesses had been withheld to prevent retaliation against them. Similarly, the Sixth Circuit noted that it is critical to protect the anonymity of students who "blow the whistle" on classmates involved in serious offenses such as drug dealing.[19]

State laws and school board policies often provide students facing expulsion with more elaborate procedural safeguards than the constitutional protections. Once such expulsion procedures are established, courts will require that they be followed.

Zero-Tolerance Policies. The growing concern about school safety has led to specific federal and state laws directed at the discipline of students who bring weapons onto school campuses. Under the Gun-Free Schools Act of 1994, all states were mandated to enact legislation requiring at least a one-year expulsion for students who bring firearms to school.[20] In expanding the scope of the law, states have added to the list of prohibitions weapons such as knives, explosive devices, hand chains, and other offensive weapons as well as drugs and violent acts. The federal law also requires state provisions to permit the local school superintendent to modify the expulsion requirement on a case-by-case basis.

Severe criticism has been directed at zero-tolerance policies when school officials fail to exercise discretion and flexibility. The American Bar Association and others have called for an end to such policies that require automatic penalties without assessing the cir-

18. Brewer v. Austin Indep. Sch. Dist., 779 F.2d 260 (5th Cir. 1985).
19. Newsome v. Batavia Local Sch. Dist., 842 F.2d 920 (6th Cir. 1988).
20. The Gun-Free Schools Act of 1994 has been repealed but the provisions have been incorporated into No Child Left Behind Act, 20 U.S.C. § 7151 (2003). Additionally, most states have enacted gun-free or weapons-free school zone laws restricting possession of firearms in or near schools.

cumstances.[21] Recent cases underscore the harsh consequences when students encounter inflexible policies. In a Virginia case, a 13-year-old student took a suicidal friend's binder containing a knife and placed it in his own locker. Upon hearing about the knife, the assistant principal asked the student to retrieve it from his locker. The student was expelled from school for four months, even though the assistant principal felt that the student was attempting to save his friend's life and at no time posed a threat to anyone. The Fourth Circuit, in upholding the expulsion, noted its harshness but found no violation of the student's due process rights.[22]

In contrast, some courts have held that invoking mandatory expulsion policies may implicate constitutional rights if administrators fail to take into consideration the individual student's history and the circumstances surrounding the conduct. For example, the Sixth Circuit noted that expelling a student for weapons possession when the student did not know that the weapon was in his car could not survive a due process challenge.[23] Other courts, however, have been reluctant to impose the *knowing possession* standard that would require the determination of a student's intent.[24]

Suspensions

Suspensions are frequently used to punish students for violating school rules and standards of behavior when the infractions are not of sufficient magnitude to warrant expulsion. Suspensions include short-term removals from school as well as the denial of participation in regular courses and activities (in-school suspension). Most legal controversies have focused on out-of-school suspensions, but it is advisable to apply the same legal principles to any disciplinary action that separates the student from the regular instructional program even for a short period of time.

In contrast to expulsions, historically state laws and judicial decisions differed widely in identifying and interpreting procedural safeguards for suspensions. In 1975, however, the Supreme Court provided substantial clarification regarding the constitutional rights of students confronting short-term suspensions. The Court majority in *Goss v. Lopez* held that minimum due process must be provided before a student is suspended for even a brief period of time.[25] **Recognizing that a student's state-created property right to an education is protected by the Fourteenth Amendment, the Court ruled that such a right cannot be impaired unless the student is afforded notice of the charges and an opportunity to**

21. Report to the ABA House of Delegates, February 19, 2001, American Bar Association, Chicago.
22. Ratner v. Loudoun County Pub. Schs., 16 Fed. Appx. 140, 143 (4th Cir. 2001), *cert. denied,* 534 U.S. 1114 (2002).
23. Seal v. Morgan, 229 F.3d 567 (6th Cir. 2000).
24. *See, e.g.,* Bundick v. Bay City Indep. Sch. Dist., 140 F. Supp. 2d 735, 740 (S.D. Tex. 2001) (holding that knowledge "can be imputed from the fact of possession").
25. 419 U.S. 565 (1975). Individuals posing a danger or threat may be removed immediately with notice and a hearing following as soon as possible. *See, e.g.,* Willis v. Anderson Cmty. Sch. Corp., 158 F.3d 415 (7th Cir. 1998).

FIGURE 8.3 ***Procedural Due Process for Student Suspensions***

- Oral or written notification of the nature of the violation and the intended punishment,
- An opportunity to refute the charges before an objective decision maker (such a discussion may immediately follow the alleged rule infraction), and
- An explanation of the evidence on which the disciplinarian is relying.

refute them before an impartial decision maker[26] (see Figure 8.3). The Supreme Court also emphasized that suspensions implicate students' constitutionally protected liberty interests because of the potentially damaging effects that the disciplinary process can have on a student's reputation and permanent record.

The *Goss* majority strongly suggested that its holding applied to all short-term suspensions, including those of only one class period. Consequently, many school boards have instituted policies that require informal procedures for every brief suspension and more formal procedures for longer suspensions.

The Supreme Court's *Goss* decision established the rudimentary procedural requirements for short-term suspensions, but students continue to seek expansion of their procedural rights. The Court specifically noted that such formal procedures as the right to secure counsel, to confront and cross-examine witnesses, and to call witnesses are not constitutionally required. The Court reiterated this stance in a later case by noting that a two-day suspension "does not rise to the level of a penal sanction calling for the full panoply of procedural due process protections applicable to a criminal prosecution."[27]

Decisions by lower state and federal courts indicate a reluctance to impose additional requirements unless mandated by state law. The *right to remain silent* has been advanced, with students arguing that school disciplinary proceedings should be governed by the Supreme Court's ruling in *Miranda v. Arizona* (that persons subjected to custodial interrogation must be advised of their right to remain silent, that any statement made may be used against them, and that they have the right to legal counsel).[28] Courts have readily dismissed these claims, finding that discussions with school administrators are noncustodial. In the *Miranda* decision, the Supreme Court was interpreting an individual's Fifth Amendment right against self-incrimination when first subjected to police questioning in connection with criminal charges. A Maine student claimed a violation of procedural due process because the school administrator denied him permission to leave during questioning and failed to advise him of his right to remain silent or to have his parents present during the interrogation.[29] The court rejected all claims, noting that there was no legal authority to substantiate any of the asserted rights. The court reasoned that to rule otherwise would, in fact, contradict the informal procedures outlined in *Goss* allowing for immediate questioning and disciplinary action.

26. The requirement of an impartial decision maker does not mean that an administrator or teacher who is familiar with the facts cannot serve in this capacity either for the informal or formal hearings. The decision maker simply must judge the situation fairly and on the basis of valid evidence.
27. Bethel Sch. Dist. No. 403 v. Fraser, 478 U.S. 675, 686 (1986).
28. 384 U.S. 436 (1966).

Although the Supreme Court in *Goss* recognized the possibility of "unusual situations" that would require more formal procedures than those outlined, little guidance was given as to what these circumstances might be. The only suggestion offered in *Goss* was that a disciplinarian should adopt more extensive procedures in instances involving factual disputes "and arguments about cause and effect."[30] Courts have declined to expand on this brief listing. The Sixth Circuit rejected a student's contention that drug charges constituted such an "unusual situation" because of the stigmatizing effect on his reputation. The court did not believe that an eighth-grade student suspended for 10 days for possessing a substance that resembled an illegal drug was "forever faced with a tarnished reputation and restricted employment opportunities."[31] More extensive procedures also were found unnecessary when a student was barred from interscholastic athletics and other activities in addition to a 10-day suspension.[32]

Students also have asserted that suspensions involving loss of course credit or occurring during exam periods require greater due process than outlined in *Goss.* The Fifth Circuit, however, did not find persuasive the argument that the loss incurred for a 10-day suspension during final examinations required more than a mere give-and-take discussion between the principal and the student. In refusing to require more formal proceedings, the court noted that *Goss* makes no distinction as to when a short-term suspension occurs, and a contrary ruling would "significantly undermine, if not nullify, its definitive holding."[33] Similarly, the Seventh Circuit rejected a student's claim that additional procedures were required because a suspension occurred at the end of the school year and precluded the student from taking his final exams and graduating.[34]

State laws, however, may require additional procedural protections for suspensions. For example, the Ohio statute, earlier found to be constitutionally defective in *Goss,* now requires that prior to suspension each student must be provided written notice of the intent to suspend and the reasons for the intended suspension.[35] Pennsylvania law also mandates written notification to parents prior to the informal hearing.[36] A Pennsylvania commonwealth court declared that a seven-day suspension violated a student's due process rights because the parents received only oral notification of the reasons for suspension.[37]

In-school suspensions or isolation may be equivalent to an out-of-school suspension, thereby necessitating due process procedures. A Mississippi federal district court noted that

29. Boynton v. Casey, 543 F. Supp. 995 (D. Me. 1982). *But see In re* R.H., 791 A.2d 331 (Pa. 2002) (holding that school police officers were required to give a student *Miranda* warnings prior to interrogation since they exercised the same powers as municipal police and the interrogation led to charges by the police, not punishment by school officials).
30. Goss v. Lopez, 419 U.S. 565, 583–584 (1975).
31. Paredes v. Curtis, 864 F.2d 426, 429 (6th Cir. 1988).
32. Palmer v. Merluzzi, 868 F.2d 90 (3d Cir. 1989).
33. Keough v. Tate County Bd. of Educ., 748 F.2d 1077, 1081 (5th Cir. 1984).
34. Lamb v. Panhandle Comm. Unit Sch. Dist. No. 2, 826 F.2d 526 (7th Cir. 1987).
35. Ohio Rev. Code § 3313.66 (2003).
36. 24 Pa. Stat. Ann. § 13–1318 (2002).
37. Mifflin County Sch. Dist. v. Steward, 503 A.2d 1012 (Pa. Commw. Ct. 1986).

whether procedural due process is required depends on the extent to which the student is deprived of instruction or the opportunity to learn.[38] The physical presence of a student at school does not conclusively relieve school officials of their duty to provide due process for disciplinary measures that exclude a student from the learning process. However, a Tennessee federal district court found that a student's placement in a classroom "time-out box" did not require due process because he continued to work on class assignments and could hear and see the teacher from the confined area.[39] The court emphasized that teachers must be free to administer minor forms of classroom discipline such as time-out, denial of privileges, and special assignments.

Closely related to suspensions are *involuntary transfers* of students to alternative educational placements for disciplinary reasons. Such transfers generally do not involve denial of public education, but they might implicate protected liberty or property interests. Legal challenges to the use of disciplinary transfers have addressed primarily the adequacy of the procedures followed. Recognizing that students do not have an inherent right to attend a given school, some courts nonetheless have held that pupils facing involuntary reassignment are entitled to minimal due process if such transfers are occasioned by misbehavior.[40]

Fundamental fairness necessitates at least minimal due process procedures when students are denied school attendance or removed from the regular instructional program. Severity of the separation dictates the amount of process due under the United States Constitution and state laws. Permanent expulsion from school triggers the most extensive process, whereas minor infractions may involve a brief give and take between school officials and students. Simply providing students the opportunity to be heard cannot only reduce mistakes but also preserve trust in the school system.

Corporal Punishment

> If not prohibited by law or school board policy, reasonable corporal punishment can be used as a disciplinary measure.

A growing number of states have banned educators' use of corporal punishment either by law or state regulation. In 1971, only one state prohibited corporal punishment; by 2001, 27 prohibited its use in schools by either state law or administrative regulation.[41] Generally, where state law permits corporal punishment, courts have upheld its reasonable application

38. Cole v. Newton Special Mun. Separate Sch. Dist., 676 F. Supp. 749 (S.D. Miss. 1987), *aff'd mem.*, 853 F.2d 924 (5th Cir. 1988).
39. Dickens v. Johnson County Bd. of Educ., 661 F. Supp. 155 (E.D. Tenn. 1987). *See also* Rasmus v. Arizona, 939 F. Supp. 709 (D. Ariz. 1996) (holding that denying a student the ability to work on class assignments during a 10-minute time-out was *de minimis* and did not violate a property right).
40. *See, e.g.*, McCall v. Bossier Parish Sch. Bd., 785 So. 2d 57 (La. Ct. App. 2001).

and have placed the burden on the aggrieved students to prove otherwise. **In evaluating the reasonableness of a teacher's actions in administering corporal punishment, courts have assessed the child's age, maturity, and past behavior; the nature of the offense; the instrument used; any evidence of lasting harm to the child; and the motivation of the person inflicting the punishment.** This section provides an overview of the constitutional and state law issues raised in the administration of corporal punishment.

Constitutional Issues

In 1977, the Supreme Court addressed the constitutionality of corporal punishment that resulted in the severe injury of two students. The Court held in *Ingraham v. Wright* that **the use of corporal punishment in public schools does not violate either the Eighth Amendment's prohibition against the government's infliction of cruel and unusual punishment or the Fourteenth Amendment's procedural due process guarantees.**[42] While recognizing that corporal punishment implicates students' constitutionally protected liberty interests, the Court emphasized that state remedies are available, such as assault and battery suits, if students are excessively or arbitrarily punished by school personnel. In essence, the Court majority concluded that state courts under provisions of state laws should handle cases dealing with corporal punishment. The majority distinguished corporal punishment from a suspension by noting that the denial of school attendance is a more severe penalty that deprives students of a property right and thus necessitates procedural safeguards. Furthermore, the majority reasoned that the purpose of corporal punishment would be diluted if elaborate procedures had to be followed prior to its use.

The Supreme Court's ruling in *Ingraham,* however, does not foreclose a successful constitutional challenge to the use of *unreasonable* corporal punishment. Most federal appellate courts have held that students' substantive due process right to be free of brutal and egregious threats to bodily security might be impaired by the use of shockingly excessive corporal punishment.[43] The Fourth Circuit concluded that although *Ingraham* bars federal litigation on procedural due process issues, excessive or cruel corporal punishment may violate students' substantive due process rights, which protect individuals from arbitrary and unreasonable governmental action. According to the appellate court, the standard for determining if such a violation has occurred is "whether the force applied caused injury so severe, was so disproportionate to the need presented, and was so inspired by malice or sadism rather than a merely careless or unwise excess of zeal that it amounted to a brutal and

41. For a listing of states, *see* Kathryn R. Urbonya, "Determining Reasonableness Under the Fourth Amendment: Physical Force to Control and Punish Students," *Cornell Journal of Law and Public Policy,* vol. 10 (Summer 2001), pp. 397–453, 427. *See also* American Academy of Pediatrics. "Corporal Punishment in Schools," *Pediatrics,* vol. 106 (August 2000), p. 343. The American Academy of Pediatrics has recommended that corporal punishment be abolished in all states because of its detrimental affect on students' self-image and achievement as well as possible contribution to disruptive and violent behavior.

42. 430 U.S. 651 (1977).

43. *See, e.g.,* Johnson v. Newburgh Enlarged Sch. Dist., 239 F.3d 246 (2d Cir. 2001); Neal v. Fulton County Bd. of Educ., 229 F.2d 1069 (11th Cir. 2000). *But see infra* text accompanying note 46.

inhumane abuse of official power literally shocking to the conscience."[44] Clearly, student challenges to the reasonable use of ordinary corporal punishment are precluded by this standard. Substantive due process claims generally are evaluated by examining the need for administering corporal punishment, the relationship between the need and the amount of punishment administered, whether force was applied to maintain or restore discipline or used maliciously with the intent of causing harm, and the extent of a student's injury.[45] The Fifth and Seventh Circuits, disagreeing with the stance of the majority of the appellate courts, concluded that substantive due process claims cannot be raised if states prohibit unreasonable student discipline and provide adequate postpunishment civil or criminal remedies for abuse.[46]

Courts allowing substantive due process claims, however, have found the threshold for recovery for the violation of a student's rights to be high. Minor pain, embarrassment, and hurt feelings do not rise to this level; actions must literally be *shocking to the conscience.* Actions courts have found *not* to rise to this level include requiring a 10-year-old boy to clean out a stopped up toilet with his bare hands,[47] two licks with a paddle that resulted in bruises to a sixth-grade boy,[48] a push to a student's shoulder causing her to fall against a door jam,[49] and the piercing of a student's upper arm with a straight pin.[50] In contrast, the Tenth Circuit ruled that substantive due process rights were implicated when a 9-year-old girl was paddled with a split paddle while she was held upside down by another teacher, resulting in severe bruises, cuts, and permanent scarring.[51] Similarly, other conscience-shocking behavior involved a coach knocking a student's eye out of the socket with a metal weight lock[52] and a teacher physically restraining a student until he lost consciousness and fell to the floor suffering significant injuries.[53]

State Law

Although the Supreme Court has ruled that the United States Constitution does not prohibit corporal punishment in public schools, its use may conflict with state constitutional provisions or local administrative regulations. As noted, the majority of states now prohibit cor-

44. Hall v. Tawney, 621 F.2d 607, 613 (4th Cir. 1980).
45. *See, e.g., Neal,* 229 F.2d 1069.
46. Moore v. Willis Indep. Sch. Dist., 233 F.3d 871 (5th Cir. 2000); Wallace v. Batavia Sch. Dist. 101, 68 F.3d 1010 (7th Cir. 1995).
47. Harris v. Robinson, 273 F.3d 927 (10th Cir. 2001).
48. Wise v. Pea Ridge Sch. Dist., 855 F.2d 560, 564 (8th Cir. 1988). *See also* Golden v. Anders, 324 F.3d 650 (8th Cir. 2003).
49. Gottlieb v. Laurel Highlands Sch. Dist., 272 F.3d 168 (3d Cir. 2001).
50. Brooks v. Sch. Bd. of Richmond, Va., 569 F. Supp. 1534 (E.D. Va. 1983). *See also* Lilliard v. Shelby County Bd. of Educ., 76 F.3d 716 (6th Cir. 1996) (holding that a single slap did not rise to the level of a constitutional violation).
51. Garcia v. Miera, 817 F.2d 650 (10th Cir. 1987).
52. Neal v. Fulton County Bd. of Educ., 229 F.3d 1069 (11th Cir. 2000).
53. Metzger v. Osbeck, 841 F.2d 518 (3d Cir. 1988).

poral punishment, and others have established procedures or conditions for its use. Teachers can be disciplined or discharged for violating these state and local provisions regulating corporal punishment. Courts have upheld dismissals based on insubordination for failure to comply with reasonable school board requirements in administering corporal punishment. In a typical case, a Michigan teacher was dismissed because he violated board policy by using corporal punishment after having been warned repeatedly to cease.[54] Teachers also have been dismissed under the statutory grounds of "cruelty" for improper use of physical force with students. In Illinois, a tenured teacher was dismissed on this ground for using a cattle prod in punishing students.[55] Other disciplinary measures also may be taken against teachers. A Nebraska teacher who "tapped" a student on the head was suspended without pay for 30 days under a state law that prohibits the use of corporal punishment.[56]

Beyond statutory or board restrictions, other legal means exist to challenge the use of unreasonable corporal punishment in public schools. Teachers can be charged with criminal assault and battery, which might result in fines and/or imprisonment. Civil assault and battery suits for monetary damages also can be initiated against school personnel.

When corporal punishment is allowed, educators should use caution in its administration, since improper use can result in dismissal, monetary damages, and even imprisonment. Corporal punishment should never be administered with malice, and the use of excessive force should be avoided. Teachers would be wise to keep a record of incidents involving corporal punishment and to adhere to minimum procedural safeguards such as notifying students of behavior that will result in a paddling, asking another staff member to witness the act, and providing parents on request written reasons for the punishment. Moreover, teachers should become familiar with relevant state laws and school board policies before attempting to use corporal punishment in their classrooms.

Academic Sanctions

> Academic sanctions should be reasonable; related to performance, absences or other academic concerns; and serve a legitimate school purpose.

It is indisputable that school authorities have the right to use academic sanctions for poor academic performance. Consistently, courts have been reluctant to substitute their own judgment for that of educators in assessing students' academic accomplishments. Failing grades, denial of credit, academic probation, retention, and expulsion from particular programs have been upheld as legitimate means of dealing with poor academic performance.

54. Tomczik v. State Tenure Comm'n, 438 N.W.2d 642 (Mich. Ct. App. 1989).
55. Rolando v. Sch. Dirs. of Dist. No. 125, 358 N.E.2d 945 (Ill. App. Ct. 1976).
56. Daily v. Bd. of Educ., 588 N.W.2d 813 (Neb. 1999).

Although courts have granted broad discretionary powers to school personnel in establishing academic standards, there has been less agreement regarding the use of grade reductions or academic sanctions as punishments for student absences and misbehavior. More complex legal issues are raised when academic penalties are imposed for nonacademic reasons. These issues are explored next in connection with grade reductions for absences and misconduct.

Absences

Excessive student absenteeism is a growing concern and has led many school boards to impose academic sanctions for absences. These practices have generated legal challenges related to students' substantive due process rights. To meet the due process requirements, the sanction must be reasonable—that is, rationally related to a valid educational purpose. Since students must attend class to benefit from the educational program, most courts have found that academic penalties for absenteeism serve a valid educational goal.

In an illustrative case, a student claimed that a school regulation stipulating that grades would be lowered one letter grade per class for an unexcused absence impaired protected rights.[57] In defending the rule, Illinois school officials asserted that it was the most appropriate punishment for the serious problem of truancy. They argued that students could not perform satisfactorily in their class work if they were absent, since grades reflected class participation in addition to other standards of performance. The appeals court was not persuaded by the student's argument that grades should reflect only scholastic achievement, and therefore concluded that the regulation was reasonable.

Similarly, the Supreme Court of Connecticut drew a sharp distinction between academic and disciplinary sanctions, noting that the school board's policy of reducing grades for unapproved absences was academic, rather than disciplinary, in intent and effect. Specifically, the court found that a board's determination that grades should reflect more than examinations and papers "constitutes an academic judgment about academic requirements."[58]

Some courts have upheld the imposition of academic penalties even though policies do not differentiate between excused and unexcused absences. For example, the Supreme Court of Arkansas upheld a board policy that disallowed course credit and permitted expulsion of students who accumulated more than 12 absences per semester.[59] The court, in refusing to substitute its judgment for the school board's, concluded that under state law this action was within the board's power to make reasonable rules and regulations for the administration of the schools. Similarly, a New York appellate court found that a policy denying course credit for absences in excess of 9 classes for semester courses and 18 absences for full-year courses was rational; students were permitted and encouraged to make up the classes before they exceeded the limit.[60]

57. Knight v. Bd. of Educ., 348 N.E.2d 299 (Ill. App. Ct. 1976).
58. Campbell v. Bd. of Educ., 475 A.2d 289, 294 (Conn. 1984).
59. Williams v. Bd. of Educ., 626 S.W.2d 361 (Ark. 1982).
60. Bitting v. Lee, 564 N.Y.S.2d 791 (App. Div. 1990).

Given the serious truancy problem confronting many school districts, it seems likely that school boards will continue to consider the imposition of academic sanctions. The legality of such policies will depend primarily on judicial interpretation of applicable state law.

Misconduct

Academic sanctions imposed for student misconduct also have been challenged. It is generally accepted that students can be denied credit for work missed while suspended from school. In fact, if students could make up such work without penalty, a suspension might be viewed as a vacation rather than a punishment. More controversy has surrounded policies that impose an additional grade reduction for suspension days, and courts have not agreed regarding the legality of this practice.

For example, a Kentucky appeals court voided a regulation whereby grades were reduced because of unexcused absences resulting from student suspensions.[61] The school board policy stated that work missed because of unexcused absences could not be made up, and that five points would be deducted for every unexcused absence from each class during the grading period. The court held that the use of suspensions or expulsions for misconduct was permissible, but the additional lowering of grades as a punitive measure was not. A Pennsylvania court also agreed with this reasoning and found grade reductions for suspensions to be beyond a school board's authority.[62] In the court's opinion, it was a clear misrepresentation of students' scholastic achievement; the penalty went beyond the five-day suspension and downgraded achievement for a full grading period. The Mississippi Supreme Court, relying on a state law mandating the maintenance of alternative schools for suspended students, concluded that students attending these schools are not absent from school.[63] Under this law, a school board cannot count suspension days as unexcused for grading purposes unless the student fails to attend the alternative school.

In contrast, the Supreme Court of Indiana upheld the denial of course credit for a high school junior expelled three days before the end of a semester after the discovery of a small amount of marijuana in his truck. The court noted that although state law did not mandate loss of credit, the board could impose such a penalty.[64] A Texas appellate court upheld a school system's right to lower course grades for suspension days imposed for misconduct in addition to giving zeros on graded class work during the suspension.[65] Relying on a state attorney general's opinion approving grade reductions, the court found the pivotal question to be whether the board had actually adopted a policy that would authorize grade reductions. According to the court, oral announcements in school assemblies explaining grade penalties constituted a valid policy. Moreover, the court noted that the grade reduction did not impair constitutionally protected property or liberty rights.

61. Dorsey v. Bale, 521 S.W.2d 76 (Ky. Ct. App. 1975).
62. Katzman v. Cumberland Valley Sch. Dist., 479 A.2d 671 (Pa. Commw. Ct. 1984).
63. Bd. of Trs. v. T.H., 681 So. 2d 110 (Miss. 1996).
64. S. Gibson Sch. Bd. v. Sollman, 768 N.E.2d 437 (Ind. 2002).
65. New Braunfels Indep. Sch. Dist. v. Armke, 658 S.W.2d 330 (Tex. Civ. App. 1983).

Generally, courts have ruled that academic course credit or high school diplomas cannot be withheld solely for disciplinary reasons. As early as 1921, the Supreme Court of Iowa held that students who had completed all academic requirements had the right to receive a high school diploma even though they refused to wear graduation caps during the ceremony.[66] The court ruled that the school board was obligated to issue a diploma to a pupil who had satisfactorily completed the prescribed course of study and who was otherwise qualified to graduate from high school. More recently, a Pennsylvania court held that a student who completed all coursework and final exams while expulsion proceedings were pending could not be denied a diploma, because state law specifies that a diploma must be issued once all requirements are met.[67]

Although the use of academic sanctions for student misconduct and truancy is prevalent, students will likely continue to challenge such practices. To ensure fairness, any regulation stipulating that grades will be lowered should be reasonable, related to absences from class, and serve a legitimate school purpose. Furthermore, students must be informed of these rules through the school's official student handbook or similar means.

Search and Seizure

> School personnel can search students' lockers or personal effects based on reasonable suspicion that the students possess contraband that is either illegal or in violation of school policy.

Search and seizure cases involving public schools have increased in recent years, with the majority resulting from the confiscation of either illegal drugs or weapons. Students have asserted that warrantless searches conducted by school officials impair their rights under the Fourth Amendment of the Constitution. Through an extensive line of decisions, the United States Supreme Court has affirmed that the basic purpose of the Fourth Amendment is to "safeguard the privacy and security of individuals against arbitrary invasions by governmental officials."[68] This amendment protects individuals against unreasonable searches by requiring state agents to obtain a warrant based on probable cause prior to conducting a search. Under the *probable cause standard,* a governmental official must have reasonable grounds of suspicion, supported by sufficient evidence, to cause a cautious person to believe that the suspected individual is guilty of the alleged offense and that the search will produce evidence of the crime committed. Governmental officials violating Fourth Amendment rights may be subject to criminal or civil liability, but the most important remedy for the aggrieved individual is the exclusionary rule.[69] This rule renders evidence of an illegal

66. Valentine v. Indep. Sch. Dist. of Casey, 183 N.W. 434 (Iowa 1921).

67. Ream v. Centennial Sch. Dist., 765 A.2d 1195 (Pa. Commw. Ct. 2001); 24 P.S. § 16-1613 (2003).

68. Camara v. Mun. Ct. of S.F., 387 U.S. 523, 528 (1967).

search inadmissible in criminal prosecutions. Also, under the *fruit of the poisonous tree* doctrine, additional evidence obtained later, resulting from the events set in motion by the illegal search, may be excluded.

Application of Fourth Amendment to Students

Since Fourth Amendment protections apply only to searches conducted by agents of the state, a fundamental issue in education cases is whether school authorities function as private individuals or as state agents. Most courts have found the Fourth Amendment applicable to public schools, but it was not until 1985 in *New Jersey v. T.L.O.* that the Supreme Court finally held that the Amendment's prohibition of unreasonable searches applies to school authorities.[70] **The Court concluded that school officials are state agents, and all governmental actions—not merely those of law-enforcement officers—come within the constraints of the Fourth Amendment.**

Although finding the Fourth Amendment applicable, the Court in *T.L.O.* concluded that educators' substantial interest in maintaining discipline required "easing" the warrant and probable cause requirements imposed on police officers. The Court reasoned that requiring educators to obtain a warrant before searching students suspected of violating school rules or criminal laws would interfere with the administration of prompt and informal disciplinary procedures needed to maintain order. In modifying the level of suspicion required to conduct a search, the Court found the public interest was best served in the school setting with a standard less than probable cause. Accordingly, **the Court held that the legality of a search should depend "simply on the reasonableness, under all the circumstances, of the search."**[71]

The Court in *T.L.O.* advanced two tests for determining reasonableness. First, is the search justified at its inception? That is, are there "reasonable grounds for suspecting that the search will turn up evidence that the student has violated or is violating either the law or the rules of the school?"[72] Second, is the scope of the search reasonable? In the Court's words, are "the measures adopted reasonably related to the objectives of the search and not excessively intrusive in light of the age and sex of the student and the nature of the infraction?"[73]

The "reasonableness" standard allows courts substantial latitude in interpreting Fourth Amendment rights. Among factors courts have considered in assessing reasonable grounds for a search are the child's age, history, and record in the school; prevalence and seriousness of the problem in the school to which the search is directed; exigency to make the search without delay and further investigation; probative value and reliability of the information used as a justification for the search; the school officials' experience with the student and with the type of problem to which the search is directed; and the type of search.

69. *See* Mapp v. Ohio, 367 U.S. 643 (1961).
70. 469 U.S. 325 (1985).
71. *Id.* at 341.
72. *Id.* at 342.
73. *Id.*

Clearly, reasonable suspicion requires more than a hunch, good intentions, or good faith. The Supreme Court, in upholding an exception to the warrant requirement for a "stop and frisk" search for weapons by police officers, concluded that to justify the intrusion, the police officer must be able to point to "specific and articulable facts."[74] In recognizing an exception for school searches, it appears that, at a minimum, the judiciary will require searches of students to be supported by objective facts.

Informants often play an important role in establishing the "specific and articulable facts" necessary to justify a search. Reliability of informants can be assumed unless school officials have reason to doubt the motives of the reporting student, teacher, parent, citizen, or anonymous caller. The amount of detail given by an informant adds to the veracity of the report—that is, identifying a specific student by name, what the student is wearing, and the specific contraband and where it is located will support a decision to search. Additionally, even with limited information, the level of danger presented by an informant's tip may require an immediate response. A California appellate court commented that "the gravity of the danger posed by possession of a firearm or other weapon on campus was great compared to the relatively minor intrusion involved in investigating" the accused students.[75]

A further requirement of reasonableness appears to be individualized suspicion. The Supreme Court in *T.L.O.* did not address individualized suspicion, but the Court did state that "exceptions to the requirement of individualized suspicion are generally appropriate only where the privacy interests implicated by a search are minimal and where 'other safeguards' are available 'to assure that the individual's reasonable expectation of privacy is not subject to the discretion of the official in the field.' "[76] **In the absence of exigency requiring an immediate search, courts have been reluctant to support personal searches lacking individualized suspicion.**

In assessing the constitutionality of searches in the public schools, two questions are central: (1) What constitutes a search? and (2) What types of searches are reasonable? According to the Supreme Court's rulings, essential considerations in determining whether an action is a search are an individual's reasonable expectation of privacy (reasonable in the sense that society is prepared to recognize the privacy)[77] and the extent of governmental intrusion.[78] The reasonableness of a specific type of search must be evaluated in terms of all the circumstances surrounding the search. This would include variables such as who initiated the search, who conducted the search, need for the search, purpose of the search, information or factors prompting the search, what or who was searched, and use of the evidence. In the next sections, various types of school searches are examined within this context.

74. Terry v. Ohio, 392 U.S. 1, 21 (1968).
75. *In re* Alexander B., 270 Cal. Rptr. 2d 342, 344 (Ct. App. 1990).
76. New Jersey v. T.L.O., 469 U.S. 325, 342 n.8 (1985) (quoting Delaware v. Prouse, 440 U.S. 648, 654-655 (1979)).
77. *Id.* at 361 (Harlan, J., concurring).
78. United States v. Chadwick, 433 U.S. 1, 7 (1977).

Lockers

Courts have singled out school lockers as generating a *lower* expectation of privacy, frequently distinguishing locker searches on the basis that a locker is school property, and students do not retain exclusive possession. This is particularly likely when they have signed a form acknowledging that the locker is school property and subject to inspection. **Under the view of joint control, school officials have been allowed to inspect lockers or even to consent to searches by law enforcement officers.**[79]

A Kansas case illustrates the general judicial view toward locker searches. The Supreme Court of Kansas held that the right of inspection is inherent in the authority granted to school officials to manage schools.[80] The court maintained that it is a proper function of school personnel to inspect the lockers under their control and to prevent the use of lockers in illicit ways or for illegal purposes. The Tenth Circuit also concluded that "school authorities have, on behalf of the public, an interest in these lockers and a duty to police the school, particularly where possible serious violations of the criminal laws exist."[81] An important point in both of these cases, however, is that school officials retained a list of the combinations and had occasionally inspected the lockers. These points have been emphasized in other cases to support the nonexclusive nature of lockers.

Most student conduct codes and some state laws specify guidelines for locker searches. These codes or laws may establish that reasonable suspicion is required prior to conducting a search. In a Pennsylvania case, the state supreme court relied on the *T.L.O.* decision and the student code in establishing a legitimate expectation of privacy in lockers. The code specified: "Prior to a locker search a student shall be notified and given an opportunity to be present. However, where school authorities have *reasonable suspicion* that the locker contains materials which pose a threat to the health, welfare, and safety of students in the school, students' lockers may be searched without prior warning [emphasis added]."[82] Although the court held that students possessed a reasonable expectation of privacy in their lockers, it was minimal. In balancing students' privacy interests and school officials' concerns, the court found the schoolwide blanket search reasonable based on the heightened awareness of drug activity that permeated the entire school and the compelling concern about drug use.

Due to recent incidents of school violence, some states have enacted broad laws eliminating any presumption of privacy in school lockers. For example, a Michigan law states: "A pupil who uses a locker that is the property of a school district . . . is presumed to have no expectation of privacy in that locker or that locker's content."[83] Furthermore, school officials can search the lockers at any time and can request the assistance of the local law-enforcement agency. Based on judicial interpretations of students' privacy rights, it is likely

79. *But see infra* text accompanying note 119, for cases addressing the involvement of law-enforcement personnel.

80. State v. Stein, 456 P.2d 1, 2 (Kan. 1969).

81. Zamora v. Pomeroy, 639 F.2d 662, 670 (10th Cir. 1981).

82. Commonwealth v. Cass, 709 A.2d 350, 353 (Pa. 1998).

83. MCLS § 380.1306 (2003).

that statutes such as these will be challenged regarding the expectation of privacy in the contents of the lockers as well as the use of law-enforcement personnel.

Search of Personal Possessions: Purses, Book Bags, and Other Property

Students have a greater expectation of privacy in their personal property or effects than in their school lockers. In the Supreme Court's *T.L.O.* decision, a teacher had reported that a student was smoking in the restroom. Upon questioning by the assistant principal, the student denied smoking and, in fact, denied that she even smoked. The assistant principal then opened the student's purse seeking evidence to substantiate that she did smoke. In the process of removing a package of cigarettes, he spotted rolling papers and subsequently found marijuana and other evidence implicating her in drug dealing. Using the "reasonable suspicion" test, the Supreme Court found that the search in *T.L.O.* was reasonable. The school official had a basis for suspecting that the student had cigarettes in her purse. Although possession was not a violation of a school rule, it was not irrelevant; discovery of cigarettes provided evidence to corroborate that she had been smoking and challenged her credibility. Characterizing this as a "common sense" conclusion, the Court noted that "the requirement of reasonable suspicion is not a requirement of absolute certainty: 'sufficient probability, not certainty, is the touchstone of reasonableness under the Fourth Amendment.' "[84]

The New York high court concluded that a security officer's investigation of a student's book bag was reasonable based on hearing an "unusual metallic thud" when the student tossed the bag on a metal shelf. Following the sound, the security officer ran his fingers over the outside of the book bag and detected the outline of a gun. The court noted that the sound alone was insufficient to justify searching the bag, but the discovery of the presence of a gunlike shape established reasonable suspicion to open the bag.[85] The Supreme Court of California, however, declined to uphold the search of a student's calculator case in the absence of articulable facts to support individualized suspicion.[86] The vice principal's search was based on the student's tardiness for class, his "furtive gestures" to hide the calculator, and his comment that the principal needed a warrant. Although the behaviors were suspicious, the actions alone did not point to the possible violation of any specific rule or law.

In a Massachusetts case, the state high court assessed whether a student had a legitimate expectation of privacy in his handwriting.[87] The charges against the student grew out of several incidents of graffiti on school property containing obscenities and racial slurs, some directed toward one teacher. Because prior occurrences made the student a potential

84. New Jersey v. T.L.O., 469 U.S. 325, 346 (1985) (quoting Hill v. California, 401 U.S. 797, 804 (1971)).

85. *In re* Gregory M., 606 N.Y.S.2d 579 (1993). *See also* DesRoches v. Caprio, 156 F.3d 571 (4th Cir. 1998) (concluding that student had a legitimate expectation of privacy in his backpack, necessitating individualized suspicion to search).

86. *In re* William G., 709 P.2d 1287 (Cal. 1985). *But see* People v. Dilworth, 661 N.E.2d 310 (Ill. 1996) (upholding the search of a student's flashlight based on a report that he was selling drugs).

87. Commonwealth v. Buccella, 751 N.E.2d 373 (Mass. 2001).

suspect, several of his homework assignments, along with two other students' papers, were analyzed to determine if they matched the graffiti. Based on a match with the student's writing, he was charged with malicious destruction of property and violation of the targeted teacher's civil rights. The court refused to suppress the handwriting analyses and samples, finding that it was reasonable for school authorities to suspect the student and that the inspection of the papers involved minimal intrusion.

A student's car, like other personal possessions, may be searched if reasonable suspicion can be established. A Texas federal district court, however, declined to uphold a general dragnet search of a school parking lot.[88] The school's interest in the contents of the cars was viewed as minimal since students did not have access to their cars during the school day. Furthermore, the search was indiscriminate, lacking any evidence of individualized suspicion. In contrast, a Florida district court upheld the search of a student's car after a school aide, who regularly patrolled the parking lot during students' lunch break, observed in plain view a water pipe, commonly used to smoke marijuana.[89] In the court's opinion, patrolling the lot fell within the school's duty to maintain order and discipline, and the search was based on individualized suspicion.

Personal Search of Students

Warrantless searches of a student's person raise significant legal questions. Unlike locker searches, it cannot be asserted that there is a lower expectation of privacy. **Students have a legitimate expectation of privacy in the contents of their pockets and their person.** The Fifth Circuit noted that "the Fourth Amendment applies with its fullest vigor against any intrusion on the human body."[90] In personal searches, not only is it necessary to have reasonable cause to search, but also the search itself must be reasonable. Reasonableness is assessed in terms of the specific facts and circumstances of a case.

A Washington appellate court declined to support the search of a student's pockets because he was in the school parking lot during the school day, a violation of the closed campus policy. The court emphasized that "there must be a nexus between the item sought and the infraction under investigation."[91] In the absence of other suspicious factors about the student, violation of the school's closed campus rule did not justify the automatic search that led to the discovery of marijuana. The Alabama Supreme Court, however, found the search of two fifth-grade students for the alleged theft of nine dollars reasonable based on the fact that they had been alone in the classroom at the time the money disappeared.[92]

88. Jones v. Latexo Indep. Sch. Dist., 499 F. Supp. 223 (E.D. Tex. 1980). *See also* Burnham v. West, 681 F. Supp. 1160 (E.D. Va. 1987).
89. State v. D.T.W., 425 So. 2d 1383 (Fla. Civ. App. 1983). *See also* Covington County v. G.W., 767 So. 2d 187 (Miss. 2000) (holding that report of a student drinking beer in the school parking lot justified search of his truck; no warrant was required).
90. Horton v. Goose Creek Indep. Sch. Dist., 690 F.2d 470, 478 (5th Cir. 1982).
91. State v. B.A.S., 13 P.3d 244, 246 (Wash. App. 2000). *See also* Commonwealth v. Damian D., 752 N.E.2d 679 (Mass. 2001) (finding that a student's truancy did not establish reasonable suspicion to support school officials' search).

Personal searches are permitted, but strip searches of students usually cannot be justified on the basis of reasonable suspicion. The Second Circuit noted that "as the intrusiveness of the search intensifies, the standard of Fourth Amendment 'reasonableness' approaches probable cause, even in the school context."[93] The Seventh Circuit, in a strongly worded statement, proclaimed in an Indiana case: "It does not require a constitutional scholar to conclude that a nude search of a thirteen-year-old child is an invasion of constitutional rights of some magnitude. More than that: it is a violation of any known principle of human decency."[94]

The Ninth Circuit found a "pat-down" search and subsequent strip search to be unlawful.[95] Such an invasion of privacy could not be justified on the basis that a bus driver saw the student exchange "what appeared to be money" for an unidentified object. Similarly, the West Virginia high court found the strip search of a 14-year-old eighth-grader suspected of stealing $100 excessively intrusive, and thus unreasonable in scope.[96] The court concluded that unless exigent circumstances necessitate an immediate search to protect the safety of other students, a warrantless strip search is impermissible.

A few strip searches have been upheld with sufficient evidence of individualized suspicion, specifically related to drug use. The Sixth Circuit upheld the strip search of a female high school student suspected of possessing drugs.[97] Among the significant facts establishing reasonable suspicion were a call from another student's mother who described a glass vial containing a white powdery substance, a student informant's tip, a teacher's report of strange behavior, and an incriminating letter detailing drug use. Similarly, the Seventh Circuit found that substantial evidence existed to search a high school student with an "unusual bulge" in his sweatpants.[98] Acknowledging that the potential impact of a strip search is substantial, the court, however, emphasized that with the administrators' suspicion that the student was "crotching drugs," a strip search was the least intrusive way to proceed. Both circuit courts considered the nature of the contraband sought and the likelihood of it being hidden on the body in determining that the scope of the searches was reasonable.

Courts have not prohibited strip searches of students, but enough caveats exist to alert school officials of the inherent risks of such intrusive personal searches. **The judicial trend indicates that reasonable suspicion alone may be inadequate to justify most strip searches; rather, the required standard approaches probable cause necessitating specific evidence of a violation linked to an individual student.** Except for emergency situ-

92. Wynn v. Bd. of Educ., 508 So. 2d 1170 (Ala. 1987). *See also* Bridgman v. New Trier High Sch. Dist. No. 203, 128 F.3d 1146 (7th Cir. 1997) (holding that student's unruly behavior, bloodshot eyes, and dilated pupils established reasonable suspicion to conduct search).
93. M.M. v. Anker, 607 F.2d 588, 589 (2d Cir. 1979).
94. Doe v. Renfrow, 631 F.2d 91, 92-93 (7th Cir. 1980).
95. Bilbrey v. Brown, 738 F.2d 1462 (9th Cir. 1984).
96. State *ex rel.* Galford v. Mark Anthony B., 433 S.E.2d 41 (W. Va. 1993). *See also* Kennedy v. Dexter Consol. Schs., 10 P.3d 115 (N.M. 2000) (concluding that the strip search of two high school students without individualized suspicion to find a missing ring violated clearly established law).
97. Williams v. Ellington, 936 F.2d 881 (6th Cir. 1991).
98. Cornfield v. Consol. High Sch. Dist. No. 230, 991 F.2d 1316 (7th Cir. 1993).

ations posing immediate danger to the safety of students, few circumstances appear to necessitate such intrusions.

Use of Metal Detectors

With the increased concern about the high rate of violence in schools, metal detectors have become more commonplace as school officials seek to maintain a safe educational environment. Moreover, the use of metal detectors is no longer limited to secondary schools. In 2000, the Chicago chief education officer approved metal detectors for all the district's 489 elementary schools.[99] **Although metal detectors are used in airports and many public buildings, their use does constitute a search for Fourth Amendment purposes.** Such public searches have been found to be reasonable in balancing the threat of violence against the minimally intrusive nature of the search. As challenges have been raised about the use of metal detectors in schools, similar reasoning has been applied. General scanning of students with metal detectors is only minimally intrusive on students' Fourth Amendment rights when weighed against school officials' interest in providing a safe school environment.

The Pennsylvania high court upheld a general, uniform search of all students for weapons as they entered the high school building; each student's personal belongings were searched, and then a security officer scanned each student with a metal detector.[100] Individualized suspicion was not required in light of the high rate of violence in the school district. The court concluded that the search involved a greater intrusion on students' privacy interests than the search of a locker, but with the nonintrusive nature of the search, it remained a minimal intrusion. Similarly, the Eighth Circuit found a search of all male students from grades 6 to 12 for dangerous weapons to be minimally intrusive based on reasonable suspicion that weapons had been brought to school that day.[101] Students were scanned with a metal detector after they removed their shoes and the contents of their pockets. If the metal detector sounded, a subsequent "pat-down" search was conducted.

An Illinois appellate court assessed the reasonableness of the use of metal detectors from the perspective of schools' "special needs."[102] In the first year of using the detectors, Chicago school officials confiscated over 300 weapons (including 15 guns) from the high schools. With continued use of these devices, they showed a reduction of about 85 percent in weapons confiscated. The court, in concluding that individualized suspicion was not required to use metal detectors, noted that the purpose of the screening was to ensure a safe school environment for all students, not to secure evidence of a crime.

In each of the cases litigated, courts pointed to the violent context that led school officials to use metal detectors and the minimally intrusive nature of these devices. With

99. Jessica Portner, "Girl's Slaying Elicits Calls for Metal Detectors," *Education Week* (March 15, 2000), p. 3.

100. *In re* F.B., 726 A.2d 361 (Pa. 1999).

101. Thompson v. Carthage Sch. Dist., 87 F.3d 979 (8th Cir. 1996).

102. People v. Pruitt, 662 N.E.2d 540 (Ill. App. Ct. 1996).

increasing use, it can be expected that courts will continue to review the constitutional issues raised by metal detectors in school searches.

Drug-Detecting Canines

The use of drug-detecting dogs in searches raises a number of controversial questions regarding Fourth Amendment rights. Does the presence of a dog sniffing students constitute a search? Must reasonable suspicion exist to justify the use of dogs? Does the alert of a dog establish reasonable suspicion? A few courts have addressed these issues.

The Tenth Circuit upheld the use of trained police dogs in the sniffing of lockers but did not directly address the constitutional issues presented by the canine searches. Rather, the court discussed generally the school administrator's duty to inspect, even to the point that an inspection may violate Fourth Amendment rights. Under this broad grant of authority, the alert of a dog three times at a locker established reasonable suspicion to conduct a search.[103]

The Fifth Circuit, on the other hand, confronted the question of whether sniffing by a dog is a search in terms of an individual's reasonable expectation of privacy.[104] The appellate court noted that most courts, including the United States Supreme Court, have held that law-enforcement use of canines for sniffing objects does not constitute a search.[105] Specifically, the court referenced cases involving checked luggage, shipped packages, public lockers, and cars on public streets. According to the court, a reasonable expectation of privacy does not extend to the airspace surrounding these objects. The court maintained that what has evolved is a doctrine of "public smell," equivalent to the "plain view" theory (that is, an object in plain view can be seized under certain circumstances). This point was illustrated by the example of a police officer detecting the odor of marijuana from an object or property. No search is involved because the odor is considered to be in "public view" and thus unprotected.

From this line of reasoning, the Fifth Circuit noted that the use of canines has been viewed as merely enhancing the ability to detect an odor, as the use of a flashlight improves vision. Accordingly, the court concluded that sniffing of student lockers and cars in public view was not a search, and therefore the Fourth Amendment did not apply. Although permitting the use of dogs to detect drugs, the court held that reasonable suspicion is required for a further search of a locker or car by school officials, and that such suspicion can be established only on showing that the dogs are reasonably reliable in detecting the actual presence of contraband.[106]

In most instances, judicial support for the use of dogs has been limited to the sniffing of objects. The Seventh Circuit, however, concluded that the presence of dogs in a classroom was not a search.[107] In this well-publicized Indiana case, school officials with the

103. Zamora v. Pomeroy, 639 F.2d 662, 670 (10th Cir. 1981).

104. Horton v. Goose Creek Indep. Sch. Dist., 690 F.2d 470 (5th Cir. 1982).

105. The Supreme Court concluded that the brief detention of a passenger's luggage at an airport for the purpose of subjecting it to a "sniff" test by a trained narcotics detection dog did not constitute a search under the Fourth Amendment. Use of canines was characterized as unique, involving a very limited investigation and minimal disclosure. United States v. Place, 462 U.S. 696 (1983).

assistance of police officers conducted a schoolwide inspection for drugs in which trained dogs were brought into each classroom for approximately five minutes. When a dog alerted beside a student, school officials requested that the student remove the contents of his or her pockets or purse. A continued alert by the dog resulted in a strip search. The appellate court, in weighing the minimal intrusion of the dogs against the school's desire to eliminate a significant drug problem, concluded that sniffing of the students by the dogs did not constitute a search invoking Fourth Amendment protections. Search of pockets and purses, however, did involve an invasion of privacy but was justified because the dog's alert constituted reasonable cause to believe that the student possessed drugs. However, as discussed previously, the court drew the line at conducting a strip search based on a dog's alert.

In contrast to the reasoning of the Seventh Circuit, a Texas federal district court concluded that the use of dogs in a blanket "sniffing" (or inspection) of students did constitute a search. The court noted that drug-detecting dogs posed a greater intrusion on personal privacy than electronic surveillance devices, which have not required individualized suspicion. According to the court, "The dog's inspection was virtually equivalent to a physical entry into the students' pockets and personal possessions."[108] In finding the dog's sniffing to be a search, the court further held that for school authorities to use dogs in a search, they must have prior individualized suspicion that a student possesses contraband that will disrupt the educational process. In essence, a dog alert cannot be used to establish such suspicion.

Similarly, the Fifth Circuit held that sniffing of students by dogs significantly intrudes on an individual's privacy, thereby constituting a search.[109] Although recognizing that the sniffing of a person is a search, the court did not prohibit such searches but held that their intrusiveness must be weighed against the school's need to conduct the search. The court concluded that even with a significant need to search, individualized suspicion is required prior to the use of dogs because of the degree of intrusion on personal dignity and security. The Ninth Circuit concurred, noting that the significant intrusion on a student's expectation of privacy posed by dogs requires individualized suspicion.[110]

Given the scope of the drug problem in public schools, it seems likely that school districts will continue to consider the use of drug-detecting canine units. Until the Supreme Court addresses whether such a practice constitutes a search in schools (requiring individualized suspicion) or whether a dog alert can establish reasonable grounds for a personal search, different interpretations among lower courts seem destined to persist.

106. Subsequently, in denying a rehearing, the court clarified the issue of the dogs' reliability. According to the court, a school district does not have to establish with "reasonable certainty that contraband is present . . . or even that there is probable cause to believe that contraband will be found." Rather, there must be some evidence to indicate that the dogs' performance is reliable enough to give rise to a reasonable suspicion. Horton v. Goose Creek Indep. Sch. Dist., 693 F.2d 524, 525 (5th Cir. 1982).

107. Doe v. Renfrow, 631 F.2d 91 (7th Cir. 1980).

108. Jones v. Latexo Indep. Sch. Dist., 499 F. Supp. 223, 233 (E.D. Tex. 1980).

109. *Horton,* 690 F.2d 470.

110. B.C. v. Plumas Unified Sch. Dist., 192 F.3d 1260 (9th Cir. 1999).

Drug Testing

In an effort to control drug use among students, some districts have considered schoolwide drug-testing programs. Such programs raise serious questions about students' privacy rights. In 1989 the Supreme Court held that urinalysis, the most frequently used means for drug testing, is a search under the Fourth Amendment.[111] Although the Court upheld the testing of government employees for drug use in these two decisions, the holdings were narrowly drawn and based on compelling governmental interests in ensuring public safety and national security. Individualized suspicion was not a precondition for conducting the urinalysis in these cases, but the narrow circumstances justifying the testing programs minimized the discretion of supervisors and the potential for arbitrariness.

The Supreme Court has rendered two decisions regarding the drug testing of students. **In 1995, the Court in *Vernonia School District 47J v. Acton* upheld a school district's drug policy authorizing random urinalysis drug testing of students participating in athletic programs.**[112] Emphasizing the district's "custodial and tutelary" responsibility for children, the Court recognized that school personnel can exercise a degree of supervision and control over children that would not be permitted over adults. This relationship was held to be pivotal in assessing the reasonableness of the district's drug policy—a policy undertaken "in furtherance of the government's responsibilities, under a public school system, as guardian and tutor of children entrusted to its care."[113] Addressing students' legitimate privacy expectations, the court noted that the lower privacy expectations within the school environment are reduced even further when a student elects to participate in sports.

In 2002, the Supreme Court in *Board of Education v. Earls* again reviewed a drug-testing policy but one that applied to students in all extracurricular activities, including athletics.[114] The policy required students to take a drug test prior to participation, to submit to random drug testing while involved in the activity, and to agree to be tested at any time when reasonable suspicion existed. Acknowledging that athletes' lower expectation of privacy was noted in *Vernonia,* the Court emphasized that the critical element in upholding the earlier policy was the school context. In sustaining the drug testing policy in *Earls,* the Court reasoned that the collection procedures, like *Vernonia,* were minimally intrusive, information was kept in confidential files with limited access, and test results were not given to law-enforcement authorities. Based on these factors, the Court concluded that the drug-testing policy was not a significant invasion of students' privacy rights. Although the students had argued that no pervasive drug problem existed to justify such an intrusive measure as drug testing, the Court responded that it had never required such evidence before allowing the government to conduct suspicionless drug testing. Moreover, in light of the widespread use of drugs nationally and some evidence of increased use in this school, the Court found it entirely reasonable to enact this specific drug-testing policy.

It is clear that specific subgroups of students, such as athletes and participants in extracurricular activities, can be subjected to drug testing, but courts have not permit-

111. Skinner v. Ry. Labor Executives' Ass'n, 489 U.S. 602 (1989); Nat'l Treasury Employees Union v. Von Raab, 489 U.S. 656 (1989).

112. 515 U.S. 646 (1995).

113. *Id.* at 665.

114. 536 U.S. 822 (2002).

ted blanket testing of *all* students.[115] A Texas federal district court did not find exigent circumstances or other demonstrated compelling interests to justify a mandatory testing program of all students in grades 6 through 12.[116] Accordingly, the federal court held the program unreasonable and unconstitutional under the Fourth Amendment. The Seventh Circuit rejected a school district's policy requiring drug and alcohol testing of all students suspended for three or more days for violating any school rule.[117] In this case, the student was suspended for fighting, and upon his return to school was informed that he was required to submit to a test for drug and alcohol use. When he refused, school officials suspended him again; refusal to take the test was treated as admission of unlawful drug use. In ruling that the policy violated the Fourth Amendment, the court did not find a connection between fighting and use of drugs. Furthermore, the suspension procedures in Indiana require school officials to meet with students prior to suspension. At that point, it is possible to determine if individualized suspicion exists to support testing a particular student for drugs or alcohol.

Although blanket or random drug testing of *all* students is not likely to withstand judicial challenge, **many schools subject students to urinalysis based on individualized suspicion, and such practices have not been invalidated by courts.**[118] Any drug-testing program, however, must be carefully constructed to avoid impairing students' Fourth Amendment privacy rights. The policy must be clearly developed, specifically identifying reasons for testing. Data collection procedures must be precise and well defined. Students and parents should be informed of the policy, and it is advisable to request students' consent prior to testing. If the test indicates drug use, the student must be given an opportunity to explain the results. Providing for the rehabilitation of the student rather than punishment strengthens the policy.

Police Involvement

A "reasonable suspicion" or a "reasonable cause to believe" standard is invoked in assessing the legality of school searches, but a higher standard generally is required when police officers are involved. The nature and extent of such involvement are important considerations in determining whether a search is reasonable. **If the police role is one of finding evidence of a crime, a warrant based on probable cause would be required.** However, searches by trained police officers employed by, or assigned to, a school district generally are governed by the *T.L.O.* reasonable suspicion standard rather than the probable cause standard.

Since the 1970s, decisions have tended to draw a sharp distinction between searches with and without police assistance. In an illustrative Illinois case, a school principal received a call that led him to suspect that three girls possessed illegal drugs.[119] Upon the superinten-

115. With the vast majority of students participating in extracurricular activities, school districts appear to be moving toward testing all students.

116. Tannahill *ex rel.* Tannahill v. Lockney Indep. Sch. Dist., 133 F. Supp. 2d 919 (N.D. Tex. 2001).

117. Willis v. Anderson Cmty. Sch., 158 F.3d 415 (7th Cir. 1998).

118. *See* Gruenke v. Seip, 225 F.3d 290 (3rd Cir. 2000) (concluding under the *Vernonia* standard that compelling a student athlete to submit to a pregnancy test, absent a legitimate health concern, was an unreasonable search).

119. Picha v. Wielgos, 410 F. Supp. 1214 (N.D. Ill. 1976).

dent's advice, he called the police to assist in the investigation. After the police arrived, the school nurse and the school psychologist searched each girl; however, no drugs were discovered. Subsequently, the students filed suit alleging that their civil rights had been violated. The court found that the police were not called merely to assist in maintaining school discipline but to search for evidence of a crime. Under the circumstances, the court concluded that the students had a constitutional right not to be searched unless the police had a warrant based on probable cause.

In contrast, the same Illinois court held that a police officer's involvement in persuading a student to relinquish the contents of his pockets did not violate Fourth Amendment rights under the *T.L.O.* standard.[120] The police officer's role was quite limited in this case. He was in the school building on another matter, and his role in the search was restricted simply to asking the student to empty his pockets. There was no police involvement in the investigation that led to detaining the student, nor was the evidence used for criminal prosecution. Similarly, the Eighth Circuit held that the assistance of a police officer assigned as a liaison officer in a high school did not subject a search for stolen property to the Fourth Amendment's probable cause standard.[121]

When police simply provide information regarding possible criminal conduct in a school, subsequent searches initiated by school administrators generally are not considered "police action" or "joint action." For example, a Pennsylvania court held that a student's Fourth Amendment rights were not violated when the principal conducted an investigation based on a report from the police.[122] Although the police informed the principal about an anonymous tip indicating that a student had brought a gun to school, school officials were not acting as agents of the police or at the behest of the police. Rather, they were carrying out their duty to protect the safety and welfare of the student body.

In a number of decisions applying the reasonable suspicion standard to school searches, courts have specifically noted or implied that this lower standard is not applicable if law-enforcement officials are involved. A Florida district court stated: "The reasonable suspicion standard does not apply in cases involving a search directed or participated in by a police officer."[123] Similarly, a Kentucky appellate court found the lower standard appropriate for searches in school settings in the absence of police participation.[124]

Although students possess Fourth Amendment rights against unreasonable searches, educators can search when suspicion exists that a student is violating a school rule or the law. Searches that are highly intrusive, however, must be supported by a greater degree of suspicion (see Figure 8.4). Additionally, school personnel can protect themselves by adhering to a few basic guidelines:

- Students and parents should be informed at the beginning of the school term of the procedures for conducting locker and personal searches.

120. Martens v. Dist. No. 220, 620 F. Supp. 29 (N.D. Ill. 1985). *See also* Shade v. City of Farmington, 309 F.3d 1054 (8th Cir. 2002).
121. Cason v. Cook, 810 F.2d 188 (8th Cir. 1987).
122. *In re* D.E.M., 727 A.2d 570 (Pa. Super. Ct. 1999).
123. State v. D.T.W., 425 So. 2d 1838, 1385 (Fla. Civ. App. 1983).
124. Rone v. Daviess County Bd. of Educ., 655 S.W.2d 28 (Ky. Ct. App. 1983).

FIGURE 8.4 ***Degree of Suspicion Required to Conduct Student Searches***

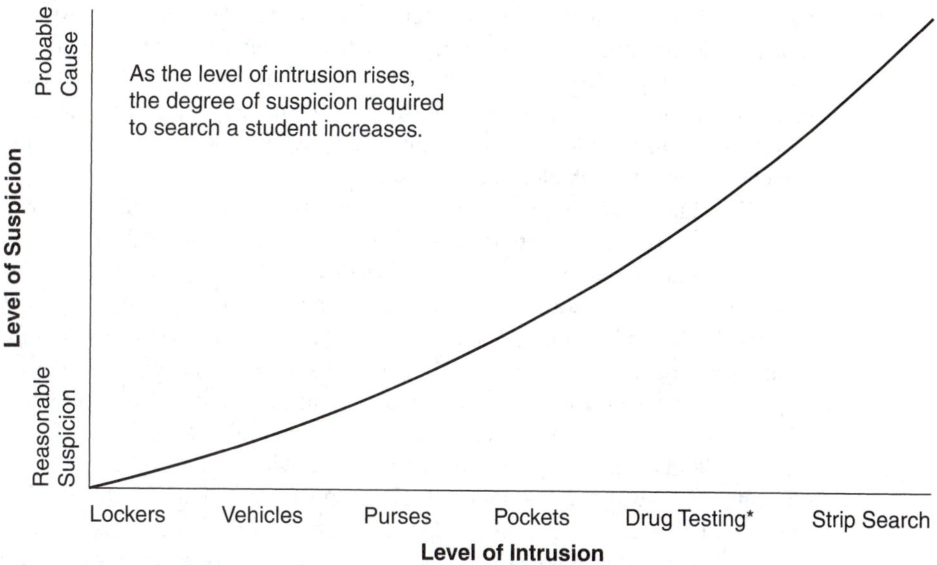

* Under school district drug-testing policies, athletes and students participating in extracurricular activities can be subjected to suspicionless drug tests.

- Any personal search conducted should be based on "reasonable suspicion" that the student possesses contraband that may be disruptive to the educational process.
- The authorized person conducting a search should have another staff member present who can verify the procedures used in the search.
- School personnel should refrain from using strip searches or mass searches of groups of students.
- If police officials conduct a search in the school, either with or without the school's involvement, it is advisable to ensure that they first obtain a search warrant.

Remedies for Unlawful Disciplinary Actions

If students are unlawfully punished, they are entitled to be restored (without penalty) to their status prior to the imposition of the punishment and to have their records expunged of any reference to the illegal punishment.

Several remedies are available to students who are unlawfully disciplined by school authorities. When physical punishment is involved, students can seek damages through assault and battery suits against those who inflicted the harm. For unwarranted suspensions or expulsions, students are entitled to reinstatement without penalty to grades and to have their school records expunged of any reference to the illegal disciplinary action. Remedies for violation of procedural due process rights generally include remand for further proceedings. If academic penalties are unlawfully imposed, grades must be restored and transcripts altered accordingly. For unconstitutional searches, illegally seized evidence may be suppressed, school records may be expunged, and damages may be awarded if the unlawful search results in substantial injury to the student. Courts also may award court costs when students successfully challenge disciplinary actions.

The Supreme Court has held that school officials can be sued for monetary damages in state courts as well as in federal courts under 42 U.S.C. Section 1983 if they arbitrarily violate students' federally protected rights in disciplinary proceedings.[125] In *Wood v. Strickland,* the Court declared that ignorance of the law is not a valid defense to shield school officials from liability if they should have known that their actions would impair students' clearly established federal rights.[126] Under *Wood,* a showing of malice is not always required to prove that the actions of school officials were taken in bad faith, but a mere mistake in carrying out duties does not render school authorities liable. The Court also recognized in *Wood* that educators are not charged with predicting the future direction of constitutional law. Other courts have reiterated school officials' potential liability in connection with student disciplinary proceedings, but to date students have not been as successful as teachers in obtaining monetary awards for constitutional violations. Courts have been reluctant to delineate students' "clearly established" rights, the impairment of which would warrant compensatory damages.

In 1978, the Supreme Court placed restrictions on the amount of damages that could be awarded to students in instances involving the impairment of procedural due process rights. In *Carey v. Piphus,* **the Court declared that students who were suspended without a hearing, but were not otherwise injured, could recover only nominal damages (not to exceed one dollar).**[127] This case involved two Chicago students who had been suspended without hearings for allegedly violating school regulations. The Supreme Court ruled that substantial damages could be recovered only if the suspensions were unjustified. Accordingly, the case was remanded for the district court to determine whether the students would have been suspended if correct procedures had been followed. This decision may appear to have strengthened the position of school boards in exercising discretion in disciplinary proceedings, but the Supreme Court indicated that students might be entitled to substantial damages if suspensions are proven to be unwarranted. In addition to damages, students also may be awarded attorneys' fees.

Educators should take every precaution to afford fair and impartial treatment to students. School personnel would be wise to provide at least an informal hearing if in doubt as to whether a particular situation necessitates due process. Liability never results from the provision of too much due process, but damages can be assessed if violations of procedural

125. Howlett v. Rose, 496 U.S. 356 (1990).

126. 420 U.S. 308 (1975). *See also* Thomas v. Roberts, 323 F.3d 950 (11th Cir. 2003) (ruling that rights can be clearly established by decisions of the Supreme Court, the appropriate federal circuit court, and the highest court of the state in which the case arose).

127. 435 U.S. 247 (1978).

rights result in unjustified suspensions, expulsions, or other disciplinary actions. Although constitutional and statutory due process requirements do not mandate that a specific procedure be followed in every situation, courts will carefully study the record to ensure that any procedural deficiencies do not impede the student's efforts to present a full defense.

Conclusion

In 1969, Justice Black noted that "school discipline, like parental discipline, is an integral and important part of training our children to be good citizens—to be better citizens."[128] Accordingly, school personnel have been empowered with the authority and duty to regulate pupil behavior in order to protect the interests of the student body and the school. Reasonable sanctions, such as suspensions and expulsions, can be imposed if students do not adhere to legitimate conduct regulations. Courts, however, will intervene if disciplinary procedures are arbitrary or impair students' protected rights.

Some type of procedural due process should be afforded to students prior to the imposition of punishments. For minor penalties, an informal hearing suffices; for serious punishments, more formal procedures are required (e.g., notification of parents, representation by counsel, opportunity to cross-examine witnesses). Legitimate punishments include suspensions, expulsions, academic sanctions, and transfer to other programs or schools. In the absence of a state law or school board prohibition, reasonable corporal punishment also can be used as a disciplinary technique. Additionally, school personnel can search students if reasonable suspicion exists that the students possess contraband that will disrupt the school.

School authorities should ensure that constraints placed on student conduct are necessary for the proper functioning of the school. If students are unlawfully punished, school officials can be held liable for damage. Educators, however, have considerable latitude in controlling student behavior to maintain an appropriate educational environment and should not feel that the judiciary has curtailed their authority to discipline students. As noted in *Goss,* courts "have imposed requirements that are, if anything, less than a fair-minded principal would impose."[129]

Points to Ponder

1. Under a school district's zero-tolerance discipline policy, a middle school student was expelled for one year for the possession of a knife on school property. A teacher discovered the knife when the student dropped his unzipped backpack and a number of items fell out, including a small Boy Scout pocketknife. The student claimed he had used the backpack for a camping trip the prior weekend and had forgotten to remove knife. The parents filed suit, arguing that the automatic one-year expulsion was arbitrary and violated their son's due process rights. What issues will the court consider? What is the likely outcome of the case?

128. Tinker v. Des Moines Indep. Sch. Dist., 393 U.S. 503, 524 (1969) (Black, J., dissenting).
129. Goss v. Lopez, 419 U.S. 565, 583 (1975).

2. A high school honor student was suspended for five days at the end of the fall semester. The suspension period included two days of the final exam period, and his request to make up three exams was denied. He asserted that the detrimental impact on his overall grade-point average demanded greater due process than an informal conversation with the principal. What procedural protections are due in this suspension?

3. A 13-year-old student, who was in the hallway without a pass, belligerently responded when a teacher ordered him to return to his classroom. The teacher responded by grabbing the student and throwing him against a locker. The boy suffered a cut to the forehead, which required stitches. He filed suit, claiming that the teacher's action impaired his substantive due process right to be free from unreasonable physical punishment. What issues are involved in this claim? Will the student succeed in his challenge?

4. A high school student discovered that his small, digital recorder was missing from his backpack. He had left the backpack open at his desk while he worked in a small group across the room. The teacher asked everyone to look around the classroom for the recorder. When it was not found, the teacher requested that the students bring their backpacks and jackets to the front of the room to be searched. Each student's possessions were searched, but the recorder was not found. The next day, the student's parents filed a complaint with the school principal, protesting the search of their son. Was this search reasonable under the circumstances? Explain.

9

Terms and Conditions of Employment

Maintenance of a uniform system of public schools is one of the preeminent functions of the state legislature. The judiciary has clearly recognized the plenary power of the legislature in establishing, conducting, and regulating all public education functions. The legislature, through statutory law, establishes the boundaries within which educational systems operate; however, the actual administration of school systems is delegated to state boards of education, state departments of education, and local boards of education. These agencies enact rules and regulations pursuant to legislative policy for the operation of public schools.

Although state statutes and regulations are prominent in defining school personnel's employment rights, they cannot be viewed independently of state and federal constitutional provisions, civil rights laws, and negotiated agreements between school boards and teacher unions. These provisions may restrict or modify options available under the state school code. For example, the authority to transfer teachers may be vested in the school board, but the board cannot use this power to discipline a teacher for exercising protected constitutional rights. The board's discretion may be further limited if it has agreed in the master contract with the teachers' union to follow certain procedures prior to transferring an employee.

Among the areas affected by state statutory and regulatory provisions are the terms and conditions of educators' employment. With the intense public pressure to improve students' academic performance, most states have enacted education reform legislation demanding greater accountability from public schools. These efforts have had an impact not only on the curriculum and operation of schools but also on expectations for educators. Local school boards must ensure that the new demands are met, and courts have recognized the board's expansive authority to fulfill these responsibilities. This chapter presents an overview of state requirements pertaining to licensure, employment, contracts, tenure, collective bargaining, and other related aspects of employment. Specific job requirements that implicate constitutional rights or antidiscrimination mandates are reviewed in subsequent chapters.

Licensure

The state establishes minimum qualifications for licensure, which may include professional preparation as well as other prerequisites.

To qualify for a teaching position in public schools, **prospective teachers must acquire a valid license or certificate[1] from their states**. Licenses are issued according to each state's statutory provisions. States have not only the right but also the duty to establish minimum qualifications and to ensure that teachers meet these standards. Although the responsibility for licensing resides with state legislatures, administration of the process has been delegated to state boards of education and departments of education.

Licenses are granted primarily on the basis of professional preparation. In most states, educational requirements include a college degree, with minimum credit hours or courses in various curricular areas. Other prerequisites to licensure may include a minimum age, U.S. citizenship, signing of a loyalty oath, and passage of an academic examination. Additionally, an applicant for certification may be required to have "good moral character." The definition of what constitutes good character often is elusive, with a number of factors entering into the determination. Courts generally will not rule on the wisdom of a certifying agency's assessment of character; they will intervene only if statutory or constitutional rights are abridged.

Certification of teachers by examination was common prior to the expansion of teacher education programs in colleges and universities. Then, for many years, only a few southern states required passage of an exam. With the emphasis on improving the quality of teachers and the strong movement toward standards-based licensure, most states now require some type of standardized test or performance-based assessment for teacher education programs, initial license, and/or license renewal.[2] **If a state establishes a test or assessment process as an essential eligibility requirement, it can deny a license to individuals who do not pass.** States using standardized tests often employ the National Teachers Examination. The U.S. Supreme Court has upheld its use even though the test has been shown to disproportionately disqualify minority applicants.[3]

1. The terms *licensure* and *certification* are used interchangeably in this chapter.
2. Almost half the states have set up professional standards boards to govern and regulate standards-based criteria and assessment for licenses. The principal purpose of these boards, whose membership is comprised primarily of teachers, is to address issues of educator preparation, licensure, and relicensure.
3. United States v. South Carolina, 445 F. Supp. 1094 (D.S.C. 1977), *aff'd sub nom.* Nat'l Educ. Ass'n v. South Carolina, 434 U.S. 1026 (1978). In challenges alleging discrimination, consent decrees between states and plaintiffs have contained agreements for the development of tests that reduce the discriminatory impact on minority candidates. *See, e.g.,* Allen v. Ala. State Bd. of Educ., 164 F.3d 1347 (11th Cir. 1999), *on remand,* Allen v. Ala. State Bd. of Educ., 190 F.R.D. 602 (M.D. Ala. 2000).

Signing a loyalty oath may be a condition of obtaining a teaching license, but such oaths cannot be used to restrict association rights guaranteed under the U.S. Constitution. The Supreme Court has invalidated oaths that require teacher applicants to swear that they are not members of subversive organizations;[4] however, teachers can be required to sign an oath pledging faithful performance of duties and support for the Federal Constitution and an individual state's constitution.[5] According to the Supreme Court, these oaths must be narrowly limited to affirmation of support for the government and a pledge not to act forcibly to overthrow the government.[6]

Some litigation has focused on legislative efforts to alter licensure standards by imposing new or additional requirements as prerequisites to renew a license. The Supreme Court of Texas held that teachers possessing life certificates could be required to pass an examination as a condition of continued employment.[7] Since the certificate was found to be a "license" rather than a "contract," the court held that new conditions for retention of the certificate could be imposed. Under statutory law, however, the Supreme Court of Rhode Island found that the State Board of Regents for Elementary and Secondary Education could not revoke valid five-year certificates for teachers' failure to meet new agency requirements.[8] Since state law provided that certificates were valid for a specified period of time and could be revoked only for cause, teachers could not be required to meet a state agency's new requirements until their certificates expired.

Licenses are issued for designated periods of time under various classifications such as emergency, temporary, provisional, professional, and permanent. Renewing or upgrading a license may require additional university coursework, other continuing education activities, or passage of an examination. Licenses also specify professional position (e.g., teacher, administrator, librarian), subject areas (e.g., history, English, math), and grade levels (e.g., elementary, high school). Where licensure subject areas have been established, a teacher must possess a valid license to teach a specific subject. A school district's failure to employ licensed teachers may result in the loss of state accreditation and financial support.

A license indicates only that a teacher has satisfied minimum state requirements; no absolute right exists to acquire a position. It does not entitle an individual to employment in a particular district or guarantee employment in the state, nor does it prevent a local school board from attaching additional prerequisites to employment. For example, an Iowa appellate court upheld a local school board's authority to require physical education teachers to complete training in cardiopulmonary resuscitation and water-safety instruction.[9] If a local board imposes additional standards, however, the requirements must be uniformly applied.

4. Keyishian v. Bd. of Regents, 385 U.S. 589 (1967).
5. Ohlson v. Phillips, 397 U.S. 317 (1970).
6. Cole v. Richardson, 405 U.S. 676 (1972); Connell v. Higginbotham, 403 U.S. 207 (1971).
7. State v. Project Principle, 724 S.W.2d 387 (Tex. 1987).
8. Reback v. R.I. Bd. of Regents for Elementary and Secondary Educ., 560 A.2d 357 (R.I. 1989).
9. Pleasant Valley Educ. Ass'n v. Pleasant Valley Cmty. Sch. Dist., 449 N.W.2d 894 (Iowa Ct. App. 1989).

Teaching credentials must be in proper order to ensure full employment rights. Under most state laws, teachers must file their licenses with the district where employed. Failure to renew a license prior to expiration or to meet educational requirements necessary to maintain or acquire a higher-grade license can result in loss of employment. Without proper licensure, a teaching contract is unenforceable.

The state is empowered not only to license teachers but also to suspend or revoke licensure. Although a local board may initiate charges against a teacher, only the state can alter the status of a teacher's license. Revocation is a harsh penalty, generally foreclosing future employment as a teacher. As such, it must be based on statutory causes with full procedural rights provided to the teacher.[10] The most frequently cited grounds for revoking licenses are immorality, incompetency, contract violation, and neglect of duty. Examples of actions justifying revocation include misrepresenting experience and credentials in a job application and altering one's license to misrepresent areas of licensure (immorality);[11] theft of drugs and money (conduct unbecoming a teacher);[12] and assault on a minor female (lack of good moral character).[13]

When revocation or suspension of a license is being considered, assessment of a teacher's competency encompasses not only classroom performance but also actions outside the school setting that may impair his or her effectiveness. An Ohio appellate court ruled that a teacher's involvement in welfare fraud constituted conduct unbecoming to a teacher, justifying revocation of her license.[14] The Supreme Court of Kansas concluded that an act of burglary was sufficiently related to a teacher's fitness to teach to warrant suspension of the license for such a crime.[15] Courts will not overturn the judgment of state boards regarding an educator's fitness to teach unless evidence clearly establishes that the decision is unreasonable or unlawful.

Employment by Local School Boards

> School boards are vested with the power to appoint teachers and to establish professional and academic employment standards above the state minimums.

As noted, a certificate or license does not guarantee employment in a state; it attests only that educators have met minimum state requirements. The decision to employ a licensed

10. *See also* text accompanying note 21, Chapter 12, for details of procedural due process.
11. Nanko v. Dep't of Educ., 663 A.2d 312 (Pa. Commw. Ct. 1995). *See also* Patterson v. Superintendent of Pub. Instruction, 887 P.2d 411 (Wash. Ct. App. 1995) (supporting six-month suspension of certificate for falsifying and omitting information from application).
12. Crumpler v. State Bd. of Educ., 594 N.E.2d 1071 (Ohio Ct. App. 1991).
13. *In re* Morrill, 765 A.2d 699 (N.H. 2001).
14. Stelzer v. State Bd. of Educ., 595 N.E.2d 489 (Ohio Ct. App. 1991).
15. Hainline v. Bond, 824 P.2d 959 (Kan. 1992).

teacher or administrator is among the discretionary powers of local school boards. Although such powers are broad, school board actions may not be arbitrary, capricious, or violate an individual's statutory or constitutional rights.[16] Furthermore, boards must comply with mandated statutory procedures as well as locally adopted procedures. Employment decisions also must be neutral as to race, religion, national origin, and gender.[17] Unless protected individual rights are abridged, courts will not review the wisdom of a local school board's judgment in employment decisions made in good faith.

The responsibility for hiring teachers and administrators is vested in the school board as a collective body and cannot be delegated to the superintendent or board members individually. In most states, binding employment agreements between a teacher or an administrator and the school board must be approved at legally scheduled board meetings. A number of state laws specify that the superintendent must make employment recommendations to the board; however, the board is not compelled to follow these recommendations unless mandated to do so by law.

School boards possess extensive authority in establishing job requirements and conditions of employment for school personnel. The following sections examine the school board's power to impose specific conditions on employment and to assign personnel.

Employment Requirements

The state's establishment of minimum licensure standards for educators does not preclude the local school board from requiring higher professional or academic standards as long as they are applied in a uniform and nondiscriminatory manner. For example, school boards often establish continuing education requirements for teachers, and a board's right to dismiss teachers for failing to satisfy such requirements has been upheld by the Supreme Court.[18] The Court concluded that school officials merely had to establish that the requirement was rationally related to a legitimate state objective, which in this case was to provide competent, well-trained teachers.

School boards can adopt reasonable health and physical requirements for school personnel. Courts have recognized that such standards are necessary to safeguard the health and welfare of students and other employees. For example, the First Circuit held that a school board could compel an administrator to submit to a psychiatric examination as a condition of continued employment because a reasonable basis existed for the board members to believe that the administrator might jeopardize the safety of students.[19] Similarly, the Sixth Circuit ruled that a school board could justifiably order a teacher to submit to mental and physical examinations when his aberrant behavior affected job performance.[20] Health and

16. *See generally* Chapter 10 for a discussion of teachers' constitutional rights.
17. *See generally* Chapter 11 for a discussion of discriminatory employment practices. Under limited circumstances, gender may be a bona fide occupational qualification (e.g., supervision of the girls' locker room).
18. Harrah Indep. Sch. Dist. v. Martin, 440 U.S. 194 (1979) (upholding policy requiring teachers to earn an additional five semester hours of college credit every three years while employed).
19. Daury v. Smith, 842 F.2d 9 (1st Cir. 1988).
20. Sullivan v. River Valley Sch. Dist., 197 F.3d 804 (6th Cir. 1999).

physical requirements imposed on school personnel, however, must not be applied in an arbitrary manner. Also, school board standards for physical fitness must be rationally related to ability to perform teaching duties. A New York court found that obesity per se was not reasonably related to ability to teach or maintain discipline.[21]

In addition, **regulations must not contravene various state and federal laws designed to protect the rights of persons with disabilities.** For example, the U.S. Supreme Court ruled that tuberculosis, a contagious disease, is a disability under federal antidiscrimination provisions that protect otherwise qualified individuals with disabilities from adverse employment consequences. Accordingly, a school district could not dismiss a teacher for chronic recurrence of tuberculosis without evidence that the teacher was otherwise unqualified to perform her job or that accommodations would place undue hardships on the school district.[22]

Under state laws, most school boards are required to conduct a criminal background check of all employees prior to employment. The screening process may require individuals to consent to fingerprinting. Concern for students' safety also has led some school districts to require teachers to submit to urinalysis based on reasonable suspicion of drug use. The Sixth Circuit has even upheld *suspicionless* drug testing of all teacher applicants and transfers, noting that teachers occupy safety-sensitive positions in a highly regulated environment with diminished privacy expectations.[23]

Unless prohibited by law, school boards also may require school personnel to live within the school district as a condition of employment. Typically, residency requirements have been imposed in urban communities and encompass all city employees, including educators. Proponents contend that the policy builds stronger community relationships and stabilizes the city tax base. The Supreme Court upheld a municipal regulation requiring all employees hired after a specified date in Philadelphia to be residents of the city, finding no impairment of Fourteenth Amendment equal protection rights or interference with interstate and intrastate travel.[24] Those already employed were not required to alter their residence. In upholding the regulation, the Court distinguished a requirement of residency of a given duration prior to employment (which violates the right to interstate travel) from a continuing residency requirement applied after employment. Lower courts have applied similar reasoning in upholding residency requirements for public educators.[25] Although residency requirements after employment do not violate the Constitution, they may be impermissible under state law.[26]

21. Parolisi v. Bd. of Exam'rs, 285 N.Y.S.2d 936 (Sup. Ct. 1967).
22. Sch. Bd. of Nassau County, Fla. v. Arline, 480 U.S. 273 (1987).
23. Knox County Educ. Ass'n v. Knox County Bd. of Educ., 158 F.3d 361 (6th Cir. 1998). For further discussion of Fourth Amendment rights of employees, *see* text accompanying note 82, Chapter 10.
24. McCarthy v. Phila. Civil Serv. Comm'n, 424 U.S. 645 (1976).
25. *See, e.g.,* Wardwell v. Bd. of Educ., 529 F.2d 625 (6th Cir. 1976).
26. *See, e.g.,* Ind. Code Ann. § 20-6.1-6.2 (2003); Mass. Gen. Laws ch. 71 § 38 (2003). As urban school systems face difficulty in recruiting teachers, some have abolished their residency requirements, such as Philadelphia, Pittsburgh, and Providence, R.I. *See* Jeff Archer, "City Districts Lifting Rules on Residency," *Education Week* (January 16, 2002), pp. 1, 13.

Unlike residency requirements, school board policies requiring employees to send their children to public schools have been declared unconstitutional. Parents have a constitutionally protected right to direct the upbringing of their children that cannot be restricted without a compelling state interest. The Eleventh Circuit held that a school board policy requiring employees to enroll their children in public schools could not be justified to promote an integrated public school system and good relationships among teachers when weighed against the right of parents to direct the education of their children.[27]

Assignment of Personnel and Duties

The authority to assign teachers to schools within a district resides with the board of education. As with employment in general, these decisions must not be arbitrary, made in bad faith, or in retaliation for the exercise of protected rights. Within the limits of a license, a teacher can be assigned to teach in any school at any grade level. Assignments designated in the teacher's contract, however, cannot be changed during a contractual period without the teacher's consent. That is, a board cannot reassign a teacher to a first-grade class if the contract specifies a fifth-grade assignment. If the contract designates only a teaching assignment within the district, the assignment still must be in the teacher's licensure area. Also, objective, nondiscriminatory standards must be used in any employment or assignment decision. Assignments to achieve racial balance may be permitted in school districts that have not eliminated the effects of school segregation. Any racial classification, however, must be temporary and necessary to eradicate the effects of prior discrimination.

School boards retain the authority to assign or transfer teachers, but such decisions often are challenged as demotions requiring procedural due process. Depending on statutory law, factors considered in determining whether a reassignment is a demotion may include reduction in salary, responsibility, and stature of position. A transfer from one grade level to another is not usually considered a demotion. The reassignment of an Ohio classroom teacher as a permanent substitute or floating teacher, however, was found to be a demotion in violation of the state tenure law.[28] The court recognized the pervasive authority of the superintendent and board to make teaching assignments, but noted that other statutory provisions, such as the state tenure law, may limit this power. This reduction in status without notice and a hearing was found to deprive the teacher of due process guarantees.

Administrative reassignments frequently are challenged as demotions because of reductions in salary, responsibility, and status of the position. Again, as in the assignment of teachers, statutory law defines an individual employee's rights. The South Carolina appellate court concluded that the reassignment of an assistant superintendent to a principal position was within the school board's discretion when it did not involve a reduction in salary or violate the district's regulations.[29] Similarly, the Seventh Circuit found that the reassignment of a principal to a central office position did not involve an economic loss requiring an

27. Stough v. Crenshaw County Bd. of Educ., 744 F.2d 1479 (11th Cir. 1984).

28. Mroczek v. Bd. of Educ., 400 N.E.2d 1362 (Ohio C.P. 1979).

29. Barr v. Bd. of Trs., 462 S.E.2d 316 (S.C. Ct. App. 1995).

opportunity for a hearing.[30] A Wisconsin principal was not removed from her position, but the school board reassigned many of her duties and responsibilities. She resigned her position and claimed that violation of her property interests in the position precipitated the resignation. The Seventh Circuit concluded that Wisconsin law did not entitle principals to perform specific duties.[31] Moreover, reassignment from an administrative to a teaching position because of financial constraints or good faith reorganization is not a demotion requiring due process unless procedural protections are specified in state law.

The assignment of noninstructional duties often is defined in a teacher's contract or the master contract negotiated between the school board and the teachers' union. In the absence of such specification, school officials can make reasonable and appropriate assignments, such as activities that are an integral part of the school program and related to the employee's teaching responsibilities. Reasonableness of an assignment is typically evaluated in terms of time involvement, teachers' interests and abilities, benefits to students, and the professional nature of the duty. Refusal to accept assigned duties can result in dismissal.

Contracts

> Teacher contracts must satisfy the general principles of contract law as well as conform to any additional specifications contained in state law.

The employment contract defines the rights and responsibilities of the teacher and the school board in the employment relationship. The general principles of contract law apply to this contractual relationship. Like all other legal contracts, it must contain the basic elements of (1) offer and acceptance, (2) competent parties, (3) consideration, (4) legal subject matter, and (5) proper form.[32] Beyond these basic elements, it also must meet the requirements specified in state law and administrative regulations.

The authority to contract with teachers is an exclusive right of the board. The school board's offer of a position to a teacher—including (1) designated salary, (2) specified period of time, and (3) identified duties and responsibilities—creates a binding contract when accepted by the teacher. In most states, only the board can make an offer, and this action must be approved by a majority of the board members in a properly called meeting. In a Washington case, the coordinator of special services extended a teacher an offer of employment at the beginning of the school year, pending a check of references from past employers. The recommendations were negative, and the teacher was not recommended to the board even though she had been teaching for several weeks. The state appellate court

30. Bordelon v. Chi. Sch. Reform Bd. of Trs., 233 F.3d 524 (7th Cir. 2000).

31. Ulichny v. Merton Cmty. Sch. Dist., 249 F.3d 686 (7th Cir. 2001).

32. For a discussion of contract elements, *see* Kern Alexander and M. David Alexander, *American Public School Law,* 5th ed. (Belmont, CA: West/Thomson Learning, 2001), pp. 667–669.

held that no enforceable contract existed; under state law, hiring authority resides with the board.[33]

Contracts also can be invalidated because of lack of competent parties. To form a valid, binding contract, both parties must have the legal capacity to enter into an agreement. The school board has been recognized as a legally competent party with the capacity to contract. A teacher who lacks a license or is under the statutorily required age for licensure is not considered a competent party for contractual purposes. Consequently, a contract made with such an individual is not enforceable.

Consideration is another essential element of a valid contract. *Consideration* is something of value that one party pays in return for the other party's performance. Teachers' monetary compensation and benefits are established in the salary schedule adopted by the school board or negotiated between the school board and the teachers' association.[34] The contract also must involve a legal subject matter and follow the proper form required by law. Most states prescribe that a teacher's contract must be in writing to be enforceable, but if there is no statutory specification, an oral agreement is legally binding on both parties.

In addition to employment rights derived from the teaching contract, provisions of any collective bargaining agreement (master contract) are part of the employment contract. Statutory provisions and school board rules and regulations also may be considered part of the terms and conditions of the contract. If not included directly, the provisions existing at the time of the contract may be implied. Moreover, the contract cannot be used as a means of waiving teachers' statutory or constitutional rights.[35]

Term and Tenure Contracts

Two basic types of employment contracts are issued to teachers: term contracts and tenure contracts. *Term contracts* are valid for a fixed period of time (e.g., one or two years). At the end of the contract period, renewal is at the discretion of the school board; nonrenewal requires no explanation unless mandated by statute. Generally, a school board is required only to provide notice prior to the expiration of the contract that employment will not be renewed. *Tenure contracts,* created through state legislative action, ensure teachers that employment will be terminated only for adequate cause and that procedural due process will be provided. **After the award of tenure or during a term contract, school boards cannot**

33. McCormick v. Lake Wash. Sch. Dist., 992 P.2d 511 (Wash. Ct. App. 2000).

34. Increasingly, legal challenges are being brought to secure health, retirement, and other benefits for domestic partners of gay and lesbian employees. Rights may exist under state constitutional and statutory provisions or institutional policies. Some courts have held that the denial of benefits discriminates on the basis of marital status. *See, e.g.,* Univ. of Alaska v. Tumeo, 933 P.2d 1147 (Alaska 1998); Baker v. State, 744 A.2d 864 (Vt. 1999). *But see* Rutgers Council of AAUP Chapters v. Rutgers State Univ., 689 A.2d 828 (N.J. Super Ct. App. Div. 1997) (finding no equal protection violation in granting benefits only to spouses of married employees). *See also* Donna Euben, *Domestic Partnership Benefits on Campus: A Litigation Update* (Washington, DC: American Association of University Professors, 2002).

35. *See, e.g.,* Denuis v. Dunlap, 209 F.3d 944 (7th Cir. 2000) (holding that a teacher was not required to relinquish constitutional privacy rights regarding medical or financial records for an employment background check).

unilaterally abrogate teachers' contracts. At a minimum, the teacher must be provided with notice of the dismissal charges and a hearing.[36]

Since tenure contracts involve statutory rights, specific procedures and protections vary among the states. Consequently, judicial interpretations in one state provide little guidance in understanding another state's law. Most tenure statutes specify requirements and procedures for obtaining tenure and identify causes and procedures for dismissing a tenured teacher. In interpreting tenure laws, courts have attempted to protect teachers' rights while simultaneously preserving school officials' flexibility in personnel management.

Prior to a school board awarding a tenure contract to a teacher, most states require a probationary period of approximately three years to assess a teacher's ability and competence. During this probationary period, teachers receive term contracts, and there is no guarantee of employment beyond each contract. Tenure statutes generally require regular and continuous service to complete the probationary period.

The authority to grant a tenure contract is a discretionary power of the local school board that cannot be delegated. Although the school board confers tenure, it cannot alter the tenure terms established by the legislature; the legislature determines the basis for tenure, eligibility requirements, and the procedures for acquiring tenure status. Thus, if a statute requires a probationary period, this term of service must be completed prior to the school board awarding tenure. When teachers meet the statutory requirements, the school board cannot refuse to carry out its obligation to award tenure nor can the board require new teachers to waive tenure rights as a precondition to employment. Moreover, a board may be compelled to award tenure if a teacher completes the statutory requirements and the school board does not take action to grant or deny tenure. Unless specified in statute, however, tenure is not transferable from one school district to another. This ensures that school officials are provided an opportunity to evaluate teachers before granting tenure.

States often limit the award of tenure to teaching positions, thereby excluding administrative, supervisory, and staff positions. Where tenure is available for administrative positions, probationary service and other specified statutory terms must be met. Although tenure as a teacher usually does not imply tenure as an administrator, most courts have concluded that continued service as a certified professional employee, albeit as an administrator, does not alter tenure rights acquired as a teacher. The Supreme Court of Wyoming noted, "It is desirable—and even important—to have people with extensive classroom teaching experience in administrative positions. It would be difficult to fill administrative positions with experienced teachers if the teachers would have to give up tenure upon accepting administrative roles."[37] In contrast to the prevailing view, the Supreme Court of New Mexico held that an individual who voluntarily resigned a teaching position for advancement to an administrative position forfeited tenure rights.[38] According to the court, state tenure rights attach to a position rather than to an individual.

36. *See* text accompanying note 21, Chapter 12, for discussion of procedural due process requirements.

37. Spurlock v. Bd. of Trs., 699 P.2d 270, 272 (Wyo. 1985).

38. Atencio v. Bd. of Educ., 655 P.2d 1012 (N.M. 1982).

Supplemental Contracts

School boards can enter into supplement contracts with teachers for duties beyond the regular teaching assignments. As with teaching contracts, authority to employ resides with the school board. Generally, these are limited contracts specifying the additional duties, compensation, and time period. Extra duties often relate to coaching, department chair, supervision of student activities or clubs, and extended school year assignments.

Supplemental service contracts are usually considered outside the scope of tenure protections. Coaches, in particular, have asserted that supplemental contracts are an integral part of the teaching position and thereby must be afforded the procedural and substantive protections of state tenure laws. Some courts have noted that tenure rights apply only to employment in licensure areas and that the lack of licensure requirements for coaches in a state negates tenure claims for such positions.[39] Other courts also have distinguished coaching and various extra duties from teaching responsibilities based on the extracurricular nature of the assignment and supplemental compensation. In denying the claim of a 10-year veteran baseball coach, the Ninth Circuit held that the coach did not have a protected interest in his coaching position, since California law specified that extra-duty assignments could be terminated by the school board at any time.[40] When both classroom teaching and extra-duty assignments are covered in the same contract, however, protected property interests may be created. Accordingly, the teacher would be entitled to due process prior to the termination of the extra-duty assignment.

Because coaching assignments generally require execution of a supplemental contract, a teacher can usually resign a coaching position and maintain the primary teaching position. School boards having difficulty in filling coaching positions, however, may tender an offer to teach on the condition that an individual assume certain coaching responsibilities. If a single teaching and coaching contract is found to be indivisible, a teacher cannot unilaterally resign the coaching duties without relinquishing the teaching position. Individual state laws must be consulted to determine the status of such contracts.

Where teaching and coaching positions are combined, a qualified teaching applicant who cannot assume the coaching duties may be rejected. This practice, however, may be vulnerable to legal challenge if certain classes of applicants, such as women, are excluded from consideration. In an Arizona case, female plaintiffs successfully established that a school district was liable for gender discrimination by coupling a high school biology teaching position with a football coaching position. The school board was unable to demonstrate a business necessity for the practice that resulted in female applicants for the teaching position being eliminated from consideration.[41]

39. Smith v. Bd. of Educ., 708 F.2d 258 (7th Cir. 1983); Coles v. Glenburn Pub. Sch. Dist. 16, 436 N.W.2d 262 (N.D. 1989).

40. Lagos v. Modesto City Schs. Dist., 843 F.2d 347 (9th Cir. 1988). *See also* Bd. of Educ. v. Code, 57 S.W.3d 820 (Ky. 2001) (ruling that basketball coach was not entitled to a formal evaluation prior to nonrenewal of his contract).

41. Civil Rights Div. of the Ariz. Dep't of Law v. Amphitheater Unified Sch. Dist. No. 10, 706 P.2d 745 (Ariz. Ct. App. 1985).

Leaves of Absence

Contracts may specify various types of leaves of absence. Within the parameters of state law, school boards have discretion in establishing requirements for these leaves. This topic often is the subject of collective negotiations, with leave provisions specified in bargained agreements. School boards, however, cannot negotiate leave policies that impair rights guaranteed by the United States Constitution and various federal and state antidiscrimination laws.[42] Similarly, where state law confers specific rights, local boards do not have the discretion to deny or alter these rights. Generally, statutes identify employees' rights related to various kinds of leaves such as sick leave, personal leave, pregnancy or child-care leave, sabbatical leave, disability leave, family leave, and military leave. State laws pertaining to leaves of absence usually specify eligibility for benefits, minimum days that must be provided, whether leave must be granted with or without pay, and restrictions that may be imposed by local school boards. If a teacher meets all statutory and procedural requirements for a specific leave, a school board cannot deny the request.

Personnel Evaluation

> A school board's broad authority to determine teacher performance standards may be restricted by state-imposed evaluation requirements.

To ensure a quality teaching staff, many states have enacted laws requiring periodic appraisal of teaching performance. Beyond the purposes of faculty improvement and remediation, results of evaluations may be used in a variety of employment decisions including retention, tenure, dismissal, promotion, salary, reassignment, and reduction-in-force. When adverse personnel decisions are based on evaluations, legal concerns of procedural fairness arise. Were established state and local procedures followed? Did school officials employ equitable standards? Was sufficient evidence collected to support the staffing decision? Were evaluations conducted in a uniform and consistent manner?

School systems have broad discretionary powers to establish teacher performance criteria, but state statutes may impose specific evaluation requirements. More than half of the states have enacted laws governing teacher evaluation. Content and requirements vary substantially across states, with some states merely mandating the establishment of an appraisal system and others specifying procedures and criteria to be employed.[43] Iowa law notes only that the local board must establish an evaluation system.[44] California, on the other hand,

42. Charges of discrimination in connection with leave policies pertaining to pregnancy-related absences and the observance of religious holidays are discussed in Chapter 11.

43. *See* Perry Zirkel, "Legal Boundaries for Performance Evaluation of Public School Professional Personnel," *Education Law Reporter,* vol. 172 (2003), pp. 1–15.

44. Iowa Code Ann. § 279.14 (2003).

specifies the intent of evaluations, areas to be assessed, frequency of evaluations, notice to employees of deficiencies, and an opportunity to improve performance.[45] Florida requires the superintendent of schools to establish criteria and procedures for appraisal, including evaluation at least once a year, a written record of assessment, prior notice to teachers of criteria and procedures, and a meeting with the evaluator to discuss the results of the evaluation.[46] Although a few evaluation systems are established at the state level, state laws usually require local officials to develop evaluation criteria, often in conjunction with teachers or other professionals. Unless prohibited by law, it also may be negotiable with the teachers' union.

Courts generally require strict compliance with evaluation requirements and procedures identified in statutes, board policies, or employment contracts. When school boards have been attentive to these requirements, courts have upheld challenged employment decisions. For example, a California appellate court found that a teacher's dismissal comported with state evaluation requirements because he received periodic appraisals noting specific instances of unsatisfactory performance.[47] The evaluation reports informed the teacher of the system's expectations, his specific teaching weaknesses, and actions needed to correct deficiencies.

Courts are reluctant to interject their judgment into the teacher evaluation process. Judicial review generally is limited to the procedural issues of fairness and reasonableness. Several principles emerge from case law to guide educators in developing equitable systems:

- Standards for assessing teaching adequacy must be defined and communicated to teachers.
- Criteria must be applied uniformly and consistently.
- An opportunity and direction for improvement must be provided.
- Procedures specified in state laws and school board policies must be followed.

Personnel Records

> Maintenance, access, and dissemination of personnel information must conform to federal and state laws and contractual agreements.

Because several statutes in each state as well as employment contracts govern school records, it is difficult to generalize as to the specific nature of teachers' privacy rights regard-

45. Cal. Code Ann. §§ 44660–44665 (2003).
46. Fla. Stat. § 1012.34 (C) (2002).
47. Perez v. Comm'n on Prof'l Competence, 197 Cal. Rptr. 390 (Ct. App. 1983). *See also* Tippecanoe Educ. Ass'n v. Tippecanoe Sch. Corp., 700 N.E.2d 241 (Ind. Ct. App. 1998) (finding that the evaluator adequately informed teacher of deficiencies).

ing personnel files. State privacy laws that place restrictions on maintenance and access to the school records typically protect personnel information. Among other provisions, these laws usually require school boards to maintain only necessary and relevant information, provide individual employees access to their files, inform employees of the various uses of the files, and establish a procedure for challenging the accuracy of information. Collective bargaining contracts may impose additional and more stringent requirements regarding access and dissemination of personnel information.

A central issue in the confidentiality of personnel files is whether the information constitutes a public record that must be reasonably accessible to the general public. Public-record, freedom of information, or right-to-know laws that grant broad access to school records may directly conflict with privacy laws, requiring courts to balance the interests of the teacher, the school officials, and the public. The specific provisions of state laws determine the level of confidentiality granted to personnel records. The federal Freedom of Information Act (FOIA),[48] which serves as a model for many state FOIAs, often is used by courts in interpreting state provisions. Unlike the federal law, however, many states do not exempt personnel records.

In the absence of a specific exemption, most courts have concluded that **any doubt as to the appropriateness of disclosure should be decided in favor of public disclosure.** The Supreme Court of Michigan held that teachers' personnel files are open to the public because they are not specifically exempt by law.[49] The Supreme Court of Washington noted that the public disclosure act mandated disclosure of information that is of legitimate public concern.[50] As such, the state superintendent of public instruction was required to provide a newspaper publisher with records specifying the reasons for teacher certificate revocations. The Supreme Court of Connecticut interpreted the state Freedom of Information Act exemption, prohibiting the release of information that would constitute an invasion of personal privacy, to exempt employees' evaluations[51] but not their sick-leave records.[52] **In general, information that must be maintained by law is a public record (i.e., personal directory information, salary, employment contracts, leave records, and teaching license) and must be released.**

Educators have not been successful in asserting that privacy interests in personnel records are protected under either the Family Educational Rights and Privacy Act (FERPA) or the U.S. Constitution. The former applies only to students and their educational records, not to employees' personnel records. Similarly, employees' claims that their constitutional privacy rights bar disclosure of their personnel records have been unsuccessful. In a case where a teacher's college transcript was sought by a third party under the Texas Open Records Act, the Fifth Circuit ruled that even if a teacher had a recognizable privacy interest in her transcript, that interest "is significantly outweighed by the public's interest in evaluating the competence of its school teachers."[53]

48. 5 U.S.C. § 552 (2003).

49. Bradley v. Bd. of Educ., 565 N.W.2d 650 (Mich. 1997).

50. Brouillet v. Cowles Pub. Co., 791 P.2d 526 (Wash. 1990).

51. Chairman v. Freedom of Info. Comm'n, 585 A.2d 96 (Conn. 1991).

52. Perkins v. Freedom of Info. Comm'n, 635 A.2d 783 (Conn. 1993).

Access to personnel files also has been controversial in situations involving allegations of employment discrimination. Personnel files must be relinquished if subpoenaed by a court. The Equal Employment Opportunity Commission (EEOC) also is authorized to subpoena relevant personnel files to investigate thoroughly allegations that a particular individual has been the victim of discriminatory treatment. The Supreme Court held that confidential peer review materials used in university promotion and tenure decisions were not protected from disclosure to the EEOC. The Court ruled that under Title VII of the Civil Rights Act of 1964, the EEOC must only show relevance, not special reasons or justifications, in demanding specific records. Regarding access to peer review materials, the Court noted that "if there is a 'smoking gun' to be found that demonstrates discrimination in tenure decisions, it is likely to be tucked away in peer review files."[54]

With respect to the maintenance of records, information clearly cannot be placed in personnel files in retaliation for the exercise of constitutional rights. Courts have ordered letters of reprimand expunged from files when they have been predicated on protected speech and association activities.[55] Reprimands, although not a direct prohibition on protected activities, may present a constitutional violation because of their potentially chilling effect on the exercise of constitutional rights.

Reporting Suspected Child Abuse

All states have laws requiring teachers to report suspected child abuse and granting immunity from liability if reports are made in good faith.

Child abuse and neglect are recognized as national problems, with reported cases remaining at a high level.[56] States, recognizing that teachers are in a unique role to detect signs of potential abuse, have enacted legislation identifying teachers among the professionals required to report signs of child abuse. Most state laws impose criminal liability for failure to report suspected abuse. Penalties may include fines ranging from $500 to $5,000, prison terms up to one year, and/or public service. Civil suits also may be initiated against teachers

53. Klein Indep. Sch. Dist. v. Mattox, 830 F.2d 576, 580 (5th Cir. 1987).
54. Univ. of Pa. v. EEOC, 493 U.S. 182, 193 (1990).
55. *See, e.g.,* Aebisher v. Ryan, 622 F.2d 651 (2d Cir. 1980) (concluding that a letter of reprimand for speaking to the press about violence in the school implicated protected speech); Columbus Educ. Ass'n v. Columbus City Sch. Dist., 623 F.2d 1155 (6th Cir. 1980) (holding that a letter of reprimand issued to a union representative for zealous advocacy of a fellow teacher violated the First Amendment).
56. In 2000, three million referrals were made to child protection agencies with almost 900,000 children found to be victims of abuse. Children's Bureau Administration on Children, Youth, & Families, *National Child Abuse and Neglect Data System* (Washington, DC: U.S. Dep't of Health and Human Services, April 2002).

for negligence in failing to make such reports.[57] Additionally, school systems may impose disciplinary measures against a teacher who does not follow the mandates of the law. The Seventh Circuit upheld the suspension and demotion of a teacher-psychologist for not promptly reporting suspected abuse.[58] The court rejected the teacher's claim to a federal right of confidentiality, noting the state's compelling interest to protect children from mistreatment.

Although specific aspects of the laws may vary from one state to another, definitions of abuse and neglect often are based on the Federal Child Abuse Prevention and Treatment Act, which provides funds to identify, treat, and prevent abuse. The Act identifies *child abuse* and *neglect* as

> the physical or mental injury, sexual abuse or exploitation, negligent treatment, or maltreatment of a child under the age of eighteen, or the age specified by the child protection law of the state in question, by a person who is responsible for the child's welfare under the circumstances which indicate that the child's health or welfare is harmed or threatened thereby.[59]

Several common elements are found in state child abuse statutes. The laws mandate that certain professionals such as doctors, nurses, and educators report suspected abuse. Statutes do not require that reporters have absolute knowledge, but rather "reasonable cause to believe" or "reason to believe" that a child has been abused or neglected. Once abuse is suspected, the report must be made immediately to the designated child protection agency, department of welfare, or law-enforcement unit as specified in state law. All states grant immunity from civil and criminal liability to individuals if reports are made in good faith.

School districts often establish reporting procedures that require teachers to report suspected abuse to their principal or school social worker. However, if statutory provisions specify that teachers must promptly report suspected abuse to another agency or law enforcement, teachers are not relieved of their individual obligation to report to state authorities. Some state laws, however, do relieve teachers of the obligation to report if someone else has already reported or will be reporting the incident. But teachers should always follow up to be sure the report was made to the appropriate agency.

State laws are explicit as to reporting requirements for suspected child abuse, but it is difficult to prove that a teacher had sufficient knowledge of abuse to trigger legal liability for failure to report. Therefore, it is desirable for school officials to establish policies and procedures to encourage effective reporting. The pervasiveness of the problem and concern about the lack of reporting by teachers also indicate a need for in-service programs to assist teachers in recognizing signs of abused and neglected children.[60]

57. The Ohio Supreme Court ruled that a school system and its employees did not have sovereign immunity for damages when state law expressly imposed liability for failure to report suspected abuse. Campbell v. Burton, 750 N.E.2d 539 (Ohio 2001). *See also* Chapter 2 for a discussion of the elements of negligence.

58. Pesce v. J. Sterling Morton High Sch. Dist. 201, 830 F.2d 789 (7th Cir. 1987).

59. 42 U.S.C. § 5101 (2003).

Collective Bargaining

> Teachers have a constitutionally protected right to form and join a union; specific bargaining rights are conferred through state statutes or judicial interpretations of state constitutions, thus creating wide divergence in teachers' bargaining rights across states.

Although basic differences in employment exist between the public and private sectors, collective bargaining laws (specifically, the National Labor Relations Act[61] and the Taft-Hartley Act[62]) in the private sector have been significant in shaping statutory and judicial regulation of public negotiations. Similarities between the two sectors can be noted in a number of areas, such as unfair labor practices, union representation, and impasse procedures. However, several basic differences distinguish bargaining in the public and private sectors. First, the removal of decision-making authority from public officials through bargaining has been viewed as an infringement on the government's sovereign power, which has resulted in the enactment of labor laws strongly favoring public employers. Public employees' rights have been further weakened by prohibitions of work stoppages. Whereas employees' ability to strike is considered *essential* to the effective operation of collective decision making in the private sector, this view has been rejected in the public sector because of the nature and structure of government services.

Bargaining rights developed slowly for public employees who historically had been deprived of the right to organize and bargain collectively. It was not until the late 1960s that public employees' constitutional right to join a union was firmly established. A large number of public employees actively participated in collective bargaining, but statutes and regulations in some states prohibited union membership. These restrictions against union membership were challenged as impairing association freedoms protected by the First Amendment. Although not addressing union membership, **the Supreme Court held in 1967 that public employment cannot be conditioned on the relinquishment of free association rights.**[63] In a later decision, the Seventh Circuit clearly announced that "an individual's right to form and join a union is protected by the First Amendment."[64] Other courts followed this precedent by invalidating state statutory provisions that blocked union mem-

60. Although sanctions have rarely been imposed on educators for failure to report abuse inflicted by parents, recent litigation has involved allegations that school employees are the abusers. For a discussion of these cases, see text accompanying note 87, Chapter 6.
61. The act states that "employees shall have the right to self-organization, to form, join or assist labor organizations, to bargain collectively through representatives of their own choosing, and to engage in concerted activities, for the purpose of collective bargaining or other mutual aid or protection." 29 U.S.C. § 157 (2003).
62. 29 U.S.C. §§ 141 *et seq.* (2003).
63. Keyishian v. Bd. of Regents, 385 U.S. 589 (1967).
64. McLaughlin v. Tilendis, 398 F.2d 287, 289 (7th Cir. 1968).

bership. School officials have been prohibited from retaliating against teachers, imposing sanctions, or denying benefits to discourage protected association rights.

Diversity in labor laws and bargaining practices among the states makes it difficult to generalize about collective bargaining and teachers' labor rights. State labor laws, state employment relations board rulings, and court decisions must be consulted to determine specific rights, because there is no federal labor law covering public school employees. Over two-thirds of the states have enacted bargaining laws, ranging from very comprehensive laws controlling most aspects of negotiations to laws granting the minimal right to meet and confer. Still other states, in the absence of legislation, rely on judicial rulings to define the basic rights of public employees in the labor relations arena. This section provides a general overview of public school teachers' employment rights under the collective bargaining process.

Although the U.S. Constitution has been interpreted as protecting public employees' rights to organize, the right to form and join a union does not ensure the right to bargain collectively with a public employer; individual state statutes and constitutions govern such bargaining rights. Whether identified as professional negotiations, collective negotiations, or collective bargaining, **the process entails bilateral decision making in which the teachers' representative and the school board attempt to reach mutual agreement on matters affecting teacher employment.** The judiciary has been reluctant to interfere with legislative authority to define the collective bargaining relationship between public employers and employees unless protected rights have been compromised.

Because of the variations in labor laws, as well as the lack of such laws in some states, substantial differences exist in bargaining rights and practices. A few states, such as New York, have a detailed, comprehensive collective bargaining statute that delineates specific bargaining rights. In contrast, negotiated contracts between teachers' organizations and school boards are prohibited in North Carolina. Under North Carolina law, all contracts between public employers and employee associations are invalid.[65]

In contrast to North Carolina, other states without legislation have permitted negotiated agreements. The Kentucky Supreme Court ruled that a public employer may recognize an employee organization for the purpose of collective bargaining, even though state law is silent regarding public employee bargaining rights.[66] The decision does not impose a duty on local school boards to bargain but merely allows a board the discretion to negotiate. This ruling is consistent with a number of other judicial decisions permitting negotiated contracts in the absence of specific legislation. The board's authority to enter into contracts for the operation and maintenance of the school system has been construed to include the ability to enter into negotiated agreements with employee organizations. Once a school board extends recognition to a bargaining agent and commences bargaining, the board's actions in the negotiation process are governed by established judicial principles.

65. N.C. Gen Stat. § 95-98 (2003).

66. Bd. of Trs. v. Pub. Employees Council No. 51, 571 S.W.2d 616 (Ky. 1978).

Teachers' Statutory Bargaining Rights

In states with laws governing teachers' bargaining rights, school boards must negotiate with teachers in accordance with the statutorily prescribed process. Generally, public employee bargaining laws address employer and employee rights, bargaining units, scope of bargaining, impasse resolution, grievance procedures, unfair labor practices, and penalties for prohibited practices. Many states have established labor relations boards to monitor bargaining under their statutes. Although the specific functions of these boards vary widely, their general purpose is to resolve questions arising from the implementation of state law. Functions assigned to such boards include determination of membership in bargaining units, resolution of union recognition claims, investigation of unfair labor practices, and interpretation of the general intent of statutory bargaining clauses. Usually, judicial review cannot be pursued until administrative review before labor boards is exhausted. Thus, decisions of labor boards are an important source of labor law since many of the issues addressed by boards are never appealed to courts. When the labor boards' decisions are challenged in court, substantial deference is given to their findings and determinations.

Like the National Labor Relations Act (NLRA) in the private sector, state statutes require bargaining "in good faith." ***Good faith bargaining*** **has been interpreted as requiring parties to meet at reasonable times and attempt to reach mutual agreement without compulsion on either side to agree.** A number of states have followed the federal law in stipulating that this "does not compel either party to agree to a proposal or to require the making of a concession."[67] Failure of the school board or teachers' organization to bargain in good faith can result in the imposition of penalties.

Statutes impose certain restrictions or obligations on both the school board and the employee organization. Violation of the law by either party can result in an unfair labor practice claim. Allegations of unfair labor practices are brought before the state public employee relations board for a hearing and judgment. Specific unfair labor practices, often modeled after those in the NLRA, are included in state statutes. The most common prohibited labor practice is that an employer or union will not interfere with, restrain, or coerce public employees in exercising their rights under the labor law. Among other prohibited *employer* practices are interference with union operations, discrimination against employees because of union membership, refusal to bargain collectively with the exclusive representative, and failure to bargain in good faith. *Unions* are prevented from causing an employer to discriminate against employees on the basis of union membership, refusing to bargain or failing to bargain in good faith, failing to represent all employees in the bargaining unit, and engaging in unlawful activities such as strikes or boycotts identified in the bargaining law.

Upon completion of the negotiation process, the members of the bargaining unit and the school board must ratify the written agreement (usually referred to as *the master contract*). These agreements often contain similar standard contract language and clauses, beginning with recognition of the exclusive bargaining representative and union security issues (i.e., fair share fees).[68] Management rights and association rights also are detailed. Management clauses emphasize the board's control over the establishment of educational

67. 29 U.S.C. § 158(d) (2003).

68. *See infra* text accompanying note 75.

policies, and union clauses may include the right to use school facilities or communication systems. Other provisions relate to the scope of bargaining, which is defined by the state's labor law or common law. These items include not only salary and fringe benefits but also may address grievance procedures, employee evaluations, preparation time, length of workday, class size, procedures for employee discipline, transfers, layoff and recall procedures, assignment of duties, and processes for filling vacancies.

Scope of Negotiations

Should the teachers' organization have input into class size? Who will determine the length of the school day? How will extra-duty assignments be determined? Will reductions-in-force necessitated by declining enrollment be based on seniority or merit? These questions and others are raised in determining the scope of negotiations. *Scope* refers to the range of issues or subjects that are negotiable, and determining scope is one of the most difficult tasks in public sector bargaining. Public employers argue that issues must be narrowly defined to protect the government's policymaking role, whereas employee unions counter that bargaining subjects must be defined broadly to have meaningful negotiations.

Restrictions on scope of bargaining vary considerably among states. Consequently, to determine negotiable items in a particular state, the state's collective bargaining law, other statutes, and litigation interpreting these laws must be examined. The specification of negotiable items in labor laws may include broad guidelines or detailed enumeration of specific issues. As noted, many states have modeled their bargaining statutes after the NLRA, which stipulates that **representatives of the employer and employees must meet and confer "with respect to wages, hours, and other terms and conditions of employment."**[69] A few states deal directly with the scope of bargaining by identifying each item that must be negotiated. Some states specify prohibited subjects of bargaining. For example, Michigan's prohibited subjects include decisions related to the establishment of the starting date for the school year, composition of site-based decision-making bodies, interdistrict and intradistrict open enrollment opportunities, authorization of public school academies, and establishment and staffing of experimental programs.[70] Generally, statutory mandates cannot be preempted by collective bargaining agreements; however, in a few states, the negotiated agreement prevails over conflicting laws, unless the laws are specifically exempted.

All proposed subjects for negotiation can be classified as mandatory, permissive, or prohibited. *Mandatory* items must be negotiated. Failure of the school board to meet and confer on such items is evidence of lack of good faith bargaining. *Permissive* items can be negotiated if both parties agree; however, there is no legal duty to consider the items. Furthermore, in most states, permissive items cannot be pursued to the point of negotiation impasse, and an employer cannot unilaterally change these items if no agreement is reached. *Prohibited* items are beyond the power of the board to negotiate; an illegal delegation of power results if the board agrees to negotiate these items. Since most statutory scope provi-

69. 29 U.S.C. § 158(d) (2003).

70. M.C.L.A. § 423.215(3)(4) (2003).

sions are general in nature, courts or labor relations boards often have been asked to differentiate between negotiable and nonnegotiable items.

Defining managerial rights is a key element in establishing limitations on negotiable subjects at the bargaining table. **State laws specify that public employers cannot be required to negotiate governmental policy matters, and courts have held that it is impermissible for a school board to bargain away certain rights and responsibilities in the public policy area.** Generally, educational policy matters are defined through provisions in collective bargaining statutes, such as "management rights" and "scope of bargaining" clauses. Policy issues—such as class size, teacher evaluation criteria, and the award of tenure—are excluded as negotiable items in a few states; however, most states stipulate only that employers are *not required* to bargain such policy rights.

Public employee labor laws requiring the negotiation of "conditions of employment" can include far-reaching policy matters, since most school board decisions either directly or indirectly affect the teacher in the classroom. The Maryland high court noted the difficulty in distinguishing between educational policy and matters relating to teachers' employment: "Virtually every managerial decision in some way relates to 'salaries, wages, hours, and other working conditions,' and is therefore arguably negotiable. At the same time, virtually every such decision also involves educational policy considerations and is therefore arguably nonnegotiable."[71] In many states, the interpretation of what is negotiable resides with the labor relations board. Often, a balancing test is employed by these boards as well as courts, beginning with an inquiry into whether a particular matter involves wages, hours, and terms and conditions of employment. If so, then the labor board or court must determine if the matter also is one of inherent managerial policy. If not, the matter is a mandatory subject of bargaining. However, if the issue also pertains to educational policy, the benefits of bargaining on the decision-making process must be balanced against the burden on the employer's authority. Accordingly, this process entails a fact-specific analysis.

Judicial decisions interpreting negotiability illustrate the range in bargainable matters. The Supreme Court of New Jersey narrowly interpreted *conditions of employment* to mean wages, benefits, and work schedules, thereby removing governmental policy items such as teacher transfers, course offerings, and evaluations.[72] A number of courts, however, have construed the phrase in broader terms. The Nevada Supreme Court ruled that items *significantly* related to wages, hours, and working conditions are negotiable.[73] Similarly, the Pennsylvania Supreme Court concluded that an issue's *impact* on conditions of employment must be weighed to determine whether it should be considered outside the educational policy area.[74]

Although courts agree that school boards cannot be *required* to negotiate inherent managerial rights pertaining to policy matters, some states view these rights as *permissive* subjects of bargaining. That is, the board may agree to negotiate a particular "right" in the

71. Montgomery County Educ. Ass'n v. Bd. of Educ., 534 A.2d 980, 986 (Md. 1987).

72. Ridgefield Park Educ. Ass'n v. Ridgefield Park Bd. of Educ., 393 A.2d 278 (N.J. 1978).

73. Clark County Sch. Dist. v. Local Gov't Employee-Management Relations Bd., 530 P.2d 114 (Nev. 1974).

74. Pa. Labor Relations Bd. v. State Coll. Area Sch. Dist., 337 A.2d 262 (Pa. 1975).

absence of statutory or judicial prohibitions. If the board does negotiate a policy item, it is bound by the agreement in the same manner as if the issue were a mandatory item.

Union Security Provisions

To ensure their strength and viability, unions attempt to obtain various security provisions in the collective bargaining contract. The nature and extent of these provisions will depend on state laws and constitutional limitations. When bargaining with employees, unions seek to gain provisions that require all employees either to join the association or to pay fees for its services. Since a union must represent all individuals in the bargaining unit, it is argued that such provisions are necessary to eliminate "free riders" (i.e., the individuals who receive the benefits of the union's work without paying the dues for membership).

Union security provisions take several forms. The *closed shop,* requiring an employer to hire only union members, does not exist in the public sector and is unlawful in the private sector. The *union shop* agreement requires an employee to join the union within a designated time period after employment to retain a position. Although union shop agreements are prevalent in the private sector, they are not authorized by most public-sector laws and are limited or proscribed in a number of states under "right-to-work" laws.[75] The security provisions most frequently found in the public sector are *agency shop* and *fair share* agreements—terms that often are used interchangeably. An agency shop provision requires an employee to pay union dues but does not mandate membership, whereas a fair share arrangement requires a nonmember simply to pay a service fee to cover the cost of bargaining activities.

Nonunion teachers have challenged mandatory fees as a violation of their First Amendment speech and association rights. The Supreme Court, however, upheld the payment of fair share fees by public employees in *Abood v. Detroit Board of Education.*[76] The Court rejected the nonunion members' First Amendment claims, noting the importance of ensuring labor peace and eliminating "free riders." Yet, the Court concluded that **employees cannot be compelled to contribute to the support of ideological causes they oppose as a condition of maintaining employment as public school teachers.** Accordingly, the fee for nonmember teachers who object to forced contributions to a union's political activities must reflect only the costs of bargaining and contract administration.[77]

75. Twenty-two states specifically declare that an individual's employment cannot be conditioned on joining a union or paying fees to a union. *See* http://nrtw.org/rtws.htm.

76. 431 U.S. 209 (1977).

77. *See also* Lehnert v. Ferris Faculty Ass'n, 500 U.S. 507 (1991) (ruling that unions may not assess nonmembers for lobbying and other political activities that are unrelated to contract ratification or implementation, for litigation that does not involve the local bargaining unit, and for public relations efforts to enhance the image of the teaching profession); Chicago Teachers' Union v. Hudson, 475 U.S. 292 (1986) (ruling that collection of fees requires an explanation of the basis for the fee, an opportunity to challenge the amount of the fee, and an escrow account for the disputed amount); Prescott v. County of El Dorado, 177 F.3d 1102 (9th Cir. 1999) (ruling that financial statements must be audited, not simply reviewed).

Although the Supreme Court has upheld fair share arrangements, they may not be permitted under some state laws. The Maine high court held that forced payment of dues was "tantamount to coercion toward membership."[78] The Maine statute ensures employees the right to join a union *voluntarily,* and the court interpreted this provision as including the right to *refrain* from joining. Similarly, the Vermont Supreme Court held that fees were prohibited under the Vermont Labor Relations for Teachers Act, which specified that teachers have the right to join or not to join, assist, or participate in a labor organization.[79] Indiana amended its labor law in 1995 to prohibit the payment of fair share fees or any other representation fees.[80]

Exclusive Privileges

The designated employee bargaining representative gains security through negotiating exclusive rights or privileges, such as dues checkoff, the use of the school mail systems, and access to school facilities. Although exclusive arrangements strengthen the majority union and may make it difficult for minority unions to survive, they often are supported by courts as a means of promoting labor peace and ensuring efficient operation of the school system.

The exclusive privilege most often included in collective bargaining contracts is dues checkoff, a provision that authorizes employers to deduct union dues and other fees when authorized by employees. Over half of the states with public employee bargaining laws specify dues checkoff as a mandatory subject for bargaining. The Supreme Court, however, has held that **employee unions have no constitutional right to payroll deductions.**[81] The Fourth Circuit ruled that state legislation permitting payroll deductions for charitable organizations but not labor unions was not an infringement of the First Amendment; the law did not deny the union members the right to associate, speak, publish, recruit members, or express their views.[82] Unless prohibited by state law, rival unions can be denied checkoff rights.

In 1983, the Supreme Court clarified one of the most controversial security rights—exclusive access to school mail facilities.[83] The case focused on an agreement between the exclusive bargaining representative and an Indiana school board denying all rival unions access to the interschool mail system and teacher mailboxes. One union challenged the agreement as a violation of the First and Fourteenth Amendments. The Supreme Court upheld the arrangement, reasoning that the First Amendment does not require "equivalent access to all parts of a school building in which some form of communicative activity

78. Churchill v. Sch. Adm'r Dist. No. 49 Teachers Ass'n, 380 A.2d 186, 192 (Me. 1977).

79. Weissenstein v. Burlington Bd. of Sch. Comm'rs, 543 A.2d 691 (Vt. 1988). *But see* Nashua Teachers Union v. Nashua Sch. Dist., 707 A.2d 448 (N.H. 1998) (interpreting state law that permits negotiation of "other terms and conditions of employment" as authorizing agency fees to promote labor peace and rejecting argument that the fees were an unfair labor practice "encouraging" union membership).

80. Ind. Code § 20-7.5-1-6 (2003).

81. City of Charlotte v. Local 660, Int'l Ass'n of Firefighters, 426 U.S. 283 (1976).

82. S.C. Educ. Ass'n v. Campbell, 883 F.2d 1251 (4th Cir. 1989).

83. Perry Educ. Ass'n v. Perry Local Educators' Ass'n, 460 U.S. 37 (1983).

occurs."[84] **The Court concluded that the school mail facility was not a public forum for communication and thereby its use could be restricted to official school business.** The fact that several community groups (e.g., Boy Scouts, civic organizations) used the school mail system did not create a public forum. The Court noted that, even if such access by community groups created a limited public forum, access would be extended only to similar groups—not to labor organizations. The Court's emphasis on the availability of alternative channels of communication (e.g., bulletin boards and meeting facilities), however, indicates that total exclusion of rival unions would not be permitted.

In most states, school boards negotiate only with the designated bargaining representative. Under this exclusive recognition, other unions and teacher groups can be denied the right to engage in official exchanges with an employer. The Supreme Court has held that nonmembers of a bargaining unit or members who disagree with the views of the representative have no constitutional right "to force the government to listen to their views."[85] The Court concluded that a Minnesota statute requiring employers to "meet and confer" only with the designated bargaining representative did not violate other employees' speech or associational rights as public employees or as citizens, because these sessions were not a public forum. According to the Court, "The Constitution does not grant to members of the public generally a right to be heard by public bodies making decisions of policy."[86]

However, in a public forum, such as a school board meeting, **a nonunion teacher has a constitutional right to address the public employer, even concerning a subject of negotiation.** The Supreme Court concluded that a Wisconsin nonunion teacher had the right to express concerns to the school board.[87] In this case, negotiation between the board and union had reached a deadlock on the issue of an agency shop provision. A nonunion teacher, representing a minority group of teachers, addressed the board at a regular public meeting and requested postponement of a decision until further study. The Court reasoned that the teacher was not attempting to negotiate, but merely to speak on an important issue before the board—a right every citizen possesses. The Court further noted that teachers have never been "compelled to relinquish their First Amendment rights they would otherwise enjoy as citizens to comment on matters of public interest in connection with the operation of the public school in which they work."[88]

Grievances

Disputes concerning employee rights under the terms of a collective bargaining agreement are resolved through the negotiated grievance procedures, which generally must be exhausted before pursuing review by state labor relations boards or courts. The exhaustion requirement ensures the integrity of the collective bargaining process, encouraging orderly and efficient dispute resolution at the local level. Grievance procedures usually provide for

84. *Id.* at 44.
85. Minn. State Bd. for Cmty. Colls. v. Knight, 465 U.S. 271, 283 (1984).
86. *Id.*
87. City of Madison v. Wis. Employment Relations Comm'n, 429 U.S. 167 (1976).
88. *Id.* at 175 (quoting Pickering v. Bd. of Educ., 391 U.S. 563, 568 (1968)).

a neutral third party, generally an arbitrator, to conduct a hearing and render a decision. *Grievance* arbitration, which addresses enforcement of contract rights, differs from *interest* arbitration, which may take place in resolving an impasse in negotiating the contract.

Depending on state law and the negotiated contract, grievance arbitration decisions may be advisory or binding. Public employers, adhering to the doctrine of the sovereign power of government, have been reluctant to agree to procedures that might result in a loss of public authority. Allowing grievance procedures to include final decision making by a third party significantly lessens a school board's power, effectively equating the positions of the teachers' organization and the school board. Nevertheless, as bargaining has expanded, **legislative bodies have favored binding arbitration to settle labor disputes.** About one-half of the states have enacted laws permitting school boards to negotiate grievance procedures with binding arbitration, and several states require binding arbitration as the final step in the grievance procedure.[89] With the widespread acceptance of grievance arbitration, it has become one of the most contested areas in collective bargaining. Suits have challenged the arbitrator's authority to render decisions in specific disputes as well as the authority to provide certain remedies.

Negotiation Impasse

An impasse occurs in bargaining when an agreement cannot be reached and neither party will compromise. When negotiations reach such a stalemate, several options are available for resolution: mediation, fact finding, and arbitration. As will be discussed, the most effective means for resolving negotiation impasse—the strike—is not legally available to the majority of public employees. Most comprehensive state statutes address impasse procedures, with provisions ranging from allowing impasse procedures to be negotiated to mandating detailed steps that must be followed.

Mediation is often the first step to reopening negotiations. A neutral third party assists both sides in finding a basis for agreement. The mediator serves as a facilitator rather than a decision maker, thus enabling the school board's representative and the teachers' association jointly to reach an agreement. Mediation may be optional or required by law; the mediator is selected by the negotiation teams or, upon request, appointed by a public employee relations board.

Failure to reach agreement through mediation frequently results in fact finding (often called advisory arbitration). The process may be mandated by law or may be entered into by mutual agreement of both parties. Fact finding involves a third party investigating the causes for the dispute, collecting facts and testimony to clarify the dispute, and formulating a judgment. Because of the advisory nature of the process, proposed solutions are not binding on either party. However, since fact-finding reports are made available to the public, they provide an impetus to settle a contract that is not present in mediation.

In a number of states, the final step in impasse procedures is fact finding, which may leave both parties without a satisfactory solution. A few states permit a third alternative—binding interest arbitration. This process is similar to fact finding except that the decision of

89. States requiring binding grievance arbitration are Alaska, Florida, Illinois, Minnesota, and Pennsylvania.

the arbitrator, related to the terms of the negotiated agreement, is binding on both parties. States that permit binding arbitration often place restrictions on its use.[90] For example, Ohio, Oregon, and Rhode Island permit binding arbitration on matters of mutual consent;[91] Maine allows binding arbitration on all items except salaries, pensions, and insurance.[92]

Although it is argued there can be no true collective bargaining without the right to withhold services, which characterizes the bargaining process in the private sector, **state statutes or common law prohibit most teachers from striking.** In those states that grant public employees a limited right to strike, certain conditions, specified in statute, must be met prior to the initiation of a work stoppage.[93] Designated conditions vary but usually include (1) the exhaustion of statutory mediation and fact-finding steps, (2) expiration of the contract, (3) elapse of a certain time period prior to commencing the strike, (4) written notice of the union's intent to strike, and (5) evidence that the strike will not constitute a danger to public health or safety. In contrast to the few states permitting strikes, most states with public employee collective bargaining statutes have specific "no-strike" provisions.

Courts consistently have upheld "no-strike" laws and generally have denied the right to strike unless affirmatively granted by the state. Several early cases still represent the dominant judicial posture on public teachers' strikes. The Connecticut high court stated that permitting teachers to strike would allow them to "deny the authority of government."[94] The court in this case denied teachers the right to strike, emphasizing that a teacher is an agent of the government, possessing a portion of the state's sovereignty. The Supreme Court of Indiana issued a restraining order against striking teachers, affirming the same public welfare issue.[95] Addressing the legality of strikes, a New Jersey appellate court declared that legislative authorization for bargaining did not reflect the intent to depart from the common law rule prohibiting strikes by public employees.[96] In contrast to the prevailing common law position, the Louisiana high court declared strikes permissible for some public employees, including teachers. The court found under state law "an intent to afford public employees a system of organizational rights which parallels that afforded to employees in the private sector."[97]

90. To avoid strikes among certain groups of public employees, interest arbitration may be mandatory. *See, e.g.,* Ohio Rev. Code § 4117.14 (D)(1) (2002).
91. Ohio Rev. Code § 4117.14(C) (2002); Or. Rev. Stat. § 243. 712(2)(e) (2001); R.I. Gen. Laws 28 § 9.3-9 (2002).
92. Me. Rev. Stat. 26 § 979.D(4) (2002). *But see* Conn. Gen. Stat. § 10-153f (2002) (providing for submission of unresolved issues to "last best offer" arbitration).
93. A statutory limited right to strike exists for public employees in Alaska, Colorado, Hawaii, Illinois, Minnesota, Montana, Ohio, Oregon, Pennsylvania, Vermont, and Wisconsin. Alaska law has been interpreted as prohibiting teachers from striking even though most other public employees are permitted to strike. Anchorage Educ. Ass'n v. Anchorage Sch. Dist., 648 P.2d 993 (Alaska 1982).
94. Norwalk Teachers Ass'n v. Bd. of Educ., 83 A.2d 482, 485 (Conn. 1951).
95. Anderson Fed'n of Teachers v. Sch. City of Anderson, 251 N.E.2d 15 (Ind. 1969).
96. Passaic Township Bd. of Educ. v. Passaic Township Educ. Ass'n, 536 A.2d 1276 (N.J. Super Ct. App. Div. 1987).
97. Davis v. Henry, 555 So. 2d 457, 464-465 (La. 1990).

A strike is more than simply a work stoppage; states define the term broadly to include a range of concerted activities such as work slowdowns, massive absences for "sick" days, and refusal to perform certain duties. For example, the Massachusetts high court found that refusing to perform customary activities, such as grading papers and preparing lesson plans after the end of the school day, constituted a strike.[98] A Missouri appellate court upheld the right of the St. Louis school superintendent to request documentation from 1,190 teachers that a "sick" day was not related to a labor dispute surrounding the negotiation of a new contract.[99] Without documentation from the teachers, the school district could deny payment for the day.

State laws, in addition to prohibiting work stoppages, usually identify penalties for involvement in strikes. Such penalties can include withholding compensation for strike days, prohibiting salary increases for designated periods of time (e.g., one year), and dismissal. Penalties for illegal strikes also are imposed on unions. Sanctions may include fines, decertification of the union, and loss of certain privileges such as dues checkoff.

Despite statutory prohibitions on strikes, many teachers, as well as other public employees, participate in work stoppages each year. Public employers can seek a court injunction against teachers who threaten to strike or initiate such action. Most courts have granted injunctions, concluding as did the Supreme Court of Alaska that the "illegality of the strike is a sufficient harm to justify injunctive relief."[100] Failure of teachers and unions to comply with such a restraining order can result in contempt of court charges and resulting fines and/or imprisonment. For example, teachers in a Maryland school district who refused to obey an injunction were found guilty of criminal contempt.[101] In South Bend, Indiana, refusal to comply with an injunction resulted in a contempt-of-court charge and fines totaling $200,000 against two unions.[102] Establishing the level of fines involves a consideration of factors such as the magnitude of the threatened harm and the association's financial condition.

Teachers illegally participating in a strike are subject to court-imposed penalties and, in most states, to statutory penalties. Refusal of teachers to return to the classroom can result in dismissal.

Conclusion

More so than in the other areas of law that have been discussed, individual state laws, school board regulations, and master contracts must be consulted to determine the specific terms and conditions of teachers' employment. Except for certain limitations imposed by constitutional provisions and federal civil rights laws, state statutes govern educators' employment. The state prescribes general requirements for licensure, contracts, tenure, and

98. Lenox Educ. Ass'n v. Labor Relations Comm'n, 471 N.E.2d 81 (Mass. 1984).

99. Franklin v. St. Louis Bd. of Educ., 904 S.W.2d 433 (Mo. Ct. App. 1995).

100. Anchorage Educ. Ass'n v. Anchorage Sch. Dist., 648 P.2d 993, 998 (Alaska 1982). *But see* Wilson v. Pulaski Ass'n of Classroom Teachers, 954 S.W.2d 221 (Ark. 1997) (requiring proof of irreparable harm to issue a preliminary injunction).

101. Harford County Educ. Ass'n v. Bd. of Educ., 380 A.2d 1041 (Md. 1977).

102. Nat'l Educ. Ass'n-S. Bend v. S. Bend Cmty. Sch. Corp., 655 N.E.2d 516 (Ind. Ct. App. 1995).

employment. Local school boards are vested with the power to appoint teachers and to establish professional and academic employment standards above the state minimums. Also, a school board may assign or transfer a teacher to any school or grade at its discretion, as long as the assignment is within the teacher's licensure area and not limited by contract terms. Under state laws, school boards confer tenure, which ensures that dismissal is based on adequate cause and accompanied by procedural due process.

In some states, employment is further defined by negotiated collective bargaining agreements (often called master contracts) between school boards and teacher unions, which limit the discretionary power of school boards to make unilateral employment decisions. Specific bargaining rights are conferred through state statutes or judicial interpretations of state constitutions, thus creating wide divergence in teachers' bargaining rights across states. Although all teachers have a constitutionally protected right to form and join a union, school boards are not required to bargain with employee organizations unless mandated to do so by state law. Negotiated agreements typically include the specification of salary and fringe benefits but also may address management and association rights, grievance procedures, employee evaluations, and procedural due process for employee discipline and reduction in force.

Points to Ponder

1. After a two-year recruitment effort, a prominent, successful basketball coach moved across the state to accept a position to coach the boys' varsity basketball team and teach science in a well-known high school program. His failure to produce a championship basketball team led the school board to terminate his coaching contract four years later. Although he retained his teaching position, he challenged the board's decision, arguing that he was recruited primarily to coach basketball and that he had moved, at great expense, to the community for the coaching opportunity. What are the teacher/coach's legal rights? For two perspectives, *see* Lagos v. Modesto City Schs. Dist., 843 F.2d 347 (9th Cir. 1988) and Kingsford v. Salt Lake City Sch. Dist., 247 F.3d 1123 (10th Cir. 2001).

2. You have been offered employment in a school district for next fall. With the offer of employment, the superintendent notes several requirements that must be met prior to final school board approval. In addition to the typical physical examination, the board requires that all new appointees consent to fingerprinting, a criminal background check, and a drug test. Do these requirements implicate protected privacy rights?

3. A high school principal refused to appoint a teacher, former president of the teachers' union, as department chair of history. The teacher questioned the decision, claiming that the denial was based on her union activities. What are the teacher's protected rights?

4. Invoking the state Freedom of Information Act, a group calling itself Concerned Citizens for Improving Our Schools requested extensive financial data as well as personnel data from the local school district. Teachers objected to the release of personal data related to their sick leave records, teaching licenses, and annual evaluations. Does this request violate teachers' privacy rights? How do freedom of information laws affect these privacy rights?

5. After several weeks of noticing prominent bruises on a 10-year-old boy, a teacher expressed her concern to the principal. The principal responded that she had no cause to worry, particularly since the boy's parents were prominent citizens in the community. What is the teacher's legal responsibility in this situation?

10

Teachers' Substantive Constitutional Rights

Although statutory law is prominent in defining specific terms and conditions of employment, substantive rights also are conferred on public employees by the Federal Constitution. These rights cannot be abridged by legislation or school board action without an overriding government interest, nor can public employment be conditioned on their relinquishment.

This chapter presents an overview of the scope of public school teachers' constitutional rights as defined by the judiciary in connection with freedom of expression and association, choice in appearance, and privacy rights. Constitutional rights pertaining to equal protection, due process, and religious guarantees as well as remedies available to aggrieved individuals when their rights have been abridged are discussed in other chapters.

Freedom of Expression

> Public employees' comments on matters of public concern are constitutionally protected expression.

Until the mid-twentieth century, it was generally accepted that public school teachers could be dismissed or disciplined for expressing views considered objectionable by the school board. The private-sector practice of firing such employees was assumed to apply to public employment as well. Since the late 1960s, however, the Supreme Court has recognized that the First Amendment limits public employers' discretion to condition employment on the expression of certain views, including those critical of government policies. Although clearly established that free expression rights are not forfeited by accepting public school employment, courts also have acknowledged that First Amendment rights must be weighed against the school district's interest in maintaining effective and efficient schools. This section reviews the evolution of legal principles articulated by the Supreme Court and their application to specific school situations.

Legal Principles

In the landmark 1968 decision, *Pickering v. Board of Education,* the Supreme Court recognized that teachers have a First Amendment right to air their views on matters of public concern.[1] Pickering wrote a letter to a local newspaper, criticizing the school board's fiscal policies, especially the allocation of funds between the education and athletic programs. The school board dismissed Pickering because of the letter, which included false statements allegedly damaging the reputations of school board members and district administrators.

Reversing the Illinois courts, the Supreme Court first identified expression pertaining to matters of public concern as constitutionally protected and reasoned that the funding and allocation issues raised by Pickering were clearly questions of public interest requiring free and open debate. **The Court then applied a balancing test, weighing the teacher's interest in expressing his views on public issues against the school board's interest in providing educational services.** The Court recognized that expression on public issues could be the basis for disciplinary action if it:

- Jeopardized Pickering's relationship with his immediate supervisor or harmony with coworkers,
- Impaired classroom performance, or
- Impeded school operations.

Concluding that Pickering's letter did not have a detrimental effect in any of these areas, the Court found no justification for limiting his contribution to public debate. Indeed, the Court noted that a teacher's role provides a special vantage point from which to develop an informed opinion on the allocation of school district funds, thus making it essential for teachers to be able to speak about public issues without fear of reprisal. Furthermore, the Court held that false statements about matters of public record, without proof that they were intentionally or recklessly made, cannot be the basis for dismissal.

In 1977, the Supreme Court established the principle that even if a teacher's expression is constitutionally protected, school officials are not prevented from discharging the employee if sufficient cause exists *independent* of the protected speech. In *Mt. Healthy City School District v. Doyle,* a school board voted not to renew the contract of a nontenured teacher who had made a telephone call to a local radio station concerning a proposed teacher grooming code. The teacher had been involved in several previous incidents, but in not renewing his contract, the board cited "lack of tact in handling professional matters," referring only to the radio call and obscene gestures made to several female students.[2] The lower courts ruled in favor of the teacher, but the Supreme Court reversed,

1. 391 U.S. 563 (1968).
2. 429 U.S. 274, 282 (1977), *on remand,* 670 F.2d 59 (6th Cir. 1982).

instructing the courts below to assess whether the school board would have reached the same decision in the absence of the teacher's exercise of protected speech. The Supreme Court reasoned that protected expression should not place an employee in a better or worse position with regard to continued employment. In short, dismissal or nonrenewal is not negated by the employee's exercise of protected speech as long as the personnel action is warranted on other grounds. On remand, the board clearly established that there were sufficient grounds other than the radio station call to justify the teacher's nonrenewal.

Under the *Mt. Healthy* test, the burden is on the employee to show that the conduct is constitutionally protected and a substantial or motivating factor in the school board's adverse employment decision. Once established, the burden then shifts to the board to show by a preponderance of evidence that it would have reached the same decision if the protected expression had not occurred. Even if proven that the school board's decision was based primarily on comments related to matters of public concern (i.e., the adverse consequences would not have happened "but for" the protected expression), the decision might still be upheld applying the *Pickering* balancing test. Expression that interferes with teaching effectiveness, relationships with superiors, or school operations can always be the basis for disciplining public employees.

For more than a decade after the *Pickering* decision, it was unclear whether public employees' *private* communications enjoyed First Amendment protection. In 1979, the Supreme Court concluded in *Givhan v. Western Line Consolidated School District* that as long as the expression pertains to matters of public concern (in contrast to personal grievances), statements made in private or through a public medium are constitutionally protected.[3] The teacher had made critical comments to her principal regarding race relations in the school, and the Court reasoned that the forum where the expression occurs does not determine whether it is of public or personal interest. The Court did note, however, that the time, place, and manner of the remarks can be considered in assessing private expression because of the nature of the employer-employee relationship.

In a significant 1983 decision, *Connick v. Myers,* the Supreme Court's interpretation of the *Pickering* balancing test narrowed the circumstances under which public employees can prevail in free expression cases.[4] The case involved an assistant district attorney who was dissatisfied with her proposed transfer and circulated among coworkers a questionnaire concerning office operations and morale. She was subsequently terminated for her actions. The Supreme Court ruled that the questionnaire related primarily to a personal employment grievance that is not protected by the First Amendment rather than to matters of public interest. Of particular importance was the Court's conclusion that **the *form* and *context* as well as the *content* of the expression should be considered in assessing whether it relates to public matters.** Thus, the Court indicated that the factors applied under the *Pickering* balancing test to determine if speech adversely affects government interests can be considered in the *initial* assessment of whether the expression informs public debate or is simply part of a private employment grievance. For expression in the latter category, no additional constitutional scrutiny is required (see Figure 10.1).

3. 439 U.S. 410 (1979).
4. 461 U.S. 138 (1983).

FIGURE 10.1 ***Analyzing Public Educators' Expression Outside the Classroom***

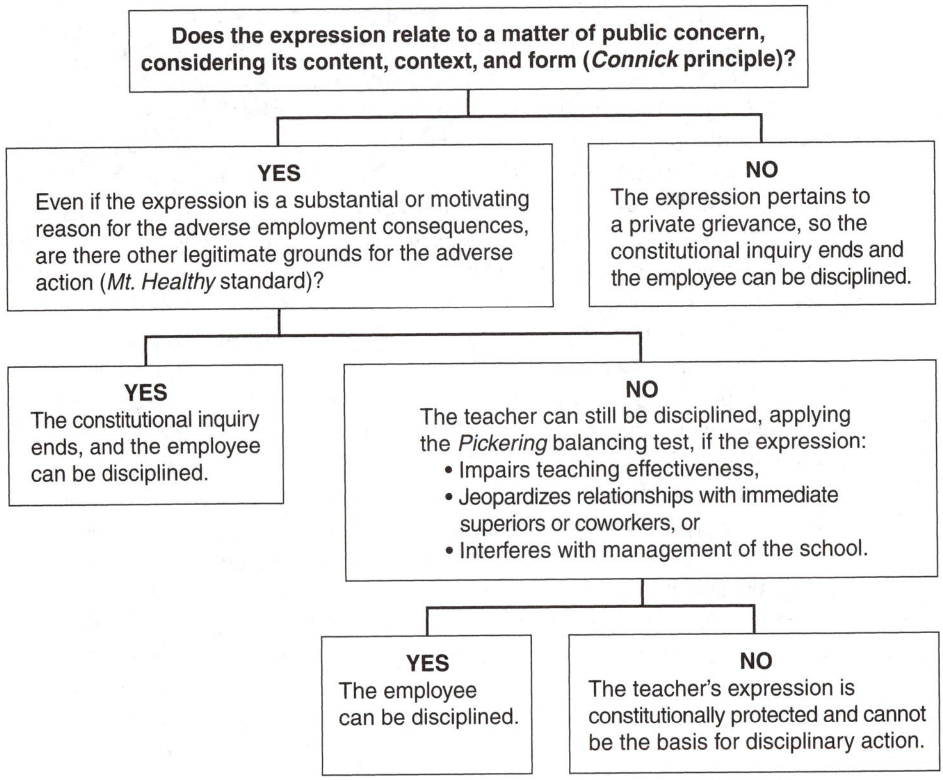

The *Connick* majority recognized that the state's burden of justifying a given discharge varies according to the nature of the employee's expression. The employer's burden increases as the employee's speech more directly involves public issues and decreases as the expression interferes with close working relationships that are essential to fulfilling public responsibilities. The majority did concede, however, that this "particularized balancing" of competing interests is a difficult task.[5]

In 1994, the Supreme Court again addressed the scope of public employees' free speech rights in *Waters v. Churchill.*[6] Churchill, a nurse at a public hospital, was discharged for making critical comments about hospital operations to a coworker during a break. The comments were overheard by other coworkers, and although the actual remarks were dis-

5. *Id.* at 150. *See also* Rankin v. McPherson, 483 U.S. 378 (1987) (assessing the context, form, and content of a public employee's pejorative statement to a coworker following the assassination attempt on President Reagan and finding no basis for dismissal in the absence of interference with work relationships or performance).

6. 511 U.S. 661 (1994).

puted, Churchill's supervisors maintained that the expression disrupted the work environment. The Supreme Court plurality categorized Churchill's expression about the hospital's training policy and its impact on patient care as criticisms of her employer rather than comments on matters of public concern. **The plurality in *Waters* further concluded that as long as the employer conducted an investigation and acted in good faith, it could discharge an employee for remarks it *believed* were made, regardless of what was actually said.** Accordingly, the government employer can reach its factual conclusions without being held to the evidentiary rules followed by courts, so the dispute over what was said did not have to be resolved by a jury. *Waters* and *Connick,* taken together, have made it more difficult for public employees to establish that adverse employment actions have impaired their First Amendment expression rights than was true in the decade following the *Pickering* decision.

Application of the Legal Principles

In the majority of cases, public educators have challenged reprisals for their speech outside the classroom. Some courts also have addressed *prior restraints* on public employees' expression and restrictions on the communication channels through which views may be aired. In addition, during the past couple of decades, educators' classroom expression has evoked considerable litigation under the Free Speech Clause.

Expression Outside the Classroom. During the 1970s and early 1980s, courts relied on the *Pickering* guidelines in striking down a variety of restrictions on teachers' rights to express views on matters of public interest. **Since the early 1980s, however, courts have seemed increasingly inclined to view teachers' and other public employees' expression as unprotected, finding that it relates to *private* employment disputes rather than to matters of public concern.** To illustrate, federal circuit courts have relied on *Connick* in concluding that protests over unfavorable performance evaluations[7] and criticisms of working conditions and low staff morale in a faculty newsletter[8] pertain primarily to private grievances. In post-*Connick* cases, courts have considered the *impact* of expression in the initial determination of whether it is protected, even if the expression touches on issues of public concern. For example, the Tenth Circuit ruled that a school nurse's criticism of the school district's student medication policy, an issue of undeniable public interest, was not constitutionally protected because the expression disrupted the school's health service program.[9]

Individuals involved in setting policy for a public agency relinquish some free speech rights to criticize their employers, because of the impact of their expression on how the agency functions. The Seventh Circuit found no impairment of free speech rights in the demotion of a principal to assistant principal for opposing the school district's efforts to secure approval of a program for disadvantaged students.[10] Similarly, the Sixth Circuit con-

7. Day v. S. Park Indep. Sch. Dist., 768 F.2d 696 (5th Cir. 1985).
8. Sanguigni v. Pittsburgh Bd. of Educ., 968 F.2d 393 (3d Cir. 1992).
9. Johnsen v. Indep. Sch. Dist. No. 3, 891 F.2d 1485 (10th Cir. 1989).

sidered the importance of a tension-free superintendent/principal relationship in concluding that a principal's complaints about the superintendent's elimination of a dress code were not protected.[11]

Although *Connick* and *Waters* have made it more difficult for public employees to establish that their expression is constitutionally protected, this burden can be satisfied. Expression that clearly relates to the welfare of students is afforded First Amendment protection. The Eighth Circuit held that a letter submitted by several teachers to the state department of education, complaining about the school district's delay in implementing programs for children with disabilities, pertained to a matter of public concern.[12] The Fifth Circuit found protected expression in teachers' protests regarding the school board's decision to cancel an art program serving predominantly minority children,[13] and in comments about efforts to raise the school's level of education.[14] In addition, federal courts have considered expression about employee safety following a workplace rape[15] and criticism in the media of the school district's instructional requirements during Black History Month[16] to pertain to matters of public concern.

Educators who blow the whistle on unlawful or unethical acts are likely to find their expression protected.[17] Political expression and union activities also are protected by the First Amendment. For example, the Sixth Circuit rejected the nonrenewal of a probationary teacher, finding that the action was based on constitutionally protected union activities rather than the asserted reasons of declining teaching evaluations and a personality conflict with the principal.[18] However, an employee cannot transform private grievances about conditions of employment into matters of public concern by simply airing the personal concerns in a union forum.[19]

It must be emphasized that courts differ as to what expression directly relates to student or school welfare, and similar factual situations may elicit different judicial responses. **Unfortunately, there is not a distinct list of "matters of public concern" versus "private grievances"; such a determination must be made on a case-by-case basis.** For example,

10. Vargas-Harrison v. Racine Unified Sch. Dist., 272 F.3d 964 (7th Cir. 2001), *cert. granted,* 123 S. Ct. 120 (2002). *See also* Love-Lane v. Martin, 201 F. Supp. 2d 566 (M.D.N.C. 2002) (finding an assistant principal's disagreements with supervisors regarding school discipline and use of a time-out room to be private grievances).
11. Sharp v. Lindsey, 285 F.3d 479 (6th Cir. 2002).
12. Southside Pub. Schs. v. Hill, 827 F.2d 270 (8th Cir. 1987).
13. Tompkins v. Vickers, 26 F.3d 603 (5th Cir. 1994).
14. Harris v. Victoria Indep. Sch. Dist. 168 F.3d 216 (5th Cir. 1999).
15. Kennedy v. Tangipahoa Parish Library Bd., 224 F.3d 359 (5th Cir. 2000).
16. Clark v. Bd. of Educ., 907 F. Supp. 826 (D.N.J. 1995).
17. *See, e.g.,* Canary v. Osborn, 211 F.3d 324 (6th Cir. 2000) (making allegations of cheating on student achievement tests); Williams v. Kentucky, 24 F.3d 1526 (6th Cir. 1994) (criticizing political patronage employment practices); DePace v. Flaherty, 183 F. Supp. 2d 633 (S.D.N.Y. 2002) (criticizing superintendent for public intoxication and driving under the influence).
18. Hickman v. Valley Local Sch. Dist. Bd. of Educ., 619 F.2d 606 (6th Cir. 1980).
19. *See, e.g.*, Hale v. Robersone, No. 96-1241-CV-W-6, 1998 U.S. Dist. LEXIS 13316 (W.D. Mo. June 25, 1998).

the Seventh Circuit concluded that a teacher's complaints about class size and student discipline constituted a private grievance.[20] In contrast, the Tenth Circuit ruled that a teacher's critical expression regarding the school district's method of disciplining students pertained to a public concern and was constitutionally protected.[21] The *form* and *context* of the expression may determine whether its purpose is to further private interests or to air public concerns.

Even if protected speech on an issue of public concern is involved, courts have relied on *Mt. Healthy* to uphold disciplinary measures where other legitimate reasons justify the personnel actions.[22] The First Circuit held that although the decision not to renew a teacher's contract was based in part on the teacher's criticism of the special education director and student placement practices at a school board meeting, the board would have taken this action for other legitimate reasons (e.g., difficulty with her supervisor, unprofessional conduct in case conference meetings).[23] More recently, the Seventh Circuit held that teachers were not dismissed for criticism of a specific academic program or the principal's interactions with teachers, but rather for legitimate reasons pertaining to their poor performance.[24] A New York federal court reasoned that a teacher's dismissal for misconduct in trying to raise her pupils' test scores did not mask retaliation for her filing a notice of claim against other city officials.[25]

School authorities cannot rely on *Mt. Healthy,* however, to justify termination if there are no other *legitimate* reasons for the personnel actions; school officials' stated reasons for decisions cannot be a pretext to restrict protected expression. For example, the Seventh Circuit held that a counselor, allegedly dismissed for 14 incidents of insubordination and unprofessional misconduct, was actually fired in retaliation for protected expression, including articles he wrote for the local paper and criticisms of various school board procedures and actions.[26]

Assuming that the employee carries the difficult burden of establishing that the adverse employment action would not have occurred *but for* the protected expression, the school still might prevail applying the *Pickering* balancing test. **If established that expres-**

20. Cliff v. Bd. of Educ., 42 F.3d 403 (7th Cir. 1994) (noting that the comments were made in response to deficiencies listed on the teacher's performance evaluations). *See also* Wales v. Bd. of Educ., 120 F.3d 82 (7th Cir. 1997) (holding that comments about student discipline and classroom management focused on the personal impact on the teacher rather than on the welfare of the class).
21. Rankin v. Indep. Sch. Dist., 876 F.2d 838 (10th Cir. 1989).
22. *See, e.g.,* Flath v. Garrison Pub. Sch. Dist., 82 F.3d 244 (8th Cir. 1996); Ingrum v. Nixa Reorganized Sch. Dist., 966 F.2d 1232 (8th Cir. 1992).
23. Wytrwal v. Saco Sch. Bd., 70 F.3d 165 (1st Cir. 1995).
24. Love v. Chi. Bd. of Educ., 241 F.3d 564 (7th Cir. 2001). *See also* Leary v. Daeschner, 228 F.3d 729 (6th Cir. 2000) (holding that teachers' transfers were not motivated by their expression pertaining to discipline and instructional strategies); Settlegoode v. Portland Pub. Schs., No. CV-00-313-ST, 2002 U.S. Dist. LEXIS 2238 (D. Or. Jan. 31, 2002) (finding that the employee's nonrenewal was for her inability to write adequate individualized education programs, rather than for her complaints about treatment of special education students).
25. Rivera v. Cmty. Sch. Dist. Nine, 145 F. Supp. 2d 302 (S.D.N.Y. 2001).
26. Dishnow v. Sch. Dist., 77 F.3d 194 (7th Cir. 1996).

sion on matters of public concern is the motivating or sole basis for adverse action, the public employer has the opportunity to establish that its interests in maintaining efficient school operations outweigh the individual's free speech rights. The Eighth Circuit found that teachers' interests in voicing concerns about incidents with special education students were outweighed by interests in efficiently administering the middle school, given that the expression caused school upheaval.[27]

In applying the principles articulated by the Supreme Court, the threshold question is whether the speech pertains to a public issue considering the content, form, and context of the expression. During the 1970s, it was generally assumed that even educators' expression involving matters of private rather than public interest could not be the basis for adverse personnel action unless the expression posed some threat of disrupting the educational process. But, post-*Connick* cases indicate that sanctions can be imposed for the expression of private concerns in the absence of any disruptive effect.[28] Thus, the threshold determination of whether the speech pertains to public or private issues has become increasingly important. Moreover, under *Waters,* the school board has considerable discretion in determining what constitutes unprotected, private expression. As long as the board makes a reasonable effort to investigate the nature of the expression and its conclusion is not clearly arbitrary, a court will accept the board's decision.

Prior Restraint and Channel Rules. The judiciary is less likely to condone prior restraints on expression than it is to uphold disciplinary action after the expression has occurred. **A key is whether the prior restraint is content based, which requires strict judicial scrutiny, or whether it is content neutral, thus receiving a "less rigorous examination."**[29] For example, the Tenth Circuit struck down a portion of an Oklahoma law authorizing the termination of teachers for "advocating . . . public or private homosexual activity in a manner that creates a substantial risk that such conduct will come to the attention of school children or school employees."[30] The Fifth Circuit also invalidated a school board policy requiring prior approval of all political, sectarian, or special-interest materials distributed in the schools, which had been applied to limit debate on one side of an issue. The board had invoked the policy to prevent distribution of documents that were critical of a proposed teacher testing program, while the school board's literature supporting the program had been distributed in the schools.[31]

Policies limiting teachers' access to the school board also have generated legal disputes. In 1976, the Supreme Court held that a nonunion teacher has a free speech right to comment on a bargaining issue at a public school board meeting.[32] Also, the Ninth Circuit awarded a teacher-coach damages for his suspension as a coach, which occurred because he

27. Fales v. Garst, 235 F.3d 1122 (8th Cir. 2001).
28. Prior to *Connick,* courts often relied on the principle that undifferentiated fear of disruption was not sufficient to curtail free expression rights. *See* Tinker v. Des Moines Indep. Cmty. Sch. Dist., 393 U.S. 503 (1969); text accompanying note 41, Chapter 5.
29. Eclipse Enter., Inc. v. Gulotta, 134 F.3d 63, 66 (2d Cir. 1997).
30. Nat'l Gay Task Force v. Bd. of Educ., 729 F.2d 1270, 1274 (10th Cir. 1984), *aff'd by an equally divided court,* 470 U.S. 903 (1985).
31. Hall v. Bd. of Sch. Comm'rs, 681 F.2d 965 (5th Cir. 1982).

did not advise the superintendent before writing a letter to school board members about an issue of public concern.[33] Similarly, the Seventh Circuit struck down a policy requiring all communication to the school board to be directed through the superintendent and ordered a reprimand for violating the policy to be removed from a teacher's personnel file.[34]

But, some constraints on employee communication in the public school's nonpublic forum have been upheld. For example, the Seventh Circuit upheld a school board's denial of a request by a group of teachers to hold religious meetings in the public school before students arrived in the morning, reasoning that the public school is not a forum for employees to hold meetings on matters of personal concern.[35] Reflecting similar reasoning, the Fourth Circuit held that public employees do not have a free speech right to use state equipment for expressive purposes not related to the agency's business. Accordingly, the appeals court upheld restrictions on state employees' access to sexually explicit internet materials on computers owned or leased by the state.[36]

In a significant 1983 decision, *Perry Education Association v. Perry Local Educators' Association,* the Supreme Court ruled that a school district is not constitutionally obligated to allow a rival teachers' union access to internal school mailboxes although the exclusive bargaining agent is granted such access. **Holding that a public school's internal mail system is not a public forum for expression, the Court declared that "the state may reserve the forum for its intended purposes, communicative or otherwise, as long as the regulation on speech is reasonable and not an effort to suppress the speaker's views."**[37] The Court determined that alternative communication channels were available to the rival union.

Subsequently, the Supreme Court affirmed a Fifth Circuit decision that a Texas school district had not created a public forum in either its schools or school mail facilities. Thus, the district could deny representatives of teachers' organizations school access during school hours and could bar their use of the school mail system.[38] However, the court found a First Amendment violation in school policies that denied teachers the right to discuss employee organizations during nonclass time or to use school mail facilities for communications, including any mention of employee organizations. Under certain circumstances, a

32. City of Madison, Joint Sch. Dist. No. 8 v. Wis. Employment Relations Comm'n, 429 U.S. 167 (1976); text accompanying note 87, Chapter 9.
33. Anderson v. Cent. Point Sch. Dist., 746 F.2d 505 (9th Cir. 1984).
34. Knapp v. Whitaker, 757 F.2d 827 (7th Cir. 1985).
35. May v. Evansville-Vanderburgh Sch. Corp., 787 F.2d 1105 (7th Cir. 1986). *But see* Secretary Roderick Paige, *Guidance on Constitutionally Protected Prayer in Public Elementary and Secondary Schools* (Washington, DC: United States Department of Education, 2003) (authorizing teachers to meet for religious purposes during lunch or other noninstructional time as long as it is clear from the context that they are not participating in devotional activities in their official capacities).
36. Urofsky v. Gilmore, 216 F.3d 401 (4th Cir. 2000), *cert. denied,* 531 U.S. 1070 (2001).
37. 460 U.S. 37, 46 (1983).
38. Tex. State Teachers Ass'n v. Garland Indep. Sch. Dist., 777 F.2d 1046 (5th Cir. 1985), *aff'd mem.,* 479 U.S. 801 (1986). *See also* Tex. State Teachers Ass'n v. Garland Indep. Sch. Dist., 489 U.S. 782 (1989) (awarding attorneys' fees for work on issues on which teachers' association prevailed).

school's mail system might be designated a public forum by school officials and thus selective access to the forum could not be denied.[39]

Although prior restraints on teachers' free speech rights are vulnerable to legal attack, courts have upheld reasonable time, place, and manner regulations. Such restrictions must not be based on the content of speech, and they must serve significant government interests and leave alternative communication channels open.

Classroom Expression. Public educators' classroom expression generally is governed by *Hazelwood School District v. Kuhlmeier,* which allows school authorities to censor school-sponsored expression for pedagogical reasons.[40] **Public school classrooms are not public forums, and school boards can restrict teachers' classroom expression based on legitimate educational concerns.**[41] As discussed in Chapter 3, teachers cannot use their classrooms to proselytize students; school board prohibitions on religious advocacy consistently have been upheld.[42] Also, courts have approved adverse employment action against teachers who discuss topics when they have received sufficient notice that such expression is inappropriate. For example, the First Circuit held that a teacher's discussion of abortion of Downs syndrome fetuses could be curtailed, noting that the school board may limit a teacher's classroom expression in the interest of promoting educational goals.[43]

Relying on *Hazelwood,* the Tenth Circuit upheld disciplinary action against a teacher who made comments during class about rumors that two students had engaged in sexual intercourse on the school tennis court during lunch hour.[44] More recently, a high school teacher did not prevail in his efforts to post material outside his classroom that denounced homosexuality and extolled traditional family values. His display was intended to offset the posted materials recognizing Gay and Lesbian Awareness Month as required by the Los Angeles Unified School District.[45] Concluding that the teacher was speaking for the school, the Ninth Circuit ruled that teachers' rights to express views off campus do not entitle them to express views in the classroom that are counter to the adopted curriculum.

39. *See, e.g.,* Ysleta Fed'n of Teachers v. Ysleta Indep. Sch. Dist., 720 F.2d 1429 (5th Cir. 1983).
40. 484 U.S. 260 (1988).
41. *See, e.g.,* Debro v. San Leandro Unified Sch. Dist., No. C-99-0676 VRW, 2001 U.S. Dist. LEXIS 17388 (N.D. Cal. Oct. 11, 2001) (holding that a teacher had no First Amendment right to depart from classroom instruction to discuss tolerance toward homosexuals, even though of public interest).
42. *See, e.g.,* Webster v. New Lenox Sch. Dist. No. 122, 917 F.2d 1004 (7th Cir. 1990); text accompanying note 36, Chapter 3.
43. Ward v. Hickey, 996 F.2d 448 (1st Cir. 1993). For a discussion of teachers' interests in academic freedom, see text accompanying note 32, Chapter 4.
44. Miles v. Denver Pub. Schs., 944 F.2d 773 (10th Cir. 1991). *But see* Scruggs v. Keen, 900 F. Supp. 821 (W.D. Va. 1995) (holding that a teacher's comments on interracial dating made in response to students' questions during study hall pertained to a public concern).
45. Downs v. L.A. Unified Sch. Dist., 228 F.3d 1003 (9th Cir. 2000), *cert. denied,* 532 U.S. 994 (2001). The Supreme Court has recognized that when the speaker is conveying a particular message on behalf of the government, content distinctions can be imposed. *See* Rosenberger v. Rector & Visitors, 515 U.S. 828, 833 (1995); Rust v. Sullivan, 500 U.S. 173, 194-200 (1991).

Espousing similar reasoning, a Virginia federal district court held that a teacher had no First Amendment right to post outside his classroom door the American Library Association's pamphlet listing banned books to "educate" his students and others who passed by.[46] The court reasoned that such expression was an extension of the curriculum and could be censored for educational reasons. The principal and superintendent felt that the pamphlets contained information with the potential to compromise the school's family life education program and other initiatives.

Departing from the general trend of evaluating teachers' instructional expression under *Hazelwood,* the Sixth Circuit applied the *Pickering/Connick* analysis to a teacher's classroom speech in a Kentucky case. The appeals court found genuine issues of material fact regarding whether the school district's proffered grounds for terminating the teacher (i.e., insubordination, conduct unbecoming a teacher, inefficiency, incompetency, and neglect of duty) were a pretext because of the notoriety surrounding her decision to invite an actor, Woody Harrelson, to give class presentations on the environmental benefits of industrial hemp.[47] The court held that although the teacher was speaking as an employee when presenting the information on industrial hemp, school authorities' interests in an efficiently run school and a harmonious workplace did not outweigh the teacher's interests in speaking about an issue of substantial concern in the state.

Freedom of Association

> A public educator's participation in political activities outside the classroom cannot be the basis for adverse employment decisions, unless the employee has policymaking responsibilities or such activities negatively affect work performance.

Although freedom of association is not specifically addressed in the First Amendment, the Supreme Court has recognized that associational rights are "implicit in the freedoms of speech, assembly, and petition."[48] The Court has consistently declared that infringements on the right to associate for expressive purposes can be justified only by a compelling government interest, unrelated to suppressing ideas, that cannot be achieved through less restrictive means.[49] Accordingly, public educators cannot be disciplined for forming or joining political, labor, religious, or social organizations.

46. Newton v. Slye, 116 F. Supp. 2d 677 (W.D. Va. 2000) (noting, however, that the teacher could still distribute the pamphlets in the classroom as part of the instructional program and students continued to have access to the pamphlets).
47. Cockrel v. Shelby County Sch. Dist., 270 F.3d 1036 (6th Cir. 2001), *cert. denied,* 123 S. Ct. 73 (2002).
48. Healy v. James, 408 U.S. 169, 181 (1972).
49. *See, e.g.,* NAACP v. Button, 371 U.S. 415 (1963).

Associational activities can be limited, however, if they disrupt school operations or interfere with teachers' professional duties. This section presents an overview of teachers' associational rights in connection with political affiliations and activities. Public educators' rights to intimate association are discussed in the section on privacy rights, and labor union issues are addressed in Chapter 9.

Political Affiliations

Conditioning public employment on partisan political affiliation has been controversial. Historically, the patronage system governed public employment; when the controlling political party changed, noncivil service employees belonging to the defeated party lost their jobs. In 1976, the Supreme Court ruled that the patronage system in an Illinois sheriff's office placed a severe restriction on political association and belief.[50] The constant threat of replacing nonpolicymaking individuals, who cannot undermine the administration's policies, was considered detrimental to government effectiveness and efficiency. The Court has subsequently extended the principle established in the political firing cases to all aspects of public employment, ruling that party affiliation cannot influence promotion, transfer, recall, and other decisions pertaining to employees who do not establish policies.[51]

Despite being insulated from partisan politics, in some instances public educators have asserted that employment decisions have been based on their party affiliation. In such cases, the school employee has the burden of substantiating that protected political affiliation was the motivating factor in the board's employment decision.[52] If an employee satisfies this burden, then the board must demonstrate by a preponderance of evidence that it would have reached the same decision in the absence of the political association.[53]

Public educators have substantial protection against politically based dismissals, but school authorities can question teachers about activities that may adversely affect teaching. In *Beilan v. Board of Public Education of Philadelphia,* the Supreme Court held that questions regarding a teacher's involvement in the Communist Party were relevant to an assessment of his classroom activities and fitness to teach, and that refusal to answer the superintendent's inquiries could result in dismissal.[54] **Although organizational membership *per se* is protected, a teacher must respond to queries about associational activities that are related to teaching fitness.**

Also, courts have upheld anti-nepotism policies that prohibit teachers from reporting to their spouses or working in the same building as their spouses. The Sixth Circuit reasoned

50. Elrod v. Burns, 427 U.S. 347 (1976). *See also* Branti v. Finkel, 445 U.S. 507 (1980).

51. Rutan v. Republican Party, 497 U.S. 62 (1990). *See also* Armour v. County of Beaver, 271 F.3d 417 (3d Cir. 2001), *cert. denied,* 535 U.S. 1079 (2002) (holding that access to confidential information alone was insufficient to establish that political affiliation was an appropriate job requirement for a secretary to the county commissioner); McCloud v. Testa, 97 F.3d 1536 (6th Cir. 1996) (rejecting public employer's immunity for violating lower level employees' constitutional protections against discrimination based on their political speech and association).

52. *See, e.g.,* Piazza v. Aponte Roque, 909 F.2d 35 (1st Cir. 1990) (finding that nonrenewal of teachers' aides because of their political party affiliation impaired associational rights).

53. *See, e.g.,* Estrada-Izquierdo v. Aponte Roque, 850 F.2d 10 (1st Cir. 1988).

54. 357 U.S. 399 (1958).

that such an anti-nepotism policy did not interfere with the fundamental right to marry, because the policy affected working conditions, not the marriage itself.[55] The fact that such policies do not apply to employees who are cohabiting or dating has not nullified anti-nepotism provisions.

Political Activity

Teachers, like all citizens, are guaranteed the right to participate in the political process. First Amendment associational as well as free speech rights have been invoked to protect public educators in expressing political views, campaigning for candidates, and running for office.

Campaigning for Issues and Candidates. Public employees are constitutionally protected from retaliation for participating in political affairs at the local, state, and federal levels. For example, the Sixth Circuit held that the coordinator of gifted education, which was not a policymaking position, could not be reassigned for the exercise of constitutionally protected political expression and association.[56] The superintendent did not demonstrate that political loyalty was essential to the duties of this position. Of course, public employees in policymaking positions may be vulnerable to adverse employment consequences for their political activities that may preclude an effective relationship with the school board.[57]

Political activity that would cause divisiveness within the school district always can be restricted.[58] A California appeals court held that a school district could prevent its employees from wearing political buttons in instructional settings, because of the presence of students, but could not place such a restriction on expression in noninstructional settings.[59] **Making campaign speeches in the classroom is clearly prohibited; teachers cannot take advantage of their position of authority with an impressionable captive audience to impose their political views.** However, if campaign issues are related to the class topic, a teacher can present election issues and candidates in a nonpartisan manner.

Holding Public Office. Certain categories of public employees have been prevented from running for political office.[60] In 1973, the Supreme Court upheld the Hatch Act, a federal law that prevents *federal* employees from holding formal positions in political parties,

55. Montgomery v. Carr, 101 F.3d 1117 (6th Cir. 1996).
56. Hager v. Pike County Bd. of Educ., 286 F.3d 366 (6th Cir. 2002). *But see* Beattie v. Madison County Sch. Dist., 254 F.3d 595 (5th Cir. 2001) (finding insufficient causal link between employee's termination and her support for the nonincumbent candidate for school superintendent).
57. *See, e.g.,* Dabbs v. Amos and Cabarrus County Bd. of Educ., 70 F.3d 1261 (4th Cir. 1995); Kinsey v. Salado Indep. Sch. Dist., 950 F.2d 988 (5th Cir. 1992).
58. *See, e.g.,* State Bd. v. Howard, 834 S.W.2d 657 (Ky. 1992).
59. Cal. Teachers Ass'n v. San Diego Unified Sch. Dist., 53 Cal. Rptr. 2d 474 (Ct. App. 1996). *See also* Green Township Educ. Ass'n v. Rowe, 746 A.2d 499 (N.J. Super. Ct. 2000).
60. *See, e.g.,* Brazil-Breashears v. Bilandic, 53 F.3d 789 (7th Cir. 1995) (finding no First or Fourteenth Amendment infractions in prohibiting certain judicial branch employees from being candidates for public office or engaging in specified political activities).

playing substantial roles in partisan campaigns, and running for partisan office.[61] The Court recognized that legitimate reasons exist for restricting political activities of public employees, such as ensuring impartial and effective government, removing employees from political pressure, and preventing employee selection based on political factors. In a companion case, the Court upheld an Oklahoma law forbidding classified civil servants from running for paid political offices.[62]

Yet, laws or policies prohibiting *all* public employees from running for *any* political office have been struck down as overly broad.[63] Several courts have held that public educators, unlike public employees who are directly involved in the operation of government agencies, have the right to hold public office. The Utah Supreme Court, for example, ruled that public school teachers and administrators were not disqualified from serving in the state legislature.[64]

Restrictions can be imposed, however, to protect the integrity of the educational system. If campaigning would interfere with job responsibilities, public educators can be required to take a leave of absence while running for a public office.[65] Courts also have recognized that certain offices are incompatible with public school employment, especially if they involve an employer-employee relationship. Common law has established that such incompatibility exists when a teacher seeks a position on the school board where employed.[66] Of course, a teacher would not be prevented from serving on the school board of another school district.

Although school boards must respect employees' associational rights, they are obligated to ensure that the political activities of public school personnel do not adversely affect the school. Employees can be disciplined if they:

- Neglect instructional duties to campaign,
- Use the classroom as a political forum, or
- Disrupt school operations because of their political activities.

But, school boards must be certain that constraints on employees' freedom of association are not based on mere disagreement with the political orientation of the activities. Personnel actions must be justified as necessary to protect the interests of students and the school.

61. United States Civil Serv. Comm'n v. Nat'l Ass'n of Letter Carriers, 413 U.S. 548 (1973), interpreting 5 U.S.C. § 7324 (2003).
62. Broadrick v. Oklahoma, 413 U.S. 601 (1973).
63. *See, e.g.,* Minielly v. State, 411 P.2d 69 (Or. 1966); Cranston Teachers Alliance v. Miele, 495 A.2d 233 (R.I. 1985).
64. Jenkins v. Bishop, 589 P.2d 770 (Utah 1978) (per curiam).
65. *See, e.g.,* White v. Dougherty County Bd. of Educ., 579 F. Supp. 1480 (M.D. Ga. 1984), *aff'd,* 470 U.S. 1067 (1985).
66. *See, e.g.,* Unified Sch. Dist. No. 501 v. Baker, 6 P.3d 848 (Kan. 2000) (invalidating election of a teacher to the school board where state legislature had not negated the common law doctrine of job incompatibility by authorizing the holding of dual offices).

Personal Appearance

School officials can place constraints on educators' personal appearance if there is a rational basis for such restrictions.

Historically, school boards often imposed rigid grooming restrictions on teachers. In the 1970s, such attempts to regulate teachers' appearance generated considerable litigation, as did grooming standards for students.[67] Controversies have subsided somewhat, but constraints on school employees' appearance continue to be challenged. School boards have defended their efforts to regulate teacher appearance on the perceived need to set an appropriate tone in the classroom and enforce similar appearance and dress codes for students. Teachers have contested these requirements as abridgments of their constitutionally protected privacy, liberty, and free expression rights.

Most courts since the mid-1970s have supported school officials in imposing reasonable grooming and dress restrictions on teachers. The Supreme Court provided some clarification of public employers' authority regarding regulation of employee appearance in a 1976 decision upholding a hair-grooming regulation for police officers.[68] The Court placed the burden on the individual to demonstrate the lack of a rational connection between the regulation and a legitimate public purpose. This reasoning has been followed by lower courts in assessing dress and appearance restrictions for teachers. For example, the Second Circuit upheld a Connecticut school board's requirement that all male teachers must wear ties as a rational means to promote respect for authority, traditional values, and classroom discipline.[69] Because of the uniquely influential role of teachers, the court noted that they may be subjected to restrictions in their professional lives that otherwise would not be acceptable. The First Circuit similarly upheld a school board's dismissal of a teacher for wearing short skirts.[70] More recently, a federal court ruled that a school board did not violate a teacher's rights by instructing her to cover her t-shirt displaying the words *Jesus 2000—J2K* or to change into another top.[71]

Restrictions will not be upheld, however, if found to be unrelated to a legitimate government concern. Although courts generally acknowledge that individuals have a protected interest in governing their appearance, this interest has not been declared a fundamental right

67. For a discussion of restrictions on student appearance, *see* text accompanying note 82, Chapter 5. For a discussion of employees' wearing religious attire in public schools, *see* text accompanying note 50, Chapter 11.

68. Kelley v. Johnson, 425 U.S. 238 (1976).

69. E. Hartford Educ. Ass'n v. Bd. of Educ., 562 F.2d 838 (2d Cir. 1977).

70. Tardif v. Quinn, 545 F.2d 761 (1st Cir. 1976). *See also* Zalewska v. County of Sullivan, 180 F. Supp. 2d 486 (S.D.N.Y. 2002) (upholding uniform policy for van drivers to project a professional appearance and ensure safety of vans with chair lifts).

71. Downing v. W. Haven Bd. of Educ., 162 F. Supp. 2d 19 (D. Conn. 2001).

requiring heightened judicial scrutiny. School officials thus can restrict employees' appearance as long as the regulations advance legitimate school objectives and are not arbitrary.

Privacy Rights

Sanctions cannot be imposed solely because school officials disapprove of teachers' private conduct, but restrictions can be placed on unconventional behavior that is detrimental to job performance or harmful to students.

Public employees have asserted constitutional and statutory rights to be free from unwarranted government intrusions in their personal activities. The Federal Constitution does not explicitly enumerate personal privacy rights, but the Supreme Court has recognized that certain *implied* fundamental rights warrant constitutional protection because of their close relationship to explicit constitutional guarantees. For example, protected privacy rights have been interpreted as encompassing personal choices in matters such as marriage, contraception, procreation, and family relations.[72] Employment decisions cannot be based on relinquishing such rights without a compelling justification. Litigation covered in this section focuses on constitutional privacy claims initiated under the Fourth Amendment (protection against unreasonable searches and seizures), the Ninth Amendment (personal privacy as an unenumerated right reserved to the people), and the Fourteenth Amendment (protection against state action impairing personal liberties without due process of law).

In some instances, public employees have asserted that government action has impaired their privacy right to intimate association related to creating and maintaining a family. To assess such claims, courts must weigh the employee's interests against the government's interests in promoting efficient public services.[73] To illustrate, public educators cannot be deprived of their jobs because of the politics or other activities of their partners or spouses. The Sixth Circuit found an inference that the superintendent's nonrenewal recommendation for an employee, whose husband disagreed with school district policies, was impermissibly based on the employee's marital relationship.[74]

The Second Circuit upheld a teacher's privacy claim in her refusal to submit to a physical examination by the school district's male physician.[75] The unreasonableness of the board's action was supported by the fact that the teacher offered to go at her own expense to

72. *See, e.g.,* Roe v. Wade, 410 U.S. 113 (1973) (right to have an abortion); Loving v. Virginia, 388 U.S. 1 (1967) (right to interracial marriage); Griswold v. Connecticut, 381 U.S. 479 (1965) (right to use birth control measures); Skinner v. Oklahoma, 316 U.S. 535 (1942) (right to procreate).

73. *See, e.g.,* Kelly v. City of Meriden, 120 F. Supp. 2d 191 (D. Conn. 2000) (upholding dismissal of a school social worker who was living with the noncustodial father of children to whom she had provided social services; the city director believed the employee may have violated the ethics code, discredited the municipal service, and hindered other school social workers in performing their work).

74. Adkins v. Bd. of Educ., 982 F.2d 952 (6th Cir. 1993).

75. Gargiul v. Tompkins, 704 F.2d 661 (2d Cir. 1983), *vacated and remanded,* 465 U.S. 1016 (1984).

any female physician the board selected. Also, the Fifth Circuit recognized that a teacher's interest in breast-feeding her child at school during noninstructional time was sufficiently close to fundamental rights regarding family relationships and child rearing to trigger constitutional privacy protection. The court acknowledged, however, that courts must determine whether school boards' interests in avoiding disruption of the educational process, ensuring that teachers perform their duties without distraction, and avoiding liability for potential injuries are sufficiently compelling to justify restrictions imposed on teachers' fundamental privacy interests.[76]

Teachers have not succeeded in asserting a privacy right to refuse physical examinations as a prerequisite to employment or as a condition of returning from medical leave.[77] Also, courts have found no privacy impairments in required observations by superiors and other strategies used to assess teaching competence. For example, a Texas appeals court upheld videotaping a teacher's performance for evaluative purposes, concluding that teachers' privacy rights do not shield them from legitimate performance evaluations.[78]

Although regulations are far less restrictive today than in the early 1900s, when some school districts prohibited female teachers from marrying or even dating, school boards still attempt to proscribe aspects of teachers' personal lives that conflict with community values. **School officials have defended constraints on some behaviors on the grounds that teachers serve as role models for students and therefore should conform to community norms to ensure an appropriate educational environment.** Recognizing that teachers are held to a higher standard of conduct than general citizens, the judiciary has upheld dismissals for behavior that jeopardizes student welfare, even if it takes place during the summer break.[79] The remainder of this section focuses on litigation in which courts have assessed the competing government and individual interests in connection with employee searches and lifestyle choices.

Search and Seizure

Public educators, like all citizens, are shielded by the Fourth Amendment against unreasonable government invasions of their person and property. This amendment usually requires police officers and other state agents to secure a search warrant (based on probable cause that evidence of a crime will be found) before conducting personal searches. The Supreme Court has not addressed teachers' rights in connection with searches initiated by public school authorities, but it has upheld warrantless personal searches of students based on *reasonable suspicion* that contraband detrimental to the educational process is concealed.[80]

76. Dike v. Sch. Bd., 650 F.2d 783 (5th Cir. 1981).

77. *See, e.g.,* Strong v. Bd. of Educ., 902 F.2d 208 (2d Cir. 1990); Daury v. Smith, 842 F.2d 9 (1st Cir. 1988).

78. Roberts v. Houston Indep. Sch. Dist., 788 S.W.2d 107 (Tex. Ct. App. 1990). *See also* Brannen v. Bd. of Educ., 761 N.E.2d 84 (Ohio Ct. App. 2001) (holding that board's use of surveillance cameras to videotape school custodians in their break room to identify unauthorized breaks was not unreasonable and did not constitute an unlawful search).

79. *See, e.g.,* Bd. of Educ. v. Wood, 717 S.W.2d 837 (Ky. 1986).

80. New Jersey v. T.L.O., 469 U.S. 325 (1985). *See* text accompanying note 70, Chapter 8, for a discussion of the reasonable suspicion standard.

The Court also has upheld a warrantless search by state hospital supervisors of an employee physician's office; the search was considered necessary to carry out hospital business.[81] Items seized from the physician's desk and file cabinets were used in administrative proceedings that resulted in his dismissal for improprieties in managing the residency program.

Although case law in the public school context is scant, the judiciary has recognized that the reasonableness of a job-related search or seizure by a supervisor rests on whether educational interests outweigh the employee's expectation of privacy. **The Fourth Amendment prohibits *arbitrary* invasions of teachers' personal effects by school officials, but in some situations courts have ruled that the school's interests are overriding.**[82]

Drug-screening programs in schools have become increasingly controversial. School boards can require employees to have physical examinations as a condition of employment, but mandatory screening for drugs has been challenged as impairing Fourth Amendment privacy rights. Several courts have struck down random or blanket urinalysis screening of public school employees, holding that school boards must have *individualized suspicion* of conduct detrimental to the school environment to subject employees to drug tests.[83]

In contrast to *blanket* testing of all personnel, support for drug testing of public employees in *safety-sensitive roles* can be found in two 1989 Supreme Court decisions upholding the mandatory drug testing of railroad employees involved in accidents[84] and customs employees who carry firearms or intercept illegal drugs.[85] The Court found that the safety and security interests served by the programs outweighed employees' privacy concerns. The District of Columbia Circuit subsequently upheld the school district's policy requiring all employees whose duties affect child safety, such as bus attendants, to submit to a drug test as part of routine medical examinations.[86] And, the Fifth Circuit ruled that a school custodian, whose performance affected almost 900 students, was in a safety-sensitive role justifying suspicionless drug testing.[87]

What constitutes safety-sensitive roles in the school context, however, remains unclear. Some courts seem more inclined than in the past to interpret expansively the posi-

81. O'Connor v. Ortega, 480 U.S. 709 (1987).

82. *See, e.g.,* Shaul v. Cherry Valley-Springfield Cent. Sch. Dist., 218 F. Supp. 2d 266 (N.D.N.Y. 2002) (upholding principal's search of suspended teacher's desk and files for educational materials). *But see* Gillard v. Schmidt, 579 F.2d 825 (3d Cir. 1978) (invalidating search of school counselor's desk by a school board member, because the search was politically motivated and lacked sufficient work-related justification).

83. *See, e.g.,* Ga. Ass'n of Educators v. Harris, 749 F. Supp. 1110 (N.D. Ga. 1990); Patchogue-Medford Congress of Teachers v. Bd. of Educ., 510 N.E.2d 325 (N.Y. 1987).

84. Skinner v. Ry. Executives' Ass'n, 489 U.S. 602 (1989) (upholding alcohol testing of employees as well).

85. Nat'l Treasury Employees Union v. Von Raab, 489 U.S. 656 (1989).

86. Jones v. McKenzie, 833 F.2d 335 (D.C. Cir. 1987), *vacated sub nom.* Jones v. Jenkins, 490 U.S. 1001 (1989), *on remand,* 878 F.2d 1476 (D.C. Cir. 1989).

87. Aubrey v. Sch. Bd., 148 F.3d 559 (5th Cir. 1998). *See also* English v. Talladega County Bd. of Educ., 938 F. Supp. 775 (N.D. Ala. 1996) (upholding random drug testing of school bus mechanics).

tions in this category.[88] In a controversial 1998 case, the Sixth Circuit upheld a school district's policy requiring suspicionless drug testing for all individuals who apply for, transfer to, or are promoted to safety-sensitive positions, including *teaching positions.*[89] Although there was no evidence that teachers exhibited an apparent drug problem, the court reasoned that teachers are entrusted with the care of children and are on the "frontline" of school security and thus are in safety-sensitive roles. The court also upheld drug testing of any individual for whom there was reasonable suspicion of drug possession or use, but it struck down the provision calling for blanket alcohol testing of all employees.[90] Other courts have not yet interpreted safety-sensitive roles this broadly.

Employees, like students, can always be subjected to alcohol and drug testing based on *reasonable suspicion* that the individual is under the influence of such substances. The Eleventh Circuit found legitimate grounds for terminating a teacher who refused to undergo urinalysis after a drug-sniffing dog detected marijuana in her car.[91] Ruling that the Fourth Amendment allows dog sniff searches of personal property in public places, the court rejected the teacher's asserted expectation of privacy in the odors emanating from her car.

Courts in some instances have found inadequate grounds for individualized suspicion. In a St. Louis case, a teacher forced to submit to a drug and alcohol test stated a valid Fourth Amendment claim; the school district's request for summary judgment was denied because of genuine issues as to whether the teacher's behavior suggested drug use and whether she consented to the test.[92] Also, the Fifth Circuit struck down policies in two Louisiana school districts that required employees injured in the course of employment to submit to urinalysis, finding an insufficient nexus between such injuries and drug impairment to create reasonable suspicion of drug use.[93] **The law is still evolving regarding what constitutes individualized suspicion of drug use and the circumstances under which certain public employees can be subjected to urinalysis without such suspicion.**

Lifestyle Choices

In recent years, teachers frequently have challenged school officials' authority to restrict personal lifestyle choices. Although the right to such personal freedom is not an enumerated constitutional guarantee, it is a right implied in the concept of personal liberty embodied in

88. Advocates of drug testing of school employees have been encouraged by Supreme Court decisions expanding suspicionless drug testing of students to those participating in any extracurricular activities. *See* Bd. of Educ. v. Earls, 536 U.S. 822 (2002); Vernonia Sch. Dist. 47J v. Acton, 515 U.S. 646 (1995); text accompanying note 112, Chapter 8.

89. Knox County Educ. Ass'n v. Knox County Bd. of Educ., 158 F.3d 361 (6th Cir. 1998).

90. *Id.* The case was remanded for a determination of whether the low level of alcohol impairment identified, .02, was reasonably related to the purpose of the testing program.

91. Hearn v. Bd. of Pub. Educ., 191 F.3d 1329 (11th Cir. 1999).

92. Warren v. Bd. of Educ., 200 F. Supp. 2d 1053 (E.D. Mo. 2001) (upholding school district's policy authorizing drug testing based on reasonable suspicion that a given employee is under the influence of alcohol or drugs; employees referred for testing are suspended pending the outcome and given back pay for the suspended days if the results are negative).

93. United Teachers of New Orleans v. Orleans Parish Sch. Bd., 142 F.3d 853 (5th Cir. 1998).

the Fourteenth Amendment. Constitutional protection afforded to teachers' privacy rights is determined not only by the *location* of the conduct but also by the *nature* of the activity.[94] The judiciary has attempted to balance teachers' privacy interests against the school board's legitimate interests in safeguarding the welfare of students and the school. Teachers can suffer adverse employment consequences for behavior that impairs job performance. Educators can be terminated based on evidence that would not be sufficient to support criminal charges,[95] but they cannot be dismissed for unsubstantiated rumors about their activities.[96] Since some cases dealing with lifestyle choices also are discussed in Chapter 12 in connection with dismissals based on charges of immorality, the following discussion is confined to an overview of the constitutional issues.

Recognizing that decisions pertaining to marriage and parenthood involve constitutionally protected privacy rights, courts have been reluctant to support dismissal actions based on teachers' unwed, pregnant status without evidence that the condition impairs fitness to teach.[97] Compelled leaves of absence for such employees similarly have been invalidated as violating constitutional privacy rights.[98]

Most courts also have reasoned that public employees, including educators, have a privacy right to engage in consenting sexual relationships out of wedlock and that such relationships cannot be the basis for dismissal unless teaching effectiveness is impaired. To illustrate, the Supreme Court of Iowa held that a teacher's adulterous relationship was insufficient to justify revocation of his teaching certificate, since no harmful effect on his teaching was substantiated.[99] Similarly, the Sixth Circuit ruled that a school board's nonrenewal of a teacher's contract, because of her involvement in a divorce, abridged constitutional privacy rights.[100]

Some courts, however, have upheld dismissals or other disciplinary actions based on public employees' lifestyle choices that involve unconventional sexual relationships. For example, a New York federal court upheld termination of a teacher for actively participating in a group supporting consensual sexual activity between men and boys, reasoning that his activities in this organization were likely to impair teaching effectiveness and disrupt the school.[101]

Conditioning employment decisions on a teacher's sexual orientation has become increasingly controversial. Among factors that courts consider are whether the homosexual

94. *See, e.g.,* Lile v. Hancock Place Sch. Dist., 701 S.W.2d 500 (Mo. Ct. App. 1985).

95. *See, e.g.,* Montefusco v. Nassau County, 39 F. Supp. 2d 231 (E.D.N.Y. 1999) (holding that although the criminal investigation did not result in criminal charges, the school board could suspend the teacher with pay and remove extracurricular assignments for his possession of candid pictures of teenagers taken at the teacher's home).

96. *See, e.g.,* Peaster Indep. Sch. Dist. v. Glodfelty, 63 S.W.3d 1 (Tex. Ct. App. 2001) (holding that gossip triggered by unproven allegations of sexual misconduct could not be the basis for nonrenewal of teachers' contracts).

97. *See, e.g.,* Avery v. Homewood City Bd. of Educ., 674 F.2d 337 (5th Cir. 1982).

98. *See, e.g.,* Ponton v. Newport News Sch. Bd., 632 F. Supp. 1056 (E.D. Va. 1986).

99. Erb v. Iowa State Bd. of Pub. Instruction, 216 N.W.2d 339 (Iowa 1974).

100. Littlejohn v. Rose, 768 F.2d 765 (6th Cir. 1985). *See also* Bertolini v. Whitehall City Sch. Dist. Bd. of Educ., 744 N.E.2d 1245 (Ohio Ct. App. 2000); text accompanying note 40, Chapter 12.

101. Melzer v. Bd. of Educ., 196 F. Supp. 2d 229 (E.D.N.Y. 2002).

conduct is public or private, the notoriety surrounding the conduct, and its impact on teaching effectiveness. The law is clear that educators can be dismissed for immorality if they engage in *public* sexual activity, whether heterosexual or homosexual in nature.[102]

However, *private* sexual behavior enjoys Fourteenth Amendment protection. In 2003, the Supreme Court in *Lawrence v. Texas* struck down a Texas law prohibiting persons of the same gender from engaging in certain sexual conduct in their own homes as violating liberty rights of consenting adults.[103] Overturning a 1986 ruling, in which the Court upheld a Georgia law criminalizing consensual sodomy,[104] the *Lawrence* Court reasoned that the earlier decision did not recognize the substantial constitutional protection afforded to adults in private matters pertaining to sexual activity.

Dismissals of public school employees based solely on sexual orientation, in the absence of criminal charges, have evoked a range of judicial interpretations.[105] **In general, courts will require a nexus between private homosexuality and impaired teaching effectiveness to justify dismissal.** To illustrate, the Utah Federal District Court ruled that the community's negative response to a teacher's homosexuality was not sufficient justification to remove the teacher as the girl's volleyball coach and instruct her not to mention her sexual orientation to students, parents, or staff.[106] Also, an Ohio federal court awarded a teacher reinstatement, back pay, and damages for his nonrenewal that was impermissibly based on his sexual orientation rather than on his teaching deficiencies as the board asserted.[107]

Yet, the Eleventh Circuit upheld revocation of a public employee's job offer after her employer, the state's chief legal officer, learned of the employee's pending same-sex marriage. The employment action was based on her illegal wedding ceremony rather than on her status as a lesbian. The court found no impairment of associational rights, given the employer's interests in hiring staff to enforce state laws.[108] The plaintiff's intimate associational rights were subordinate to the employer's interest in the effective functioning of the

102. *See, e.g.,* Nat'l Gay Task Force v. Bd. of Educ., 729 F.2d 1270 (10th Cir. 1984), *aff'd by an equally divided court,* 470 U.S. 903 (1985) (upholding Oklahoma law allowing teachers to be discharged for public homosexual activity, but not for mere advocacy of homosexual rights), *supra* text accompanying note 30; Morgan v. State Bd. of Educ., 2002 Ohio 2738 (Ct. App. 2002) (upholding revocation of teaching certificate for disorderly conduct conviction stemming from his participation in a public sex act).

103. No. 02-102, 2003 U.S. LEXIS 5013 (June 26, 2003).

104. Bowers v. Hardwick, 478 U.S. 186 (1986).

105. There also has been litigation regarding the rights of homosexual employees in the private sector. *See* Boy Scouts of Am. v. Dale, 530 U.S. 640 (2000) (protecting expressive association rights in connection with the Boy Scouts' official position barring homosexuals from being troop leaders); text accompanying note 80, Chapter 5.

106. Weaver v. Nebo Sch. Dist., 29 F. Supp. 2d 1279 (D. Utah 1998). *See also* Miller v. Weaver, 66 P.3d 592 (Utah 2003) (rejecting citizen group's standing to challenge Weaver's status as a teacher for presumably violating the state's antisodomy law).

107. Glover v. Williamsburg Local Sch. Dist., 20 F. Supp. 2d 1160 (S.D. Ohio 1998).

108. Shahar v. Bowers, 114 F.3d 1097 (11th Cir. 1997). *See also* Rowland v. Mad River Local Sch. Dist., 730 F.2d 444 (6th Cir. 1984) (upholding the nonrenewal of a guidance counselor who told other school personnel about her bisexuality as well as the homosexuality of two student advisees); Gaylord v. Tacoma Sch. Dist. No. 10, 559 P.2d 1340 (Wash. 1977) (upholding a teacher's dismissal after he admitted his homosexuality to a school administrator).

government office. Some rights of teachers in this regard similarly may be overridden, if private choices adversely affect their teaching effectiveness or management of the school.

Conclusion

The U.S. Constitution places constraints on government, not private, action. Thus, public employees, but not usually those working in the private sector, can challenge employment decisions as violating their constitutional rights. If public employees can show that they have suffered adverse employment consequences because of the exercise of protected expression, association, or privacy rights, then the burden shifts to the employer to justify the restriction on protected rights as necessary to carry out the work of the government agency. In the school context, this means that the employee's action has impaired teaching effectiveness, relations with superiors, or school operations. The public employer also can prevail by showing that there are legitimate reasons for the personnel action aside from the exercise of protected expression or other constitutional rights. In short, under certain circumstances, restrictions on constitutional freedoms can be justified by overriding government interests.

Points to Ponder

1. A nontenured teacher has received mediocre evaluations for two years. The principal has provided him some instructional assistance but feels that the teacher is not making sufficient progress. Thus, the principal recommends that the teacher's contract not be renewed. Before the school board acts on the recommendation, the teacher writes a letter to the newspaper, criticizing the school board's adoption of a new math program for elementary grades. Is protected expression involved? Can the school board decline to renew the teacher's contract?
2. A teacher complained to her principal that children with disabilities were being placed in the regular classroom for fiscal reasons, when the children needed more restrictive placements. Can the teacher be disciplined for such expression?
3. A school board is concerned about the mounting drug problem in the community and particularly in the public schools. To address the problem, the school has instituted a drug-education program and a drug-testing program for all students who participate in extracurricular activities. Now, the board wants to adopt a requirement that all new teachers as part of their preemployment medical exams must submit to urinalysis screening for drug use. Are teachers in safety-sensitive roles? Can such a drug-screening program be justified without individualized suspicion?
4. A homosexual tenured middle school teacher has not mentioned his sexual orientation to his students. Yet, he has been prominent in gay rights rallies and has been a guest on a radio talk show to advocate a law authorizing homosexual marriages. As a result, several parents have complained to the principal and asked that the teacher be dismissed. Can the homosexual teacher be removed from the classroom?

11

Discrimination in Employment

All persons and groups are potential victims of discrimination in employment. People of color and women claim discrimination in traditionally segregated job categories, whereas Caucasians and males claim that affirmative action has denied them the right to compete on equal grounds. The young argue that the old already hold the good jobs and that entry is nearly impossible; the old contend that they often are released when "downsizing" occurs and that reemployment at the same level and salary is unlikely. Religious minorities contend that their religious needs are seldom accommodated; coworkers counter that seniority or performance should determine eligibility for work assignments (e.g., evenings, weekends), personal leave, and the like, rather than one's professed religion. Likewise, persons with disabilities often complain that they are not given the opportunity to show what they can do, whereas existing employees at times complain that they are required to perform supplemental duties due to the limited performance of a coworker with a disability. Given these diverse and conflicting interests, it is not surprising that literally hundreds of employment discrimination suits are filed each year.

Legal Context

> Numerous federal laws prohibit discrimination in public and private employment.

Most, but not all, forms of employment discrimination violate either federal or state law. Foremost among these legal protections are the Fourteenth Amendment to the United States Constitution and Title VII of the Civil Rights Act of 1964; both are discussed here, given their broad application. Other more narrowly tailored statutes are reviewed in the respective sections addressing discrimination based on race and national origin, gender, religion, age, and disability (see Table 11.1).

TABLE 11.1 ***Selected Federal Laws Prohibiting Employment Discrimination***

	Applies To:				*Prohibits Discrimination Based On:*					
Federal Law	*Public Schools*	*Private Schools*	*Recipients of Federal Financial Assistance*	*Number of Employees Necessary for Law to Apply*	*Race*	*National Origin, Alienage*	*Sex*	*Age*	*Religion*	*Disability*
14th Amendment U.S. Constitution	X				X	X	X	X	X	X
42 U.S.C. § 1983	X				X	X	X	X	X	X
42 U.S.C. § 1981	X	X			X	X Ethnicity				
Title VII of Civil Rights Act of 1964	X	X		15	X	X	X		X	
Equal Pay Act of 1963		X		20			X			
Section 504 of Rehabilitation Act of 1973			X							X
Americans with Disabilities Act	X	X		15						X
Age Discrimination in Employment Act	X	X		20				X		

Fourteenth Amendment

The Fourteenth Amendment to the United States Constitution mandates that no state shall deny to any person within its jurisdiction equal protection of the laws. This provision has been interpreted as prohibiting intentional discrimination and applies to subdivisions of the state, including public school districts. Districts may be found guilty of facial discrimination (e.g., where an administrative position is reserved for a female applicant), or facially neutral discrimination (e.g., where the district's use of standardized test scores in hiring results in disparate impact based on race).

Title VII

Title VII prohibits employers with 15 or more employees from discriminating on the basis of race, color, religion, gender, or national origin and covers hiring, promotion, and compensation practices as well as fringe benefits and other terms and conditions of employment.[1] This statute prohibits claims of both disparate treatment (i.e., where an individual plaintiff purports to be a victim of discrimination) and disparate impact (i.e., where plaintiff's class has allegedly been discriminated against because of the differential impact of a neutral policy or practice).

Hiring discrimination based on disparate treatment can be established by showing that the applicant or employee is a member of a protected class, applied for and was qualified for the job, and was denied the position, while the employer continued to seek applicants with the plaintiff's qualifications. These criteria were articulated by the Supreme Court in 1973 in *McDonnell Douglas Corporation v. Green*[2] and also are applied in discrimination claims involving promotion, termination, nonrenewal, and tenure.

Once a plaintiff has supported a claim, the burden shifts to the employer to state a reason for its action that does not violate Title VII. Such a reason may be either objective (e.g., requirement that the successful candidate possess a graduate degree upon hiring), subjective (e.g., assessment of interpersonal skills), or a combination in determining which applicant is best qualified. If the employer is unable to produce a nondiscriminatory reason for the action, a decision for the plaintiff most likely would be granted. But, given the comparative ease of presenting a nondiscriminatory reason, employers in nearly every instance provide a response.

After the employer provides a rebuttal, the plaintiff then has the additional burden of proving that the proffered reason was false and served as a pretext for prohibited intentional discrimination. In most instances of alleged discrimination, the plaintiff is unable to show that the employer's purported nondiscriminatory basis was pretextual.

In contrast to disparate treatment, **to establish disparate impact the plaintiff is not initially required to prove discriminatory intent but must establish that an employer's facially neutral practice had a disproportionate impact on the plaintiff's protected**

1. 42 U.S.C. § 2000e *et seq.* (2003). Furthermore, it is important to consider "combinations" of protected categories. For example, it might be that an employer would discriminate against Asian women but not against all women or Asian men.
2. 411 U.S. 792, 802 (1973).

class. This generally is accomplished through the use of statistics. Once this type of claim is supported, the employer then must show that the challenged policies or practices (or its employment practices in the aggregate) are job related and justified by a business necessity. Accordingly, an employer's nondiscriminatory reason for the act is insufficient to rebut a claim of discriminatory impact. Moreover, even if a business necessity is identified, a plaintiff still may prevail by showing that the employer's facially neutral practice had a discriminatory purpose. The Supreme Court has recognized, however, that mere awareness of a policy's adverse impact on a protected class does not constitute proof of unlawful motive. A discriminatory purpose "implies that the decisionmaker . . . selected or reaffirmed a particular course of action at least in part 'because of,' not merely 'in spite of,' its adverse effects upon an identifiable group."[3] Nonetheless, foreseeably discriminatory consequences can be considered by courts in assessing intent, although more will be needed to substantiate unlawful motive. Furthermore, the employee may prevail if it is shown that the employer refused to adopt an alternative policy identified by the employee that realistically would have met the employer's business needs without resulting in disparate impact.

Protection against discriminatory employment practices is not absolute for individuals within these classifications, for both Congress and courts have identified exceptions. In creating and amending Title VII over the years, Congress has expressly permitted employers to facially discriminate based on religion, gender, or national origin (but not on race or color) if they can show the existence of a *bona fide occupational qualification* that is reasonably necessary to the normal operation of their particular enterprise (e.g., that the head of a Catholic school be Catholic). Additionally, courts have specified that employers may use facially neutral employment practices that result in a disparate impact on a protected class, but only if a *business necessity* is identified in the use of that practice and there are no less discriminatory ways of meeting that need.

Title VII also prohibits acts of retaliation (e.g., termination, demotion, harassment) taken against persons who have filed complaints or suits. When this occurs, the employee may file a second claim alleging retaliation. To support this type of case, three things must have occurred:

- The employee must have engaged in statutorily protected activity (i.e., the filing of a complaint or suit),
- The employer must have taken an adverse employment action against the employee, and
- There must be a causal connection between the protected activity and the adverse action.[4]

3. Personnel Adm'r of Mass. v. Feeney, 442 U.S. 256, 279 (1979).
4. *See, e.g.,* Greer v. Bd. of Educ., 267 F.3d 723 (7th Cir. 2001) (finding that the plaintiff had been denied reemployment due to a consent decree and not as an act of retaliation); Sharma v. Ohio State Univ., 25 Fed. Appx. 243 (6th Cir. 2001) (concluding that the plaintiff failed to show that his comparatively low salary was due to filing discrimination complaints).

If the employee can show that filing the complaint was the basis for the adverse employment decision, even if the original complaint of discrimination fails, the court will provide appropriate relief. Showing that the retaliatory action followed soon after engagement in the protected activity often is critical to supporting a retaliation claim.[5] Furthermore, demonstrating that the administrator responsible for the adverse action knew of the original filing is essential to proving that the employer retaliated against the employee in response to the filing.[6]

If it is proven that the employee was a victim of prohibited discrimination, courts have the authority to require a *make-whole remedy,* in which the person is placed in the same position he or she otherwise would have been, absent discriminatory activity. In meeting this objective, courts may:

- Provide injunctive and declaratory relief;
- Require that a person be reinstated, hired, tenured, or promoted;
- Direct the payment of back pay, interest on back pay, or front pay;[7]
- Assign retroactive seniority;
- Provide attorneys' fees, expert witness fees, and court costs; and
- Require compensatory and punitive damages, in cases where intentional discrimination is proven.

But, an employer may not be held liable for the discriminatory acts of its managerial staff if their decisions are contrary to the employer's good faith efforts to comply with Title VII.[8]

In mixed-motive cases where legitimate as well as discriminatory motives influence the employer's decision (e.g., poor job performance as well as gender), an employer will be held liable for decisions based in part on impermissible considerations. However, if the same decision would have resulted notwithstanding the discriminatory factors, Title VII limits the legal remedy to ensure that employees will not be placed in better positions than they would have been absent the influence of an illegal motive.

5. *See, e.g.,* Ahmed v. Am. Red Cross, 218 F.3d 932 (8th Cir. 2000) (noting that a four-year period between the protected conduct and the allegedly retaliatory response suggests that the two events are not related).
6. *See, e.g.,* Tinsley v. First Union Nat'l Bank, 155 F.3d 435 (4th Cir. 1998) (noting that the plaintiff failed to show that the adverse action was based on filing an Equal Pay Act complaint 14 years earlier or that the supervisor was even aware of the filing).
7. For example, if a teacher were denied a principalship due to race, the court may direct the district to hire the teacher for the next available position. Also, if the principal position provided greater compensation than did the teacher position, the court could require as part of a make-whole remedy that the difference in salary be awarded to the teacher up to the time of promotion. That portion of the salary paid in the future is termed *front pay,* whereas that portion due the teacher at the time of the judgment for the previous period is termed *back pay.*
8. *See, e.g.,* Kolstad v. Am. Dental Ass'n, 527 U.S. 526 (1999).

Race and National-Origin Discrimination

> Without a proven history of prior discrimination, race may not play a factor in making employment decisions.

Race and national-origin discrimination in employment continues in spite of more than 135 years of protective statutes and constitutional amendments. For most of that period, however, the relief plaintiffs received was typically limited to a make-whole remedy and seldom penalized the employer sufficiently to discourage future discrimination. Due to changes in statutes and case law, it now is easier for plaintiffs to vindicate their rights in court and to receive substantial monetary awards. Race and national-origin lawsuits are usually filed under the Fourteenth Amendment or Title VII.[9]

Hiring and Promotion Practices

The desire to provide a racially diverse faculty or role models for specific populations within the student body will not justify current acts of discrimination without a proven history of prior discrimination. Only when a court of law determines that a school district has engaged in prior discrimination will the court narrowly tailor a remedy that will correct, to the degree possible, any lingering effects of the discriminatory conduct. Even then, however, the court order may not go beyond the constitutional violation and may persist only long enough to correct the prior discrimination. When the district has not engaged in a proven history of prior discrimination, race may neither advantage nor disadvantage an applicant or employee at any time in the employment relationship.

If discrimination is alleged in a disparate treatment case, a plaintiff must prove that the employer intended to discriminate. In attempting to support such a claim, many plaintiffs have difficulty overcoming employers' purported nondiscriminatory reasons for their decisions (e.g., better qualifications or experience),[10] even when they can show that persons of another race or national origin were eventually selected or treated more favorably. But, at times plaintiffs are able to show that no legitimate bases supported the employer's decision and that the selection was based on impermissible factors.[11]

9. Suits also may be filed under 42 U.S.C. § 1981. This law originally was § 1 of the Civil Rights Act of 1866. At one time, it prohibited only race discrimination in making and enforcing contracts, but now § 1981 applies when either race or ethnicity discrimination is alleged in making, performing, modifying, and terminating contracts, as well as in the enjoyment of all benefits, privileges, terms, and conditions of the contractual relationship.
10. *See, e.g.,* Cooper v. Murphysboro Bd. of Educ., 6 Fed. Appx. 438 (7th Cir. 2001) (determining that the plaintiff failed to support a claim because he lacked sufficient experience and certification for the position), *cert. denied,* 534 U.S. 1042 (2001).
11. *See, e.g.,* Stern v. Trs. of Columbia Univ., 131 F.3d 305 (2d Cir. 1997).

Because most qualifications for initial employment (e.g., degree, licensure) are clearly required to perform school jobs satisfactorily and to meet state standards and accountability mandates, disparate impact claims also are difficult to win. Among the more controversial objective measures is the use of standardized test scores. Employers are required to conduct validity studies for tests used in making employment decisions if they result in adverse impact on a protected class. Adverse impact exists when:

- One group succeeds at a rate that is less than four-fifths, or 80 percent, of that achieved by the group with the highest passing rate (e.g., adverse impact results if 90 percent of Caucasians pass a test, but fewer than 72 percent of African Americans do so); or
- For small populations, the difference in scores between two groups is statistically significant.

For tests with a disparate impact to be used, they must be reliable, be valid, and qualify as a business necessity.[12] Moreover, they may not be discriminatorily administered, nor may their results be discriminatorily used (e.g., the use of different cutoff scores or adjusted scores based on race is prohibited, whether used to advantage or disadvantage a population).

Adverse Decisions

Employers may not dismiss, decline to renew, or demote employees on the basis of race or national origin; legitimate, nondiscriminatory bases must be used. In 1993, the Supreme Court reviewed a significant race-based termination case, *St. Mary's Honor Center v. Hicks,*[13] in which a minority employee of a halfway house was demoted and eventually fired. The Court first noted that the employee had met his initial burden of proof (i.e., he was African American, he was qualified for the position, he was demoted and later discharged, and the position remained open until ultimately filled by a Caucasian). Accordingly, the burden then shifted to the employer to produce a nondiscriminatory reason for its action. The employer argued that the decision to terminate was necessary because of the employee's poor supervision of his subordinates, his failure to conduct a proper investigation of a brawl between inmates, and his use of threatening words with his immediate superior. Given this response, the burden shifted to the employee to show both that the proffered reasons were not to be believed *and* that the true basis for the termination was race.

The district court had determined that the employer's reasons were untrue, noting that the employee was the only supervisor disciplined for violations committed by his subordinates; that similar and at times more severe violations by others were either treated more leniently or disregarded; and that the supervisor provoked the employee into threatening him. The district court noted, and the Supreme Court agreed, however, that even though the

12. *See, e.g.,* Griggs v. Duke Power Co., 401 U.S. 424, 432 (1971) (holding that a private company's use of both a high school diploma requirement and a test of general intelligence as prerequisites to initial employment and a condition of transfer violated Title VII; neither requirement was shown to be related to successful job performance, and both operated to disqualify minority applicants at a higher rate than those who were Caucasian).

13. 509 U.S. 502 (1993).

employee was able to show that the purported reasons were not to be believed, he failed to show that race was a factor in his termination. Because the plaintiff was unable to meet his entire burden of persuasion, he could not prove a Title VII violation.[14] Similar decisions have been reached by other courts when adverse decisions were based on legitimate nonpretextual factors such as stalking and rape, neglect of duty, incompetence, lack of punctuality, insubordination, falsification of records, theft, unprofessional conduct, reduced need, and the like.[15]

Affirmative Action

***Affirmative action* has been defined as "steps taken to remedy the grossly disparate staffing and recruitment patterns that are the present consequences of past discrimination and to prevent the occurrence of employment discrimination in the future."**[16] Correcting such imbalances requires the employer to engage in activities such as:

- Expanding its training programs,
- Becoming actively involved in recruitment,
- Eliminating invalid selection criteria that result in disparate impact, and
- Modifying collective bargaining agreements that impermissibly restrict the promotion and retention of minorities.

Courts will uphold most strategies that the Equal Employment Opportunity Commission (EEOC) has identified as affirmative action under Title VII (for which the EEOC has regulatory authority). However, courts will prohibit the use of affirmative action plans that provide a discriminatory "preference" rather than an "equal opportunity," unless there is a proven history of institutional discrimination.

In 1989, the Supreme Court began to question a variety of public-sector practices that provided racial preferences.[17] **In the aggregate, these cases discredited societal discrimination as a justification for such programs; required showing specific discriminatory action to impose a race-based remedy; and allowed only narrowly tailored plans that would further a compelling governmental interest.** Given this precedent, existing public-sector affirmative action plans that provide racial preferences in employment without a

14. *See also* Silvera v. Orange County Sch. Bd., 244 F.3d 1253 (11th Cir. 2001), *cert. denied,* 535 U.S. 1013 (2002) (upholding termination of an employee convicted for child molestation and multiple counts of assault and battery; the plaintiff was unable to show that his race resulted in termination); Conward v. Cambridge Sch. Comm., 171 F.3d 12 (1st Cir. 1999) (upholding termination of the teacher for handing a student a document entitled "Application for a Piece of Ass"; plaintiff failed to show that treatment was race related or that persons of another race were treated differentially).
15. *See, e.g.,* Shaw v. Monroe, 20 Fed. Appx. 563 (7th Cir. 2001) (stalking and rape); Clearwater v. Indep. Sch. Dist. No. 166, 231 F.3d 1122 (8th Cir. 2000) (tardiness).
16. United States Commission on Civil Rights, *Statement of Affirmative Action for Equal Employment Opportunities* (Washington, DC: United States Commission on Civil Rights, 1973).

proven history of discrimination, or that are based only on underrepresentation of minority involvement, will likely be found unconstitutional.

In addition to affirmative action in hiring and promotion, there also have been efforts to protect the diversity gained through court order and voluntary affirmative action by providing a preference when an organization is downsizing. When a reduction in school staff is necessary due to financial exigency, declining enrollment, or a change in education priorities, it generally is based, at least in part, on seniority rankings. Accordingly, it is important for all employees to be in their rightful place on the seniority list. To obtain their rightful place, victims of discrimination have been awarded varying levels of retroactive seniority in addition to those years accrued while on the job.[18]

In some cases, plaintiffs have proposed the modification of seniority systems to give an overall preference to all minorities regarding eligibility for promotion and other job benefits or in protection from a reduction-in-force. Such affirmative action plans are similar to awards of retroactive seniority, but in contrast to seniority adjustments for individual discrimination victims, class remedies benefit class members who may not have been victims of prior acts of discrimination. Courts will prohibit such class remedies, even if the employer is found guilty of a pattern or practice of racial discrimination.[19] The appropriate form of relief is to award competitive seniority to individual victims so as to restore them to their rightful place. Furthermore, courts may not disregard a negotiated seniority system in fashioning a class remedy.

Gender Discrimination

> Although there are a few instances where gender will qualify as a bona fide occupational qualification, it generally may not be used as a basis in determining whom to hire, what salary to provide, or any other term or condition of employment.

Prior to 1963, there were no federal statutes prohibiting discrimination based on gender. Women were commonly denied employment if a qualified male applicant was in the pool, were offered less money for the same or similar job, or were expected to do work that would not have been asked of a man. Today, most forms of gender discrimination are legally pro-

17. *See, e.g.,* Adarand Constructors v. Pena, 515 U.S. 200 (1995); Northeastern Fla. Chapter of the Associated Gen. Contractors of Am. v. City of Jacksonville, 508 U.S. 656 (1993); Martin v. Wilks, 490 U.S. 755 (1989). However, the Supreme Court proclaimed in 2003 that the benefits derived from a diverse student body represent a compelling interest and may justify a university's affirmative action admissions plan if shown to be narrowly tailored. The impact of these cases on employment is yet to be determined. Grutter v. Bollinger, No. 02-241, 2003 U.S. LEXIS 4800 (Sup. Ct. June 23, 2003); Gratz v. Bollinger, No. 01-516, 2003 U.S. LEXIS 4801 (Sup. Ct. June 23, 2003).
18. *See, e.g.,* Franks v. Bowman Trans. Co., 424 U.S. 747 (1976).
19. *See, e.g.,* Firefighters Local Union No. 1784 v. Stotts, 467 U.S. 561 (1984).

hibited. The Fourteenth Amendment and Title VII, among other provisions, have played significant roles in allowing victims of gender discrimination to vindicate their rights in court.

Hiring and Promotion Practices

Gender discrimination is facial when an employer openly seeks a person of a particular gender (e.g., the posting of a position for a male guidance counselor). It becomes illegal discrimination when being male or female is unrelated to meeting job requirements (e.g., hiring only females as kindergarten teachers). At other times, employment practices are facially neutral (e.g., requiring head coaching experience in football in order to qualify as athletic director), but nevertheless result in nearly the same level of exclusion as when the discrimination is facial. Where this occurs, an action will be upheld only if found to qualify as a business necessity and other less discriminatory options do not meet the needs of the organization. However, employers have the discretion to choose among equally qualified candidates, as long as the decision is not based on unlawful criteria. They are not required to restructure employment practices to maximize the number of males or females, even if one gender is shown to be underrepresented.[20]

If a particular applicant or employee has been allegedly treated unfairly solely because of gender, the person must:

- Present evidence of membership in a protected class,
- Apply and be qualified for the job,[21] and
- Demonstrate that the employer denied the applicant and continued to seek additional candidates with the same qualifications until a person of the opposite sex was hired.

When such a case is established, the employer then must identify a basis other than gender for its decision (e.g., showing that the successful applicant is better qualified or that the plaintiff is unqualified).[22] Rejected applicants have prevailed where employers based their decisions on stereotypic attitudes about the capabilities of their gender (e.g., that the turnover rate among women is higher); where job advertisements included phrases, "prefer male" or "prefer female"; and where job descriptions were specifically drafted to exclude qualified applicants of a particular gender.

Not all gender-based distinctions are prohibited, however, as Title VII explicitly allows for a bona fide occupational qualification (BFOQ) exception. For a BFOQ to be upheld, it needs to be narrowly defined and applied only when necessary to achieve the employer's objectives. Since either males or females can perform the vast majority of jobs in education, there have been few BFOQ school cases. The only readily identifiable BFOQ in education would be the hiring of a female to supervise the girls' locker room and the hiring of a male to supervise the boys' locker room.

20. *See, e.g.,* Tex. Dep't of Cmty. Affairs v. Burdine, 450 U.S. 248 (1981).
21. Lockridge v. Bd. of Trs., 315 F.3d 1005 (8th Cir. 2003) (finding no race or gender discrimination where plaintiff failed to apply for a promotion).
22. *See, e.g.,* Bickerstaff v. Vassar Coll., 196 F.3d 435 (2d Cir. 1999) (finding that the plaintiff failed to meet the criteria for promotion to full professor).

Moreover, where gender does not qualify as a BFOQ, a position may not be left vacant when qualified persons of the nonpreferred gender are available in the labor pool. In such a case, the Seventh Circuit in 1999 concluded that a reasonable jury had sufficient data to conclude that the plaintiff, a male, was discriminated against solely because of gender when the dean refused to accept his nomination for a position that the dean hoped would be filled by a female.[23] The dean based his decision on the need to meet the affirmative action target for his college. The target was established to create a diversified staff, but not to eradicate the consequences of prior discrimination.

Compensation Practices

Claims of gender-based compensation discrimination involving entry salaries, raises, supplemental or overtime opportunities, or other perquisites and benefits are not uncommon within business, industry, and even higher education. However, because most K–12 salary decisions are based on objective criteria such as seniority, degree level, and civil service classification, the number of public school cases has been comparatively small.[24]

In addition to the Fourteenth Amendment and Title VII, plaintiffs who claim that their salaries are based on gender may file suit under the Equal Pay Act (EPA) of 1963.[25] However, the EPA applies only when the dispute involves gender-based wage discrimination claims of unequal pay for equal work. The act does not apply when race, national origin, disability, religion, or age-based salary differences are challenged, or when the work is not substantially equal. Also, because the EPA is restricted to those circumstances where there are male and female workers performing substantially the same work, it will apply only where both genders are represented, regardless of how abysmal the salaries are for the identified occupation (e.g., school kitchen workers).

In determining whether the jobs in question are equal, courts look at more than position titles (e.g., custodian versus cleaner; assistant principal versus assistant to the principal) and will examine the comparative skills, effort, responsibilities, and working conditions associated with each job as well as the nature of required tasks. **When the jobs are found substantially equal (although not identical) with unequal pay, the employer then must show by a preponderance of evidence that the different salaries were justified by seniority, merit, quantity or quality of production, or any factor other than gender.**[26]

If the employer purports to be using a merit system, it should be uniformly applied and be based on established criteria.[27] Under the EPA, the plaintiff need not prove that the employer intended to discriminate; proof that the compensation is different and not based on factors other than gender will suffice. Where violations are discovered, compensatory

23. Hill v. Ross, 183 F.3d 586 (7th Cir. 1999).

24. *See, e.g.,* Buntin v. Breathitt County Bd. of Educ., 134 F.3d 796 (6th Cir. 1998) (remanding the case to see if differential in "extended employment days" for which additional compensation is provided was due to gender).

25. 29 U.S.C. § 206(d) (2003).

26. *See, e.g.,* Wollenburg v. Comtech Mfg. Co., 201 F.3d 973 (7th Cir. 2000) (identifying experience as a legitimate basis for pay difference).

27. *See, e.g.,* Port Auth. v. Ryduchowski, 530 U.S. 1276 (2000).

damages may be awarded.[28] Furthermore, the law prohibits the lowering of the salaries for the higher paid group (generally men) and therefore requires the salaries for the lower paid group (generally women) to be raised. Importantly, EPA suits against states are not barred by Eleventh Amendment immunity.[29]

Moreover, gender-based wage discrimination claims are not confined exclusively to violations of the EPA; they also may be filed under Title VII. As with race-based cases, intent will have to be proven in a disparate treatment case, whereas salary differences will have to be statistically significant for plaintiffs to prevail in a disparate impact case.[30] In such a statistical analysis, variables that affect salary within the particular school district must be included (e.g., seniority, degree level, merit, administrative assignments, supplemental duties). For example, the Fourth Circuit ruled in favor of male faculty members who claimed Title VII and EPA violations when their university voluntarily increased the salaries of female faculty, allegedly to eliminate salary inequities.[31] The study did not include performance criteria used for merit, consider the impact of prior administrative experience on salary, or include career interruptions when measuring academic experience.

Termination, Nonrenewal, and Denial of Tenure

Title VII prohibits arbitrary termination, nonrenewal, and denial of tenure based on gender.[32] In disparate treatment cases, the employee is required to prove that the employer's adverse action was due to gender. As in most cases where proof of intent is required, employees claiming gender discrimination often have difficulty supporting their claims, even if true. Occasionally, however, officials responsible for making personnel decisions (e.g., school board members, superintendents) will inadvertently provide corroborating evidence (both written and oral).

In a 1994 Tenth Circuit decision, a female former principal was "bumped" by an associate superintendent, who assumed her position as well as his own. The district initially proposed that the reduction-in-force was necessary due to financial exigency but later claimed that the female principal had continuing difficulty with her faculty, which allegedly was the basis for her contract not being renewed. The appeals court found the evidence to be contradictory, including the superintendent's annual evaluation of the principal where she received high marks for establishing and maintaining staff cooperation and creating an environment conducive to learning. Given such discrepancies, the appeals court reversed the lower court's grant of summary judgment for the board.[33]

28. *See, e.g.,* West v. Gibson, 527 U.S. 212 (1999).
29. *See, e.g.,* Siler-Khodr v. Univ. of Tex. Health Sci. Ctr. San Antonio, 261 F.3d 542 (5th Cir. 2001).
30. *See, e.g.,* Chance v. Rice Univ., 989 F.2d 179 (5th Cir. 1993).
31. Smith v. Va. Commonwealth Univ., 84 F.3d 672 (4th Cir. 1996).
32. *See, e.g.,* Weinstock v. Columbia Univ., 224 F.3d 33 (2d Cir. 2000) (holding that a female professor failed to show that gender rather than performance was the basis for her tenure denial).
33. Cole v. Ruidoso Mun. Sch., 43 F.3d 1373 (10th Cir. 1994).

Pregnancy Discrimination

Under the Pregnancy Discrimination Act,[34] **employers may not discriminate based on pregnancy, childbirth, or related medical conditions.** As such, pregnancy may not be used as a basis for refusing to hire an otherwise qualified applicant; denying disability, medical, or other benefits; or terminating or nonrenewing employment. It is inappropriate for an employer even to ask questions regarding an employee's intent to have children or how the employee plans to take care of her children if she were hired. Nonetheless, it is the plaintiff's responsibility to show that pregnancy rather than some other factor was the basis of an adverse decision.[35]

In addition, if an employer requires a doctor's statement for other conditions, it may require one for pregnancy prior to granting leave or paying benefits.[36] And, if employees are unable to perform their jobs due to pregnancy, the employer is required to treat them the same as any other temporarily disabled person. Possible forms of accommodation may be to modify tasks, alternate assignments, or provide disability leave (with or without pay). If a pregnant employee takes a leave of absence, her position must be held open the same length of time that it would be if she were sick or disabled. Moreover, maternity leave cannot be considered an interruption in employment for the purposes of accumulating credit toward tenure or seniority if employees retain seniority rights when on leave for other disabilities.[37] Finally, mandatory pregnancy leave policies requiring public school teachers to take a leave of absence prior to the birth of their children and specifying a return date also violate the Due Process Clause by creating an *irrebuttable presumption* that all pregnant teachers are physically incompetent as of a specified date.[38]

Sexual Harassment

Sexual harassment generally refers to repeated and unwelcome sexual advances, sexually suggestive comments, or sexually demeaning gestures or acts. Both men and women have been victims of sexual harassment from persons of the opposite or same sex.[39] The harasser may be a supervisor, an agent of the employer, a supervisor of another area, a coworker, a nonemployee, or even a student. Critical to a successful claim is proof that the harassment is indeed based on gender, rather than sexual preference, being transsexual, transvestism, or personal dislike.[40] There are two types of harassment that can be challenged under Title VII:[41] quid pro quo and hostile environment. Each is reviewed briefly here.

34. 42 U.S.C. § 2000e(k) (2003).
35. *See, e.g.,* Piraino v. Int'l Orientation Res., 137 F.3d 987 (7th Cir. 1998).
36. *See, e.g.,* Hoeflinger v. W. Clermont Local Bd. of Educ., 478 N.E.2d 251 (Ohio Ct. App. 1984).
37. *See, e.g.,* Nashville Gas Co. v. Satty, 434 U.S. 136 (1977).
38. *See, e.g.,* Cleveland Bd. of Educ. v. LaFleur, 414 U.S. 632 (1974).
39. *See, e.g.,* Oncale v. Sundowner Offshore Servs., 523 U.S. 75 (1998).
40. Succar v. Dade County Sch. Bd., 229 F.3d 1343 (11th Cir. 2000) (concluding that an adulterous male teacher was not harassed by his former lover due to being male, but for terminating the relationship).
41. In addition to Title VII, plaintiffs may file charges under state employment or tort law. Tort claims may include intentional infliction of emotional distress, assault and battery, invasion of privacy, and defamation. *See* Chapter 2.

Quid Pro Quo. ***Quid pro quo* harassment literally means giving something for something.** To establish a prima facie case of quid pro quo harassment against an employer, the employee must show that:

- He or she was subjected to unwelcome sexual harassment in the form of sexual advances and requests for sexual favors,
- The harassment was based on gender, and
- Submission to the unwelcome advances was an express or implied condition for either favorable actions (e.g., promotion) or avoidance of adverse actions (e.g., termination) by the employer.

Although only a preponderance of evidence is required in such cases, acquiring the necessary proof can be difficult, particularly given that the violator is unlikely to provide corroborating testimony. Also, the alleged behavior usually takes place behind closed doors so as to limit the opportunity for others to observe the conduct. When the employee succeeds, however, the law imposes strict liability on the employer, given the harasser's authority to alter the terms and conditions of employment.[42]

Hostile Environment. **To prevail under this theory, the plaintiff must show that the environment in fact is hostile—it needs to be severe *or* pervasive,[43] and unreasonably interfere with an individual's work performance.[44]** Title VII is violated if the environment is reasonably perceived as hostile and abusive, although psychological injury need not be proven.[45] The following criteria should be used in assessing if a hostile environment exists:

- Whether the victim solicited or initiated the conduct;
- Whether the victim considered the conduct undesirable and offensive;
- Whether the victim contributed to creating the environment;
- Whether the victim informed the harasser that the unwelcome conduct was offensive;
- Whether the behavior was physically threatening or humiliating, or merely represented an offensive utterance; and
- Whether the conduct unreasonably interfered with an employee's work performance.

Although employer liability in hostile environment claims is more difficult to establish than in quid pro quo harassment claims, it appears to be getting easier. In 1998, in *Burlington Industries v. Ellerth*[46] *and Faragher v. City of Boca Raton,*[47] the Supreme Court

42. *See, e.g.,* Highlander v. K.F.C. Nat'l Mgmt. Co., 805 F.2d 644, 648 (6th Cir. 1986).
43. *See, e.g.,* Haugerud v. Amery Sch. Dist., 259 F.3d 678 (7th Cir. 2001) (noting that one extremely serious act of harassment could rise to an actionable level as could a series of less severe acts).
44. *See, e.g.,* Meritor Sav. Bank v. Vinson, 477 U.S. 57 (1986).
45. Harris v. Forklift Sys., 510 U.S. 17 (1993).
46. 524 U.S. 742 (1998).
47. 524 U.S. 775 (1998).

proclaimed that an employer is subject to liability for the acts of its supervisors with immediate authority over an alleged victim. However, the employer may raise an affirmative defense to liability if the employee suffered no tangible employment loss. Such a defense requires that the employer exercise reasonable care to prevent or promptly correct harassing behavior *and* that the employee failed to take advantage of preventive and corrective opportunities provided by the employer. Accordingly, to guard against liability, school districts should:

- Prepare and disseminate sexual harassment policies;
- Provide appropriate staff training;
- Establish appropriate grievance procedures, including at least two avenues for reporting in case one is blocked by the harasser;
- Take claims seriously and investigate promptly;
- Initiate corrective action in a timely manner;
- Keep all information confidential; and
- Maintain thorough records of all claims and activities.

Furthermore, investigators should have no stake in the outcome of the proceedings, and both male and female investigators should be available.

Retirement Benefits

Although the longevity figures for men and women have narrowed over the past 20 years, it remains true that women on average live longer than men. Recognition of female longevity historically resulted in differential treatment of women with respect to retirement benefits since employers either required women to make a higher contribution or awarded them lower benefits upon retirement. The process resulted in providing women with the same lifetime benefit, but a lower annual payment. **The Supreme Court rejected the use of gender-segregated actuarial tables in retirement benefits programs** when it invalidated a retirement program requiring women to make a higher contribution to receive equal benefits on retirement, noting that gender was the only factor considered in predicting life expectancy.[48] Similarly, the Court also has prohibited a state from administering a deferred compensation program by contracting with insurance companies that used sex-segregated actuarial tables to determine benefits.[49] In the latter case, female employees received lower monthly annuity payments than did males who contributed the same amount.

Discrimination based on gender will foreseeably continue, notwithstanding federal and state laws making such practices illegal. Women are graduating from high schools, colleges, and professional programs at a higher rate than are males and will continue to make gains in employment. Some employers will attempt to protect traditionally gender-segregated occupations or practice various forms of harassment.

48. City of L.A. Dep't of Water & Power v. Manhart, 435 U.S. 702 (1978).
49. Ariz. Governing Comm. for Tax Deferred Annuity & Deferred Comp. Plans v. Norris, 463 U.S. 1073 (1983).

Religious Discrimination

> An employee's religion may not be used as a basis for negative employment decisions; however, neither may it be used by the employee to acquire benefits or opportunities that are rightfully determined by seniority or negotiated agreement.

The United States is now more culturally and religiously diverse than at any time in its history, with most of the world's religions present somewhere within its boundaries. When discrimination occurs, or the employer fails to provide reasonable accommodations, suits have been filed under the First and Fourteenth Amendments as well as Title VII.

Hiring and Promotion Practices

Religion does not qualify as a bona fide occupational qualification in public education, and public employers may not inquire as to an applicant's religious beliefs, use the interview process as an opportunity to indoctrinate, or require prospective employees to profess a belief in a particular faith or in God.[50] A person's religious affiliation or practice, if any, should not be a consideration in making an employment decision.

Accommodation

Recommended forms of religious accommodation include activities such as accepting voluntary substitutions and assignment exchanges, using a flexible schedule, and modifying job assignments. Tests, interviews, and other selection procedures should not be scheduled at times when an applicant cannot attend for religious reasons. However, if requested accommodations would compromise the constitutional, statutory, or legitimate contractual rights of other employees (e.g., interfere with a bona fide seniority system) or result in undue hardship for the employer, Title VII does not require compliance. **In this instance, undue hardship results when extensive changes are required in business practices or when the costs of religious accommodations are more than minimal.** Some of the more often litigated controversies regarding religious accommodation in public education involve dress codes, personal leave, and job assignments.

Attire Restrictions. As a general rule, public school district restrictions on the wearing of religious apparel, even if also purportedly cultural, will be upheld if young and impressionable students would perceive the garment as religious. In an illustrative case, the Third Circuit held that a district's refusal to accommodate a Muslim substitute teacher who sought to

50. *See, e.g.,* Torcaso v. Watkins, 367 U.S. 488 (1961) (holding that to require an appointee to the office of notary public to declare a belief in God before he received his commission violated the First Amendment).

wear religious attire in the public school classroom did not violate Title VII.[51] The district's action was pursuant to a state statute that regarded the wearing of religious clothing as a significant threat to the maintenance of a religiously neutral public school system.

Personal Leave. Although most public school calendars allow time off for Christmas and Easter to coincide with semester and spring breaks, it also is true that the holy days of religions other than Christianity are not so routinely accommodated. Given this problem, public schools often provide a variety of accommodations to avoid unduly burdening the religious beliefs of their employees (e.g., use of personal leave days, flexible schedules).

Modest requests for religious absences are typically met, but others may result in undue hardship both for the district as well as for students. School officials often have had difficulty in determining appropriate limits and procedures. The Supreme Court in *Trans World Airlines v. Hardison* provided some guidance, where a member of the Worldwide Church of God challenged his dismissal for refusing to work on Saturdays in contravention of his religious beliefs.[52] The employer asserted that the plaintiff could not be accommodated because shift assignments were based on seniority in conformance with the collective bargaining agreement. Evidence also showed that supervisors had taken appropriate steps in meeting with the plaintiff and in attempting to find other employees to exchange shifts. The Court found no Title VII violation and reasoned that an employer was not required to bear more than minimal costs in making religious accommodations or to disregard a bona fide seniority system in the absence of proof of intentional discrimination.[53]

Some employees have been satisfied with time off without compensation; others have requested that leave be accompanied with full or partial pay. In *Ansonia Board of Education v. Philbrook,* a teacher asserted that the negotiated agreement violated Title VII by permitting employees to use only three days of paid leave for religious purposes, while three additional days of paid personal business leave could be used for specified secular activities. The plaintiff proposed either permitting the use of the personal business leave days for religious observances or allowing employees to receive full pay but cover the costs of substitute teachers for each additional day missed for religious reasons. The Supreme Court, in upholding the agreement, held that the employer was not required to show that each of plaintiff's proposed alternatives would result in undue hardship. The Court noted that the employer could satisfy Title VII by offering a reasonable accommodation, which may or may not be the one the employee preferred.[54]

Job Assignments and Responsibilities. If an employee is hired to perform a certain job, he or she must be willing and able to perform all the essential functions of the job. In a somewhat unique case, an interpreter for the hearing impaired refused to sign or translate cursing or bad language and used her religious beliefs as a basis for her nonperformance.[55] Given

51. United States v. Bd. of Educ., 911 F.2d 882 (3d Cir. 1990).
52. 432 U.S. 63 (1977).
53. *See also* Graff v. Henderson, 30 Fed. Appx. 809 (10th Cir. 2002) (finding that undue hardship would result if the employer were required to accommodate a member of the Worldwide Church of God who was unable to work between sundown Friday and sundown Saturday).
54. 757 F.2d 476 (2d Cir. 1985), *aff'd,* 479 U.S. 60 (1986).

her refusal to follow district policy and administrative directives, her contract was terminated. The Missouri appeals court upheld her termination under state law and concluded that the teacher could not have been accommodated without compromising the educational entitlements of her students and that requiring a literal translation of classroom dialogue was not unreasonable.

Adverse Employment Decisions

Employees at times have claimed religious discrimination when they have been transferred, demoted, nonrenewed, terminated, or denied tenure.[56] As with other claims of employment discrimination, the burden is on the plaintiff to prove that the adverse action was motivated by an impermissible reason (e.g., the employee's religious beliefs, practices, or affiliation). Plaintiffs experience difficulty in winning such cases, as employers typically can identify one or more legitimate bases for the adverse action (e.g., lack of commitment, excessive absenteeism).

Age Discrimination

> Under the Age Discrimination in Employment Act, persons age 40 and over may claim age discrimination in employment; they may not, however, claim age discrimination when the criteria used to make the adverse decision is only correlated with age (e.g., seniority, vesting in retirement).

Unlike other characteristics that generate charges of discrimination, age is unique in that everyone is subject to the aging process and eventually will fall within the age-protected category. The mean age of the American population has climbed steadily in recent years, and this phenomenon has been accompanied by an increase in judicial activity pertaining to age discrimination in employment. Such individuals are afforded protection under the Fourteenth Amendment, the Age Discrimination in Employment Act (ADEA),[57] and additional federal and state statutes.

55. Sedalia # 200 Sch. Dist. v. Mo. Comm'n on Human Rights, 843 S.W.2d 928 (Mo. Ct. App. 1992). *See also* Shelton v. Univ. of Med. & Dentistry, 223 F.3d 220 (3d Cir. 2000) (finding that a hospital accommodated a nurse who refused to participate in abortions due to her religious beliefs by permitting her to trade assignments unless an emergency existed; upholding her termination when she failed to treat pregnant patients who were experiencing life-threatening situations).
56. *See, e.g.,* Habib v. NationsBank, 279 F.3d 563 (8th Cir. 2001) (upholding termination for insubordination when an employee refused to bring a doctor's statement supporting her need for a leave; she had claimed that the real reason for her firing was her need to pray 5 times per day, lasting 5 to 15 minutes each).
57. 29 U.S.C. § 621 *et seq.* (2003).

The intent of the ADEA is to promote the employment of older persons based on their ability rather than their age, and to prohibit arbitrary age discrimination in employment. The ADEA specifically stipulates that "it shall be unlawful for an employer . . . to fail or refuse to hire or to discharge any individual or otherwise discriminate . . . with respect to his compensation, terms, conditions, or privileges of employment, because of such individual's age."[58] For a violation to be substantiated, age must play a role in the decision-making process *and* have a determinative influence on the outcome.[59]

The ADEA applies to most employers that have 20 or more employees for 20 or more weeks in the current or preceding calendar year. Where violations of the ADEA are found, courts may provide for injunctive relief; compel employment, reinstatement, or promotion; and provide back pay (including interest), liquidated damages,[60] and attorneys' fees. Punitive damages, however, are not available.[61] Moreover, future application of the ADEA in public school cases on occasion may be limited. The Supreme Court in *Kimel v. Florida Board of Regents* held that Eleventh Amendment immunity may be claimed as a defense in federal court when money damages will be paid out of the state treasury.[62] This ruling, however, will limit public school ADEA suits only in the rare instance where a district is viewed as an arm of the state, rather than a subdivision; even then, expect plaintiffs simply to sue under the Fourteenth Amendment or comparable state statutes to vindicate their rights.

Hiring and Promotion Practices

Under the ADEA, except where age qualifies as a bona fide occupational qualification (BFOQ), selection among applicants for hiring or promotion may be based on any factor other than age. When a BFOQ is proposed, the employer carries the burden of persuasion to demonstrate that there is reasonable cause to believe that all, or substantially all, applicants beyond a certain age would be unable to safely perform a job (e.g., drive a bus).

As with Title VII cases, most employers who are alleged to have engaged in age discrimination simply respond that a better qualified applicant was hired, irrespective of age. To prove that such a rebuttal is pretext to discrimination, a plaintiff need not discredit each and every proffered reason for the rejection. Nevertheless, a plaintiff still is required to cast substantial doubt on many, if not most, of the purported bases so that a fact-finder then could rationally disbelieve the remaining reasons, given the employer's loss of credibility.[63]

58. 29 U.S.C. § 623(a)(1) (2003).
59. *See, e.g.,* Hazen Paper Co. v. Biggins, 507 U.S. 604, 617 (1993).
60. *Liquidated damages* represent a reasonable amount agreed to in contract that one party would pay to the other if it were to breach a contract.
61. 29 U.S.C. § 626(b) (2003).
62. 528 U.S. 62 (2000).
63. *See, e.g.,* Narin v. Lower Merion Sch. Dist., 206 F.3d 323 (3d Cir. 2000).

Compensation and Benefits

Few public school employees have alleged age-based salary discrimination. In large part, this is due to the fact that teachers and staff primarily are paid on salary schedules based on seniority and/or degree level. As most school personnel become older, they concomitantly gain seniority and receive a higher scheduled salary. When age discrimination is alleged, the burden of proof remains with the employee to prove that age, rather than performance or other factors, was used to determine the level of compensation. Additionally, a district may not spend less on the benefits package of older workers than for younger employees. The cost of the benefits package must be the same.[64]

Adverse Employment Actions

Courts often are asked to determine whether an employee's age was used as a basis to terminate, nonrenew, downsize, fail to rehire following a layoff, demote, or transfer an employee. Courts generally support the employers' reasons for their adverse decisions, although there are occasions when the bases for making adverse decisions have been found pretextual.[65] For a plaintiff to prevail, the reason submitted by the employer must be refuted and age must be shown to have been the basis for the adverse action. To establish a case under the ADEA, plaintiffs must show that they:

- Were age 40 or over,
- Applied for and were qualified for the position,
- Were subjected to adverse action, and
- Were replaced by a substantially younger person.[66]

The removal of an employee from the workforce is relatively simple for at-will employees[67] (e.g., kitchen workers), but may prove difficult for those with continued employment expectations (e.g., a tenured teacher). For those employees who are tenured or working within a long-term contract, a hearing is required for the district to show cause as to why the removal of the employee is necessary. Although many factors may be considered in making such decisions (e.g., morality, efficiency), the employee's age may not be considered, unless age qualifies as a BFOQ. In a 2000 Supreme Court case, *Reeves v. Sanderson Plumbing Products,* a 57-year-old former employee was terminated and replaced with persons in their thirties.[68] In ruling that the company was not entitled to judgment as a matter of law, the Court noted that the plaintiff was able to establish a claim, create a jury issue

64. 29 C.F.R. § 1625.10(a)(1) (2003).
65. *See, e.g.,* Ware v. Howard Univ., 816 F. Supp. 737 (D.D.C. 1993).
66. *See, e.g.,* Brennan v. Metro. Opera Ass'n, 192 F.3d 310 (2d Cir. 1999) (noting that replacement with someone who is substantially younger than the plaintiff is a more valuable indicator of age discrimination than whether the replacement was over age 40).
67. At-will employees have no contract or job expectation and may leave or be terminated at any time.
68. 530 U.S. 133 (2000).

concerning the falsity of the employer's basis for the action, and introduce additional evidence showing that the director was motivated by age-related animus.

At times, employees allege that they were *constructively discharged.* This could occur when the individual resigns due to being harassed on the job or when the job is altered arbitrarily to ensure poor performance or nonperformance by the plaintiff. To succeed, the employee must show that the conditions created by the employer were such that a reasonable person similarly situated would find the work intolerable and that the employer acted with the intent of forcing the employee to quit.

Another type of adverse action that is used by school officials is a transfer. If an employee challenges an involuntary transfer as age discrimination, he or she will be required to show that such transfer was based on age and that the new assignment was:

- Materially less prestigious,
- Less suited to current skills and expertise, or
- Less conducive to career advancement.

The fact that the employee preferred one position over another does not establish an ADEA violation. Most courts have ruled for school districts when transfers have been challenged, because they seldom view a change of school or a change of grade level to represent a materially significant disadvantage or to be tantamount to a demotion.[69]

Retirement

Given that the mandatory retirement of school employees has been eliminated, districts have attempted to entice older employees to retire through attractive retirement benefits packages. **Under the ADEA, employers can follow the terms of a bona fide retirement plan as long as the plan is not a subterfuge to evade the purposes of the act.** Also, employers may not reduce annual benefits or cease the accrual of benefits after employees attain a certain age as an inducement for them to retire.[70]

Furthermore, legal challenges also may occur when an employee is terminated prior to becoming eligible for full retirement benefits (i.e., prior to becoming vested). In a 1993 Supreme Court decision, *Hazen Paper Co. v. Biggins,* the plaintiff was fired at age 62, only a few weeks before completing 10 years of service and vesting in his pension plan.[71] Two issues before the Supreme Court were whether the employer's interference with the vesting of pension benefits violated the ADEA *and* whether the standard for liquidated damages applied to informal age-based decisions by employers in addition to those that were based on formal, facially discriminatory policies.

In a unanimous opinion, the Court vacated and remanded the lower court decision for a determination of whether the jury had sufficient evidence to find an ADEA violation. **The**

69. *See, e.g.,* Galabya v. New York City Bd. of Educ., 202 F.3d 636 (2d Cir. 2000).
70. 29 U.S.C. § 623(i)(1) (2003). *See also* Solon v. Gary Cmty. Sch. Corp., 180 F.3d 844 (7th Cir. 1999) (finding an ADEA violation in offering early retirement to teachers aged 58 to 61, where employees received less money the longer they waited to retire after reaching 58).
71. 507 U.S. 604 (1993).

Court made it clear, however, that disparate treatment is not supported when the factor motivating the employer is something other than the employee's age, even if it is correlated with age (e.g., vesting or pension status). Because age and years of service are distinctly different factors, an employer at times may take one into account, yet ignore the other.

Disability Discrimination

> Federal disability law protects only those individuals who can show that they are otherwise qualified for the job, although reasonable accommodations at times may be needed.

Two primary federal statutes prohibit disability discrimination in employment: the Rehabilitation Act of 1973[72] and the Americans with Disabilities Act (ADA).[73] The former was the first federal civil rights law protecting the rights of the disabled. **Section 504 of the act provides that no "otherwise qualified individual with a disability . . . shall . . . be excluded from participation in, be denied the benefits of, or be subjected to discrimination under any program or activity receiving federal financial assistance."**[74] In regard to employment, a recipient of federal financial assistance may not discriminate regarding any term, condition, or privilege of employment.

The ADA is substantially the same as the Rehabilitation Act in regard to definitions (e.g., individual with a disability, undue hardship, reasonable accommodation) and general provisions. The statute provides great specificity regarding preemployment activities (e.g., the limited use of medical examinations, testing, preemployment interviewing) as well as terms and conditions of employment and applies to employers with 15 or more employees, including those that do not receive federal funds.[75]

The ADA may be used in suits filed against school districts, unless the district is found to be an "arm of the state."[76] In such rare instances, the district may claim Eleventh Amendment immunity.[77] When this occurs, however, persons who have been subjected to disability discrimination in employment are not powerless to vindicate their rights. The ADA still prescribes standards that are applicable to state employers. These standards could be enforced by the United States in federal judicial actions for monetary damages and by employees in actions seeking injunctive relief. Furthermore, many state disability laws provide identical

72. 29 U.S.C. § 794 (2003).
73. 42 U.S.C. § 12101 *et seq.* (2003).
74. 29 U.S.C. § 794(a) (2003).
75. *See, e.g.,* Owens v. S. Devel. Council, 59 F. Supp. 2d 1210 (M.D. Ala. 1999).
76. *See, e.g.,* Mt. Healthy City Sch. Dist. v. Doyle, 429 U.S. 274 (1977) (concluding that the school district was not entitled to assert Eleventh Amendment immunity since under state law the board was more like a county or a city, rather than an arm of the state).
77. *See, e.g.,* Bd. of Trs. v. Garrett, 531 U.S. 356 (2001).

or at least similar coverage to that mandated by the ADA and permit monetary damages under certain circumstances. Moreover, because all (or nearly all) public schools are recipients of federal financial assistance, they must meet substantially similar obligations under the Rehabilitation Act—a law that at times permits the awarding of money damages. When cases are filed, courts often are asked to resolve questions regarding whether the plaintiff is in fact disabled and, if so, what type of accommodation is required.

Qualifying as Disabled

A person qualifies as disabled under Section 504 and the ADA if he or she:

- Has a physical or mental impairment that substantially limits one or more major life activities;
- Has a record of impairment (e.g., having been hospitalized due to tuberculosis, alcoholism, or drug addiction); or
- Is regarded as having an impairment (e.g., when the person is discriminatorily treated for being HIV-positive,[78] but does not have any type of current physical impairment limiting a major life activity).[79]

Qualifying as "disabled" requires a two-step process: identifying a physical or mental impairment and then determining whether the impairment *substantially limits* a major life activity (e.g., working).[80] Not all impairments limit a major life activity (e.g., a hearing-impaired employee may have average or near-average hearing due to the use of a hearing aid). **Performance is substantially limited when an employee is unable to perform, or is significantly restricted in performing, a major life activity that can be accomplished by the average person in the general population.** The nature, severity, duration, and long-term impact of the impairment are considered in making the determination. An impairment that is substantially limiting for one individual may not be for another,[81] and those impair-

78. *Compare* Merillat v. Mich. State Univ., 523 N.W.2d 802 (Mich. Ct. App. 1994) (determining that a university dispatcher qualified as disabled when she was treated as though she had a mental and emotional impairment) *with* Amadio v. Ford Motor Co., 238 F.3d 919 (7th Cir. 2001) (noting that it is not enough for a plaintiff to show that the employer knew of his or her impairment; the plaintiff also must show that the employer believed that the impairment substantially limited a major life activity).
79. *See also* Sch. Bd. v. Arline, 480 U.S. 273 (1987) (determining that a teacher with three relapses of tuberculosis was qualified as disabled due to her record of impairment, but remanding the case for the district court to determine whether risks of infection to others precluded her from being otherwise qualified and whether her condition could be reasonably accommodated without an undue burden on the district).
80. *See, e.g.,* Kelly v. Drexel Univ., 94 F.3d 102 (3d Cir. 1996) (holding that an employee who had suffered a hip injury was not substantially limited in the major life activity of walking so as to qualify as disabled under the ADA).
81. *Compare* Williams v. Toyota Motor Mfg., 224 F.3d 840 (6th Cir. 2000) (denying summary judgment, as a reasonable jury might determine that the plaintiff's tendonitis substantially limited the major life activity of working) *with* Chanda v. Engelhard/ICC, 234 F.3d 1219 (11th Cir. 2000) (finding that the plaintiff's tendonitis was not substantially limiting).

ments that do limit some activity are not necessarily substantially limiting, since they often restrict the ability to perform only one job rather than a broad range of jobs. And finally, in assessing whether an applicant or employee is disabled, mitigating and corrective measures (both positive and negative[82]) must be considered.[83]

In one of the more unusual cases where the plaintiff attempted to claim protection based on disability, a teacher purported to have a compulsive sexual addiction that caused him to harass students and seek out the services of prostitutes. He contended that his behavior was a manifestation of his disability and that his rights under the ADA and Section 504, among others, were violated when he was fired. The court disagreed, however, and upheld his termination.[84]

Otherwise Qualified

If a person is identified as disabled, it then must be determined whether he or she is "otherwise qualified." **To be an otherwise qualified individual with a disability, the applicant or employee must be able to perform the essential functions of the job in spite of the disability, although reasonable accommodation at times may be necessary.** In identifying the essential functions of the job, courts will give consideration to what the employer perceives to be essential. As long as each identified requirement for employment is either training related (for initial employment) or job related, the employer should not have difficulty in substantiating its claim of business necessity. For example, being on time to work and being at work on a regular daily basis can qualify as a business necessity for most positions in education as well as elsewhere. Employees often have claimed that their respective disabilities were the basis for their lateness or nonarrival. Although this may have been true, courts generally have not found such employees to be otherwise qualified.[85]

Reasonable Accommodation

Persons with disabilities must be able to perform all essential functions of the position, either with accommodation or without. Employers are responsible for providing accommodations considered reasonable that do not cause undue hardship.[86] They are not, however, required to violate seniority rights, bump a current employee to allow a person with a disability to fill the position, fill a vacant position it did not intend to fill, or create a new unnecessary position.[87] Moreover, an employer need not transfer the employee to a better position

82. Corrected vision through use of contact lenses is a positive mitigating measure; side effects of medication represent a negative one.
83. *See, e.g.,* Sutton v. United Airlines, 527 U.S. 471 (1999); Murphy v. United Parcel Serv., 527 U.S. 516 (1999).
84. Winston v. Me. Technical Coll. Sys., 631 A.2d 70 (Me. 1993). *See also* Motzkin v. Trs. of Boston Univ., 938 F. Supp. 983 (D. Mass. 1996) (upholding the termination of a professor who sexually harassed several female students, sexually assaulted a colleague, and provided alcohol to minors in violation of both the university's drug and alcohol policy and state criminal code; rejecting his defense that a "disinhibitory psychological disorder" limited his control and ability to refrain from engaging in intolerable conduct).
85. *See, e.g.,* Tyndall v. Nat'l Educ. Ctrs., 31 F.3d 209 (4th Cir. 1994).

(i.e., promote the person because he or she is disabled) or select a less qualified or unqualified applicant solely because of disability.[88] Such forms of accommodation may be theoretically possible but would result in undue hardship to the employer and discriminate against other employees.

Courts determine whether undue hardship results after a review of:

- The size of the program and its budget,
- The number of employees,
- The type of facilities and operation, and
- The type and cost of accommodation.

Because there is no fixed formula for calculations, courts have differed markedly in identifying what they consider reasonable.

To support a case of failure to provide reasonable accommodation, plaintiffs must prove that their employers were aware of their respective disabilities.[89] At other times, employees have had difficulty showing that reasonable accommodations existed that would enable them to fulfill job requirements. In a 1998 Sixth Circuit case, an HIV-positive surgical technician was laid off. In addition to preparing and handling surgical instruments, he at times was required to put his hands in an incision to make room for the surgeon to work or to provide visibility. In the process, he would have regular exposure to blood and could incur eventual needle pricks (or possibly even cuts). As an alternative, the medical center offered him a position as cart-instrument coordinator. The plaintiff refused this proposal and was terminated. In upholding the granting of summary judgment for the employer, the court held that no reasonable accommodation would eliminate the direct threat the plaintiff posed and that he was not otherwise qualified for the position.[90]

Termination and Nonrenewal

More individuals with disabilities are in the workplace today than ever before with many achieving leadership positions. Not all persons with disabilities have fared well, however, as some were not selected for initial employment, failed to receive tenure or promotion, received less pay, or were terminated. At times, such adverse decisions were due to inadequate qualifications or skills, better-qualified applicants, poor job performance, posing a risk, or criminal wrongdoing.[91] At other times, the employee's disability was found to be the

86. *See, e.g.,* Vollmert v. Wis. Dep't of Trans., 197 F.3d 293 (7th Cir. 1999) (finding that the employer failed to accommodate a staff member with learning disabilities when it transferred her to a position with fewer opportunities for promotion; such transfer was inappropriate because accommodations had not been provided for the previous job).
87. *See, e.g.,* Ozlowski v. Henderson, 237 F.3d 837 (7th Cir. 2001).
88. *See, e.g.,* EEOC v. Humiston-Keeling, 227 F.3d 1024 (7th Cir. 2000).
89. *See, e.g.,* Whitney v. Bd. of Educ., 292 F.3d 1280 (10th Cir. 2002).
90. Estate of Mauro v. Borgess Med. Ctr., 137 F.3d 398 (6th Cir. 1998).
91. *See, e.g.,* Haulbrook v. Michelin N. Am., 252 F.3d 696 (4th Cir. 2001); Borgialli v. Thunder Basin Coal Co., 235 F.3d 1284 (10th Cir. 2000).

basis for the adverse decision or the environment had become so hostile that the employee was constructively discharged.[92]

To support a disparate treatment adverse action claim, employees generally must establish that they:

- Have a qualifying disability that substantially limits a major life activity as compared to the average person in the population,
- Applied for and were otherwise qualified for their respective jobs (although accommodations may be required), and
- Were denied employment or retention in employment due to disability.

The cost of many accommodations, along with the tightening of state and local budgets, should make disability accommodation cases among the more volatile in the years to come. Although comparatively few plaintiffs are likely to prevail on such claims, expect school districts to devote significant resources in (1) providing reasonable accommodations and (2) defending related policies and practices.

Conclusion

Federal law requires that employment decisions be based on qualifications, performance, merit, seniority, and the like, rather than factors such as race, national origin, gender, religion, age, or disability. Statutes vary considerably, however, as to what they require. Moreover, federal regulations are extensive, complex, and at times confounding.

When preparing a policy related to personnel, it will be important to consider (1) whether it facially discriminates only in legal and appropriate ways (e.g., female supervisor of the girl's locker room) and (2) whether it adversely affects a protected class, even though the policy may be facially neutral. Treating all persons the same may not accommodate individual needs and may inadvertently result in subtle forms of discrimination. In the alternative, treating persons differently may advantage some over others. The bottom line is that there is no simple solution.

Points to Ponder

1. A math and science teacher at an elite (selective admissions), public magnet school had a knowledge base measured at the 99th percentile of all persons taking a standardized math test. He was hired because of his knowledge of math and his ability to teach (as evidenced by the exceptional evaluations he received at his former school in China, his native country). Unfortunately, little effort was made to determine his English language speaking skills, although his written English proficiency scores were satisfactory. After two semesters of unsuccessful teaching, his contract was not renewed. He was not tenured and did not have the guarantee of employment beyond the one-year contract that had just expired. He then

92. *See, e.g.,* Spells v. Cuyahoga Cmty. Coll., 889 F. Supp. 1023 (N.D. Ohio 1994), *aff'd without published opinion,* 51 F.3d 273 (6th Cir. 1995).

sued the school under Title VII and the Fourteenth Amendment. School officials claimed that he was nonrenewed because of his horrible teaching evaluations (based overwhelmingly on poor verbal communication skills) and not because of national origin. Two other Chinese teachers remained on staff. Is the nonrenewed teacher likely to win this suit? Why or why not?

2. All candidates for promotion are required to take a standardized test. Only persons scoring in the top 10 percent make the first cut and are allowed to proceed to the interview portion of the promotion process. You did poorly on the test, as did several others within your racial classification. In fact, only 2 percent of those within your race were in the top 10 percent, notwithstanding the fact that your race represents 25 percent of those in the pool of candidates with the seniority to be considered for promotion. Performance on the test has been shown to be predictive of success on the job. You sued under Title VII, claiming disparate impact. Will you be successful in this suit? Why or why not?

3. A physically disabled school maintenance worker was terminated because of poor job performance. As a form of accommodation, he had requested additional time (with additional compensation) to perform the job or an assistant to do a portion of the work for him—he could perform two-thirds of the daily work assignment within an eight-hour day. Following his termination, he filed suit under Section 504 of the Rehabilitation Act of 1973. The school district, which receives federal funds, claimed that he was not otherwise qualified to meet the essential functions of the job. How will this legal challenge be decided?

4. A well-qualified male applicant for a first-grade teaching position was not hired admittedly because of gender. There were no other applicants for the position. The male principal made it clear that only females historically had been first-grade teachers and that they, by their nature, were better suited for such positions. Moreover, he encouraged the male to apply for a middle school position, for which he also was licensed, and virtually guaranteed the applicant that he would be selected. Following his initial rejection, the male applicant filed suit against the district under Title VII. Is he likely to win this case? Why or why not?

12

Termination of Employment

State laws delineate the authority of school boards in terminating school personnel. Generally, these laws specify the causes for which a teacher may be terminated and the procedures that must be followed. The school board's right to determine the fitness of teachers is well established; in fact, courts have declared that school boards have a duty as well as a right to make such determinations.

The first section of this chapter provides an overview of due process in connection with nonrenewal and dismissal. Since due process is required only if a teacher is able to establish that a constitutionally protected property or liberty interest is at stake, this section explores the dimensions of teachers' property and liberty rights in the context of employment termination. In the next section, specific procedural requirements are identified and discussed. A survey of judicial interpretations of state laws regarding causes for dismissal is presented in the third section. The concluding section provides an overview of remedies available to teachers for violation of their protected rights.

Procedural Due Process in General

> A teacher is entitled to procedural due process if termination of employment impairs a property or liberty interest.

Basic due process rights are embodied in the Fourteenth Amendment, which guarantees that no state shall "deprive any person of life, liberty, or property without due process of law."[1] Due process safeguards apply not only in judicial proceedings but also to acts of governmental agencies such as school boards. As discussed in Chapter 1, constitutional due process entails *substantive* protections against arbitrary governmental action and *procedural* protections when the government threatens an individual's life, liberty, or property interests. Most teacher termination cases have focused on procedural due process requirements.

The individual and governmental interests at stake and applicable state laws influence the nature of procedural due process required. **Courts have established that a teacher's interest in public employment may entail significant "property" and "liberty" rights necessitating due process prior to employment termination.** A *property interest* is a legitimate claim of entitlement to continued employment that is created by state law.[2] The granting of tenure conveys such a right to a teacher. Also, a contract establishes a property right to employment within its stated terms. A property interest in continued employment, however, does not mean that an individual cannot be terminated; it simply means that an employer must follow the requirements of due process and substantiate cause.

The judiciary has recognized that Fourteenth Amendment liberty rights encompass fundamental constitutional guarantees, such as freedom of speech. Procedural due process always is required when a termination implicates such fundamental liberties. A liberty interest also is involved when termination creates a stigma or damages an individual's reputation in a manner that forecloses future employment opportunities.[3] If protected liberty or property interests are implicated, the Fourteenth Amendment entitles the teacher at least to notice of the reasons for the school board's action and an opportunity for a hearing.

Employment terminations are classified as either dismissals or nonrenewals. The distinction between the two has significant implications for teachers' procedural rights. In this section, the procedural safeguards that must be provided the tenured teacher and the nontenured teacher are distinguished. Specific attention is given to the conditions that may give rise to a nontenured teacher's acquiring a protected liberty or property interest in employment, thereby establishing a claim to procedural due process.

Dismissal

The term *dismissal* refers to the termination for cause of any tenured teacher or a probationary teacher within the contract period. Both tenure statutes and employment contracts establish a property interest entitling teachers to full procedural protection.[4] Beyond the basic constitutional requirements of appropriate notice and an opportunity to be heard, state laws and school board policies often contain detailed procedures that must be followed. Failure

1. As noted in Chapter 1, the Fourteenth Amendment restricts state, in contrast to private, action. The Supreme Court has recognized that mere regulation by the state will be insufficient to evoke constitutional protections in private school personnel matters. The Court rejected a suit for damages against a private school for allegedly unconstitutional dismissals, reasoning that there was no "symbiotic relationship" between the private school and the state. Rendell Baker v. Kohn, 457 U.S. 830 (1982).
2. *See* Bd. of Regents v. Roth, 408 U.S. 564 (1972).
3. *See infra* text accompanying note 14.
4. If a statute conferring specific property rights (e.g., tenure) is rescinded or amended to eliminate those rights, individuals are not entitled to procedural due process related to that deprivation; statutory benefits can be revoked without due process unless the change impairs contractual rights. *See, e.g.,* Indiana *ex rel.* Anderson v. Brand, 303 U.S. 95 (1938); Pittman v. Chi. Bd. of Educ., 64 F.3d 1098 (7th Cir. 1995). However, school boards generally cannot amend, repeal, or circumvent statutory rights (e.g., entitlement to procedural due process) through the employment contract. *See, e.g.,* Parker v. Indep. Sch. Dist. No. I-003 Okmulgee County, Okla, 82 F.3d 952 (10th Cir. 1996).

to provide these additional procedures, however, results in a violation of state law, rather than constitutional law. Statutory procedures vary as to specificity, with some states enumerating detailed steps and others identifying only broad parameters. In addition to complying with state law, a school district must abide by its own procedures, even if they exceed state law. For example, if school board policy provides for a preliminary notice of teaching inadequacies and an opportunity to correct remediable deficiencies prior to dismissal, the board must follow these steps.

A critical element in dismissal actions is a showing of justifiable cause for termination of employment. If causes are identified in state law, a school board must base dismissal on those grounds. Failure to relate the charges to statutory grounds can invalidate the termination decision. Because statutes typically list broad causes—such as incompetency, insubordination, immorality, unprofessional conduct, and neglect of duty—notice of discharge must indicate specific conduct substantiating the legal charges. Procedural safeguards ensure not only that a teacher is informed of the specific reasons and grounds for dismissal but also that the school board bases its decision on evidence substantiating those grounds. Detailed aspects of procedural due process requirements and dismissal for cause are addressed in subsequent sections of this chapter.

Nonrenewal

Unless specified in state law, procedural protections are not accorded the probationary teacher when the employment contract is not renewed. At the end of the contract period, employment can be terminated for any or no reason, as long as the reason is not constitutionally impermissible (e.g., denial of protected speech).[5] The most common statutory requirement is notification of nonrenewal on or before a specified date prior to the expiration of the contract. When a statute designates a deadline for nonrenewal, a school board must notify a teacher on or before the established date. The timeliness of nonrenewal notices is strictly construed. The fact that the school board has set in motion notification (e.g., mailed the notice) generally does not satisfy the statutory requirement; the teacher's actual receipt of the notice is critical. A teacher, however, cannot avoid or deliberately thwart delivery of notice and then claim insufficiency of notice. Failure of school officials to observe the notice deadline may result in a teacher's reinstatement for an additional year or even the granting of tenure in some jurisdictions.

In the nonrenewal of teachers' contracts, some states require a written statement of reasons and may even provide an opportunity for a hearing at the teacher's request. Unlike evidentiary hearings for dismissal of a teacher, the school board is not required to show cause for nonrenewal; a teacher is simply provided the reasons underlying the nonrenewal and an opportunity to address the school board. When a school board is required to provide reasons, broad general statements such as "the school district's interest would be best served," "the district can find a better teacher," or "the term contract has expired" will not suffice. If state law establishes specific requirements and procedures for nonrenewal, failure to abide by these provisions may invalidate a school board's decision. Also, a school board must follow not only state law but also must comply substantially with its own nonrenewal procedures.

5. *See* Chapter 10 for a discussion of teachers' constitutional rights.

Although state laws may not provide the probationary teacher with specific procedural protections, a teacher's interest in continued public employment may be constitutionally protected if a liberty or property right guaranteed by the Fourteenth Amendment has been abridged. Infringement of these interests entitles a probationary teacher to due process rights similar to the rights of tenured teachers. These rights are delineated next.

Establishing Protected Property and Liberty Interests

The United States Supreme Court addressed the scope of protected interests encompassed by the Fourteenth Amendment in two significant decisions in 1972: *Board of Regents v. Roth*[6] and *Perry v. Sindermann.*[7] These decisions addressed whether the infringement of a liberty or property interest entitles a probationary teacher to due process rights similar to the rights of tenured teachers. The cases involved faculty members at the postsecondary level, but the rulings are equally applicable to public elementary and secondary school teachers.

In Roth, the question presented to the Court was whether a nontenured teacher had a constitutional right to a statement of reasons and a hearing prior to nonreappointment. Roth was hired on a one-year contract, and the university elected not to rehire him for a second year. Since Roth did not have tenure, there was no entitlement under Wisconsin law to an explanation of charges or a hearing; the university simply did not reemploy him for the succeeding year. Roth challenged the nonrenewal, alleging that failure to provide notice of reasons and an opportunity for a hearing impaired his due process rights.

The Supreme Court held that nonrenewal did not require procedural protection unless impairment of a protected liberty or property interest could be shown. To establish infringement of a liberty interest, the Court held that the teacher must show that the employer's action (1) resulted in damage to his or her reputation and standing in the community or (2) imposed a stigma that foreclosed other employment opportunities. The evidence presented by Roth indicated that there was no such damage to his reputation or future employment. Accordingly, the Court concluded, "It stretches the concept too far to suggest that a person is deprived of 'liberty' when he simply is not rehired in one job but remains as free as before to seek another."[8]

The Court also rejected Roth's claim that he had a protected property interest to continued employment. The Court held that in order to establish a valid property right, an individual must have more than an "abstract need or desire" for a position; there must be a "legitimate claim of entitlement."[9] Property interests are not defined by the Federal Constitution, but rather by state laws or employment contracts that secure specific benefits. An abstract desire or unilateral expectation of continued employment alone does not constitute a property right. The terms of Roth's one-year appointment and the state law precluded any claim of entitlement.

6. 408 U.S. 564 (1972).
7. 408 U.S. 593 (1972).
8. *Roth,* 408 U.S. at 575.
9. *Id.* at 577. *See also* Lautermilch v. Findlay City Schs., 314 F.3d 271 (6th Cir. 2003) (finding that a substitute teacher without a contract did not have a protected property interest in continued employment).

On the same day it rendered the *Roth* decision, the Supreme Court in the *Sindermann* case explained the circumstances that might create a legitimate expectation of reemployment for a nontenured teacher.[10] Sindermann was a nontenured faculty member in his fourth year of teaching when he was notified, without a statement of reasons or an opportunity for a hearing, that his contract would not be renewed. He challenged the lack of procedural due process, alleging that nonrenewal deprived him of a property interest protected by the Fourteenth Amendment and violated his First Amendment right to freedom of speech.

In advancing a protected property right, Sindermann claimed that the college, which lacked a formal tenure system, had created an informal, or *de facto,* tenure system through various practices and policies. Specifically, Sindermann cited a provision in the faculty guide stating that "the College wishes the faculty member to feel that he has permanent tenure as long as his teaching services are satisfactory."[11] The Supreme Court found that Sindermann's claim, unlike Roth's, may have been based on a legitimate expectation of reemployment promulgated by the college. According to the Court, the lack of a formal tenure system did not foreclose the possibility of an institution fostering entitlement to a position through its personnel policies.

In assessing Sindermann's free speech claim, the Supreme Court confirmed that a teacher's lack of tenure does not void a claim that nonrenewal was based on the exercise of constitutionally protected conduct. Procedural due process must be afforded when a substantive constitutional right is violated. In a later case, however, the Supreme Court held that if a constitutional right is implicated in a nonrenewal, the teacher bears the burden of showing that the protected conduct was a substantial or motivating factor in the school board's decision.[12] Establishing an inference of a constitutional violation then shifts the burden to the school board to show that it would have reached the same decision in the absence of the protected activity.

The *Roth* and *Sindermann* cases are the legal precedents for assessing the procedural rights of nontenured teachers. To summarize, the Supreme Court held that a nontenured teacher does not have a constitutionally protected property right to employment requiring procedural due process before denial of reappointment. Certain actions of the school board, however, may create conditions entitling a nontenured teacher to notice and a hearing similar to the tenured teacher. Such actions would include:

- Nonrenewal decisions damaging an individual's reputation and integrity,
- Nonrenewal decisions foreclosing other employment opportunities,
- Policies and practices creating a valid claim to reemployment, and
- Nonrenewal decisions violating fundamental constitutional guarantees (e.g., freedom of expression).

Since the Supreme Court has held that impairment of a teacher's property or liberty interests triggers procedural protections, the question arises as to what constitutes a violation of these interests. Courts have purposely avoided precisely defining the concepts of

10. 408 U.S. 593 (1972).
11. *Id.* at 600.
12. Mt. Healthy City Sch. Dist. Bd. of Educ. v. Doyle, 429 U.S. 274 (1977). *See* text accompanying note 2, Chapter 10, for a discussion of the First Amendment issue in this case.

"liberty" and "property," preferring to allow experience and time to shape their meanings. Since 1972, the Supreme Court and federal appellate courts have rendered a number of decisions that provide some guidance in understanding these concepts.

Property Interest. In general, a nontenured employee does not have a property claim to reappointment unless state or local governmental action has clearly established such a right. Protected property interests are not created by mere longevity in employment. Both the Fourth and Tenth Circuits found that issuing an employee a series of annual contracts did not constitute a valid claim to continued employment in the absence of a guarantee in state law, local policy, or an employment contract.[13] Similarly, a statute or collective bargaining agreement providing a teacher, upon request, a hearing and statement of reasons for nonrenewal does not confer a property interest in employment requiring legally sufficient cause for termination. Such a provision simply gives the teacher an opportunity to present reasons why the contract should be renewed.

Liberty Interest. As noted previously, liberty interests encompass fundamental constitutional guarantees such as freedom of expression and privacy rights. If governmental action in the nonrenewal of employment threatens the exercise of these fundamental liberties, procedural due process must be afforded. Most nonrenewals, however, do not overtly implicate fundamental rights, and thus, the burden is on the aggrieved employee to prove that the proffered reason is pretextual to mask impermissible grounds.

A liberty interest also may be implicated if the nonrenewal of employment damages an individual's reputation. The Supreme Court established in *Roth* that damage to a teacher's reputation and future employability could infringe Fourteenth Amendment liberty rights. In subsequent decisions, the Court identified prerequisite conditions for establishing that a constitutionally impermissible stigma has been imposed. According to the Court, procedural protections must be afforded only if stigma or damaging statements are related to loss of employment, publicly disclosed, alleged to be false, and virtually foreclose opportunities for future employment.[14]

Under this *stigma-plus test,* governmental action damaging a teacher's reputation, standing alone, is insufficient to invoke the Fourteenth Amendment's procedural safeguards.[15] Although many employment actions may stigmatize and affect a teacher's reputation, they do not constitute a deprivation of liberty in the absence of loss of employment. As the Ninth Circuit noted, "Nearly any reason assigned for dismissal is likely to be to some extent a negative reflection on an individual's ability, temperament, or character," but circumstances giving rise to a liberty interest are narrow.[16] Charges must be serious implications against character, such as immorality and dishonesty, to create a stigma of

13. Martin v. Unified Sch. Dist. No. 434, 728 F.2d 453 (10th Cir. 1984); Robertson v. Rogers, 679 F.2d 1090 (4th Cir. 1982).

14. *See, e.g.,* Codd v. Velger, 429 U.S. 624 (1977); Bishop v. Wood, 426 U.S. 341 (1976); Bordelon v. Chi. Sch. Reform Bd. of Trs., 233 F.3d 524 (7th Cir. 2000).

15. State constitutions, however, may provide greater protection of due process rights encompassing damage to reputation alone. *See, e.g.,* Kadetsky v. Egg Harbor Township Bd. of Educ., 82 F. Supp. 2d 327 (D.N.J. 2000).

16. Gray v. Union County Intermediate Educ. Dist., 520 F.2d 803, 806 (9th Cir. 1975).

constitutional magnitude that virtually forecloses other employment. According to the Fifth Circuit, a charge must give rise to "a 'badge of infamy,' public scorn, or the like."[17]

Among accusations that courts have found to necessitate a hearing are a serious drinking problem, emotional instability, mental illness, immoral conduct, accusation of child molestation, and extensive professional inadequacies.[18] Reasons held to pose no threat to a liberty interest include job-related comments such as personality differences and difficulty in working with others, hostility toward authority, incompetence, aggressive behavior, ineffective leadership, and poor performance.[19] Charges relating to job performance may have an impact on future employment but do not create a stigma of constitutional magnitude.

Procedural Requirements in Discharge Proceedings

When a liberty or property interest is implicated, the Fourteenth Amendment requires that a teacher be notified of charges and provided with an opportunity for a hearing that usually includes representation by counsel, examination and cross-examination of witnesses, and a record of the proceedings.

Since termination of a tenured teacher or a nontenured teacher during the contract period requires procedural due process, the central question becomes: *What process is due?* Courts have noted that no fixed set of procedures apply under all circumstances. Rather, due process entails a balancing of the individual and governmental interests affected in each situation. Minimally, the Fourteenth Amendment requires that dismissal proceedings be based on established rules or standards. Actual procedures will depend on state law, school board regulations, and collective bargaining agreements, but they cannot drop below constitutional minimums. For example, a statute requiring tenured teachers to pay half the cost of a hearing that constitutionally must be provided by the school board violated federal rights.[20]

In assessing the adequacy of procedural safeguards, the judiciary looks for the provision of certain basic elements to meet constitutional guarantees.[21] Courts generally have

17. Ball v. Bd. of Trs., 584 F.2d 684, 685 (5th Cir. 1978).
18. Donato v. Plainview-Old Bethpage Cent. Sch. Dist., 96 F.3d 623 (2d Cir. 1996); Vanelli v. Reynolds Sch. Dist. No. 7, 667 F.2d 773 (9th Cir. 1982); Carroll v. Robinson, 874 P.2d 1010 (Ariz. Ct. App. 1994).
19. Lybrook v. Members of Farmington Mun. Schs. Bd., 232 F.3d 1334 (10th Cir. 2000); Hayes v. Phoenix-Talent Sch. Dist. No. 4, 893 F.2d 235 (9th Cir. 1990); Robertson v. Rogers, 679 F.2d 1090 (4th Cir. 1982).
20. Rankin v. Indep. Sch. Dist. No. I-3, Noble County, Okla., 876 F.2d 838 (10th Cir. 1989). *See also* Cal. Teachers Ass'n v. State, 975 P.2d 622, 643 (Cal. 1999) (concluding that imposing cost of hearing "chills the exercise of the right to a hearing and vigorous advocacy on behalf of the teacher").
21. *See, e.g.,* Clark County Sch. Dist. v. Riley, 14 P.3d 22 (Nev. 2000).

held that a teacher facing a severe loss such as termination must be afforded full procedural due process (see Figure 12.1 for elements).[22] Beyond the constitutional considerations, courts also strictly enforce any additional procedural protections conferred by state laws and local policies. Examples of such requirements might be providing detailed performance evaluations prior to termination, notifying teachers of weaknesses, and allowing an opportunity for improvement before dismissal. Although failure to comply with these stipulations may invalidate the school board's action under state law, federal due process rights *per se* are not violated if minimal constitutional procedures are provided. Except in limited circumstances, individuals are required to exhaust administrative procedures, or the grievance procedures specified in the collective bargaining agreement, prior to seeking judicial review. Pursuing an administrative hearing promotes resolution of a controversy at the agency level.

Various elements of due process proceedings may be contested as inadequate. Questions arise regarding issues such as the sufficiency of notice, impartiality of the board members, and placement of the burden of proof. The aspects of procedural due process that courts frequently scrutinize in assessing the fundamental fairness of school board actions are examined next.

Notice

In general, a constitutionally adequate notice is timely, informs the teacher of specific charges, and allows the teacher sufficient time to prepare a response.[23] Beyond the constitutional guarantees, state laws and regulations as well as school board policies usually

FIGURE 12.1 ***Procedural Due Process Elements in Teacher Termination Proceedings***

- Notification of charges,
- Opportunity for a hearing,
- Adequate time to prepare a rebuttal to the charges,
- Access to evidence and names of witnesses,
- Hearing before an impartial tribunal,
- Representation by legal counsel,
- Opportunity to present evidence and witnesses,
- Opportunity to cross-examine adverse witnesses,
- Decision based on evidence and findings of the hearing,
- Transcript or record of the hearing, and
- Opportunity to appeal an adverse decision.

22. This chapter focuses on procedural protections required in teacher terminations. It should be noted, however, that other school board decisions (e.g., transfers, demotions, or mandatory leaves) may impose similar constraints on decision making.

23. *See, e.g.*, Farley v. Bd. of Educ., 365 S.E.2d 816 (W. Va. 1988) (finding that notice of termination received by teachers one to two days prior to hearing date set by school board was not a "meaningful notice" to prepare for a hearing).

impose very specific requirements relating to form, timeliness, and content of notice.[24] In legal challenges, the adequacy of a notice is assessed in terms of whether it meets constitutional as well as other requirements. Failure to comply substantially with mandated requisites will void school board action.

The form or substance of notice is usually stipulated in statutes. In determining appropriateness of notice, courts generally have held that substantial compliance with form requirements (as opposed to strict compliance required for notice deadlines) is sufficient. Under this standard, the decisive factor is whether the notice adequately informs the teacher of the pending action rather than the actual form of the notice. For example, if a statute requires notification by certified mail and the notice is mailed by registered mail or is personally delivered, it substantially complies with the state requirement. However, oral notification will not suffice if the law requires written notification. If the form of the notice is not specified in statute, any timely notice that informs a teacher is adequate.

Although form and timeliness are important concerns in issuing a notice, the primary consideration is the statement of reasons for an action. With termination of a teacher's contract, school boards must bring specific charges against the teacher, including not only the factual basis for the charges but also the names of accusers. State laws may impose further specifications such as North Dakota's requirement that reasons for termination in the notice must be based on issues raised in prior written evaluations.[25] If the state law identifies grounds for dismissal, charges also must be based on the statutory causes. But, a teacher cannot be forced to defend against vague and indefinite charges that simply restate the statutory categories, such as incompetency or neglect of duty. Notice must include specific accusations to enable the teacher to prepare a proper defense. Finally, only charges identified in the notice can form the basis for dismissal.

Hearing

In addition to notice, some type of hearing is required *before* an employer makes the initial termination decision; posttermination hearings do not satisfy federal constitutional due process requirements.[26] Courts have not prescribed in detail the procedures to be followed in administrative hearings. Basically, the fundamental constitutional requirement is fair play—that is, an opportunity to be heard at a meaningful time and in a meaningful manner. Beyond this general requirement, the specific aspects of a hearing are influenced by the circumstances of the case, with the potential for grievous losses necessitating more extensive safeguards. According to the Missouri Supreme Court, a hearing generally should include a meaningful opportunity to be heard, to state one's position, to present witnesses, and to cross-examine witnesses; the accused also has the right to counsel and access to written reports in advance of the hearing.[27] Implicit in these rudimentary requirements are the assumptions that the hearing will be conducted by an impartial decision maker and will

24. *See, e.g.,* Stills v. Ala. State Tenure Comm'n, 718 So. 2d 1145 (Ala. Civ. App. 1998) (holding that when a statute specified that notice must be received by the last day of the school term, receipt of a notice three days later was inadequate).

25. Hoffner v. Bismarck Pub. Sch. Dist., 589 N.W.2d 195 (N.D. 1999).

26. Cleveland Bd. of Educ. v. Loudermill, 470 U.S. 532 (1985).

result in a decision based on the evidence presented. This section examines issues that may arise in adversarial hearings before the school board.

Adequate Notice of Hearing. As noted, due process rights afford an individual the opportunity to be heard at a meaningful time. This implies sufficient time between notice of the hearing and the scheduled meeting. Unless state law designates a time period, the school board can establish a reasonable date for the hearing, taking into consideration the specific facts and circumstances. In a termination action, the school board would be expected to provide ample time for the teacher to prepare a defense; however, the teacher bears the burden of requesting additional time if the length of notice is insufficient to prepare an adequate response.

Waiver of Hearing. Although a hearing is an essential element of due process, a teacher can waive this right by failing to request a hearing, refusing to attend, or walking out. Voluntary resignation of a position also waives an individual's entitlement to a hearing. In some states, a hearing before the school board may be waived by an employee's election of an alternative hearing procedure such as a grievance mechanism or an impartial referee. For example, the Third Circuit held that an employee's choice of *either* a hearing before the school board *or* arbitration under the collective bargaining agreement met the constitutional requirements of due process; the school board was not required to provide the individual a hearing in addition to the arbitration proceeding.[28]

Impartial Hearing. A central question raised regarding hearings is the school board's impartiality as a hearing body. This issue arises because school boards often perform multiple functions in a hearing; they may investigate the allegations against a teacher, initiate the proceedings, and render the final judgment. Teachers have contended that such expansive involvement violates their right to an unbiased decision maker. Rejecting the idea that combining the adjudicative and investigative functions violates due process rights, courts generally have determined that prior knowledge of the facts does not disqualify school board members.[29] In addition, the fact that the board makes the initial decision to terminate employment does not render subsequent review impermissibly biased. Neither is a hearing prejudiced by a limited, preliminary inquiry to determine if there is a basis for terminating a teacher. Since hearings are costly and time consuming, such a preliminary investigation may save time as well as potential embarrassment.

27. Valter v. Orchard Farm Sch. Dist., 541 S.W.2d 550 (Mo. 1976). *See also* McClure v. Indep. Sch. Dist. No. 16, 228 F.3d 1205 (10th Cir. 2000) (holding that a teacher was deprived of due process rights when she was not allowed to cross-examine witnesses who provided testimony by affidavit at termination hearing).
28. Pederson v. S. Williamsport Area Sch. Dist., 677 F.2d 312 (3d Cir. 1982).
29. *See, e.g.,* Withrow v. Larkin, 421 U.S. 35 (1975). *See also* Yukadinovich v. Bd. of Sch. Trs., 278 F.3d 693 (7th Cir. 2002) (concluding that a teacher did not establish bias in a termination hearing held in front of the school board that he had publicly criticized); Moore v. Bd. of Educ., 134 F.3d 781 (6th Cir. 1998) (finding that a superintendent's dual roles as presiding officer at the hearing and investigator did not deprive teacher of due process).

In *Hortonville Joint School District No. 1 v. Hortonville Education Association,* the United States Supreme Court firmly established that the school board is a proper review body to conduct dismissal hearings.[30] The Court held that a school board's involvement in collective negotiations did not disqualify it as an impartial hearing board in the subsequent dismissal of striking teachers. The Court noted that "a showing that the Board was 'involved' in the events preceding this decision, in light of the important interest in leaving with the board the power given by the state legislature, is not enough to overcome the presumption of honesty and integrity in policymakers with decision-making power."[31]

Although the school board is the proper hearing body, bias on the part of the board or its members is constitutionally unacceptable. A teacher challenging the impartiality of the board has the burden of proving actual, not merely potential, bias. This requires the teacher to show more than board members' pre-decision involvement or prior knowledge of the issues. A high probability of bias, however, can be shown if a board member has a personal interest in the outcome of the hearing or has suffered personal abuse or criticism from a teacher.

Evidence. Under teacher tenure laws, the burden of proof is placed on the school board to show cause for dismissal. The standard of proof generally applied to administrative bodies is to produce a "preponderance of evidence" or "substantial evidence." Administrative hearings are not held to the more stringent standards applied in criminal proceedings (i.e., clear and convincing evidence beyond a reasonable doubt). Proof by a preponderance of evidence simply indicates that the majority of the evidence supports the board's decision or, as the New York high court stated, "such relevant evidence as a reasonable mind might accept as adequate to support a conclusion."[32] If the board fails to meet this burden of proof, the judiciary will not uphold the termination decision. For example, the Nebraska Supreme Court, in overturning a school board's dismissal decision, concluded that dissatisfaction of parents and school board members was not sufficient evidence to substantiate incompetency charges against a teacher who had received above-average performance evaluations during her entire term of employment.[33]

Only relevant, well-documented evidence presented at the hearing can be the basis for the board's decision. Unlike formal judicial proceedings, hearsay evidence may be admissible in administrative hearings. Courts have held that such evidence provides the background necessary for understanding the situation. Comments and complaints of parents have been considered relevant, but hearsay statements of students generally have been given little weight.[34]

30. 426 U.S. 482 (1976).
31. *Id.* at 496-497.
32. Altsheler v. Bd. of Educ., 476 N.Y.S.2d 281, 281 (1984).
33. Schulz v. Bd. of Educ., 315 N.W.2d 633 (Neb. 1982).
34. *See, e.g.,* Daily v. Bd. of Educ., 588 N.W.2d 813 (Neb. 1999).

Dismissal for Cause

> Causes for dismissal vary widely among the states, but usually include such grounds as incompetency, immorality, insubordination, unprofessional conduct, and other good and just cause.

Tenure laws are designed to assure competent teachers continued employment as long as their performance is satisfactory. With the protection of tenure, a teacher can be dismissed only for cause, and only in accordance with the procedures specified by law. Tenure rights accrue under state laws and therefore must be interpreted in light of each state's provisions.

When grounds for dismissal of a permanent teacher are identified by statute, a school board cannot base dismissal on reasons other than those specified. To cover unexpected matters, statutes often include a catch-all phrase such as "other good and just cause." Causes included in statutes vary considerably among states and range from an extensive listing of individual grounds to a simple statement that dismissal must be based on cause. The most frequently cited causes are incompetency, immorality, and insubordination.

Since grounds for dismissal are determined by statute, it is difficult to provide generalizations for all teachers. The causes are broad in scope and application; in fact, individual causes often have been attacked for impermissible vagueness. It is not unusual to find dismissal cases with similar factual situations based on different grounds. In addition, a number of grounds often are introduced and supported in a single termination case. Illustrative case law is examined here in relation to the more frequently cited grounds for dismissal.

Incompetency

Incompetency is legally defined as the "lack of ability, legal qualifications, or fitness to discharge the required duty."[35] Although incompetency has been challenged as unconstitutionally vague, courts have found the term sufficiently precise to give fair warning of prohibited conduct. These cases often involve issues relating to teaching methods, grading procedures, classroom management, and professional relationships.

Dismissals for incompetency are generally based on a number of factors or a pattern of behavior rather than isolated incidents. In a Minnesota case, indicators of incompetency included poor rapport with students, inappropriate use of class time, irrational grading of students, and lack of student progress.[36] A Pennsylvania court interpreted incompetency as deficiencies in personality, composure, judgment, and attitude that have a detrimental effect on a teacher's performance.[37] Incompetency in this case was supported by evidence that the

35. Henry Black, *Black's Law Dictionary,* 7th ed. (St. Paul, MN: West Publishing, 1999).
36. Whaley v. Anoka-Hennepin Indep. Sch. Dist. No. 11, 325 N.W.2d 128 (Minn. 1982).
37. Hamburg v. N. Penn Sch. Dist., 484 A.2d 867 (Pa. Commw. Ct. 1984).

teacher was a disruptive influence in the school; could not maintain control of students; and failed to maintain her composure in dealing with students, other professionals, and parents.

Immorality

Immorality, one of the most frequently cited causes for dismissal, is generally not defined in state laws. The judiciary, in defining the term, has tended to interpret *immorality* broadly as unacceptable conduct that affects a teacher's fitness. Traditionally, the teacher has been viewed as an exemplar whose conduct is influential in shaping the lives of young students.

Sexually related conduct *per se* between a teacher and a student has consistently been held to constitute immoral conduct justifying termination of employment. The Supreme Court of Colorado stated that when a teacher engages in sexually provocative or exploitative conduct with students, "a strong presumption of unfitness arises against the teacher."[38] Similarly, a Washington appellate court found that a male teacher's sexual relationship with a minor student justified dismissal.[39] The court declined to hold that an adverse effect on fitness to teach must be shown. Rather, the court concluded that when a teacher and a minor student are involved, the board might reasonably decide that such conduct is harmful to the school district.

In addition to sexual improprieties with students, which clearly are grounds for dismissal, other conduct that sets a bad example for students may be considered immoral under the "role model" standard. Courts, however, generally have required school officials to show that misconduct or a particular lifestyle has an adverse impact on fitness to teach. They have recognized that allowing dismissal merely upon a showing of immoral behavior without consideration of the nexus between the conduct and fitness to teach would be an unwarranted intrusion on a teacher's right to privacy. For example, an Ohio appellate court found that school officials had not produced evidence to show that an adulterous affair with another school employee constituted immorality when it did not have a hostile impact on the school community.[40]

Sexual orientation has been an issue in several controversial teacher dismissal cases. Although these cases often have raised constitutional issues related to freedom of expression and privacy, courts also have confronted the question of whether homosexuality *per se* is evidence of unfitness to teach or whether it must be shown that this lifestyle impairs teaching effectiveness.[41] According to the Supreme Court of California, immoral or unprofessional conduct or moral turpitude must be related to unfitness to teach to justify termination.[42] Gen-

38. Weissman v. Bd. of Educ., 547 P.2d 1267, 1273 (Colo. 1976).

39. Denton v. S. Kitsap Sch. Dist. No. 402, 516 P.2d 1080 (Wash. Ct. App. 1973). *See also* DeMichele v. Greenburgh Cent. Sch. Dist. No. 7, 167 F.3d 784 (2d Cir. 1999) (ruling that termination of a teacher for sexual misconduct with students occurring 24 years earlier did not violate his due process rights).

40. Bertolini v. City Sch. Dist. Bd. of Educ., 744 N.E.2d 1245 (Ohio Ct. App. 2000). *But see* Parker-Bigback v. St. Labre Sch., 7 P.3d 361 (Mont. 2000) (upholding termination of a counselor for cohabitation with a man to whom she was not married).

41. *See* text accompanying note 102, Chapter 10, for a discussion of teachers' privacy rights and sexual orientation.

erally, other courts have adopted a similar position, requiring school boards to establish a connection between private homosexuality and impaired teaching effectiveness to sustain dismissal.[43]

Whereas many teacher terminations for immorality involve sexual conduct, immorality is broader in meaning and scope. As one court noted, it covers conduct that "is hostile to the welfare of the school community."[44] Such hostile conduct has included, among other things, dishonest acts, criminal conduct, and drug-related conduct. Specific actions substantiating charges of immorality have included misrepresenting absences from school as illness,[45] being involved in the sale of illegal drugs,[46] possessing cocaine,[47] altering student transcripts,[48] and instructing a student to lie and cheat during a wrestling tournament.[49]

Insubordination

Insubordination is generally defined as the willful disregard of or refusal to obey school regulations and official orders. Teachers can be dismissed for violation of administrative regulations and policies even though classroom performance is satisfactory; school officials are not required to establish a relationship between the conduct and fitness to teach.

With the plethora of regulations enacted by school districts, wide diversity is found in types of behavior adjudicated as insubordination. Dismissals based on insubordination have been upheld in cases involving refusal to abide by specific school directives, unwillingness to cooperate with superiors, unauthorized absences, and numerous other actions. Since conduct is measured against the existence of a rule or policy, a school board may more readily document insubordination than most other legal causes for dismissal.

Many state laws and court decisions require that acts be "willful and persistent" to be considered insubordinate. A Minnesota teacher's continuous refusal to complete program evaluation forms resulted in *insubordination* charges. The Minnesota Supreme Court, upholding the dismissal, defined insubordination as "constant or continuing intentional refusal to obey a direct or implied order, reasonable in nature, and given by and with proper

42. Morrison v. State Bd. of Educ., 461 P.2d 375 (Cal. 1969). *But see* Rowland v. Mad River Local Sch. Dist., 730 F.2d 444 (6th Cir. 1984). *See also* text accompanying note 108, Chapter 10; Gaylord v. Tacoma Sch. Dist. No. 10, 559 P.2d 1340 (Wash. 1977).
43. *See, e.g.,* Glover v. Williamsburg Local Sch. Dist., 20 F. Supp. 2d 1160 (S.D. Ohio 1998) (ordering reinstatement when a teacher's nonrenewal was based on his sexual orientation rather than his teaching effectiveness); Weaver v. Nebo Sch, Dist., 29 F. Supp. 2d 1279 (D. Utah 1998) (concluding that a community's negative response to a teacher's homosexuality did not justify her removal as the girls' volleyball coach).
44. Jarvella v. Willoughby-Eastlake City Sch. Dist., 233 N.E.2d 143, 145 (Ohio 1967).
45. Riverview Sch. Dist. v. Riverview Educ. Ass'n, 639 A.2d 974 (Pa. Commw. Ct. 1994). *See also* Dohanic v. Commonwealth Dep't of Educ., 533 A.2d 812 (Pa. Commw. Ct. 1987) (holding that lying to school officials constituted immoral conduct).
46. Woo v. Putnam County Bd. of Educ., 504 S.E.2d 644 (W. Va. 1998).
47. Gedney v. Bd. of Educ., 703 A.2d 804 (Conn. App. Ct. 1997).
48. Hill v. Indep. Sch. Dist. No. 25, 57 P.3d 882 (Okla. Civ. App. 2002).
49. Florian v. Highland Local Sch. Dist. Bd. of Educ., 493 N.E.2d 249 (Ohio Ct. App. 1983).

authority."[50] In some instances, however, a severe or substantial single incident may be adequate for dismissal action. For example, state courts upheld a Missouri teacher's termination for refusal to teach an assigned course[51] and a Colorado teacher's dismissal for showing an R-rated movie without submitting a request for approval under the district's "controversial materials" policy.[52]

Teachers cannot ignore reasonable directives and policies of administrators or school boards. If the school board has prohibited corporal punishment or prescribed procedures for its administration, teachers must strictly adhere to board requirements. Repeatedly failing to follow official directives in administering corporal punishment resulted in the termination of a Texas teacher.[53] In upholding the termination of a Colorado teacher, the state supreme court ruled that tapping a student on the head with a three-foot pointer supported termination when the teacher had been warned and disciplined previously for using physical force in violation of school district policy.[54] The Eleventh Circuit found that insubordination was established when a teacher refused to take a urinalysis drug test within two hours of the discovery of marijuana in her car in the school parking lot, as required by school board policy.[55] The Eighth Circuit upheld the dismissal of a teacher for violating a school board policy that prohibited students' use of profanity in the classroom; students had used profanity in various creative-writing assignments such as plays and poems.[56] The key determinant generally is whether the teacher has persisted in disobeying a *reasonable* school policy or directive.

Unprofessional Conduct

A number of states identify either *unprofessional conduct* or *conduct unbecoming a teacher* as cause for dismissal. A teacher's activities both inside and outside of school can be used to substantiate this charge when it interferes with teaching effectiveness. Dismissals for unprofessional conduct, neglect of duty, and unfitness to teach often are based on quite similar facts. Facts that establish unprofessional conduct in one state may be deemed neglect of duty in another state. Most courts have defined *unprofessional conduct* as actions directly related to the fitness of educators to perform in their professional capacity. The working definition adopted by the Supreme Court of Nebraska specified unprofessional conduct as breaching the rules or ethical code of a profession or "unbecoming a member in good standing of a profession." Under this definition, the court reasoned that a teacher engaged in

50. Ray v. Minneapolis Bd. of Educ., 202 N.W.2d 375, 378 (Minn. 1972). *See also* Trimble v. W. Va. Bd. of Dirs., 549 S.E.2d 294 (W. Va. 2001) (concluding that termination for a minor incident of insubordination denied individual constitutional due process; progressive disciplinary sanctions should have been imposed to correct insubordinate conduct prior to termination proceedings).
51. McLaughlin v. Bd. of Educ., 659 S.W.2d 249 (Mo. Ct. App. 1983).
52. Bd. of Educ. v. Wilder, 960 P.2d 695 (Colo. 1998).
53. Burton v. Kirby, 775 S.W.2d 834 (Tex. Ct. App. 1989).
54. Bd. of Educ. v. Flaming, 938 P.2d 151 (Colo. 1997).
55. Hearn v. Bd. of Pub. Educ., 191 F.3d 1329 (11th Cir. 1999).
56. Lacks v. Ferguson Reorganized Sch. Dist. R-2, 147 F.3d 718 (8th Cir. 1998).

unprofessional conduct when he "smacked" a student on the head hard enough to make the student cry, thereby violating the state prohibition against corporal punishment.[57]

Courts have upheld dismissal for unprofessional conduct based on a number of grounds, such as permitting students to kick or hit each other for violations of classroom rules,[58] engaging in sexual harassment of female students,[59] wrapping a student in an electrical cord and verbally humiliating him in front of other students,[60] losing complete control of the classroom,[61] showing a sexually explicit film to a classroom of adolescents without previewing it,[62] and stealing pills labeled methylphenidate (generic name for Ritalin) from the school office.[63] As with dismissals based on incompetency, courts often require prior warning that the behavior may result in dismissal.

Unfitness to Teach

Unfitness to teach covers a wide array of teacher behavior. In a Montana case, the high court found nine incidents of inappropriate comments and conduct related to sex or gender to support dismissal of a teacher for unfitness even though he was considered an outstanding educator.[64] An Illinois appellate court, defining *unfitness* as "conduct detrimental to the operation of the school," held that improper sexual conduct toward students constituted unfitness.[65] A California appellate court interpreted "evident unfitness for service" in state law to require that unfitness be attributed to a defect in temperament. As such, a teacher's termination for unfitness was supported by a number of confrontations with other teachers and administrators and sarcastic and belittling comments on student disciplinary slips.[66]

Two decisions from the Supreme Court of Maine dealt with dismissals for one-time incidents that allegedly affected fitness to teach. In the first case, a teacher who was also a

57. Daily v. Bd. of Educ., 588 N.W.2d 813, 824 (Neb. 1999). Following a hearing to consider termination of employment, the school board instead imposed a 30-day suspension on the teacher.
58. Roberts v. Santa Cruz Valley Unified Sch. Dist. No. 35, 778 P.2d 1294 (Ariz. Ct. App. 1989).
59. Conward v. Cambridge Sch. Comm., 171 F.3d 12 (1st Cir. 1999). *See also* Baltrip v. Norris, 23 S.W.3d 336 (Tenn. Ct. App. 2000) *review denied,* No. E1998-00745-SC-R11-CV, 2000 Tenn. LEXIS 416 (July 24, 2000).
60. Johanson v. Bd. of Educ., 589 N.W.2d 815 (Neb. 1999).
61. Walker v. Highlands County Sch. Bd., 752 So. 2d 127 (Fla. Dist. Ct. App. 2000), *review denied,* 773 So. 2d 58 (2000).
62. Fowler v. Bd. of Educ., 819 F.2d 657 (6th Cir. 1987).
63. Lannom v. Bd. of Educ., No. M 1999-00137-COA-R3-CV, 2000 Tenn. App. LEXIS 133 (Mar. 6, 2000).
64. Baldridge v. Bd. of Trs., 951 P.2d 1343 (Mont. 1997).
65. Lombardo v. Bd. of Educ., 241 N.E.2d 495, 498 (Ill. App. Ct. 1968). *See also* Elvin v. City of Waterville, 573 A.2d 381 (Me. 1990) (concluding that a female teacher's sexual relationship with a 15-year-old male student rendered her unfit to teach); Johnson v. Bd. of Trs., 771 P.2d 137 (Mont. 1989) (ruling that a teacher's sexual contact with two students supported dismissal for unfitness to teach and immorality).
66. Woodland Joint Unified Sch. Dist. v. Comm'n on Prof. Competence, 4 Cal. Rptr. 2d 227, 236 (App. Ct. 1992).

licensed gunsmith inadvertently brought a gun and ammunition to school in his jacket. The gun was stolen from his room but later returned. The school board initiated dismissal proceedings for "grave lack of judgment." Overturning the board action, the court held that one isolated incident does not represent such "moral impropriety, professional incompetence, or unsuitability" to constitute unfitness to teach.[67] The second case involved a teacher striking a student across the face with his hand during a basketball game.[68] The blow was severe, causing the loss of one tooth, damage to another, and extensive bruises. Here, the court concluded that the single incident was sufficient to justify dismissal because of its direct impact on the teacher's effectiveness as a coach. Dismissals for one-time incidents, regardless of the grounds, are always scrutinized closely by courts.

Mental, emotional, or physical disorders can constitute unfitness or incapacity to teach. To establish incapacity, health conditions must be severe and interfere with a teacher's ability to perform in the classroom. It should be noted, however, that dismissals based on physical disabilities might impair federally protected rights of employees with disabilities. As discussed in Chapter 11, the United States Supreme Court held that a teacher with tuberculosis was "handicapped" under federal antidiscrimination provisions and thus could not be summarily dismissed because of the disease.[69]

Other Good and Just Cause

Not unexpectedly, *other good and just cause* as grounds for dismissal often has been challenged as vague and overbroad. Courts have been faced with the task of determining whether the phrase's meaning is limited to the specific grounds enumerated in the statute or whether it is a separate, expanded cause. An Indiana appellate court interpreted it as permitting termination for reasons other than those specified in the tenure law, if evidence indicated that the board's decision was based on "good cause."[70] As such, dismissal of a teacher convicted of a misdemeanor was upheld even though the teacher had no prior indication that such conduct was sufficient cause. A Connecticut court found *good cause* to be any ground that is put forward in good faith that is not "arbitrary, irrational, unreasonable, or irrelevant to the board's task of building up and maintaining an efficient school system."[71] Terminating a

67. Wright v. Superintending Comm., Portland, 331 A.2d 640, 647 (Me. 1975).
68. McLaughlin v. Machias Sch. Comm., 385 A.2d 53 (Me. 1978).
69. Sch. Bd. of Nassau County v. Arline, 480 U.S. 273 (1987).
70. Gary Teachers Union, Local No. 4, AFT v. Sch. City of Gary, 332 N.E.2d 256, 263 (Ind. Ct. App. 1975). *See also* Hierlmeier v. N. Judson-San Pierre Bd., 730 N.E.2d 821 (Ind. Ct. App. 2000) (ruling that sexual harassment of female students and other inappropriate conduct toward students substantiated good and just cause for termination). *But see* Trs. Lincoln County Sch. Dist. No. 13 v. Holden, 754 P.2d 506 (Mont. 1988) (concluding that two instances of calling students crude names did not support good cause for dismissal).
71. Hanes v. Bd. of Educ., 783 A.2d 1 (Conn. App. Ct. 2001). *See also* Oleske v. Hilliard City Sch. Dist., 764 N.E.2d 1110, 1116 (Ohio Ct. App. 2001) (concluding that a teacher's dismissal for telling dirty jokes and calling another teacher an offensive name in front of students constituted a "fairly serious matter" supporting good and just cause for dismissal).

teacher for altering students' responses on state mandatory proficiency tests was held to be relevant to that task.

The Second Circuit found *other due and sufficient cause* as a ground for dismissal to be "appropriate in an area such as discipline of teachers, where a myriad of uncontemplated situations may arise and it is not reasonable to require a legislature to elucidate in advance every act that requires sanction."[72] The court declined to rule on the vagueness of the term but rather noted that courts generally assess the teacher's conduct in relation to the statutory grounds for dismissal. That is, if the specific behavior is sufficiently related to the causes specified in state law, it is assumed that the teacher should have reasonably known that the conduct was improper. In this case, where a teacher repeatedly humiliated and harassed students (and school administrators had discussed the problem with him), the court concluded that the teacher was aware of the impropriety of his conduct. The Supreme Court of Iowa applied a statute permitting teachers to be terminated during the contract year for "just cause" to support the termination of a teacher for shoplifting.[73] Although the teacher claimed that her compulsion to shoplift was related to a mental illness, the court found substantial evidence to terminate the teacher's employment, weighing the teacher's position as a role model, the character of the illness, and the school board's needs.

Reduction-in-Force

In addition to dismissal for causes related to teacher performance and fitness, legislation generally permits the release of teachers for reasons related to declining enrollment, financial exigency, and school district consolidation. Whereas most state statutes provide for such terminations, a number of states also have adopted legislation that specifies the basis for selection of released teachers, procedures to be followed, and provisions for reinstatement. These terminations, characterized as *reductions-in-force (RIF),* also may be governed by board policies and negotiated bargaining agreements.

Unlike other termination cases, the employee challenging a RIF decision shoulders the burden of proof. There is a presumption that the board has acted in good faith with permissible motives. Legal controversies in this area usually involve questions related to the necessity for the reductions, board compliance with mandated procedures, and possible subterfuge for impermissible termination (such as denial of constitutional rights, subversion of tenure rights, discrimination).

If statutory or contractual restrictions exist for teacher layoffs, there must be substantial compliance with the provisions. One of the provisions most frequently included is a method for selecting teachers for release. In general, reductions are based on seniority, and a tenured teacher, rather than a nontenured teacher, must be retained if both are qualified to fill the same position. State statutes usually require that both licensure and seniority be considered; a teacher lacking a license in the area would not be permitted to teach, while a permanent teacher with proper credentials, but less seniority, was dismissed. Along with seniority, merit-rating systems may be included in the determination of reductions. The Nebraska Supreme Court concluded that school boards have broad discretion in deciding

72. diLeo v. Greenfield, 541 F.2d 949, 954 (2d Cir. 1976).

73. Bd. of Dirs. v. Davies, 489 N.W.2d 19 (Iowa 1992).

what factors to use in its RIF policy and how to weight those factors.[74] Guidelines or criteria established by state or local education agencies, however, must be applied in a uniform and nondiscriminatory manner.

The Fourteenth Amendment requires minimal procedural protections in dismissals for cause, but courts have not clearly defined the due process requirements for RIF. The Eighth Circuit noted that tenured teachers possess a property interest in continued employment, and thereby must be provided notice and an opportunity to be heard.[75] Specific procedural protections for employees vary according to interpretations of state law, bargaining agreements, and board policy. A Michigan court found no need for a hearing over staff reductions, because there were no charges to refute.[76] The court emphasized that the law protected the released teacher, who, subject to qualifications, was entitled to the next vacancy. In contrast, a Pennsylvania commonwealth court held that a hearing must be provided to assure the teacher (1) that termination was for reasons specified by law and (2) that the board followed the correct statutory procedures in selecting the teacher for discharge.[77]

State law or other policies may give preference to teachers who are released due to a reduction-in-force. Typically, under such requirements, a school board cannot hire a non-employee until each qualified teacher on the preferred recall list is reemployed. Although statutes often require that a teacher be appointed to the first vacancy for which licensed and qualified, courts have held that reappointment is still at the board's discretion. Additionally, a board is generally not obligated to realign or rearrange teaching assignments to create a position for a released teacher.

Remedies for Violations of Protected Rights

> Wrongfully terminated employees may be entitled to compensatory and punitive damages, reinstatement with back pay, and attorneys' fees for the violation of their constitutional rights.

When established that school districts or officials have violated an employee's rights protected by federal or state law, several remedies are available to the aggrieved individual. In some situations, the employee may seek a court injunction ordering the unlawful action to cease. This remedy might be sought if a school board has unconstitutionally imposed restraints on teachers' expression. If terminations, transfers, or other adverse employment consequences are unconstitutionally imposed, courts will order school districts to return the affected employees to their original status with back pay.

74. Nickel v. Saline County Sch. Dist. No. 163, 559 N.W.2d 480 (Neb. 1997).
75. Boner v. Eminence R-1 Sch. Dist., 55 F.3d 1339 (8th Cir. 1995).
76. Steeby v. Sch. Dist. of Highland Park, 224 N.W.2d 97 (Mich. Ct. App. 1974).
77. Fatscher v. Bd. of Sch. Dirs., 367 A.2d 1130 (Pa. Commw. Ct. 1977).

In addition to these remedies, educators are increasingly bringing suits to recover damages for actions that violate their federally protected rights. Suits are usually based on 42 U.S.C. Section 1983, which provides that any person who acts under color of state law to deprive another individual of rights secured by the Federal Constitution or laws is subject to personal liability. This law, which was originally enacted in 1871 to prevent discrimination against African American citizens, has been broadly interpreted as conferring liability on school personnel and school districts, not only for racial discrimination but also for actions that may result in the impairment of other federally protected rights.[78]

Suits alleging Section 1983 violations can be initiated in federal or state courts,[79] and exhaustion of state administrative remedies is not required before initiating a federal suit.[80] When a federal law authorizes an exclusive nondamages remedy, however, a Section 1983 suit is precluded.[81] This section focuses on the liability of school officials and districts for the violation of protected rights and on the types of damages available to aggrieved employees.

Liability of School Officials

Under Section 1983, public school employees acting under color of state law can be held personally liable for actions abridging students' or teachers' federal rights. The Supreme Court, however, has recognized that government officials cannot be held liable under Section 1983 for the actions of their subordinates, thus rejecting the doctrine of *respondeat superior,* even where school officials have general supervisory authority over the activities of the wrongdoers. In order to be held liable, the officials must have personally participated in, or had personal knowledge of, the unlawful acts or promulgated official policy under which the acts were taken.[82] Furthermore, the Supreme Court in 1998 ruled that public officials are absolutely immune from suit under Section 1983 for their legislative activities.[83] These actions involve discretionary, policymaking decisions, and enactment of regulations, often with budgetary implications. Subsequently, courts have clarified that employment decisions related to individual employees (such as hiring, dismissal, or demotions) are administrative, not legislative, in nature.[84]

The Supreme Court has recognized that in some circumstances school officials can claim qualified immunity to shield them from personal liability when they have acted in good faith. The Court has declared that "government officials performing discretionary

78. Maine v. Thiboutot, 448 U.S. 1 (1980).

79. The Supreme Court has rejected the assertion that school officials are immune from a § 1983 suit initiated in a state court. Howlett v. Rose, 496 U.S. 356 (1990).

80. Patsy v. Bd. of Regents, 457 U.S. 496 (1982).

81. *See, e.g.,* Gonzaga Univ. v. Doe, 536 U.S. 496 (2002); Blessing v. Freestone, 520 U.S. 329 (1997); text accompanying note 91, Chapter 4.

82. *See* Am. Mfrs. Mut. Ins. Co. v. Sullivan, 526 U.S. 40 (1999); Rizzo v. Goode, 423 U.S. 362 (1976).

83. Bogan v. Scott-Harris, 523 U.S. 44 (1998).

84. *See, e.g.,* Canary v. Osborn, 211 F.3d 324 (6th Cir. 2000); Harhay v. Blanchette, 323 F.3d 206 (2d Cir. 2003).

functions generally are shielded from liability for civil damages insofar as their conduct does not violate clearly established statutory or constitutional rights of which a reasonable person would have known."[85] The Second Circuit, noting that unlawfulness must be apparent, stated:

> A right is clearly established if the contours of the right are sufficiently clear that a reasonable official would understand that what he or she is doing violates that right. The question is not what a lawyer would learn or intuit from researching case law, but what a reasonable person in the [school official's] position should know about the constitutionality of the conduct.[86]

The Seventh Circuit emphasized that the individual alleging violation of a clearly established right bears the burden of demonstrating the existence of the right.[87] In determining whether a right is clearly established, the court stated that first it examines controlling Supreme Court precedent and its own circuit decisions related to the case and then reviews all relevant case law. According to the appellate court, a split among courts in assessing similar conduct points to unsettled law.

Liability of School Districts

In 1978, the Supreme Court ruled that local governments are considered "persons" under Section 1983.[88] In essence, school districts can be assessed damages when action taken pursuant to official policy violates federally protected rights.

The governmental unit (like the individual official), however, cannot be held liable under the *respondeat superior* doctrine for the wrongful acts committed solely by its employees. Liability under Section 1983 against the agency can be imposed only when execution of official policy by an individual with final authority impairs a federally protected right.[89] The Supreme Court has held that a single egregious act of a low-level employee does not infer an official policy of inadequate training and supervision,[90] but an agency can be liable if "deliberate indifference" in ensuring adequately trained employees is established.[91]

Although school officials can plead good faith immunity, this defense is not available to school districts. The Supreme Court has ruled that school districts and other governmental subdivisions cannot claim qualified immunity based on good faith actions of their officials. The Court acknowledged that under certain circumstances sovereign immunity can shield municipal corporations from state tort suits, but concluded that Section 1983 abrogated governmental immunity in situations involving the impairment of federally protected rights.[92]

85. Harlow v. Fitzgerald, 457 U.S. 800, 818 (1982).
86. McCullough v. Wyandanch Union Free Sch. Dist., 187 F.3d 272 (2d Cir. 1999).
87. Denius v. Dunlap, 209 F.3d 944 (7th Cir. 2000).
88. Monell v. Dep't of Soc. Servs., 436 U.S. 658 (1978).
89. *See, e.g.*, Collins v. City of Harker Heights, 503 U.S. 115 (1992); Langford v. City of Atlantic City, 235 F.3d 845 (3rd Cir. 2000); Seamons v. Snow, 206 F.3d 1021 (10th Cir. 2000).
90. Oklahoma City v. Tuttle, 471 U.S. 808 (1985).
91. City of Canton, Ohio v. Harris, 489 U.S. 378 (1989).

To avoid liability for constitutional violations, school districts have introduced claims of Eleventh Amendment immunity. The Eleventh Amendment, explicitly prohibiting citizens of one state from bringing suit against another state without its consent, has been interpreted as also precluding federal lawsuits against a state by its own citizens.[93] A state can waive this immunity by specifically consenting to be sued, and Congress can abrogate state immunity through legislation enacted to enforce the Fourteenth Amendment. Such congressional intent, however, must be explicit in the federal legislation.[94]

School districts have asserted Eleventh Amendment protection based on the fact that they perform a state function. Admittedly, education is a state function, but it does not necessarily follow that school districts gain Eleventh Amendment immunity against claims of constitutional abridgments. For the Eleventh Amendment to be invoked in a suit against a school district, the state must be the "real party in interest." In many states, the Eleventh Amendment question with respect to school district immunity was resolved in the *Mt. Healthy* case.[95] The Supreme Court concluded that the issue in this case hinged on whether, under Ohio law, a school district is considered an arm of the state as opposed to a municipality or other political subdivision. Considering the taxing power and autonomy of school district operations, the Supreme Court found school districts to be more like counties or cities than extensions of the state.

Remedies

Judicial remedies for the violation of protected rights depend on employment status, federal and state statutory provisions, and the discretion of courts. Federal and state laws often identify damages that may be recovered or place limitations on types of awards. Unless these provisions restrict specific remedies, courts have broad discretionary power to formulate equitable settlements.

Damages. When a school official or school district is found liable for violating an individual's protected rights, damages are assessed to compensate the claimant for the injury. Actual injury, however, must be shown for the aggrieved party to recover damages; without

92. Owen v. City of Independence, Mo., 445 U.S. 622 (1980). *See* text accompanying note 25, Chapter 2, for a discussion of governmental immunity under tort law.
93. *See, e.g.,* Hans v. Louisiana, 134 U.S. 1 (1890). *See also* Will v. Mich. Dep't of State Police, 491 U.S. 58 (1989) (holding that § 1983 does not permit a suit against a state; Congress did not intend the word *person* to include states, but it does include political subdivisions such as school districts).
94. Most recently, the Supreme Court held that the Family Educational Rights and Privacy Act of 1974 does not explicitly confer individually enforceable rights. Gonzaga Univ. v. Doe, 536 U.S. 273 (2002). Also, in deciding whether an individual can sue a state for money damages in federal court under the Americans with Disabilities Act of 1990, the Supreme Court ruled that Congress did not act within its constitutional authority when it abrogated Eleventh Amendment immunity. Bd. of Trs. v. Garrett, 531 U.S. 356 (2001).
95. Mt. Healthy City Sch. Dist. v. Doyle, 429 U.S. 274 (1977). *But see* Belanger v. Madera Unified Sch. Dist., 963 F.2d 248 (9th Cir. 1992) (holding that California school boards are indivisible agencies of the state and thus entitled to Eleventh Amendment immunity).

evidence of monetary or mental injury, the plaintiff is entitled only to nominal damages (not to exceed one dollar), even though an impairment of protected rights is established.[96] Significant monetary damages, however, may be awarded for a wrongful termination if a teacher is able to demonstrate substantial losses. At the same time, individuals must make an effort to mitigate damages by seeking appropriate employment.

In some instances, aggrieved individuals have sought punitive as well as compensatory damages. The judiciary has ruled that school officials can be liable for punitive damages (to punish the wrongdoer) if a jury concludes that the individual's conduct is willful or in reckless and callous disregard of federally protected rights.[97] Punitive as well as compensatory damages were assessed against a principal and superintendent who, without authority, discharged a teacher in retaliation for the exercise of protected speech.[98]

In 1981, the Supreme Court ruled that Section 1983 does not authorize the award of punitive damages against a municipality.[99] Recognizing that compensation for injuries is an obligation of a municipality, the Court held that *punitive* damages were appropriate only for the *individual* wrongdoers and not for the municipality itself. The Court also noted that punitive damages constitute punishment against individuals to deter similar conduct in the future, but they are not intended to punish innocent taxpayers. This ruling does not bar claims for punitive damages for violations of federal rights in school cases, but such claims must be brought against individuals rather than against the school district itself.

Reinstatement. Whether a court orders reinstatement as a remedy for school board action depends on the protected interests involved and the discretion of the court, unless specific provision for reinstatement is specified in state law. If a tenured teacher is unjustly dismissed, the property interest gives rise to an expectation of reemployment; reinstatement in such instances is usually the appropriate remedy. A nontenured teacher, wrongfully dismissed during the contract period, however, is normally entitled only to damages, not reinstatement.

A valid property or liberty claim entitles a teacher to procedural due process, but the teacher can still be dismissed for cause after proper procedures have been followed. If a teacher is terminated without proper procedures and can establish that the action is not justified, however, reinstatement will be ordered. If proven that the actual reason for the nonrenewal of a teacher's contract is retaliation for the exercise of constitutional rights (e.g., protected speech), reinstatement would be warranted, although substantiation of such a claim is difficult.

96. *See, e.g.,* Farrar v. Hobby, 506 U.S. 103 (1992) (concluding that an award of nominal damages is mandatory when a procedural due process violation is established but no actual injury is shown); Carey v. Piphus, 435 U.S. 247 (1978) (holding that pupils who were denied procedural due process in a disciplinary proceeding would be entitled only to nominal damages unless it was established that lack of proper procedures resulted in actual injury to the students).

97. *See, e.g.,* Smith v. Wade, 461 U.S. 30 (1983). In 1991, the Supreme Court refused to place a limit on the amount of punitive damages that properly instructed juries can award in common-law suits, but it did note that extremely high awards might be viewed as unacceptable under the Due Process Clause of the Fourteenth Amendment. Pac. Mut. Life Ins. Co. v. Haslip, 499 U.S. 1 (1991).

98. Fishman v. Clancy, 763 F.2d 485 (1st Cir. 1985).

99. City of Newport v. Fact Concerts, 453 U.S. 247 (1981).

The failure to comply with statutory requirements in nonrenewals and dismissals may result in reinstatement. When statutory dates are specified for notice of nonrenewal, failure to comply strictly with the deadline provides grounds for reinstatement of the teacher. Courts may interpret this as continued employment for an additional year or reinstatement with tenure if nonrenewal occurs at the end of the probationary period. In contrast to the remedy for lack of proper notice, the remedy for failure to provide an appropriate hearing is generally a remand for a hearing, not reinstatement.

Attorneys' Fees. Attorneys' fees are not automatically granted to the teacher who prevails in a lawsuit, but are generally dependent on statutory authorization. At the federal level, the Civil Rights Attorneys' Fees Award Act gives federal courts discretion to award fees in civil rights suits.[100] In congressional debate concerning attorneys' fees, it was stated that "private citizens must be given not only the right to go to court, but also the legal resources. If the citizen does not have the resources, his day in court is denied him."[101]

To receive attorneys' fees, the teacher must be the prevailing party; that is, damages or some form of equitable relief must be granted to the teacher. The Supreme Court has held that a prevailing party is one who is successful in achieving some benefit on any significant issue in the case, but not necessarily the primary issue. At a minimum, the Court ruled that "the plaintiff must be able to point to a resolution of the dispute which changes the legal relationship between itself and the defendant."[102] If a plaintiff achieves only partial success, the fees requested may be reduced.

Although it has been established that the plaintiff who prevails in a civil rights suit may, at the court's discretion, be entitled to attorneys' fees, the same standard is not applied to defendants. When a plaintiff teacher is awarded attorneys' fees, the assessment is against a party who has violated a federal law. Different criteria must be applied when a prevailing defendant seeks attorneys' fees. The Supreme Court has held that such fees cannot be imposed on a plaintiff unless the claim was "frivolous, unreasonable, or groundless."[103] Although awards of damages to prevailing defendants have not been common, in some situations such awards have been made to deter groundless lawsuits.

Conclusion

Through state laws and the Federal Constitution, extensive safeguards protect educators' employment security. Most states have adopted tenure laws that precisely delineate teachers' employment rights in termination and disciplinary proceedings. Additionally, in the absence of specific state guarantees, the Fourteenth Amendment ensures that teachers will be afforded procedural due process when property or liberty interests are implicated. At a minimum, the employee is entitled to notice of the charges and an opportunity to be heard. Legal decisions interpreting both state and federal rights in dismissal actions have estab-

100. 42 U.S.C. § 1988 (2003).
101. 122 Cong. Rec. 33313 (1976).
102. Tex. State Teachers Ass'n v. Garland Indep. Sch. Dist., 489 U.S. 782, 792 (1989).
103. Christiansburg Garment Co. v. EEOC, 434 U.S. 412, 422 (1978).

lished broad guidelines as to when due process is required, the types of procedures that must be provided, and the legitimate causes required to substantiate dismissal action.

Causes for dismissal vary widely among the states, but usually include such grounds as incompetency, neglect of duty, immorality, insubordination, unprofessional conduct, and other good and just cause. These causes relate not only to classroom performance but also to other conduct that may have a negative impact on a teacher's effectiveness in the school system. If educators' constitutional rights are impaired in connection with termination actions, school officials and school districts can be held liable for damages. An individual, however, can recover only nominal damages for such impairment unless monetary, emotional, or mental injury can be proven.

Points to Ponder

1. An elementary teacher's contract was not renewed for failure to meet the school district's teaching expectations as she completed her third year of employment. A mentor teacher had worked closely to assist the teacher in pedagogical and classroom management issues, but little progress had been made. Her sixth-grade students consistently scored lower than other students in the school district, and parents frequently complained to the principal about her teaching. Upon receipt of the nonrenewal notice, the teacher asked for a hearing, claiming that the school board's decision severely damaged her reputation and affected her ability to obtain another position. Is she entitled to a hearing? Why or why not? Does the school board's action violate her protected liberty interests?
2. A school board sent a tenured teacher a notice of its intent to terminate him for insubordination after he repeatedly refused to develop a personal growth plan as required by school district policy. Even though he had not complied with the policy, the principal had given the teacher good teaching evaluations each year. Can the school board terminate his employment? Why or why not? What are the teacher's rights if the school board pursues termination?
3. A tenured, veteran teacher received a notice from the school board of its intent to terminate her employment for lack of teaching effectiveness. The brief letter cited the statutory language permitting teacher termination for cause and indicated that a hearing would be held in 10 days. Does this constitute adequate notice? Explain.
4. After two convictions for driving while intoxicated, a tenured, middle school teacher was dismissed on grounds of immorality. The teacher argued that the convictions did not relate to his teaching effectiveness, the students had been unaware of the incidents until his termination, and he was in a treatment program for his drinking problem. Do you think his termination will be upheld? Support your answer.
5. A male teacher was arrested and charged with propositioning a male undercover police officer. Subsequently, the charges were dropped, but the school board, with no statement of reasons, did not renew the teacher's contract at the end of the school year. Although state law and local policies do not provide for a hearing in nonrenewals, the teacher requested an opportunity to appear before the school board. Is he entitled to such a hearing? Why or why not?

13

Summary of Legal Generalizations

In the preceding chapters, principles of law have been presented as they relate to specific aspects of teachers' and students' rights and responsibilities. Constitutional and statutory provisions, in conjunction with judicial decisions, have been analyzed in an effort to depict the current status of the law. Many diverse topics have been explored, some with clearly established legal precedents and others where the law is still evolving.

The most difficult situations confronting school personnel are those without specific legislative or judicial guidance. In such circumstances, educators must make judgments based on their professional training and general knowledge of the law as it applies to education. The following broad generalizations, synthesized from the preceding chapters, are presented to assist educators in making such determinations.

Generalizations

The Legal Control of Public Education Resides with the State as One of Its Sovereign Powers. In attempting to comply with the law, school personnel must keep in mind the scope of the state's authority to regulate educational activities. Courts consistently have held that state legislatures possess plenary power in establishing and operating public schools; this power is restricted only by federal and state constitutions and civil rights laws. Of course, where the federal judiciary has interpreted the U.S. Constitution as prohibiting a given practice in public education, such as racial discrimination, the state or its agents cannot enact laws or policies that conflict with the constitutional mandate unless justified by a compelling governmental interest. In contrast, if the Federal Constitution and civil rights laws have been interpreted as permitting a certain activity, states retain discretion in either restricting or expanding the practice. Under such circumstances, standards vary across states, and legislation becomes more important in specifying the scope of protected rights.

For example, the Supreme Court has rejected the assertion that probationary teachers have an inherent federal right to due process prior to contract nonrenewal, but state legislatures have the authority to create such a right under state law. Similarly, the Supreme Court has found no Fourth Amendment violation in blanket or random drug testing of public school students who participate in extracurricular activities; however, state law may place restrictions on school authorities in conducting such searches. Also, the Supreme Court has found no Establishment Clause violation in the participation of sectarian schools in state-supported voucher programs to fund education, but these programs might run afoul of state constitutional provisions prohibiting the use of public funds for religious purposes.

Unless constitutional rights are at stake, courts defer to the will of legislative bodies in determining educational matters. State legislatures have the authority to create and redesign school districts, to collect and distribute educational funds, and to determine teacher qualifications, curricular offerings, and minimum student performance standards. With such pervasive control vested in the states, a thorough understanding of the operation of a specific educational system can be acquired only by examining an individual state's statutes, administrative regulations, and judicial decisions interpreting such provisions.

Certain prerequisites to public school employment are defined through statutes and state board of education regulations. For example, all states stipulate that a teacher must possess a valid teaching license based on satisfying specified requirements. State laws also delineate the permanency of the employment relationship, dismissal procedures for tenured and nontenured teachers, and the extent to which teachers can engage in collective bargaining.

State laws similarly govern conditions of school attendance. Every state has enacted a compulsory attendance statute to ensure an educated citizenry. These laws are applicable to all children, with only a few legally recognized exceptions. In addition to mandating school attendance, states also have the authority to prescribe courses of study and instructional materials. Courts will not invalidate such decisions unless constitutional rights are abridged. Comparable reasoning also is applied by courts in upholding the state's power to establish graduation requirements, including the use of proficiency tests as a prerequisite to receipt of a diploma. Courts have recognized that the establishment of academic standards is within the state's scope of authority.

It is a widely held perception that local school boards control public education in this nation, but local boards hold only those discretionary powers conferred by state law. Depending on the state, a local board's discretionary authority may be quite broad, narrowly defined by statutory guidelines, or somewhere in between. School board regulations enacted pursuant to statutory authority are legally binding on employees and students. For example, school boards can place conditions on employment (e.g., continuing education requirements, residency requirements) beyond state minimums, unless prohibited by law.

In some states, policymaking authority in certain domains (e.g., curriculum, personnel) has been delegated to school-based councils, and the relationship between local boards and school-based councils is still being defined. Courts will not overturn decisions made by school boards or site-based councils unless clearly arbitrary, discriminatory, or beyond their scope of authority.

School board and/or council discretion, however, may be limited by negotiated contracts with teachers' associations. Negotiated agreements may affect terms and conditions of employment in areas such as teacher evaluation, work calendar, teaching loads, extra-duty assignments, and grievance procedures. It is imperative for educators to become familiar with all these sources of legal rights and responsibilities.

All School Policies and Practices That Impinge on Protected Personal Freedoms Must Be Substantiated as Necessary to Advance the School's Educational Mission. The state and its agents have broad authority to regulate public schools, but policies that impair federal constitutional rights must be justified by an overriding public interest. Although courts do not enact laws as legislative bodies do, they significantly influence educational policies and practices by interpreting constitutional and statutory provisions. Both school attendance and public employment traditionally were considered privileges bestowed at the will of the state, but the Supreme Court has recognized that teachers and students do not shed their constitutional rights at the schoolhouse door. The state controls education, but this power must be exercised in conformance with the Federal Constitution.

It is important to keep in mind that the Bill of Rights places restrictions on governmental, not private, action that interferes with personal freedoms. To illustrate, the Establishment Clause prohibits public school employees from directing or condoning devotional activities in public education. However, student-initiated religious groups in secondary schools that do not represent the public school must be treated like other student groups in terms of school access during noninstructional time. Furthermore, community religious groups, even those involved in religious instruction targeting elementary school children, must be provided the same school access as other community groups during nonschool hours.

In balancing public and individual interests, courts weigh the importance of the protected personal right against the governmental need to restrict its exercise. For example, courts have reasoned that there is no overriding public interest to justify compelling students to salute the American flag if such an observance conflicts with religious or philosophical beliefs. In contrast, mandatory vaccination against communicable diseases has been upheld as a prerequisite to school attendance, even if opposition to immunization is based on religious grounds. Courts have reasoned that the overriding public interest in safeguarding the health of all students justifies such a requirement.

Restrictions can be placed on students' activities if necessary to advance legitimate school objectives. For example, the judiciary has recognized that students' constitutional rights must be assessed in light of the special circumstances of the school. Consequently, school authorities can restrict attire inconsistent with the school's objectives and can impose dress codes, even uniforms, if shown to advance those objectives rather than directed at stifling expression. School authorities, although considered state officials, can conduct warrantless searches of students based on reasonable suspicion that contraband posing a threat to the school environment is concealed. Similarly, vulgar expression that might be protected by the First Amendment for adults can be curtailed among public school students to further the school's legitimate interest in maintaining standards of decency. Student expression that gives the appearance of representing the school also can be censored to ensure its consistency with educational objectives. And even personal student expression of ideological views that merely happens to take place at school can be restricted if linked to a disruption of the educational process.

Similarly, constraints can be placed on school employees if justified by valid school objectives. Prerequisites to employment, such as examinations and residency requirements, can be imposed if necessary to advance legitimate governmental interests. Furthermore, restrictions on teachers' rights to govern their appearance and make lifestyle choices outside the classroom can be justified when it impinges on their effectiveness in the classroom. Although teachers enjoy a First Amendment right to express views on matters of public concern, expression relating to private employment grievances can be the basis for disciplinary action. Even teachers' expression on public issues can be curtailed if it impedes the management of the school, work relationships, or teaching effectiveness.

Every regulation that impairs individual rights must be based on valid educational considerations and be necessary to carry out the school's mission. Such regulations also should be clearly stated and well publicized so that all individuals understand the basis for the rules and the penalties for infractions.

School Policies and Practices Must Not Disadvantage Selected Individuals or Groups. The inherent personal right to remain free from governmental discrimination has been emphasized throughout this book. Strict judicial scrutiny has been applied in evaluating state action that creates a suspect classification, such as race. In school desegregation cases, courts have charged school officials with an affirmative duty to take whatever steps are necessary to overcome the lingering effects of past discrimination. Similarly, intentional racial discrimination associated with student grouping practices, testing methods, or suspension procedures, as well as with employee hiring or promotion practices, has been disallowed.

However, neutral policies, uniformly applied, are not necessarily unconstitutional even though they may have a disparate impact on minorities. For example, prerequisites to employment, such as tests that disqualify a disproportionate number of minority applicants, have been upheld as long as their use is justified by legitimate employment objectives and not accompanied by discriminatory intent. Also, the placement of a disproportionate number of minority students in lower instructional tracks is permissible if such assignments are based on legitimate educational criteria that are applied in the best interests of students. Likewise, school segregation that results from natural causes rather than intentional state action does not implicate constitutional rights.

In addition to racial classifications, other bases for distinguishing among employees and students have been invalidated if they disadvantage individuals. Federal civil rights laws, in conjunction with state statutes, have reinforced constitutional protections afforded to various segments of society that traditionally have suffered discrimination. Indeed, the judiciary has recognized that legislative bodies are empowered to go beyond constitutional minimums in protecting citizens from discriminatory practices. Accordingly, laws have been enacted that place specific responsibilities on employers to ensure that employees are not disadvantaged on the basis of gender, age, religion, national origin, or disabilities. If an inference of discrimination is established, employers must produce legitimate nondiscriminatory reasons to justify their actions. School officials can be held liable for damages if substantiated that benefits have been withheld from certain individuals because of their inherent characteristics.

Federal and state mandates also stipulate that students cannot be denied school attendance or otherwise disadvantaged based on characteristics such as gender, disabilities, national origin, marriage, or pregnancy. Eligibility for school activities, such as participation on interscholastic athletic teams, cannot be denied to a certain class of students. In addition, disciplinary procedures that disproportionately disadvantage identified groups of students are vulnerable to legal challenge. Educators should ensure that all school policies are applied in a nondiscriminatory manner.

Courts will scrutinize grouping practices to ensure that they do not impede students' rights to equal educational opportunities. Nondiscrimination, however, does not require identical treatment. Students can be classified according to their unique needs, but any differential treatment must be justified in terms of providing more appropriate services. Indeed, judicial rulings and federal and state laws have placed an obligation on school districts to provide appropriate programs and services to meet the needs of children with disabilities and to eliminate the language barriers of those with English-language deficiencies.

Due Process Is a Basic Tenet of the United States System of Justice—The Foundation of Fundamental Fairness. The notion of due process, embodied in the Fifth and Fourteenth Amendments, has been an underlying theme throughout the discussion of teachers' and students' rights. The judiciary has recognized that due process guarantees protect individuals against arbitrary governmental action impairing life, liberty, or property interests and ensure that procedural safeguards accompany any governmental interference with these interests.

In the absence of greater statutory specificity, courts have held that the U.S. Constitution requires, at a minimum, notice of the charges and a hearing before an impartial decision maker when personnel actions impair public educators' property or liberty rights. A property claim to due process can be established by tenure status, contractual agreement, or school board action that creates a valid expectation of reemployment. A liberty claim to due process can be asserted if the employer's action implicates constitutionally protected rights (e.g., freedom of speech), damages the teacher's reputation, or forecloses the opportunity to obtain other employment. Many state legislatures have specified procedures beyond constitutional minimums that must be followed before a tenured teacher is dismissed. The provision of due process does not imply that a teacher will not be dismissed or that sanctions will not be imposed. But it does mean that the teacher must be given the opportunity to refute the charges and that the decision must be made fairly and supported by evidence.

Students, as well as teachers, have due process rights. Students have a state-created property right to attend school that cannot be denied without procedural requisites. If this right to attend school is withdrawn for disciplinary reasons, due process is required. The nature of the proceedings depends on the deprivation involved, with more serious impairments necessitating more formal proceedings. If punishments are arbitrary or excessive, students' substantive due process rights may be implicated. Children with disabilities have due process rights in placement decisions as well as in disciplinary matters. Since school authorities are never faulted for providing too much due process, at least minimum procedural safeguards are advisable when making any nonroutine change in a student's status.

Inherent in the notion of due process is the assumption that all individuals have a right to a hearing if state action impinges on personal freedoms. Such a hearing need not be elaborate in every situation; an informal conversation can suffice under some circumstances, such as brief student suspensions from school. The crucial element is for all affected parties to have an opportunity to air their views and present evidence that might alter the decision. Often, an informal hearing can serve to clarify issues and facilitate agreement, thus eliminating the need for more formal proceedings.

Educators Are Expected to Follow the Law, to Act Reasonably, and to Anticipate Potentially Adverse Consequences of Their Actions. Public school personnel are presumed to be knowledgeable of federal and state constitutional and statutory provisions as well as school board policies affecting their roles. The Supreme Court has emphasized that ignorance of the law is no defense for violating clearly established legal principles. For example, ignorance of the Supreme Court's interpretation of Establishment Clause restrictions would not shield educators from liability for conducting devotional activities in public schools.

Educators hold themselves out as having certain knowledge and skills by the nature of their special training and certification. Accordingly, they are expected to exercise sound professional judgment in the performance of their duties. Reasonable actions in one situation may be viewed as unreasonable under other conditions. To illustrate, in administering pupil punishments, teachers are expected to consider the student's age, mental condition, and past behavior as well as the specific circumstances surrounding the rule infraction. Failure to exercise reasonable judgment can result in dismissal or possibly financial liability for impairing students' rights.

Teachers also are expected to make reasonable decisions pertaining to the academic program. Materials and methodology should be appropriate for the students' age and educational objectives. If students are grouped for instructional purposes, teachers are expected to base such decisions on legitimate educational considerations.

In addition, educators are held accountable for reasonable actions in supervising students, providing appropriate instructions, maintaining equipment in proper repair, and warning students of any known dangers. Teachers must exercise a standard of care commensurate with their duty to protect students from unreasonable risks of harm. Personal liability can be assessed for negligence if a school employee should have foreseen that an event could result in injury to a student.

Educators also are expected to exercise sound judgment in personal activities that affect their professional roles. Teachers do not relinquish their privacy rights as a condition of public employment, but private choices that impair teaching effectiveness or disrupt the school can be the basis for adverse personnel action. As role models for students, teachers and other school personnel are held to a higher level of discretion in their private lives than expected of the general public.

Conclusion

One objective of this book, as noted in the introduction, has been to alleviate educators' fears that the scales of justice have been tipped against them. It is hoped that this objective has been achieved. In most instances, courts and legislatures have not imposed on school personnel any requirements that fair-minded educators would not impose on themselves. Courts have consistently upheld reasonable policies and practices based on legitimate educational objectives. If anything, legislative and judicial mandates have clarified and supported the authority as well as the duty of school personnel to make and enforce regulations that are necessary to maintain an effective and efficient educational environment. Yet, courts continue to invalidate school practices and policies if they are arbitrary, unrelated to educational objectives, or impair protected individual rights without an overriding justification.

Because reform is usually easier to implement when designed from within than when externally imposed, educators should become more assertive in identifying and altering those practices that have the potential to generate legal intervention. Internet censorship, peer sexual harassment, and zero-tolerance policies are a few issues now requiring educators' attention. Furthermore, school personnel should stay abreast of legal developments, since new laws are enacted each year and courts are continually reinterpreting constitutional and statutory provisions.

In addition to understanding basic legal rights and responsibilities, educators are expected to transmit this knowledge to students. Students also need to understand their constitutional and statutory rights, the balancing of interests that takes place in legislative and judicial forums, and the rationale for legal enactments, including school regulations. Only with increased awareness of fundamental legal principles can all individuals involved in the educational process develop a greater respect for the law and for the responsibilities that accompany legal rights.

Glossary

absolute privilege protection from liability for communication made in the performance of public service or the administration of justice.

additur the trial court's power to assess damages or increase the amount of an inadequate jury award, which can be a condition of denying a motion for a new trial.

appeal a petition to a higher court to alter the decision of a lower court.

appellate court a tribunal having jurisdiction to review decisions on appeal from inferior courts.

arbitration (binding) a process whereby an impartial third party, chosen by both parties in a dispute, makes a final determination regarding a contested issue.

assault the placing of another in fear of bodily harm.

battery the unlawful touching of another with intent to harm.

certiorari a writ of review whereby an action is removed from an inferior court to an appellate court for additional proceedings.

civil action a judicial proceeding to redress an infringement of individual civil rights, in contrast to a criminal action brought by the state to redress public wrongs.

civil right a personal right that accompanies citizenship and is protected by the Constitution (e.g., freedom of speech, freedom from discrimination).

class action suit a judicial proceeding brought on behalf of a number of persons similarly situated.

common law a body of rules and principles derived from usage or from judicial decisions enforcing such usage.

compensatory damages monetary award to compensate an individual for injury sustained (e.g., financial losses, emotional pain, inconvenience) and restore the injured party to the position held prior to the injury.

concurring opinion a statement by a judge or judges, separate from the majority opinion, that endorses the result of the majority decision but offers its own reasons for reaching that decision.

consent decree an agreement, sanctioned by a court, that is binding on the consenting parties.

consideration something of value given or promised for the purpose of forming a contract.

contract an agreement between two or more competent parties that creates, alters, or dissolves a legal relationship.

criminal action a judicial proceeding brought by the state against a person charged with a public offense.

damages an award made to an individual because of a legal wrong.

declaratory relief a judicial declaration of the rights of the plaintiff without an assessment of damages against the defendant.

de facto segregation separation of the races that exists but does not result from action of the state or its agents.

defamation false and intentional communication that injures a person's character or reputation; slander is spoken and libel is written communication.

defendant the party against whom a court action is brought.

de jure segregation separation of the races by law or by action of the state or its agents.

de minimis something that is insignificant, not worthy of judicial review.

de novo a new review.

dictum a statement made by a judge in delivering an opinion that does not relate directly to the issue being decided and does not embody the sentiment of the court.

directed verdict the verdict provided when a plaintiff fails to support a prima facie case for jury consideration or the defendant fails to produce a necessary defense.

discretionary power authority that involves the exercise of judgment.

dissenting opinion a statement by a judge or judges who disagree with the decision of the majority of the justices in a case.

en banc the full bench; refers to a session where the court's full membership participates in the decision rather than the usual quorum of the court.

fact finding a process whereby a third party investigates an impasse in the negotiation process to determine the facts, identify the issues, and make a recommendation for settlement.

fraudulent conveyance a transfer of property intended to defraud or hinder a creditor or to put such property beyond the creditor's reach.

friend-of-the-court briefs briefs provided by nonparties to inform or perhaps persuade the court (also termed *amicus curiae* briefs).

governmental function activity performed in discharging official duties of a federal, state, or municipal agency.

governmental immunity the common law doctrine that governmental agencies cannot be held liable for the negligent acts of their officers, agents, or employees.

impasse a deadlock in the negotiation process in which parties are unable to resolve an issue without assistance of a third party.

injunction a writ issued by a court prohibiting a defendant from acting in a prescribed manner.

in loco parentis in place of parent; charged with rights and duties of a parent.

liquidated damages contractual amounts representing a reasonable estimation of the damages owed to one of the parties for a breach of the agreement by the other.

mediation the process by which a neutral third party serving as an intermediary attempts to persuade disagreeing parties to settle their dispute.

ministerial duty an act that does not involve discretion and must be carried out in a manner specified by legal authority.

negligence the failure to exercise the degree of care that a reasonably prudent person would exercise under similar conditions; conduct that falls below the standard established by law for the protection of others against unreasonable risk of harm.

per curiam a court's brief disposition of a case that is not accompanied by a written opinion.

plaintiff the party initiating a judicial action.

plenary power full, complete, absolute power.

precedent a judicial decision serving as authority for subsequent cases involving similar questions of law.

preponderance of evidence a standard that requires more evidence to support than refute a claim; it also is termed the *51 percent rule.*

prima facie on its face presumed to be true unless disproven by contrary evidence.

probable cause reasonable grounds, supported by sufficient evidence, to warrant a cautious person to believe that the individual is guilty of the offense charged.

procedural due process the fundamental right to notice of charges and an opportunity to rebut the charges before a fair tribunal if life, liberty, or property rights are at stake.

proprietary function an activity (often for profit) performed by a state or municipal agency that could as easily be performed by a private corporation.

punitive damages a monetary punishment where the defendant is found to have acted with either malice or reckless indifference.

qualified immunity an affirmative defense that shields public officials performing discretionary functions from civil damages if their conduct does not violate clearly established statutory or constitutional rights.

qualified privilege protection from liability for communication made in good faith, for proper reasons, and to appropriate parties.

reasonable suspicion specific and articulable facts, which, taken together with rational inferences from the facts, justify a warrantless search.

remand to send a case back to the original court for additional proceedings.

remittitur the trial court's power to reduce a jury's excessive award of damages, which may be a condition of denying a motion for a new trial.

respondeat superior a legal doctrine whereby the master is responsible for acts of the servant; a governmental unit is liable for acts of its employees.

save harmless clause an agreement whereby one party agrees to indemnify and hold harmless another party for suits that may be brought against that party.

stare decisis to abide by decided cases; to adhere to precedent.

statute an act by the legislative branch of government expressing its will and constituting the law within the jurisdiction.

substantive due process requirements embodied in the Fifth and Fourteenth Amendments that legislation must be fair and reasonable in content as well as application; protection against arbitrary, capricious, or unreasonable governmental action.

summary judgment disposition of a controversy without a trial when there is no genuine dispute over factual issues.

tenure a statutory right that confers permanent employment on teachers, protecting them from dismissal except for adequate cause.

tort a civil wrong, independent of contract, for which a remedy in damages is sought.

ultra vires beyond the scope of authority to act on the subject.

vacate to set aside; to render a judgment void.

verdict a decision of a jury on questions submitted for trial.

Selected Supreme Court Cases

Index